MEDIA, FEMINISM, CULTURAL STUDIES

Liv Tyler
by Thomas A. Christie

The Cinema of Richard Linklater
by Thomas A. Christie

Walerian Borowczyk
by Jeremy Mark Robinson

Stepping Forward: Essays, Lectures and Interviews
by Wolfgang Iser

Wild Zones: Pornography, Art and Feminism
by Kelly Ives

'Cosmo Woman': The World of Women's Magazines
by Oliver Whitehorne

Andrea Dworkin
by Jeremy Mark Robinson

Cixous, Irigaray, Kristeva: The Jouissance of French Feminism
by Kelly Ives

*The Erotic Object: Sexuality in Sculpture
From Prehistory to the Present Day*
by Susan Quinnell

Women in Pop Music
by Helen Challis

Detonation Britain: Nuclear War In Great Britain
by Jeremy Mark Robinson

Julia Kristeva: Art, Love, Melancholy, Philosophy, Semiotics
by Kelly Ives

Luce Irigaray: Lips, Kissing, and the Politics of Sexual Difference
by Kelly Ives

Helene Cixous I Love You: The Jouissance of Writing
by Kelly Ives

The Sacred Cinema of Andrei Tarkovsky
by Jeremy Mark Robinson

Marvelous Names
P. Adams Sitney

Jean-Luc Godard: The Passion of Cinema / Le Passion de Cinéma
by Jeremy Mark Robinson

Jackie Collins

Jackie Collins

Queen of the Blockbuster Novel

Jeremy Mark Robinson

Crescent Moon

Crescent Moon Publishing
P.O. Box 1312
Maidstone, Kent
ME14 5XU, Great Britain
www.crmoon.com

First published in 1993, as *Sex, Death, Glitter, Gore and Lots of Money: Jackie Collins and the Blockbuster Novel*.
This edition 2024.
© Jeremy Mark Robinson 2024.

Set in Lucida Bright 9 on 14pt.
Designed by Radiance Graphics.

The right of Jeremy Mark Robinson to be identified as the author of this book has been asserted generally in accordance with sections 77 and 78 of the Copyright, Designs and Patents Act 1988.

All rights reserved. No part of this book may be reprinted or reproduced, stored in a retrieval system, or transmitted, in any form or by any means, electronic, mechanical, photocopying, recording or otherwise, without permission from the publisher.

British Library Cataloguing in Publication data available for this title.

ISBN-13 9781861712837
ISBN-13 9781861719201

Contents

Acknowledgements ★ 9
Prologue ★ 13
Preface To the New Edition ★ 15

1 Jackie Collins, Queen of Hollywood ★ 18
2 The Blockbuster Novel ★ 38
3 Money and Work ★ 76
4 Characters ★ 88
5 Language, Form, Structure ★ 117
6 Sex ★ 129
7 Aspects of Jackie Collins' Work ★ 148
8 Manners and Morals ★ 192
9 The Blockbuster Novel In Literature ★ 200
10 The Novels of Jackie Collins ★ 208
11 'Never Fuck With a Santangelo': The *Lucky Santangelo* Series ★ 262
12 The *Hollywood* Novel Series ★ 322
13 Jackie Collins At the Movies (and On TV Too) ★ 349

Epilogue ★ 403
Appendices ★ 405
Quotes By Jackie Collins ★ 406
Quotes From Jackie Collins' Books ★ 408
Real-Life Jackie Collins Characters ★ 409

Fans On Jackie Collins ★ 414
Bibliography ★ 417

Acknowledgements

To Jackie Collins for her books.
To the authors and publishers quoted.
To the copyright holders of the illustrations.
To Collins' publishers: Simon & Schuster, Pan Books, Macmillan, Book Club Associates and Pocket Books.

Images are used for information and research purposes, with no infringement of copyright or rights intended.

...girls do it big, girls soar, girls burn, girls take big not puny...

Andrea Dworkin, *Mercy*

Prologue

Summer, 1976 (or was it 1986... or 1996...or 2006...?)

He was a bad boy from the wrong side of town. He was so cool and handsome in his denim jacket and dirty jeans, he made all the girls cream.

He wanted to be star. A big star.

One day he read a book by a famous, glamorous author, Jackie Collins (she was hot! What a babe!). He loved her work. The glam. The glitter. The fame. The movies. The violence. The sleaze.

Yeah, and the sex.

Some day, he thought as he swaggered along the streets of Iowa doing his best Marlon Brando impression, I'm gonna get out this nowhere town and write the best goddam study of Jackie Collins' books ever!!

And he did.

And this is it.

Preface To the New Edition

Come fly with me, let's fly, let's fly away,
If you can use some exotic booze,
There's a bar in far Bombay,
Come fly with me, let's fly, let's fly away.

Come fly with me, let's float down to Peru,
In llama land there's a one-man band,
And he'll toot his flute for you,
Come fly with me, let's take off in the blue.

Sammy Cahn and James van Heusen

It has been great fun rewriting this book on Jackie Collins and the blockbuster novel from start to finish (which I wrote using a pseudonym, Cassidy Hughes). Between the first edition in 1993 and today, it has been business as usual for Jackie Collins and her world of glitz, glam and gore. She has published 14 more books, and they are pretty much the same sort of fictions as her previous works. (I began rewriting this book in 2008, up to 2010, and again in 2013-14).

Jackie Collins' stories are still easy to read and entertaining, but if you've read other authors who take in the same sort of territory, Collins' works can appear tame at first. But then you recognize the cynical humour, particularly when dealing with celebrity, and vanity, and Hollywood. And you love it! Collins can dish the dirt; she can gossip like mad; and she can bitch, bitch, bitch!

I have changed my views of Jackie Collins' work between then and now only a little, and still enjoy it just as much. The main thing I've altered in this second edition is the rather pompous and occasionally self-righteous condemnation of certain aspects of her writing.

Why do lengthy critical studies of James Joyce, Marcel Proust, Samuel Beckett, D.H. Lawrence, and Fyodor Dostoievsky exist, but none whatsoever on Jackie Collins – or Dan Brown, Dean Koontz, Catherine Cookson or John Grisham? The snobbery surrounding blockbuster fiction is impossible to miss. Yet Collins, King, Brown, Cookson, Koontz *et al* do pretty much the same things the 'high art' authors do. Only they're often far more enjoyable: how many people have started the multi-volume *Remembrance of Times Past* and stalled halfway through Book One, *How Squirrels Gather Nuts*? 'High' or 'low' art, novels are simply stories, they are storytelling. Same themes, same character types.

Jackie Collins can tell a story, and she possesses that magical element that readers appreciate and publishers seek high and low for: the Page-Turner. It's the Holy Grail of books and publishing and literature – and of stories in any media: creating the desire to know what happens next.

This is a study of an author and their works in a lighter, casual style, to reflect the content and tone of Collins' novels. (Be warned: bad language, crudity and slang are part of this approach).

Jeremy Robinson
Los Angeles and Kent, England

One

Jackie Collins, Queen of Hollywood

There is something very exciting about the beginning of the evening – well, the beginning of my evening, usually about ten-thirty, eleven o'clock. Every night at 'Hobo' is like a party – a great party where everyone knows and likes everyone else.

Jackie Collins, *The Stud* (5)

JACKIE COLLINS: BIOGRAPHY

Jacqueline Jill Collins was born in Hampstead, London on October 4, 1937. Her mother was Elssa Bessant and her father (Joseph William Collins, d. 1988) was a theatrical agent.[1] Collins has been married twice (to Wallace Austin[2] (1959-64), and Oscar Lerman (1965-92)).[3] Collins' partners have also included Frank Calcagnini[4] (d. 1998). She has three daughters (Tracy, born 1961, Tiffany, born 1967, and Rory, born 1969); her books are often dedicated to 'my three incredible, amazing daughters'. Collins has a famous sister – actress Joan Collins (b. 1933), and a brother, Bill Collins (b. 1946).[5] In 2011, Collins was estimated to be worth $90 million (thus, she was one of the richest authors in the world). She received an O.B.E. in 2013. Collins died aged 77 on September 19, 2015, in Beverly Hills.

Jackie Collins was famously expelled from school in London aged 15 in 1952 (and apparently she threw her school uniform in the River Thames). Why? Look at the internet for some of the fans' ideas (she was caught smoking! She cut classes! She wrote a dirty story in a school essay!). So, yeah, Collins wasn't a university student, a Greek philosophy nerd or an Emily Dickinson groupie, and didn't study literature at Sarah Lawrence College or Cambridge; she went into acting. (But of course plenty of Great Authors left school in their mid-teens, or had patchy schooling, including the Greatest Writer In History, William Shakespeare, who left school at 15 – *and he hailed from a tiny, dull town in the Midlands of England, not some great, seething megalapolis*).

Jackie Collins worked for a time as an actress (mainly in British television, in the 1950s and thru the mid-1960s, on shows such as *Passport To Shame*, *Intent To Kill*, *Undercover Girl*, and *The Shakedown*, and I.T.C.'s *The Saint* and *Danger Man*, where she sometimes appeared as Lynn Curtis). Collins has spent much of her life in Los

---

[1] So Collins was close to the entertainment business from an early age. Her father was Jewish, and born in South Africa. Her mother was British.
[2] Wallace Austin committed suicide in 1964 (he suffered from manic depression).
[3] Lerman died in 1992.
[4] Calcagnini is often cited in the dedications of Collins' books, including books after his death.
[5] Jackie Collins' sister Joan Collins has also written many books: novels: *Prime Time*, *Love & Desire & Hate*, *Infamous*, *Star Quality* and *Misfortune's Daughters*; lifestyle books: *The Joan Collins Beauty Book*, *My Secrets*, *My Friends' Secrets* and *Joan's Way: The Art of Living Well*, and memoirs: *Past Imperfect*, *Katy: A Fight for Life* and *Second Act*.

Angeles (since the 1980s), and usually employs North American characters and settings for her books (nearly always in the later books).

Jackie Collins is known as the Queen of Trash, the Duchess of Dirty Books. The critics call Collins the 'Proust of nips and tucks' and 'unarguably the Victor Hugo of our time'.

By the time of her death in 2015, Jackie Collins had published 32 novels,[6] her first novel being *The World Is Full of Married Men* (1968), when she was 31 (she published under her own name, not a pseudonym; I don't know if she has written works using pen names; she had a pen name as an actress). Collins' other novels include *The Stud, The Bitch, Sinners, The World Is Full of Divorced Women, Rock Star, Thrill!*, the *Hollywood* series: *Hollywood Wives* (her biggest seller, with 15m copies), *Hollywood Husbands, Hollywood Kids, Hollywood Divorces* and *Hollywood Wives: The New Generation*, the *Madison Castelli* series, and the series of novels centred around Lucky Santangelo, the daughter of a mob boss: *Chances, Lucky, Lady Boss, Vendetta, Dangerous Kiss, Goddess of Vengeance*, etc.

Some of Jackie Collins' works have been turned into movies (*The Stud, The Bitch, The World Is Full of Married Men*), and TV series (*Hollywood Wives, Lucky Chances, Lady Boss,* and *Hollywood Wives: The New Generation*).[7] *Paris Connections* (2010) was a direct-to-DVD movie of the further adventures of the recent Collins heroine, Madison Castelli.[8] The TV and film adaptations of Collins' fiction have been very disappointing. Partly, perhaps, because Collins' stories are *already* very cinematic, very movie-ish. The best movie of a Jackie Collins novel is... the novel itself. (And Collins provides the soundtrack, with references to pop and rock music; her action scenes are like movie action scenes; her characters are compared to movie stars (and often *are* movie stars); her prose and structures are very movie-like, with rapid cutting (and parallel editing to keep the many plots in the air); the stories and the melodramas echo those of films, etc).

The most well-known Jackie Collins adaptation is the big, splashy production *Hollywood Wives* (1985). It was produced by Aaron Spelling, Howard Koch, Robert McCullough, Steven Milkis, J.

---

6 Most of her books have been published with Simon & Schuster in the U.S.A.
7 She also wrote *Yesterday's Hero* (1979), and there's a series, *Jackie Collins Presents* (2004).
8 Nicole Steinwedell appeared as Madison Castelli; Charles Dance and Trudie Styler also appeared. Amber Entertainment and British supermarket chain Tesco produced.

David Williams, Douglas Cramer and E. Duke Vincent, and featured Rod Steiger, Anthony Hopkins, Candice Bergen, Stephanie Powers, Angie Dickinson, and Suzanne Somers.

As well as a novelist, TV presenter and regular chat show participant, Jackie Collins has also worked as a producer and writer in film and television (but only on her own novels). She wrote (and co-wrote) scripts for *The Stud, Lucky Chances, Lady Boss* and *Yesterday's Hero,* and co-produced *Lucky Chances, Lady Boss, Hollywood Wives: The New Generation* and *Jackie Collins Presents.*

As a youth, Ms Collins consumed Harold Robbins, Mickey Spillane, Raymond Chandler and *Playboy.* Collins has cited Charles Dickens, Mario Puzo and F. Scott Fitzgerald among her favourite authors. Collins' literary influences are easy to spot.

There are many nods and *hommages* to *The Godfather* in the *Lucky Santangelo* series (and other Jackie Collins novels), as Collins rewrites Mario Puzo. For instance, in *Vendetta: Lucky's Revenge* the ageing Gino Santangelo is gunned down in a very similar way to Don Corleone in *The Godfather:* it's on the street, near Gino's car, in daytime in an everyday context (he's with Lucky's daughter, they're buying a puppy). Then follows a hospital scene that also replays *The Godfather,* complete with Lucky Santangelo setting guards.

La Collins' own rags-to-riches move to becoming published is like something out of one her own novels:

> I was never confident about finishing a book, but friends encouraged me. When I finished my first book, it was accepted by a publisher right away and became an instant bestseller. One male critic called it the most shocking book he ever read.

No rejections from every major publisher in town, then, as with J.K. Rowling (*Harry Potter*), and zillions of other authors.

Jackie Collins has her own website (as everyone does): jackiecollins.com. It's one of the better author websites – Collins is an entertaining host.

Unlike many writers, Jackie Collins has not published plays, poetry, letters, essays, travel books, cook books,[9] gift books, guidebooks, biographies, or non-fiction (her autobiography is surely a book many fans would like to read).[10] Collins' work consists primarily of novels (not short stories), and some TV and film scripts.

---

9 Ah, but a cookbook featuring Lucky Santangelo appeared in 2014.
10 I would imagine that Collins will have quite a bit of unpublished material; I wouldn't be surprised if she had been writing her memoirs.

(Her novels are medium-length, tho' the printing, on thick paper in hardcovers with large fonts (and fewer words per page), gives the impression that they are longer, a common trick in publishing).

Among alternative careers, certainly Jackie Collins could've been a designer or stylist (adviser to the stars), a P.R. agent, or a costume designer (or make-up artist) for movies.

When Jackie Collins is interviewed on TV or radio (where she is a regular guest), she is often portrayed as a pundit who can comment expertly[11] on Hollywood and celebrity culture, just as much as a novelist who's plugging her books. Collins has hosted TV shows, including talk shows and specials.

And what about Jackie Collins' influence, and her legacy? Anybody who sells 500 million books (according to some accounts, or even 100 million, or 1 million books), is going to have some influence, somewhere. And you can spot it – in television (chat shows, celebrity shows, soaps and dramas), in magazine publishing, and in movies.

★

BOOKS BY THE QUEEN OF BLOCKBUSTERS

Books by Jackie Collins include:

- *The World Is Full Of Married Men* (1968)
- *The Stud* (1969)
- *Sinners* (a.k.a. *The Hollywood Zoo*, a.k.a. *Sunday Simmons & Charlie Brick*) (1971)
- *The Love Killers* (a.k.a. *Lovehead*) (1974)
- *The World Is Full Of Divorced Women* (1975)
- *Lovers & Gamblers* (1977)
- *The Bitch* (1979)
- *Chances* (1981)
- *Hollywood Wives* (1983)
- *Lucky* (1985)
- *Hollywood Husbands* (1986)

---

11 There are no professional qualifications for becoming an 'expert' in the world of celebrity, no courses at Harvard or Yale on 'Fame and Fashion, 1960-1990'.

- ★ *Rock Star* (1988)
- ★ *Lady Boss* (1990)
- ★ *American Star* (1993)
- ★ *Hollywood Kids* (1994)
- ★ *Vendetta: Lucky's Revenge* (1996)
- ★ *L.A. Connections* (1998)
- ★ *Thrill!* (1998)
- ★ *Dangerous Kiss* (1999)
- ★ *Lethal Seduction* (2000)
- ★ *Hollywood Wives: The New Generation* (2001)
- ★ *Deadly Embrace* (2002)
- ★ *Hollywood Divorces* (2003)
- ★ *Lovers & Players* (2005)
- ★ *Drop Dead Beautiful* (2007)
- ★ *Married Lovers* (2008)
- ★ *Poor Little Bitch Girl* (2009)
- ★ *Goddess of Vengeance* (2011)
- ★ *The Power Trip* (2012)
- ★ *Confessions of a Wild Child* (2014)
- ★ *The Lucky Santangelo Cookbook* (2014)
- ★ *The Santangelos* (2015)

Some of these novels have been grouped into series:

- ★ THE *HOLLYWOOD* SERIES:
  Hollywood Wives, Hollywood Husbands, Hollywood Kids, Hollywood Wives: The New Generation and *Hollywood Divorces.*
- ★ THE *MADISON CASTELLI* SERIES:
  L. A. Connections, Lethal Seduction and *Deadly Embrace.*
- ★ THE *LUCKY SANTANGELO* SERIES:
  Chances, Lucky, Lady Boss, Vendetta: Lucky's Revenge, Dangerous Kiss, Drop Dead Beautiful, Goddess of Vengeance, Confessions of a Wild Child and *The Santangelos.*

The *Madison Castelli* novels cross over into the *Lucky Santangelo* series and the *Hollywood* series. Characters go to the same casinos (the Magiriano resort in Las Vegas in *Deadly Embrace*, for instance).

The *Hollywood* novel series are self-enclosed stories, with new characters each time (one or two minor figures re-appear). In the *Madison Castelli* series, characters recur, grouped around the heroine, Madison Castelli, but each book is self-contained. The *Lucky Santangelo* series is a regular, on-going family saga, though each book can also stand alone (Ms Collins fills in enough back-story and plot summaries for the reader to keep up).

(The titles of Collins' books form clusters of themes: love/ lovers/ relationships (and words like *stud, married, divorce, wives, husbands, sinners, embrace, seduction, kiss*); murder (words like *killers, revenge, vengeance, lethal, dead, deadly, dangerous*); and of course fame and celebrity (words like *star, Hollywood, power*).

Many of Collins' novels are short – 100-200 pages: *The World Is Full Of Married Men*, the *Madison Castelli* books, and the movie-related books such as *The Bitch, The Stud, The Power Trip* etc.

★

WRITING IS A DRUG

I don't know how much $-$-$-$ Jacqueline Jill Collins made, but it isn't cheap living in Beverly Hills. I guess she could've written less, not published 32 novels, and still been OK. But, like so many authors, Collins is entranced – as we all are – by the act of writing. She has remarked:

> I really fall in love with my characters, even the bad ones. I love getting together with them. They tell me what to do; they take me on a wild and wonderful trip.

Of course: because one of the main reasons writers become writers is that they get hooked on the fantasies and characters they conjure up. Writers lose themselves in their worlds. It really is close to a trance, a literal fantasy: writing is a drug. (Which's one reason why some writers get edgy and nervous when they've been away from writing for a while, even when they are on vacation. Indeed, some authors, such as André Gide, liked to write something every-day. And J.R.R. Tolkien dragged his feet over finishing *The Lord of the Rings* partly because he enjoyed losing himself in his invented world of Middle-earth.)

> I love what I do [said Jackie Collins]. I fall in love with my characters. They become me, and I become them.

★

ASPECTS OF JACKIE COLLINS' ART

THE AUTHOR AS SUPERSTAR.
Jackie Collins is one of those writers who are superstars. Like Vincent van Gogh or Leonardo da Vinci or Pablo Picasso, she is as famous as her art. This is demonstrated so piquantly on the covers of her books. Collins appears on the cover, in the 1970s Star (British.) editions (trade paperback). In the Pan Books versions (also G.B.), she is on the back.

Her lips smothered with deep red lipstick and shiny lip gloss, cheekbones puffed over with heaps of blusher, her eyes outlined with black kohl and brown eye shadow, hair carefully blowdried and teased into casual cascades, 5'7" Jackie Collins looks like one of her characters – and how she describes her characters, particularly the charas that're identified with the narrator and the author (she is styled and primped like a supermodel by make-up artists and stylists).

Here the boundaries between author and text blur. No one is more like a Jackie Collins character than Jackie Collins herself. Except maybe perhaps her older sister, Joan Collins (who has of course appeared in films of her sister's books, as well as written her own novels. Joan Collins seems a rather foolish sort of person to me – she is often lampooned in the press – and I can't bring myself to read one of her books, just to see how they compare to her younger sister's work).

Her Majesty J.C. appears in a variety of outfits to sell her books: a faded, denim shirt; a black, silk jacket; and, best of all, a delicious, leopard-skin[12] dress, complete with leopard-skin cushions to recline upon. In the cult of personality or celebrity (in our Warholian era), the artist is everything. Jackie Collins herself sums up her texts, the plethora of meanings and attitudes embedded in her

---
12 'My weakness is wearing too much leopard print'.

books as well as her characters. There is an Ur-Collins at the centre of her art.[13]

Jackie Collins valorizes her art, in the same way that big-name authors such as Stephen King or Jeffrey Archer do. Punters go to see 'a Steven Spielberg Film', hears the latest 'Madonna Album', and reads 'a Catherine Cookson Romance'. The artist's name is enough. The author or celebrity becomes their own brand, their own logo, their own product.[14]

These are the artists that automatically guarantee sales (usually), box office receipts, million dollar advances and high TV ratings. Just as only a few female film stars can 'open' a movie, so Collins can 'open' a book on her name alone.[15] (If you ask people what they're reading at the moment, they often know the title but can't remember the author's name. With Collins it's the opposite: they're reading 'a Jackie Collins novel'. That's all you need to know).

Jackie Collins is her own brand to the extent that the book titles become inter-changeable, and all you need to know buying a book in a store is that it's 'the latest Jackie Collins book' (like 'the latest Meryl Streep movie'). One book merges into another, like a group of movie sequels, like a long-running TV show: and so do the characters: Collins employs the same types, in the same situations, doing the same things.

Yeah but what d'you expect? Read any of the Big Name Writers, the world-class, critically-exalted authors, and they *all* use the same characters, the same situations, the same incidents, the same settings, time after time. Samuel Beckett did (the shambling, self-hating, eternally-debating loner). Thomas Hardy did (the too-passionate young lover, the neurotic city girl, the predatory, older Casanova, the crumbly, aged coot). D.H. Lawrence did (the would-be super-macho lover, the cynical, boho type, the close-to-nature poet, the useless, weedy, mummy's boy). I could go on: Dante Alighieri, Francesco Petrarch, Leo Tolstoy, Alexander Dumas, Stendhal, Thomas Mann, Fyodor Dostoievsky, Jane Austen, Johann Wolfgang von Goethe, James Joyce, the Brontës, George Eliot, F. Scott Fitzgerald, the Grimm Brothers, *A Thousand and One Nights*, the *Bible* – they *all* use the same characters and types in work after

---

13 As there is an Ur-Tess at the heart of Thomas Hardy's *Tess of the d'Urbervilles*.
14 In the art world, a similar cult has grown up around painters such as Claude Monet and Michelangelo Buonarroti.
15 Cleo is delighted when her name appears on the cover of *Image* magazine in *The World is Full of Divorced Women* (a big deal for a journalist).

work.

But that's part of the fun, ain't it? Do you really want (or need) a totally new scenario and totally new characters and totally new incidents every time, for each new book, from the same author?

Not possible, kid.[16] No author can deliver that.

But you can *change* authors. If you are in the mood for manic depression in an abstract mindscape, you can read Samuel Beckett. Or if you fancy some intensely romantic fumblings amid the crusty, miserable denizens of rural, 19th century Dorset, Thomas Hardy's the man for you. But if you want to veg out on fun fiction, if you want a slick, fast ride, if you want bitchy gossip and hyper-neurotic, glam and OTT characters, then Jackie Collins does it better than most.

❤

CULTURAL INFLUENCES.

Jackie Collins' books have also reflected numerous trends in Western popular culture – reality TV, for instance, of the 2000s, or the increase in cosmetic surgery and beauty treatments in the 1990s, or trends in health, diets and lifestyles, or the influx of 'reality' in magazine publishing (for example, the German magazines, *Bella, Best* and *Take a Break* came onto the magazine scene in the 1970s and 1980s with T.L.S. (true life stories) and T.O.T. (triumph over tragedy) stories), which Collins' plots somewhat emulate.)

A striking aspect of Jackie Collins' fiction is how multi-racial it is: while many North American and European blockbuster novels are very white, Collins happily includes many African-American characters, often in starring roles, plus plenty of Mexicans, Russians, Italians, Chinese, etc. Of course, some of Collins' black and African-American charas do follow cultural stereotypes – supermodels *à la* Naomi Campbell, comedians like Eddie Murphy and Martin Lawrence, soul singers like Al Green and Luther Vandross.

The influence of Russian culture/ society on Jackie Collins' later fiction is interesting – this is Russia following the end of the Cold War, Russia destabilized, with new streams of revenue and the exploitation by organized crime. Thus, when Collins has a character taking up the familiar rags-to-riches journey, they often come from Russia (via Amsterdam, for instance). There are Russian charas in books such as *The Power Trip* and *Married Lovers* (and the movie *Paris Connections*).

Also: Mexican and South American society/ culture: there are

---

16 'Kid'?!

several Chicano/ Hispanic characters in Jackie Collins' fiction: some are supermodels, some are drug lords (inevitably, in keeping with the thriller and crime genres and ethnic stereotypes), and some are maids or live-in housekeepers (also inevitable – in Los Angeles society, at least). Particularly enjoyable are Collins' feisty, fiery Mexican/ Chicano characters – especially when they're women, like firecracker Mercedes in *The Power Trip*. Plus jaunts down to Acapulco and Mexico City. (If Collins deviates from the New York <-> Los Angeles <-> Las Vegas axis – the Big Three Cities in her work (her home-from-home), it's usually South, to Mexico or South America, rather than North. Somehow, going to Canada just ain't got the glitzy sheen that Collins needs! Like, is a glamorous supermodel going to slink away for a sexy weekend in cold, rainy Ontario or the palm trees and beaches of Acapulco?).

There is a strong Italian cultural component in Jackie Collins' fiction. Altho' most of her novels are set in the Land of the Free, if there is an excursion, it's often to Italy; many of the fashions and accessories that her charas wear are Italian (and the cars they drive); and there are Italian characters such as photographers, fashion models, and actors. Superstar Venus Maria in the *Santangelo* series is Italian-American. And of course don't forget all of those Italian-American gangsters. And Collins' signature character, Lucky Santangelo, is an Italian-American.

Vengeance is a very prominent theme and plot device in Jackie Collins' fiction – sometimes her work reads like an Italian opera or a Sicilian mafia novel (hell, the word *vengeance* is in three of her book titles). The Sicilian, Italian and Italian-American cultural strand is everywhere in Collins' fiction. Usually, it's tied to the villains and the rivals, who plot getting back at the heroes and heroines, but getting revenge also works within the tangled erotic relationships and betrayals (so that wives hope to enact revenge on their cheating husbands). 'Revenge – Sicilian style – was extremely sweet', the narrator says in *Vendetta* (246).

JACKIE COLLINS AS A POET.

Who says that Jackie Collins can't write? She can. I'll prove it, incontestably. This is good writing, I think:

> Falling in love is like getting hit by a large truck and yet not being mortally wounded. Just sick to your stomach, high one minute, low the next. Starving hungry but unable to eat. Hot, cold, forever horny, full of

hope and enthusiasm, with momentary depressions that wipe you out.
    It is also not being able to remove the smile from your face, loving life with a mad passionate intensity, and feeling ten years younger. (*Lucky*, 449)

Wow! This is the closest that Jackie Collins comes to poetry.[17] You could even print Collins' passage as poetry:

FALLING IN LOVE

Falling in love is like
Getting hit by a large truck
And yet not being mortally wounded.

Just sick to your stomach,
High one minute, low the next.

Starving hungry but unable to eat.
Hot, cold, forever horny.

Full of hope and enthusiasm,
With momentary depressions
That wipe you out.

It's not quite a sonnet, but eat your heart out, William Shakespeare, it's Poetry Time!

Francesco Petrarch, Dante Alighieri and the troubadours would often write of being in love like this: the 'hot' and 'cold' tropes, for instance, are classic, Petrarchan, poetic conceits (along with light/ dark, near/ far, eyes like stars, and all the rest of the courtly love poetic tradition of the 11th and 12th centuries). Those poetic conceits are everywhere in Elizabethan poetry, in Metaphysical poetry, in 19th century and Victorian poetry, and into the modern era (they also form the basic material of pop music lyrics).

The literary conceits echo the dichotomy that is always present in Francesco Petrarch's *Canzoniere* poetic cycle and in the troubadours' lyrics – between Heaven and Earth, between fear and desire, between sexuality and spirituality, between distance and nearness, between yearning and disgust, between memory and hope for the future. This is a typical sonnet from Petrarch's *Rime Sparse*:

veggio, penso, ardo, piango; et chi mi sface
sempre m' è inanzi per mia dolce pena:
guerra è 'l mio stato, d'ira e di duol piena,
et sol di lei pensando o qualche pace.
(I am awake, I think, I burn, I weep; and she who destroys me is always

---

[17] As far as I know, Collins has not published poetry.

before me, to my sweet pain: war is my state, full of sorrow and suffering, and only thinking of her do I have any peace.)[8]

THE READERS.

Who reads Jackie Collins' books?

Judging by the marketing, book packaging,[19] presentation and debates about Collins' books, it is probably chiefly women (as far as the publishers are concerned). I would imagine the audience, seen from a marketing p.o.v. (i.e., the advertizing folk of Madison Avenue who always emphasize economics and buying power), is the same as upmarket women's magazines such as *Vogue, Elle* and *Allure*,[20] the people who buy 'chick lit' books, watch *Sex and the City*, rom-com movies and TV soap operas. Collins' audience is probably educated, relatively affluent, urban and suburban, with a relatively good job.

A JACKIE COLLINS QUIZ.

Maybe Jackie Collins' books will survive two hundred years, and will crop up in exam papers at colleges and schools around the world in the future (if Charles Dickens and Edgar Allan Poe can survive, why not Collins?). So there'll be footnotes explaining what the terms 'Armani suit', 'Cristal champagne' and 'Rodeo Drive' mean. There will be university courses with titles like *Postmodern Consumerism and Post-Heterosexuality In the Fiction of Jackie Collins and Stephenie Meyer*.

Typical exam questions 200 years in the future will include:

127. Explain the meaning of the phrase 'give good party'.

Or:

509. What does the term 'blowjob' refer to? –
   A. Employment at a hairdresser's salon.
   B. Terrorist slang for a bomb attack.
   C. A drug dealer's appointment.

---

[18] Francesco Petrarch, *Rime Sparse,* sonnet 164: 5-8, in *Petrarch's Lyric Poems: The Rime Sparse and Other Lyrics*, tr. Robert M. Durling, Harvard University Press, Cambridge, Mass, 1976

[19] Plenty of girlie and 'feminine' elements're included. Little graphic symbols decorate Jackie Collins' books, in silhouette: a panther, a sports car, a rose, palm trees, hearts, or stars.

[20] For an insight into how magazines regard their readers,*Cosmopolitan*'s editor of the 1980s (Linda Kelsey) said that the '*Cosmo* girl' has evolved into a 'highly sophisticated young woman': she owns an apartment in some urban area, has a career, is more affluent, and is or wants to be in a relationship (B. Braithwaite, 141-6).

D. Oral sex.
E. A kind of firearm.

♥

Back when I wrote this book in the early Nineties (oh man, halcyon days!), Jackie Collins had sold more than 100 million copies worldwide, the blurb informed us at the front of her books. But today the publishers and ad-men are crowing of book sales of 400 million – no, wait – it's now 500 million books[21].

500 MILLION BOOKS! You gotta be kidding![22]

That's on a par with *Harry Potter!* – and *Harry Potter* is without doubt the most extraordinary phenomenon in publishing of recent times.[23] (Other blurbs boast of 200 million sales. But that's still a lot of paper!).

(Accurate statistics on best-selling authors are difficult to obtain. Among fiction writers, Barbara Cartland sold between 500 million and 1 billion copies; Danielle Steel between 500 million and 800 million; Harold Robbins sold 750 million; Georges Simenon sold 500-700 million; Sidney Sheldon sold 370-600 million; and J.K. Rowling sold 450-500 million. Jackie Collins' sales are 250-500 million (putting her 15th on the list of best-selling writers).)

OK, let's say Jackie Collins hasn't sold 400-500 million books, as the publishers claim. Let's say it was 2 million. Truth is, you can't *force* 2 million people to buy a book if they don't want to.

Have a go, if you think you can! Good luck!

But you also can't force 200,000 people to buy a book, or 20,000 people, or 2,000 people or even 200 people. Or put it like this: there must be summat about Jackie Collins' books for them to sell even 2,000 copies.

---

21 With translations into 40 languages.
22 That's what Gino Santangelo would yell to Lucky if she said she'd sold 500 million books: 'you gotta be kidding?!'
23 13 million copies were printed of *Harry Potter and the Order of the Phoenix* for its first print-run. Nielsen BookScan estimated that *Harry Potter and the Order of the Phoenix* sold 1,777,541 copies in Britain alone on its first day (an extraordinary figure by any standards). *Harry Potter and the Order of the Phoenix* was the most successful first run book in publishing history.

Some images of Jackie Collins on the following pages.

Jackie Collins, 1988 (Mirrorpix/ Everett).

Jackie Collins at home in California.

Joan Collins (at the time of The Bitch).

Two

The Blockbuster Novel

Nova and her husband, Marcus, lived part of the year on Novaroen, a magnificent twenty-five-acre estate, perched on the top of a high bluff overlooking the Pacific Ocean a few miles past Malibu. The estate boasted two separate mansions – one especially for guests – an Olympic-size swimming pool, three north-south tennis courts, a recording studio, a fully equipped gym, a luxurious movie theatre, stables for their expensive Arabian horses, and garage space for Marcus's collection of immaculately restored antique cars.

Jackie Collins, *Rock Star* (8-9)

In this book I am going to counter some of the negative critical reactions of Jackie Collins and other blockbuster novelists - from fans and readers as well as from critics. In the following discussion, on the right ('Worthy', 'Important') side of the field we have the Great Authors, and the left ('Populist', 'Trashy') side of the field we find the Blockbuster Authors.

Great Authors vs. Blockbuster Authors.

Literature vs. pulp.

Great art vs. low art.

Let battle commence!

PLOTS.

So many readers, including fans of Jackie Collins, complain that her plots are 'predictable'.

Huh? What do they mean? I think they mean they can guess what's going to happen, that there aren't enough unexpected twists and turns or reversals, or that Collins organizes the narrative structure along lines that're too formulaic and too, well, 'predictable'.

However, there are thousands of Classic Novels, (a.k.a. Great, Worthy, Serious, Significant Novels) which have wholly predictable plots. In fact, in most cases the success (and pleasure) of those Classic Novels derives in large part from the very fact that they *are* predictable (or clichéd, another term for the same sort of thing).

Take the Great Novels - *Wuthering Heights, Jane Eyre, Pride and Prejudice, Great Expectations, The Great Gatsby, Far From the Madding Crowd, Tom Sawyer, Vanity Fair* - they are predictable. (Wonderful, glorious, yes - but predictable).[1]

Take the Great Narrative Poems - *Paradise Lost, The Divine Comedy, The Illiad, The Canterbury Tales* - they are very predicable. (Wonderful, awesome, yes - but predictable).

And the detractors are making the wrong comparisons: Jackie Collins' work is in a particular *genre*: it's relationship fiction, it's romantic fiction, it's melodramatic fiction, it's family saga fiction, and it's thriller fiction.

---

[1] Some Great Novels do twist and turn and relish being unpredictable: *Frankenstein, The Count of Monte Cristo, Dracula,* etc.

In all of those kinds of fiction, genre mechanisms, rules, laws, and forms are at work. A certain degree of being 'predictable' and clichéd is part of those fictions. They are stories in which 'predictability', you might say, is built-in, just as it is in fairy tales or horror stories or actually any goddam story you can think of.

Or put it like this: is there a completely *un*-predictable story? A story in which *every* element is *un*-predictable? A story that jumped around events/ plots/ characters/ genres/ styles/ themes wholly unpredictably?[2]

No. I repeat: *no.* Because a story is a *form*, it is a *genre*, it is something *written* or *told* or *shown*, it is *composed*, it is *made up*, and it is *structured* (like language itself).

DIALOGUE.

Another common complaint is that Jackie Collins and blockbuster novelists can't write dialogue, or nobody speaks like that. You think the Celebrated Writers don't also deliver bad, inept or unbelievable dialogue? They all do, I would suggest. Have a look at how people speak in the fiction of Jane Austen, D.H. Lawrence or Edith Wharton. Or William Shakespeare or Christopher Marlowe or Geoffrey Chaucer. I'm not talking about the differences in historical time periods or changing fashions in vocabulary and language, either, or the literary contexts and forms. I'm talking about stylization and artifice.

In fact, I would suggest that the dialogue in many of Jackie Collins' novels is wittier, sharper, more concise, more to the point, less pretentious, less waffly, less pompous, and less speechifying than the dialogue in many Great Authors' works. (I could prove this by citing lotsa examples, but it's easy to do yourself: pick up and squint into a Great Novel and pick up a Collins Novel!).

Indeed, the dialogue in Jackie Collins' work is one of its chief delights. It's rapid-fire, it doesn't hang around, and it avoids many pitfalls. Such as: people speaking in ridiculously long sentences, without being interrupted by anyone else. Talk about 'unrealistic'! It's the same in drama, in cinema, in television: characters speak in lengthy paragraphs. But in 'real life', everyone speaks *over* everyone else. All the time. (Yet nobody ever remarks on this *very* artificial

---

[2] Even radical fiction, such as by Williams Burroughs, conforms to formal constraints. (In fact, Burroughs self-consciously explores and sends-up literary forms, and part of the impact of his incredible fiction is that he is derailing the genres and the forms in an explosive manner).

element in all drama and all fiction.)

Another pitfall: characters using words the author has dug out of a dictionary. Words that aren't in keeping with their characterizations. William Shakespeare is one of the worst culprits – it's accepted as a convention that characters in a play by the Immortal Bard say lines such as:

> Come, civil night,
> Thou sober-suited matron, all in black,
> And learn me how to lose a winning match,
> Play'd for a pair of stainless maidenhoods;
> Hood my unmann'd blood, bating in my cheeks,
> With thy black mantle, till strange love, grown bold,
> Think true love acted simple modesty.
>   (Juliet, in *Romeo and Juliet*)

Gimme a break! Nobody calls night a 'sober-suited matron'! Especially not a 14 year-old girl! (Nobody looks out of the window and remarks, 'Gee, it's so dark out there, just like a sober-suited matron!').

STYLE.

Many readers/ fans/ crrritics bemoan what they dub the poor prose style in Jackie Collins' fiction. It's true, she doesn't have an ornate, highly-worked style like Lawrence Durrell, James Joyce, and Virginia Woolf. And while I enjoy those writers, they are also showing off, being clever, and being so self-conscious they frequently disappear up their own kazoo.

There are plenty of Great Writers who work themselves up into paroxysms of overly-intellectual, hi-falutin' literary style: Francesco Petrarch, Dante Alighieri, André Gide, Paul Verlaine, Gertrude Stein, Samuel Beckett, John Keats, Thomas Hardy, John Cowper Powys, Homer, Torquato Tasso, Edmund Spenser, Walt Whitman, Maurice Scève, etc.

Doesn't matter. Who cares?

Because Jackie Collins' prose style does the job. It *delivers*. It gets across information and description, but it's also entertaining (it's much more fun to read than Virginia Woolf), and it's concise (it's far more economical than Walt Whitman, Dante Alighieri, John Milton or Alexander Pope, writers who, while great, over-write).

CHARACTERS.

Nobody would deny that the 32 novels written by Jackie Collins contain some stereotypes, some clichés, and some characters who are repetitions of some of her earlier characters.

OK. Fine.

Now go read all twelve of Thomas Hardy's novels. Or Jane Austen's novels. Or Fyodor Dostoievsky. Or André Gide. Or Aldous Huxley. Or H.G. Wells. Or Mark Twain. Or Jules Verne. Or Robert Louis Stevenson. Or William Faulkner.

Read every single one, one after another.

I guarantee that you will find characters that are very similar from one novel to another (some will be *incredibly similar*),[3] situations that repeat, themes that repeat, descriptions that repeat, and settings that crop up time after time.[4]

Or try this: find me an author who's written 32 novels (i.e., 32 long stories) *without* characters or situations or scenes or themes repeating themselves.

THEMES.

Ah, the Big One... *Themes*... beloved of lit'ry critics the world over, philosophy students, cultural theorists and nerds who mull over the Important Themes in the plays of Sophocles and Aeschylus and the novels of Leo Tolstoy and Victor Hugo.

Well, the fiction of Jackie Collins has themes as Important and Serious as any of the Great Authors. And, I should add, explored as richly as many of those Great Authors.

Oh, I'm not suggesting that Jackie Collins has examined certain themes as successfully as William Shakespeare (the theme of royalty and kingship and divinity, for instance), or alienation and Existentialism (André Gide, Albert Camus and Jean-Paul Sartre), or the poetic significance of Ancient Greek culture in the modern era (Friedrich Hölderlin).

But J. Collins' fiction, taken as a whole, all 32 novels, does represent a thorough exploration of all sorts of Big Themes, including love, romance, sexuality, double standards and sexism, loneliness, death, loss, separation, families, marriage, parents, children, work, capitalism, society, vanity, avarice, jealousy, and revenge.

---

3 The ardent, young lovers in the fiction of Thomas Hardy, for example, are the same type, and inter-changeable.
4 How about Lawrence Durrell: we're in another boho café amongst intellectuals and artists in another cultural capital (Paris, Alexandria, Venice, etc).

Or how about cinema in the Art vs. Trash debate? Many of the most revered film directors produced plenty of sleazy, nasty, trashy material: D.W. Griffith, Steven Spielberg, Alfred Hitchcock, Fritz Lang, Tim Burton, James Cameron, Federico Fellini, Martin Scorsese, Johns Ford and Woo... a nude woman attacked in the sea by a shark... a nude woman stabbed in a shower in a frenzy... 100s of sick serial killers... venal gangsters... gruesome tortures... horror, gore and blood...

JACKIE COLLINS AND WILLIAM SHAKESPEARE.

However, Jackie Collins *has* used some Big Themes directly from the work of William Shakespeare: *King Lear*, for example: Collins' novels contain stories of ageing patriarchs surrounded by squabbling offspring fighting over the spoils, right out of *King Lear*. I know some folk might find it preposterous, putting *King Lear* – for some people the greatest play in the English language – next to Jackie Collins' novels. But why not? Critics have done the same with *King Lear* and the *Godfather* movies, for instance. (It's no stretch to place a modern-day king in the middle of Gotham and make him a billionaire, perhaps with gangster origins).[5]

Is it bogus? Not at all! Because Shakey was also writing in a popular medium (theatre) for a popular audience. And his plays're full of the same lusts, desires, fears, anxieties, greeds, and jealousies.

Yes, and similar inconsistencies, repetitions, unbelievable co-incidences, dull bits, mistakes, and predictable endings.

Even William Shakespeare, the Greatest Writer In The World, wasn't perfect, and sometimes wrote below his gifts. Yes, and even Shakey could be corny (the young love and lovers in *Romeo and Juliet*), clichéd, exploitative, hokey (the witches in *Macbeth*), crass, mawkish and violent (Gloucester having his eyes gouged out on stage in *King Lear*), and plain dumb (the not-always-funny comedy between Sir Toby Belch, Sir Andrew Aguecheek and Malvolio in *Twelfth Night*).

I do think that William Shakespeare was probably the Greatest Author In The World, and he's a writer I love endlessly, and I've put Jackie Collins next to Shakespeare to be deliberately provocative. But when you think about it, so many of the negative criticisms

---

5 Jean-Luc Godard did that in his 1987 movie *King Lear*. As Francis Coppola pointed out, the *Godfather* movies, especially the third one of 1990, consciously employed *King Lear*. Yes, and there's some *Macbeth* in Michael Corleone's rise to power, too.

launched at Collins can also be aimed at many other writers. And you can also see that there are authors, even Great Authors, who in certain areas are far less successful than Collins.

Why is it OK for William Shakespeare to use ridiculous plots? But not for Jackie Collins or other blockbuster novel authors? Is it because the Bard of Stratford creates amazing characters? Because his dialogue is so ornate and allusive? Because his plays' structures are intricate?

Case in point: how about the Greatest Love Story In World Literature, *Romeo and Juliet*? It's two crazy teenagers (she's only 14!) who fall in love despite being from warring households. After misunderstandings involving letters, poisons, street brawls and accidental murders, he kills himself, then she does! A double love suicide! And you're telling me that isn't silly, hokey and trashy?!

Admittedly, *Romeo and Juliet* is *very* high class hokum – the highest there is. And man, that guy can write! And it does have incredible scenes, amazing speeches, marvellous characters and full-on tragedy. But the concept and story is pure silliness and cliché. (Look at those coincidences and mis-timings, for instance, with the business with poisons, the Friar, and Romeo's return from Mantua. With the aid of the apothecary and the Friar, Juliet pretends to be dead, but when Romeo discovers her in the tomb, he kills himself!).

★

POPULAR CULTURE VS. HIGH CULTURE

The oppositions in the critical debate about blockbuster fiction include:

High art	Low art
Highbrow	Lowbrow
Elitist	Popular
Culture	Trash
Royalty	Celebrity
Old money	New money
Bourgeois	Working-class
Tradition	Modernity
New York	Hollywood
Europe	North America
Classical music	Pop music

Art cinema   Popular cinema
Letters   E-mails
Novels   Internet
Classic novels   Blockbuster novels

The snobbery surrounding critical views of blockbuster novelists, including the Queen of them all, Jackie Collins, can be found everywhere. Have a look on the internet, and you'll see reviews and writing by fans and readers which talk about 'guilty pleasures', about Collins' books being 'trashy' but enjoyable.

Readers seem to feel 'guilty', they always apologize, they always talk down reading Jackie Collins - as if they should be reading Hermann Hesse or Torquato Tasso or Mikhail Bakhtin or Gayatri Chakravorty Spivak (what's stopping them?). Or doing summat useful like Saving The Earth (it doesn't *need* saving - I mean the *planet* itself, not *humanity*; the planet's been around for 5 billion years!).

Yeah, but reading novels isn't *homework*, it isn't meant to be a chore. If you're not in school or college, you don't *need* to read novels to pass exams or write essays. Nobody's gonna test you on the ideological, post-deconstructionist themes in Jackie Collins' *Hollywood Wives* or E.L. James's *50 Shades of Sh*i*t*!

So why all this guilt? Why this embarrassment or shame surrounding blockbuster novels? You could say that readers are demeaning themselves - that they are 'lowering' themselves in reading what they regard as 'trash'. But why feel 'guilty', why call it 'trash'? It's fiction, it's entertainment - come on folks, reading is just another one of 10,000 things you could be doing. But don't feel 'guilty' about it!

If you feel 'guilty' about reading Jackie Collins, then *read something else*, by the gods! There are at least two or three thousand novels that are regarded as classics in the Western tradition. Read them, dear, sweet reader, and don't feel 'guilty' about reading 'trash'. Why waste your time? You only have 80 years (if you're lucky!).

If you want to read a classic novel with plots that resemble a Collins novel, try *Tess of the d'Urbervilles* or *The Count of Monte Cristo* or *Great Expectations*. Then you won't feel shameful!

★

So you die.
You go to Heaven.

St Peter's there at the Gates (with 2,000 bouncer-angels wearing dark glasses and armed with holy spears).

He asks you, 'Did you or did you not[6] read a Jackie Collins book during your life? When you should have been reading St Augustine and Dionysius the Areopagite?'

You mumble that maybe you glanced at *Hollywood Wives* once when you were fifteen and on vacation and it was raining.

St Peter sighs. Then thunders, 'DAMN YOU TO HELL. YOU HERETIC!'

And down to Hell you go.

★

This will not happen.

★

One of the consumer reviews on the American Amazon website of *Thrill!* (1998) by Jackie Collins commented: 'good God this book was awful', adding: 'there's 6 hours of my life I'll never get back'. But what sane human *chooses* to spend six hours doing something they don't enjoy?! (Was an Italian-American wise guy holding a gun to their head?!).

I'm reminded here of genius film director Jean-Luc Godard: when someone says, 'I saw a bad film', Godard's retort is to say, 'it's your own fault. What did you do to improve the dialogue?' Only Godard could tell someone it was their own fault if they saw a bad film! And then go on to suggest that they improve the dialogue. Applying this crazy Godardism to the disgruntled reader of Collins' *Thrill!* – why didn't he or she start rewriting the book? In six hours, you could rewrite several chapters of Collins!

Critics attack books all the time, but they never offer to rewrite them or to propose 100 ideas for changing a story. Fans don't, either. A review might be 500 words of bile, but it is never 200 words of bile and 300 words of ideas for improvements. Any decent writer can come up with plenty of ways in which a text or a story could be altered, but critics never bother.

As I go along, adding to this book and rewriting it, I find myself defending Jackie Collins even more from her critics (although she doesn't need defending! Also, I would imagine that bad reviews don't affect her book sales one iota). For example, some critics (and fans) have complained that (some of) her books are badly

---

[6] For some reason, St Peter sounds like Senator Joseph McCarthy at the H.U.A.C. trials.

written.

No. Not true: Jackie Collins is a professional writer who's lived much of her life from writing. Her novels might be all sorts of things (OTT, 'unrealistic', 'predictable', as detractors insist), but they are not badly written.[7]

Anyhoo, I've already mentioned how the Big Name Authors and the Classic Books of the past three thousand years use clichés, sleaze, sex, unbelievable plot twists, unconvincing coincidences, dumb dialogue, out-size characters and everything else that the blockbuster novel uses (and is castigated for). Dante does. *Beowulf* does. Cervantes does. Shakespeare does. Gogol does. Eliot does. Twain does. Homer does.

In *Buzzine* (March, 2010), Jackie Collins said of the high culture-low culture divide:

> I am a popular culture[8] junkie. I love everything about it. I love popular television shows, popular movies, popular music... All this about "you've got to love opera" and "you've got to love ballet..." It's fine for some people, good for them! I don't criticize them for it. Yet my books, which I know are gonna be around in 100 years, people go, "It's just flash and trash," and it's not. It's saying a very important message to women, which is: you can be stronger, don't let the double standard get you down. I've hit the double standard on its head, and that's what I've always wanted to do.

What does a character in a blockbuster novel read? Other blockbuster novelists, of course: Lucky Santangelo, one of the key alter-egos in the Collinsverse, reads Mario Puzo (no surprises there!), Joseph Wambaugh and early Harold Robbins ('always a kick to reread *A Stone For Danny Fisher* and *The Adventurers*' [147]). Another of Collins' alter-egos, Madison Castelli, reads Mario Puzo and Tom Wolfe:

> She loved their books. *The Godfather* was her all-time favourite, and she'd just finished reading *The Bonfire of the Vanities*, which she'd devoured over two nights. (*Deadly Embrace*, 436).

---

[7] In some editions the copy-editing is patchy.
[8] Mainly Jackie Collins' taste in popular culture is on the nail; she knows who to name-drop, who to skip, and who to trash. However, sometimes her keen eye for talent eludes her: in *Hollywood Wives: The New Generation*, the gossip coven that meets monthly sorts thru good film directors: Stella says she prefers Guy Ritchie (*Snatch*) and Sam Mendes (*American Beauty*), two of the dullest, dreariest British film directors of recent times. As I like to put it: America has Martin Scorsese and Woody Allen, Britain has Guy Ritchie and Shane Meadows.

So, yeah, Collins' characters actually *read* – and they read *books!* (Even Gino Santangelo gets into reading books, starting with *The Great Gatsby*).

LOW AND HIGH ART.

This complaint is often trotted out:

- It's trash.
- So? And your point is?
- It's trash.
- But so is 99.99% of everything the global media churns out, in any era, any nation, anywhere.

If you regard Jackie Collins' books and blockbuster novels as 'trash' or 'low art' or 'populist culture', then you have to apply that same simplistic judgement to everything else you consume that is also 'low art' and 'popular culture'. It means that all of the following must also be seen as trash:

- Pop music
- Movies
- Television
- Radio
- Magazines and newspapers
- Theatre
- Internet
- Advertizing

This means, using your simplistic terms, that *all* of pop music is trash – pop music meaning soul, hip-hop, rap, rock, jazz, folk, metal, dance, drum and bass, whatever genre. It means that 99.99% of the movies you love are junk. It means *all* of television. It means 99.99% of radio. It means *all* of magazines and newspapers, lifestyle mags, consumer mags, whatever mags, except maybe some academic journals, which are 'high culture' (but even upscale newspapers are filled with 'low culture'). It means nearly all theatre, except Shakespeare, Ibsen, Chekhov, and 'serious' plays, etc. It means 99.99% of the internet. *All* advertizing and anything commercial, naturally.

If you were serious about avoiding all kinds of 'trash' and 'low culture', you would only partake of: ballet, opera, classical music, art, museums, and straight theatre. You would never enter a supermarket, never surf the web, never glance at a billboard, never go to the cinema, never watch TV, never listen to the radio or pop music, never go to a pop concert, never read a magazine or newspaper, never consume advertizing of any kind, and so on.

EMBOSSED COVERS

The 'blockbuster' novel, the 'airport' novel, the 'trashy' novel, the 'beach' novel, or the 'vacation' novel,[9] can be spotted a mile off in any bookstore or supermarket: they sport embossed covers, loud colours, and sexy, direct cover images. The letters are gaudily coloured – in gold, red, silver and white. The author's name is huge on the cover, having precisely the same effect as over-the-top storefronts on main streets, or hoardings placed above cinemas, or the billboards lining Sunset Boulevard.

Like a movie star appearing above the title of a film, the author of the blockbuster novel is displayed to maximum effect. The cult of personality is as highly developed here as in any other part of the media:

> JACKIE COLLINS - SHIRLEY CONRAN - JILLY COOPER - BARBARA TAYLOR BRADFORD - JUDITH KRANTZ - E.L. JAMES - VIRGINIA ANDREWS.

These are some of the well-known women authors, while among male authors we find:

> MICHAEL CRICHTON - DEAN KOONTZ - TOM CLANCY - JOHN GRISHAM - DAN BROWN - STEPHEN KING - HAROLD ROBBINS - ROBERT LUDLUM - JOHN LE CARRE - JEFFREY ARCHER - JAMES HERBERT - JACK HIGGINS - DICK FRANCIS - FREDERICK FORSYTH.

The blockbuster novel is not confined to one particular genre: the movie star/ celebrity treatment occurs with authors in horror, thrillers, detective fiction, sci-fi, war and others. The blockbuster novel itself subsumes something of family saga, soap opera, historical and domestic romance.

A glance at the covers of the blockbuster novel reveals the nature of the narratives. Jackie Collins' *Sinners*, for instance, features a young, nude woman in a luxurious, blue swimming pool; an archetypal blockbuster image (when you fly into LAX, you look

---

[9] Other terms applied to blockbuster fiction, including Jackie Collins' books, include 'potboilers', 'hack', and 'junk'.

down and see thousands of nude women in swimming pools, don't you? Sure you do!). *The Stud*'s cover depicts a zip sliding down bare, tanned flesh (very Rolling Stones). The cover of *Princess Daisy* by Judith Krantz features a soft-focus shot of an enigmatic woman. Inside the cover, however, is a child-like, poster-colour picture guide to the book's characters. The text reads: 'Stash – Daisy's father, Ram – Daisy's half-brother', and so on. The characters are portrayed like those in movie advertizing: the evil stepmother, the hunky hero, the dark-haired rival, etc. One meets the author first, then the title, then the characters: typically, a brief description of the main characters appears on the back cover (a format followed by Collins' books to the letter).

Book covers change with fashion and style like everything else in the entertainment industry: more recent book covers of Jackie Collins' books feature artwork by Jacqueline Bissett (an artist, not the actress) of generic women (young, attractive, glamorous) in high fashion outfits (pastel shades, reds, pinks, blues). The Bissett-Collins covers recall magazine covers, as generalized figureheads for the product: but they're not images of any particular character or situation in the novels (which is a pity in a way – it would be great if there was a whole strand of illustrations for Collins' characters, like there is of, say, *Harry Potter* or the Arthurian legends).

As publishers have long known, the cover of a book is one of the primary selling tools. It is all-important, and will sometimes go through a number of iterations, like a movie poster or a logo for a new business, before the final image is settled upon. (And authors do not have much say, usually, with this side of the publishing business. However, keeping a big-selling author happy is obviously essential, and they're not going to put something on the cover that really irks the writer. However, some writers are astonished by some of the cover images their publishers come up with).

Like most blockbuster novels, Jackie Collins' books come frieghted with puff pieces and rave reviews, on the jacket or at the front and back. And ads for her other books. They also contain short extracts of future books, which act like movie trailers or previews or teasers (printed at the back of the book, without page numbers).

BACK COVERS

The back cover of Jackie Collins' 1988 novel *Rock Star* introduces the reader to exotic people; KRIS PHOENIX - the legendary and wildly sexy guitar hero. BOBBY MONDELLA - black soul superstar with a past. RAFAELLA - an exotically 'beautiful girl who comes between them with a vengeance.' The back of Judith Krantz's modern fairy tale *Princess Daisy* reads: 'Daisy's life was a fairy-tale filled with parties and balls, priceless jewels, money and love.'

The plot of the blockbuster/ airport/ vacation novel is hinted at on the back cover in a language now familiar, sprinkled with words such as 'steamy', 'glittering', 'vengeance' and 'stardom'. In over-size capitals and coloured type, newspaper quotes back up the marketing exercise:

- 'SEXUAL ATHLETICS AMONG THE IN-CROWD', yells the London *Sunday Times* of *The Stud*
- 'SENSATIONAL, BITTER, COMPLETELY COMPULSIVE', asserts *She* magazine of *The Love-Killers*
- 'A SEXY SIZZLER', crows *USA Today* of *Hollywood Wives*.

The blockbuster novel is sold like a new Broadway musical or a tentpole movie: 'BRILLIANT', 'SUPERB' and 'DAZZLING!' are the typical effusions plastered all over theatres and hoardings. The merchandizing mechanism is so familiar, it is difficult to imagine these kitsch best-selling books without their glittering covers (or anyone being fooled for a moment by the hype). Imagine a scholarly edition of Jackie Collins, clad in sombre, black hardback, complete with footnotes, annotations and index and bibliography: an improbable (but not impossible) item.[10]

★

BEYOND GENRE

The blockbuster-campy-airport-beach-vacation-tune-out novel is not a genre. It's more a way of approaching and selling fiction (that is,

---

10 Yeah, in the future there'll be scholarly editions of *Poor Little Bitch Girl* (priced at $79.95 in hardcover), with footnotes and introductions from the latest trendy eggheads of lit'ry philosophy. Students will need to buy the book for their Yale University course *Race and Ethnicity In Jackie Collins*.

it's a marketing construct, because booksellers – and the media – like to know where to put the books on the shelf, and how to categorize their products). Thus, one finds a horror blockbuster or a fantasy blockbuster beside each other on the bookshelves. The marketing devices meld the genres together. There are some genres suited to the blockbuster novel: crime and thrillers, sci-fi, historical romance, family saga and Gothic horror. A blockbuster novel is rarely a comedy or a satire. The blockbuster novel instead aspires to a pseudo-realism. After all, these books are called 'novels', which gives them a certain (though sometimes spurious) dignity.

'Blockbuster fiction realism' – the term itself is a contradiction. How can something be real *and* over-the-top, in the blockbuster tradition? Quite easily, when it is written about, when it is manufactured in words, in a fantastical fiction. Blockbuster novel realism is not the gritty realism of working-class streets and race-torn neighbourhoods, even though many blockbuster protagonists begin their ambitious, colourful lives in the gutter or the ghetto (that's the 'dark past' a million characters have, including those of Jackie Collins).

But all fiction is *fiction*. Made-up stuff. Play-acting. Putting on silly clothes and fooling around.

(Or put it like this: a term like 'realism' is pretty useless (like naturalism). Instead, think of fiction as building different worlds, of worlds-within-worlds. Some worlds might relate to the so-called 'real world'. But they don't have to, or need to. As Ursula Le Guin commented, writing about the 'real world' in a slanted or altered manner (sometimes in reverse), as in science fiction and fantasy fiction, is a great way of looking at it).

The blockbuster novel draws together fictional forms such as the epic, the saga, the romance and the soap opera. Blockbuster novels claim to have a 'sweeping' view of life (the same ad-man phrases occur all the time: 'sweeping', 'epic', 'dark', 'steamy', 'thrilling'). Janet Bailey's *Tangled Vines* is advertised in *Cosmopolitan* magazine thus: 'From the valleys of California to the buzzing newsrooms of New York – a sweeping story of glamour, intrigue and romance'.

The blockbuster novel is a yarn, a tale, a story in the time-honoured tradition (i.e., they are very conventional novels, in the 18th century or 19th century tradition, and not in the modernist or *avant garde* tradition). There are also many elements of the fairy tale and the folk tale, of getting the prince, of overcoming obstacles, of achieving a quest, and being rewarded with wealth and marriage. The blockbuster novel also updates the 'bodice-ripper' (a sub-genre of romantic fiction), infusing it with titillation and sex.

The Penny Dreadful,[11] the 'blood and thunder' and the 'bloods' of the Victorian era and Victorian melodrama are also ancestors of Jackie Collins' books and the blockbuster novel – quick, cheap, sensational and lurid publishing in weekly installments.

Of all the genres among bestselling books, thrillers out-number everything else. In 1995, a list of the genres for the top-selling books included: thrillers: 27, crime: 7, romance: 6, sagas: 5, autobiographies: 5, humour: 4, fantasy: 3, TV tie-in books: 3, film tie-in books: 2, horror: 2, science: 2, gardening 2, short stories: 1, with genres such as travel, drink and biography having 1 book each. In the 1990s, thrillers took between 20% and 25% of the share of bestselling novels each year. Thriller/ crime fiction continues to dominate fiction publishing. (And in movies and television, yes, thrillers are everywhere).

The blockbuster novel is a fusion of genres, taking in the romance and family saga, elements of the thriller or crime novel, and sometimes adventure or sci-fi, and often with the relationship story, uppermost. Jackie Collins' books are pretty much her own genre, but her fictions draw on relationships, romances and family sagas most notably, with plenty of thriller and crime elements, plus there are occasional flights into adventure (And some of Collins' most enjoyable outings are when she allows herself to write a full-on adventure/ action scenario – like the plane crash in the Amazon jungle in *Lovers and Gamblers*).

One of the tendencies of the blockbuster novel is towards the soap opera, a day-to-day story of the lives of the Rich and Famous (or the Weird and the Down-trodden). Not surprisingly, blockbuster

---

11 The 'penny dreadfuls' and the 'penny bloods' were deliberately shocking and gory, and low brow and populist (just like TV and cinema – indeed, television and movies took up the same sort of area of trashy entertainment, and has continued to exploit the same territory for 115 years).

The 'penny dreadfuls' or 'bloods' were at the height of their popularity in the 1840s and 1850s. It was quick, cheap and sensational publishing in serial (often weekly) form in periodicals and newspapers.

The penny bloods and 'penny dreadfuls' exploited new printing technology which could produce thousands of copies of magazines and newspapers, as well as cheap distribution, which fed into the rise in literacy as well as the huge acceleration in population in London. (The comics industry in Japan is a comparable phenomenon).

novels are eminently suitable for TV and film adaptation. They become television 'mini-series', extended fairy tales in modern dress.

But blockbuster novels are *already* their own TV and movie adaptations: they don't need to be turned ino movies and television: they are already there. (An adaptation of a Jackie Collins novel is unnecessary – you can imagine what those characters look and sound like, which actor would play them, and even where the commercial breaks would come after the suspenseful build-up to another cliff-hanger).

Another part of this world is the glossy or upmarket soap opera on the tube – *Dallas, Dynasty, The Colbys,* and *Sex and the City,* etc. These North American TV soaps and shows, with their ambitious characters, exotic locations and moneyed lifestyles, are the small screen versions of the blockbuster novel.

> *She'd watched* Sex and the City *many times and noted that the girls on the show slept with different men all the time. And not only did they sleep with them, they were treated with respect and handsomely rewarded. None of them appeared to have serious jobs, yet the money seemed to flow. They all lived in luxury apartments, they all wore beautiful clothes.* (*Married Lovers,* 232-3)

★

CHARACTERS

The cast of characters in a Jackie Collins novel (and in many a blockbuster novel) are very familiar types:

* there's the young actor or actress eager to break into the business (who often stoops to hustling or prostitution);
* the young actor might also be a young stud, oh-so cool, so attractive, so squeezable;
* there's the ageing Hollywood star or director worrying about their looks, career and marriages;
* there's always a young woman, 15 or 16, who's rebellious but very desirable (Collins' beloved 'wild child' persona);[12]
* there's always a weirdo or psycho intent on revenge;

---
[12] If Collins' biographical statements are to be believed, she was the original Wild Child.

★ there's a gambler who gets into big debts;
★ there are wise guys, vain actors and cocky twentysomethings who chase women and good times;
★ there's a weasely brother/ sister/ cousin who sells out their famous relatives (often to the tabloids);
★ there's always a powerful, middle-aged woman, successful in a man's business world;
★ and always gangsters, often small-time, who hang about Vegas.

And there are numerous secondary characters who crop up in every book. These include:

★ over-weight assistants and hairdressers, who're permanently man-hunting (whether they're male or female);
★ young chauffeurs on the make;
★ photographers (often Italian and/ or gay);
★ gay stylists;
★ agents and managers;
★ maids and housekeepers who're Puerto Rican or Mexican.[13]

Yes, and Jackie Collins' characters have terrific and often silly names – like those of porn stars or pop stars: Charlie Brick, Jeff Stoner, Tim Wealth, Charlie Dollar, Joey Lorenzo, Jack Python, Wes Money, Silver Anderson, Orville Gooseberger, Steve Valentine, etc. You know you're in Blockbusterland when the people are called Jack Python or Nick Angel. And when Morton Sharkey is a lawyer! (Collins also favours the dumb names favoured by celebrities naming their offspring: Heaven, Summer, Sunday, etc – even Military!).[14]

Jackie Collins is great with titles: *Hollywood Wives, American Star, Rock Star, Lovers & Gamblers, The World Is Full of Married Men,* and *Poor Little Bitch Girl.* (1971's *Sunday Simmons and Charlie Brick* is a terrible title, and was duly changed to *Sinners* in 1984, a much more appropriate Jackie Collins title).

★

---

[13] Collins' books do not question the racial status quo, where Mexican and Hispanic people still do many of the menial jobs in North America.
[14] One of Brigette's exes, Paul, calls his kid Military in *Vendetta: Lucky's Revenge* (63).

THE TRUTH AND THE LIE

Jackie Collins tells the truth, and truth is stranger than fiction, the newspaper quotes on the covers of her books inform us. 'I write about real people in disguise,' she says, 'If anything, my characters are toned down – the real thing is much more bizarre.' (*Sinners,* 1) The truth is so strange, she hints, that no one would believe her if she described it (we all know that!). But 'believe me, in my books you are getting the real truth', she asserts in "A special interview with Jackie Collins" printed at the back of *Rock Star* (460).

It is a watered-down version of glittering reality that she give us. In fact it is a fantasy, a lie, a construct, like all art and all fiction. There isn't an ounce of 'truth' in it as everybody knows. But it is the illusion of 'truth', the 'truth' of art, like a Constantin Brancusi sculpture, or a symphony by Gustav Mahler. But there's no 'reality' in any art; there are simulations or illusions of 'realism' or 'naturalism'.

Jackie Collins has sometimes claimed to possess an authoritative overview of Hollywood, but of course hers is an extremely selective, highly-edited view (as anyone's is). As expressed in her novels, it is fiction, a fantasy in the tradition of a Walt Disney fairy tale. The many moral lessons in traditional 16th-19th century fairy tales – that you will get your prince, that men can be noble, that decent behaviour wins, that hard work is rewarded, that goodness will be recognized in the end – are propounded again and again in Collins' books. Her stories are fairy tales with sex and violence added. Or rather, fairy tales as they always were – full of sex and violence. Because fairy tales before they were sanitized or censored by teachers, educationalists, religious groups and parents (throughout the 19th century), were often 'steamy' and 'racy' and violent.

★

FICTION: IT'S MAKING STUFF UP

What you don't remember – make up.

Jean-Luc Godard (1968)

Far-fetched? Unbelievable? Over-the-top? Certainly the world of Jackie Collins' work is OTT and wild. That is, if you apply the rules and regulations of the so-called 'real world' and/ or 'realism' to her fiction (but 'realism', as you soon find out, can mean anything. Whose 'realism' are we talking about? 'Realism' in relation to what? Social 'realism'? If so, which society?). But Collins' books are *novels*. They are *stories* (published within a particular social, economic and historical context). They were never meant to be 'real', or interpreted as 'reality'. Yet so many detractors and critics use the rules of the 'real world' and apply them to Collins' characters and situations. 'Silly!' they cry. 'No one behaves like that in real life!' they complain.

Wrong.

Think of Jackie Collins' books as creating a *fictional and imaginary world*, like *any* novel, like *any* story – like *all* stories. Consider the world of Collins' novels like a fantastical realm. Like the fantasy realms such as Middle-earth in J.R.R. Tolkien's books, or the secret service/ political spy worlds of Ian Fleming or John Le Carré, or the late 19th century Dorset of Thomas Hardy, or the WW1 Nottinghamshire of D.H. Lawrence, or the 1800s Russia of Leo Tolstoy, or the prehistoric Greece of Homer's *Odyssey* and *Iliad*.

Right.

Then you can see that *within* the rules and laws that Ms Collins creates for herself in her fictional worlds, her characters and situations and settings are convincing. In fact, Collins' characters are just as convincing as any I can think of in contemporary fiction or in fiction of the 18th century to the present. Or the past few thousand years. (Maybe the *events* and the *lifestyles* stretch credibility, but we've all met *characters* like the people in Collins' fiction).

Yes.

Take *The Odyssey*. No one complains about the best adventure story and myth in world literature that gods like Athena or Poseidon appearing and speaking to Odysseus is silly or unbelievable. Or that Odysseus could never have had all those adventures with the Cylops and Circe and dragons and magic and all the rest. Or even been away for 19 years from Penelope (did she really keep the suitors busy in her home for 19 years?! Even a Hollywood super-hostess in a Jackie Collins novel would be running outta ideas!).

All those things are part of the mythology, the magic, the mystery and the poetry of Homer's *Odyssey*. You don't take it all literally and seriously (although some folk do, and archaeologists have spent years researching the real places in the Mediterranean mentioned in Homer's epic poem. Which is literalizing the metaphor, a big mistake, as happens with the *Bible*. It's the 'masks of God', as Joseph Campbell put it).

You go along for the ride.

You accept that Gods and Goddesses materialize in front of characters in an Ancient Greek, mythological story like the *Odyssey* or the *Iliad*. You accept that Dante and Virgil chat to tormented sinners as they take a guided tour through Hell in Dante Alighieri's mediæval poem *The Divine Comedy*. You accept that a story can involve soldiers on the front line *and* aristocrats having grand balls and dinner parties then fleeing Moscow *and* Napoleonic politics in Leo Tolstoy's *War and Peace*.

And what works for Homer works for Miguel de Cervantes or Charlotte Brontë or F. Scott Fitzgerald... or Jackie Collins.

Fiction is *fiction.* Made-up stuff. Like movies are *fiction.*

Writers make up stuff as their profession: they are professional liars.

Or put it like this: what *you* think is 'realistic' ain't the same as what *I* think is 'realistic' or *someone else* regards as 'true to life'. What you (or me) think of as the most 'gritty', 'realistic' and 'true to life' book or movie or poem or whatever, might be for someone else the silliest, corniest, most unbelievable thing ever created.

The whole notion of 'realism' or 'naturalism' is very complex – and very subjective. Too complicated to get into here.

Maybe it's partly due to critics and detractors of Jackie Collins' work getting confused between the fictional world she has created and the so-called 'real world', our 'real world', in particular the 'real world' of the media, of Hollywood, of celebrity culture, of stardom. And we all know just how *fake* and *phoney* all of that is. Because Hollywood and the media and celebrity culture is *also* a *fictional world.* In this respect, like any fictional book about Hollywood or the media, Collins' books are fictions about other fictions. (But Collins includes references to 'real' people (Mel Gibson), 'real' places (LAX), and 'real' events (WW2).)

Also, I wonder if readers and fans as well as critics and detractors of Jackie Collins' novels are confused about the celebrities and stars they read about in gossip magazines and on television shows like *Entertainment Tonight* or *Access Hollywood*, and the characters that Collins creates in her stories. Collins' characters are completely, utterly *fictional*. But the movie stars and rock stars and supermodels seen in those TV shows and in those supermarket gossip magazines are also to a large extent *fictional*. Because for readers and TV viewers they only exist in magazines and on television.

Everything you know about Madonna or Princess Diana or Donald Trump or Rupert Murdoch comes from television or books or newspapers or magazines or radio or the internet (information which is then repeated between people). They only exist as photographs, images, representations, sounds. That is, unless you've met those people. Maybe you have. But I bet 99.99% of the readers of Jackie Collins' books have *not* met those people in person, and only know about them from books and magazines and newspapers and the web and TV.

So if Jackie Collins' books are fictions about fictions, how can terms such as 'realism' or 'authenticity' or 'believability' be used at all?

★

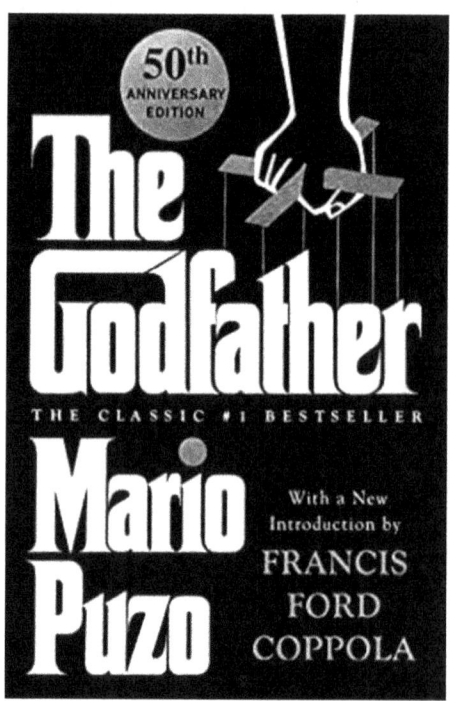

Some blockbuster novels (this page and over).

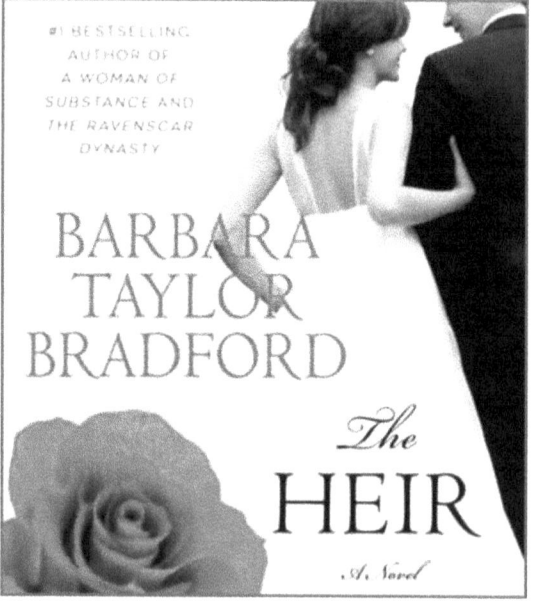

EXTREMISM

One of the most obvious elements of the blockbuster novel is not its tendency to fuse genres, but its relentless extremism. Lifestyles are so much larger than life, cars are huge stretch limos, hotels and apartments are exotically plush, obsessions are suitably odd and passionate. 'Epic' is a typical term applied to the blockbuster novel, as is the word 'sweeping'. So many books (and films) are described as 'set against the sweeping/ epic backdrop of such-and-such a place and time' (in movie-land, the model for this is definitely *Gone With the Wind*, a book and movie which's the template for much of contemporary blockbuster fiction and movies). Such bland statements of advertizing reveal the mechanisms of so much popular entertainment: the story and characters become subordinate to the background, the locations, the exotic *mise-en-scène*. Image triumphs over psychology, fashion and lifestyle transcend motive and emotion, the exotic continually displaces the humdrum, and politics and ideology are actively suppressed.

This is a fantasy world, recognizable from fairy tales as much as from teleivision soap opera. Certainly escapism features prominently (but escape *from* what? And escape *to* what?). Out of *this* life, into *that* life. Into something Other.

Maybe one of art's (entertainment's) primary functions is to take you out of yourself, to take you anywhere. In which case, any movement, any escape, will do – into fantasy, into 'reality', into love, into death, whatever – as long as it's elsewhere. (Perhaps this is because being yourself, all the time, is exhausting, or boring. So you take a break from yourself, or the dull parts of your life).

Blockbuster novels are not mirrors, in the sense that TV soap operas would like to be (but patently aren't). Theirs is a different kind of verisimilitude (a different kind of fantasy).

The blockbuster novel enhances, enlarges and colourfully embroiders so-called 'ordinary life'. The emotions of everyday life are flashily exaggerated in blockbuster stories to become consuming passions. Blockbuster novels do not exist in a day-to-day world, a workaday world; they are not the diaries of 'ordinary people', in the way that newspapers and soap operas purport to be (but patently aren't – what *is* an 'ordinary' person? Only what a particular society at a particular time and place in a particular context regards as 'ordinary'. And not everyone within that society or community would agree on what is 'ordinary' anyway. In a postmodern world (i.e., based on/ using postmodern theory), there are no 'grand narratives' or 'totalities' any more. So there's no universal person, or 'ordinary person'.)

The aim of the best-selling novel is largely to *entertain*. It is a noble and difficult goal: I don't have the disdain that some critics have for entertainment, whether populist or high-brow – because entertainment/ leisure/ laughter/ enjoyment is immensely important. Yeah, and the blockbuster novel is supremely successful.[1]

★

SUN, SEA, SAND AND SEX

> 'Paying for pussy? In *this* town!' he'd exclaimed. 'LA is a free pussy heaven!'
>
> Jackie Collins, *Lady Boss* (221)

A clichéd image is of some bourgeois book reader/ tourist tanning themselves on a Mediterranean or Florida beach, consuming a glossy, trashy book. The blockbuster novel is an object of luxury and relaxation. It is not to be taken seriously, but to be enjoyed – for fun, for kicks, for thrills. Pleasure's a goal of the blockbuster character and perhaps also the blockbuster reader. You dip your hand into a huge box of chocolates or popcorn poolside in Vegas or on the porch. Similarly, you dip into a blockbuster novel. You don't take Arthur Schopenhauer's *Essays and Aphorisms* down to the hotel pool in the morning in Vegas.

> Vegas blew him away: the long parade of neon lights and the huge gambling palaces, not to mention the unbelievably gorgeous showgirls and dancers, vast hotels and lavish shows. (104-5)

I would put the blockbuster novel and Jackie Collins' books in the same category as a box of chocolates, or a body massage, or watching a movie or pornography: it's escapism, it's fantasy, it's fun, it's silly, and it's not meant to be taken seriously ever.

---

[1] If William Shakespeare hadn't entertained audiences in the Globe and Rose Theatres of Elizabethan London, he wouldn't have been able to write play after play.

In *Cosmopolitan* (September, 1992), Lis Leigh's novel *Greed* is advertized thus: 'The world's first gastronomic blockbuster: bonk appetit!' How neatly this advert fits in with the foody sections of a magazine. It makes the age-old connections between food and sex (more recent examples of the foody-sexy novel include *Chocolat* (1999), by Joanne Harris).[2] The blockbuster novel is a decadent feast, naughty but nice, so bad for you, yet oh-so good as well, an indulgence, a weakness, a drug.

★

GLITTERING BACKDROPS

> Las Vegas. City of lights. City of sin. A magical mystery town where anything could happen, and usually did.
>
> *Goddess of Vengeance* (170)

The worlds of the blockbuster novel are largely those of the media: fashion and television, theatre and newspapers, pop music and Hollywood. Not radio (far too boring), nor classical music or ballet or painting or museum culture (a Jackie Collins novel set in a classical ballet theatre[3] in Moscow? I don't think so! Backstage at a topless show in Vegas, yes!). A typical blockbuster novel will draw together characters from cinema, fashion, modelling, pop music, TV and magazines. Often big business is featured, because of the allure of money. The clichéd underworld of the mafia, crime and drug culture is used too, but it is the glittering, glamorous, gorgeous worlds that rule supreme.

Rags-to-riches is the typical plot (it's the one Jackie Collins uses most) – so the seedier the poverty at the beginning of the tale, the richer the riches at the end. Having humble origins is noble, too, and carries authenticity, sympathy, sacrality. To make it to the top from the bottom of the pile is especially good, and endorses good Christian and Protestant (and fairy tale) values. And it's the Great American Dream.

Typically, the blockbuster novel opposes its glamorous richness

---
2 *Chocolat* was made into a truly abysmal movie in 2000.
3 In *Deadly Embrace*, Michael Castelli, another authorial stand-in, regards ballet and opera 'one big yawn' (375).

with (an idealized) poverty and suffering. From so many depressed and deprived streets and ghettos rise so many shining stars, actresses, singers, models and business people. For any hero/ine, a certain stylized poverty works wonders, as Heathcliff showed in *Wuthering Heights*.

The worlds of the blockbuster novel include bars, hotels, swimming pools, movie sets and movie offices, theatres, cinemas, jet planes, penthouses and limousines. Blockbuster novels describe the best in everything: stores, women, cars, casinos, clothes, champagne, cuisine, make-overs, jewellery, houses, furniture, travel.

Kris Phoenix, the guitar hero of *Rock Star* by Jackie Collins, lives in a typical blockbuster fictional world: he sleeps in an 'oversized California King bed, in his over-sized Bel Air mansion' (1). The goal is to attain as much wealth and as much pleasure as possible. This quote from *Rock Star* illustrates the emphasis on wealth, and on the rags-to-riches striving:

> His Bel Air mansion stood on two acres of impeccably kept ground. Flowing lawns, sumptuous flower beds, lemon and orange trees, brilliant bougainvillea, and the obligatory Hollywood swimming pool and tennis court. Not bad for an English lad who was chucked out of school at fifteen[4] without two pennies to rub together. (57)

One word sums it up: *Hollywood*.

> 'Ah... Hollywood. Nirvana. Paradise. Palm trees, sunshine, and agents.' (*Lady Boss*, 69)

★

IMAGES, MAGAZINES, FASHION

> Zipping along the Pacific Coast Highway in her red Ferrari, vintage Marvin Gaye blasting on her CD player, Lucky felt pretty good about everything.
>
> Jackie Collins, *Dangerous Kiss* (24)

I am going to discuss women's magazines and fashion for a moment here because the world of the women's magazines and fashion is the same as that of the blockbuster novel, and Jackie Collins' output.

The blockbuster novel trades on the visual image. Images

---
[4] We recall that Collins ankled school at 15.

preside over all things: the blockbuster novel takes many of its cues from the world of high fashion, as mediated mainly through magazines (and also television, cel phones and the internet). The term 'shopping and fucking'[5] emphasizes the shopping as much as the fucking (and there's usually plenty more shopping and voracious consumerism than sex in blockbuster novels, including the novels that advertize themselves as full of sex, and including Jackie C.'s books).

> Fontaine zipped through the New York stores at an alarming pace. When it came to shopping for clothes there was nobody better at spending money than she was – except perhaps Jackie Onassis. (*The Bitch*, 34)

Cleo James indulges in several bouts of shopping-as-therapy in *The World is Full of Divorced Women*:

> Two pairs of Yves Saint Laurent shoes, three silk shirts, one pair of Oliver Goldsmith sunglasses tinted green, and a Chloe dress later, she felt a lot better. Ease the tension by releasing some hard earned cash, there was nothing like it. (68)

Characters in blockbuster fiction amass designer labels. That is, all the cultural references must be exactly the *right* ones. To name the wrong label, carry the wrong bags, wear the out-of-date fashion accessory, is instant death. Blockbuster fiction characters are fashion victims, slaves to the Look. Image <> perception <> surface. It's postmodern, self-reflexive, narcissistic, and also about controlling other people's perception of oneself. Wearing a particular item of clothing is about saying: 'this is how I'm going to control how *you* look at *me*'. It's all about *me*, putting self before society, before other people.

> Poppy Soloman had changed her outfit five times. She was in a panic and simply could not make up her mind. Should she wear the Valentino? The Chanel? The Saint Laurent?
> She stamped her foot and let out a blood-curdling yell of frustration. (*Hollywood Husbands*, 237)

Make-up is also exalted: 'Over Pater Thomas Roth went Estée Lauder, with a touch of Revlon around the eyes' (*Vendetta: Lucky's Revenge*, 304).

The visual image dominates the fashion world. Fashion models don't talk – not because they are bimbos and have nothing to say,

---

[5] 'Hoarding and humping' is another term.

but because words (written or spoken) ruin the mystery and romance of it all. It's about *beauty*, and beauty goes a long, long way.

And beauty goes beyond words. Can you put beauty into words? You can try, but you can't wholly capture the beauty of a particular face in words. Nope, not even the greatest writers in the world can do it. (That's partly why we have photographs, paintings, movies – going back to prehistoric cave drawings – to express what we can't say or write).

Fashion is built on fantasy, and serious talk punctures the dream-bubbles. Images do the talking, and in high fashion, the Look is everything.

Beauty.

The image and beauty.

The pleasure of the image, the pleasure of *looking*.

Fashion magazines and women's magazines are full of women portrayed in romantic, sexual, dominant, subservient, idiotic, funny and serious roles. The attitudes these magazines extol are the same as those of the Hollywood entertainment industry: money is wonderful; materialism is wonderful; one must always look incredible; sex is heterosexual, pre-natal and helps one acquire money and men; the best life is one led in exotic places, in palatial houses, eating gorgeous food off pretty furniture.

In magazines such as *Vogue, Elle, Glamour* and *Tatler*, one finds items on fashion; fashion tips; beauty and health; hair; food and living; wine; movies; music; books; horoscopes; motoring; travel; and features on movie stars, pop stars, models and royalty. In magazines such as *Harpers & Queen*, royalty is exalted. The homes of the (European) royals, the lives and loves of the royals, what they wear, what they drive and what they eat, are all slavishly celebrated. The U.S.A. has the Kennedy dynasty, and Britain has the Royal Family. And magazines such as *Hello, National Enquirer, People, Voici, Globe* and *OK* and the gossip magazines have features on the equivalent celebrities in every territory that contains an audience with money to buy the magazines.

In women's magazines, the emphasis is on life – improving it, in having what you want. The magazines tell you how to get what you want. They tell you how to dress, how to talk, how to walk, how to exercise – in short, how to do everything, and how to think about everything. Sometimes the tone is patronizing and didactic: 'London is simply the place to live', is a typical statement. Or: 'the colour red is the colour of the moment.'

Fashion is fickle: next year the colour might be blue, or apricot, or lilac. The colour itself doesn't matter: the self-important, pseudo-authoritative tone is. What's 'in' is 'in', and one must be filled with awe for fashion gurus and gods. Fashion magazines are continually sorting through what is 'in' and what is 'out'.

> 'I want a Ferrari, two mink coats, lots of diamonds, a beautiful penthouse in New York, and a villa on the Riviera!' (*The World Is Full of Married Men*, 24)

The cult of the celebrity, of fame, of glamour, in the modern era chimes with (and partly comes out of) the art of the Andy Warhol and Pop Art. Bland, alienating, depersonalized and vacuous, and wittily, intentionally so, of course, Warhol's art adored glamour, particularly stars such as Marilyn Monroe, Liz Taylor and Elvis Presley (stardom and celebrity is enshrined everywhere in Jackie Collins' fiction). Warhol made icons out of movie and pop stars. Warhol's blank repetitions of electric chairs, Campbell soup cans, car crashes and movie stars seem to be cleverly ironic commentaries on the hedonism of consumerism, the pleasure of mass culture (the 'trash' that Warhol loved, the 'trash' that readers of Collins 'guiltily' consume). Warhol showed one didn't have to be as skilled as a Leonardo da Vinci to be able to produce 'great art'. One needed to be a good publicist, good with mass mechanical production techniques, good at organizing other people. (Meanwhile, Warhol's coterie and the Factory have provided inspiration for numerous subsequent artists, from David Bowie to Jackie Collins).

★

HOLLYWOOD

> People are intrigued by fame, power and wealth and I think Hollywood is the only place where you get all three together.
>
> Jackie Collins

The places favoured are the cities of high fashion, the destinations of jet-setters: London, Paris, New York, Tokyo. But one word sums them all up: **HOLLYWOOD**, the dream factory, where sleaze and sex and glamour seethe, where gangsters, whores, tycoons and starlets hang out. The fascination of the blockbuster novel stems partly from its setting, and nowhere is more glittering and more wannabe (and more cynical and crushing) than Tinseltown. From the seedy bars on the Strip to the remote and plush palaces tucked away in Beverly Hills and Bel Air, Hollywood has all the locations necessary for a good blockbuster yarn. As Jackie Collins put it:

> ...Hollywood is a magic name – a name that conjures up glamour, great romance, mystery, the movies and scandal. (ib. 460)

Fashion magazines and lifestyle magazines and women's magazines and general interest magazines trade a good deal on Hollywood, the mythology, ethics, gossip, history and poetry of Hollywood. Models are made up to look like movie stars; they pose in movie sets; the pictures are often narrative in nature, as if they were film stills; black-and-white prints refer not to the history of photography, not to Eugène Atget, Julia Cameron, Richard Avedon or Edward Weston, but to old, Hollywood movies of the 1940s and 1950s (you can see the posters and memorabilia in the stores along Hollywood Boulevard). Fashion constantly regurgitates the past, and presents it as the new. In many photo spreads in magazines there are references made to the act of making pictures: cables, lights, mirrors and props will be included in the shot, to draw the attention of the reader/ viewer to the manufacture of what s/he is consuming. Such self-reflexive signs indicate again where the fashion spread is coming from: Hollywood. Jackie Collins' novels play with all of that mythology,[6] as well as the crossover between the fashion industry and the Hollywood movie industry.

★

---

[6] Collins' books feature numerous photo shoots, for instance, or scenes on film sets, where entertainment and Hollywood is produced.

The first time (there is always a *first time*) a character reaches Los Angles is a magic moment (ah, it was for me). It has to be. This is **HOLLYWOOD**, La-La Land, Tinseltown, the Dream Factory. When future superstar Nick Angelo reaches the Angelic City in *American Star*, Jackie Collins writes:

> On the ride he took in the scenery. Wide streets, tall, dusty palm trees, and a proliferation of gas stations, fast food chains and used car lots. Pedestrians were sparse on the street, but cars were everywhere.
> As they got closer to the town the greenery overwhelmed him. Every garden seemed to be filled with exotic plants, and every street lined with trees.
> He couldn't help feeling excited. After all, this was the real thing, he was in Los Angeles for chrissake. Hollywood. Land of the movies. Jeez! If he was lucky he might even bump into Dustin Hoffman or Al Pacino walking down the fucking street! (239)

The ingredients in this highly artificial, fictional world are, simply: 'glamour, sex, great power and huge fortunes' (ib., 462). Conveniently, Hollywood has all that, or *seems* to have it all (*seeming* is as good as reality in the blockbuster novel, where it's all about appearances and surfaces and perceptions). **HOLLYWOOD** is a fantasy, and a very lucrative one – and Jackie Collins trades on everything to do with Hollywood. She feeds off it all, and feeds it herself, with her books.

> The first I knew of L.A. was from the books of Raymond Chandler. I thought it was romantic – the tall palm trees, the art deco buildings. I don't like the earthquakes. Something in the back of my mind says, this place is going to disappear.
>
> Terence Chang, film producer

☆

Side-note on Kenneth Anger and *Hollywood Babylon*:

Published in 1959 (with editions in 1965 and 1971), *Hollywood Babylon* by Kenneth Anger mined similar bitchy, gossipy territory to Jackie Collins' fiction. *Hollywood Babylon* was one of those tabloid-style, coffee-table books aimed at a youth and bourgeois market – it would sit nicely beside books on the paranormal or horror movies, yes, but also recipe books and gardening books. (Many of the stories have since been debunked, however). *Hollywood Babylon* wasn't published in the U.S.A. until 1975 (and a later edition in 1985).

A descent into the underworld of Tinseltown, *Hollywood Babylon* revels in its camp, excesses and decadence in a rather self-conscious and patronizing manner, which masks Kenneth Anger's obvious affection for all things Hollywood. But Anger, like Jackie Collins, is a perfect chronicler of the unreality and narcissism of Hollywood.

Meanwhile, Kenneth Anger himself (born 1927, Santa Monica, CA), is a remarkable figure – far stranger than anything that Jackie Collins has cooked up. Anger is known as one of the chief North American, *avant garde* filmmakers, alongside Stan Brakhage, Jordan Belson, Maya Deren, Hollis Frampton and Michael Snow. Anger is a film legend and, like Orson Welles, Werner Herzog and Donald Cammell, he liked to embellish and mythologize his own life.[7] If you can't remember it, make it up, as Jean-Luc Godard used to say. As well as *Lucifer Rising*, Anger is known for films such as *Fireworks* (1947), *Eaux d'Artifice* (1950/ 1953), *Rabbit's Moon* (1950/ 1972), and many others. His most famous piece is *Scorpio Rising* (1963) – once seen, never forgotten.

★

TEENAGE ROMANCE

In women's magazines aimed at older audiences (the young moms and middle-aged women represented as well as targetted in *Woman, Allure, Essentials, W, Best* and *Bella*), the emphasis is not on an urban-centred, escapist fantasy, but an easily-attainable domestic unity, grouped around the traditional family unit. However, Hollywood glamour and celebrity is just as strong a presence here, in domestic magazines and lifestyle magazines. The features dwell on movie and TV stars, as if theirs are the lifestyles one must aspire to; it is the same with the tabloid newspapers in Europe and the U.S.A. This is the world of *Hello, Voici, Us, People, Gente, National Enquirer, OK* magazines and the Sunday newspaper supplements, the biographies of famous people and the TV chat shows. Gossip is the word for this kind of information, although the titbits are presented with a quasi-seriousness. (And *paparazzi* are still bugging celebs today as they have done since the 1950s).

In teen magazines (but also in *all* women's magazines), the time-

---

[7] 'Anger's cultivated image is as important as the films he makes', opines Raymond Murray (9).

worn values of Western romance and heterosexuality[8] are zappily, brashly, ludicrously exalted. 'We've got BOYS BOYS BOYS' yells *J-17*. 'YOU WANT LOVE? Our new model boys – what makes their hearts go ping'. *J-17* (in the 1990s) had a free poster with it: 'GIANT BOYS POSTER – stick it on yer wall: Drool!' Men – 'boys', 'guys' – are portrayed as hunks, muscular, good-looking, witty, friendly, sometimes shy people. Fairy tale princes.

In fairy tales, the prince often arrives at the end of a story to marry the princess, and to conclude the narrative.[9] From early ages, modern, Western societies encourage women (and men) to think of men as princes, as hunks and heroes, people who will round off and complete life with marriage. Teen magazines are full of clean-cut boys, and maybe one or two 'wild boys'. But always boys, always men marketed as studs, the objects of fantasy, potential spouses, would-be princes. Jackie Collins' fictions are full of such types – the princes, the princesses, the poor kids and the starlets (some of Collins' charas are fond of bad boys).

Later, in magazines aimed at women in their late teens and twenties (the in-betweener years) – *Elle, Cosmopolitan, Marie Claire* – the boys disappear. Instead, one finds images of women as strong and beautiful beings. The message is clear: you can become like this, like one of these affluent, successful, pretty and slim women. The objects of lust, men, are still there, but are displaced by self-achieving women. The capitalist myths have been re-orientated: now it's OK to be single and career-minded, but the emphasis is still on attainment, on striving (the endless *desire* of advanced capitalism and the middle-classes).

How does one become a rich, attractive, slim person? The solutions are provided in the ads next to the photo spreads in women's and lifestyle magazines. By purchasing make-up, clothes, jewellery, houses, furniture and vacations. Becoming a consumer. Buying happiness and fulfilment. That is the all-too simple message of advertizing.

---

8 Janet Lee remarked of *Cosmopolitan* that it 'always assumes its readers are part of a heterosexual couple, or aspiring to be; whatever the text says, there's no mistaking the images. The 'new woman', *Cosmo* version is the sexy woman. Sex equals not only fun, but independence and success' ("Care to join me in an Upwardly Mobile Tango? Postmodernism and the 'New Woman'", in L. Gamman, 168).

9 That is the view of fairy tale expert Jack Zipes (1989), and also many second wave feminists who've analyzed fairy tales. I don't wholly agree: I think the prince does function like that, but more often it's the protagonists doing things on their own (or with magical aid) that is more significant.

It does not work like that, however. It cannot possibly work like that. If you understand the nature of image-making in the media, you'll know that you can never look like a supermodel, you can never look like those glamorous people pictured there (unless you have the opportunity to be made-up and dressed and coiffured by professionals, like the models themselves, and then have yourself photographed by professional photographers. All of that is possible.)

But the single most important element is *to have yourself appearing in the magazines themselves*: you must become *an image*. That way, you could become part of the media landscape itself, part of the magazines as products and commercials, part of the imagery of advanced capitalism. You would become another fantasy and image in a world entirely made up from fantasies and images.

There is another way, though, of becoming a fabulous supermodel: by suspending one's belief and rationality, and using one's *imagination*. Fashion magazines operate in that blurred zone somewhere between desire and gratification, between fantasy and reality, between possibility and actuality. By closing one's eyes, one can enter into the glittering world of *Vogue* or *Allure*. Again, Jackie Collins' books operate in the same fantasy zone (and Collins herself has become part of the imagery of the media, the never-ending fantasy of magazines, commercials and TV chat shows).

★

WORLDS AWAY: INSIDE AND OUTSIDE WORLDS

These lush, sensual worlds occur now, right now, and right here, in the present. Or rather, just a little in the future, and just slightly out of reach.

The Jackie Collins novel is full of jealousies, desires, disappointments, ambitions and battles, just like the school playground. From an early age, children in Western territories are deluged with idealized images of people: the images say what boys should be like, what girls should be like, what they should be yearning for, what they should wear, buy, watch, and hear (for some, the social impact, particularly on young girls, can be damaging). It is the same in a Collins book: there are the Beautiful People, the Winners and the Haves, and there are the Ugly Losers, the Have-Nots.

The idea is, clearly, to be a Winner, a Have. The blockbuster book trades on school playground ethics, on the ethics of capitalism and materialism – to have, to get, to win, to be admired, to be the best. Losing is not noble – it's nowhere near, it's nothing. Nobody respects a loser. These are not the moralities of any particular decade or time, but of all capitalism, all materialism, all of history, from the hunter-gatherers of prehistory onwards (remember the Stone Age, folks? – the prehistoric competitions for who's got the biggest cave, with wall-to-wall animal skins?). It is the morality of dog-eat-dog, the Darwinian 'survival of the fittest', the Nietzschean Superman. In short, the morality of patriarchy, of men. In sum, Western capitalism (and, beyond capitalism – survival).

★

IMAGE-MAKING

Luscious, fashionable people only exist in the global media, only when mediated by television, cameras, digital technology, the web, cel phones, and printing presses. If you switch off the electricity, if you're out of the range of cel phone towers, and there's no wi-fi, the media fizzles out into the white dot of nothingness (all modern technology requires a constant supply of fuel – in which case, the most important people of all are the oil, gas and electricity companies, the power stations, the mining operations, etc). The quick route to becoming a rich, famous, fashionable person is by closing one's eyes and imagining it all. This is what blockbuster fiction does: it helps fantasies to unfold.

Going out and buying a load of make-up and clothes won't work. Fashion is a fantasy that only exists in people's imaginations, and in magazines, billboards and TV shows. When you understand the mechanics of the media you see through the lies, the veils, the banalities, the cover-ups, the double standards, the ambiguities, the selling and the 'romance'. The pretence of it all (and the desperation of it all). We're in Fantasy Land, folks, the Land of Oz. The blockbuster novel is a capitalist theme park. (We know that, but we pretend we don't; we allow ourselves to pretend).

Blockbuster novels work because, as with fashion, fame and wealth, people yearn so desperately to believe in them (and hence the fundamental significance of the rags-to-riches narrative). The superstructure of lies can only be maintained by massive amounts of yearning. You *do* want to be like that, don't you? The audience must desire things madly. Only when they do can the lies become truths (or at least have some substance), only then will the crowds roar, girls scream, boys grunt and millions of people be fleeced of millions of dollars. Belief, faith and desire are central to exploitation – you only have to look at the history of religion and politics to see that.[10]

---

[10] Film director Ken Russell hates the lie of advertizing vehemently, and has satirized it in his movies. It's the great disease of modern times, for Russell, where lies of beauty and achievement are perpetuated. For Jean-Luc Godard, advertizing was prostitution, and an encouragement to prostitution.

Three

Money and Work

…the power of money is a distinctly male power. Money speaks, but it is with a male voice. In the hands of women, money stays literal; count it out, it buys what it is worth or less. In the hands of men, money buys women, sex, status, dignity, esteem, recognition, loyalty, all manner of possibility. In the hands of men, money does not only buy; it brings with it qualities, achievements, honor, respect.

Andrea Dworkin, *Pornography* (20)

THE BLISS OF MATERIALISM

> Taylor drove her car directly to Neiman's and indulged herself with two hours of ferocious shopping to calm herself down. Everyone was getting what they wanted.
> When was it *her* turn?
>
> Jackie Collins, *Hollywood Wives: The New Generation* (95)

Shopping is *jouissance*; people have spoken about getting a kick, a high that is nearly sexual, from buying something. Shopping lifts your spirits, we're told ('retail therapy' – you buy your way out of depression and loneliness – yeah, it's *that* easy!). Similarly, chocolate has an orgasmic effect, and is consumed by love-lorn souls, like drink and drugs. Drugs become interchangeable – alcohol, cocaine, sleeping pills, tranquillizers, uppers, downers, sugar, sex, whatever.

> And there sat Howie in a three-thousand-dollar Brioni suit, four-hundred-dollar Lorenzini shirt, and a hundred-and-fifty-dollar Armani tie. (*L.A. Connections*, 178)

What is shopping? Acquiring objects, becoming a 'Have', a winner. Shopping is materialism in action. And it is blissful. In the act of shopping one enjoys the acquisition of wealth. The artefacts signify wealth, jewellery, tasteful clothes, cars, etc (pop music is full of such imagery, like hip-hop with its fads for 'bling'). To be a successful shopper one must carry the right kind of bags with the right kind of labels and logos on them. Image is everything. Being unique is crucial – one must be the only person with a particular item of clothing, for instance. No duplications, even though most objects for sale are mass-produced.[11] (But it's not survival, it's not food, it's not hunter-gathering to survive).

(And made in the People's Republic of China. Everything you are wearing right now was made in China. Or India. or Taiwan.)

But Jackie Collins also pinpoints the vacuity of a life lived in the world of fashion and shopping: in *The Bitch*, Fontaine Khaled thinks:

> God! Was this what her life was all about? Fashion and Getting Fucked. Both were beginning to pall. (124)

★

---

[11] And most are manufactured in the People's Republic of China.

NAMING NAMES

Typical names/ brands/ logos in a Jackie Collins novel include Reebok (shoes), Perrier and Evian (water), Cristal (champagne),[12] *People, Rolling Stone* and *Billboard* (magazines), Mercedes (stretch limos), Ferraris and Porsches, and Johnny Carson (television). Numerous Italian designers (Armani, Versace, Gucci). Plenty of *haute couture* (Yves St Laurent, Chanel, Valentino). There are so many mentions of certain logos and brands, you wonder if Collins had product placement deals.[13] A typical concoction of materialism occurs in Collins' *The World Is Full of Divorced Women* (in 1975):

> She dressed, slowly, dark brown gauchos, Sonia Rykel sweater, Biba boots, Gucci leather belt, Oliver Goldsmith brown-tinted sunspecs to cover her prune eyeshadowed eyes. (2)

And in *Lovers & Players* (30 years later, in 2005):

> She was featuring her Italian supermodel look – a Roberto Cavalli outfit that was totally wild. It consisted of a long gypsy-style skirt, a suede and leather-studded vest worn over a skimpy python-print bra, multiple ivory and gold crosses strung round her swan-like neck, plus fourteen ivory and silver bangles. There was plenty of toned, taut skin on display. (232)

As well as always mentioning jewellery and clothes, Jackie Collins' fiction always draws attention to hair and make-up. In Collins' work, women are continually getting in or out of the shower, sitting by their dressing tables and preparing for a night out, and spending ages deciding what to wear in walk-in closets. In *Lucky*, Collins describes the make-up routine of Eden Antonio:

> As a former model she had the drill down pat. Out of the shower, towel dry, plug in the heated rollers, splurge with the Estee body cream, spray on the Estee scent. Naked, she sat in front of her dressing table mirror, cleansed her face with cotton wool and astringent, applied moisturizer, skin-tone base, shading, powder, blusher, eye shadow, eye-liner, mascara, eyebrow pencil, lip-liner, lipstick and lip gloss. (378)

---

12 Nobody guzzles more Cristal champers than a Collins character.
13 In the early 1990s, movie product placement deals might include fees between $5,000 and $250,000, with escalation clauses for prominent or wide-ranging advertizing. Fox charged between $20,000 and $100,000 for product placement in a film. In 1989, Pepsi-Cola's Entertainment Marketing Group, its in-house product placement department, claimed they had appearances for the Pepsi trademark in 70 films. For advertizers, it means they are reaching a huge audience: not just in the theatrical release (which might reach 13 million viewers in the cinema), but in the cable, satellite, DVD and video releases, which could take the audience reach up to 25-30 million spectators.

Food and eating is another recurring motif – these are charas who eat out a lot, and dine at fancy restaurants a lot. Collins thus often mentions the menu, and cites particular restaurants (Spago's, Ma Maison, Morton's, the Bistro), as well as famous chefs (such as Wolfgang Puck).

Nowadays, in the 2020s, one might safely allude to mainstream merchandizing names such as Ralph Lauren, Chanel, Benetton, Gap and Gaultier. Naming certain names involves an élitism, a snobbery. Authors show how knowing they are, how streetwise, how sussed. In this passage from Lis Leigh's *Greed,* one finds a character surveying a hotel room in the following bemused, snobbish manner:

> No-one could object to the decor. Dark green (masculine) striped wallpaper. Pink (feminine) flowers. Patterned dark green and pink carpet, fitted. Drapes and drapes over drapes, and fringes and ties and bows in pink and borage green wild silk (luxury touches). Gold framed pictures of 1, primulas 2, daisies – no, marguerites. Do you mind? Daisies – 3, roses. Old varieties of. 4, the Hunt in Full Cry (hand-coloured engraving). Three TVs (for the ménage à trois?), cream furniture in cane, repro bergere, four four-seater traditional settees (useful for penthouse cocktail parties). Sheik-sized bed. Cream acres of fitted wardrobe. Terrace downstairs. Plastic garden furniture. (Plastic? Heavens!). Own lawn with own pine tree. China cabinets with china. Floral. Two low tables, mahogany, repro. His and hers bathrooms. His grey marble hers pink. Jacuzzis in both.[14]

At times the blockbuster novel becomes a literature of lists, endless lists of glossy objects. Nothing could be more boring, more deathly. Yet consumerism has a buzz, and most blockbuster fiction characters are addicted to it. As Cleo thinks in Jackie Collins' *The World is Full of Divorced Women*: 'Ease the tension by releasing some hard earned cash, there was nothing like it' (58). Indeed, *The World is Full of Divorced Women* opens with a scene in a store, with Cleo trying on a dress.

In the capitalist, consumerist world, everyone is a pimp, and everyone is a whore.

★

---

[14] L. Leigh, *Greed*, 392.

LIFESTYLE

> This was the life! A beautiful woman in beautiful surroundings, champagne, what more could a man ask?'
>
> Jackie Collins, *The World Is Full of Married Men* (148).

The preferred lifestyle in the world of the blockbuster novel – of the super-capitalist variety – is one of fame, fortune and decadence. Everything to excess. Opulence all round. Men must be princes or villains, women must be hags or princesses. Extravagance is a touchstone. The hero in the Mills and Boon romance *Kiss of the Falcon*, by Stephanie Howard, lives in a huge palace on an Italian island. Naturally, this aristocratic hero is 'a tall-shouldered figure in an immaculate pale linen suit' with 'forceful features deeply bronzed'.[15] *Oooh, baby!*

The spoiled, Hollywood Wife routine in *The Santangelos* is described as:

> Pilates, spinning, yoga, daily sessions with a life coach and a shrink, weekly visits to a dermatologist. And of course the Hollywood Wife basics – shopping, lunches, putting together exclusive dinner parties. (27)

The gorgeous body is as much a part of the materialism of the blockbuster novel as the gorgeous car or the luxurious house. And, in common with most blockbuster novel heroes, this one is powerful, forceful, tanned, slightly sinister and ever so slightly gorgeous. (So get in the gym!).

Time and again, the sumptuous locations tumble from the pages of blockbuster novels. In *The Rich and the Beautiful*, by Ruth Harris, we find another aristocratic stronghold. It is described in the clichéd terms of a fairy tale castle, set amidst birch and pine trees, Autumnal mists blurring its outline, a fire crackling in the great hall (272). How many times have we been here? Similarly, how often have we visited trendy, New York apartments overlooking Central Park, or exotic, Malibu mansions (with their own beachfront), or opulent, French chateaux?

Are you bored yet?

Jackie Collins employs the same big houses in Bel Air and the Hollywood Hills, the same hotel suites in Vegas, the same beach houses in Malibu, the same apartments or plush hotels overlooking

---

15 S. Howard, *Kiss of the Falcon*, 12.

Central Park in novel after novel.

In which case fame and celebrity and wealth is another trap, another cage: everybody who achieves fame and money buys the same cars, the same houses, the same clothes, the same everything. They go to the same parties, have the same desires, and think the same thoughts. Fame and money are as mass-produced as a packet of Oreos. There is little individuality. It is the sterility of conformity. (In rap and hip-hop culture, the trappings of success and wealth express conformity to the max).

All the paraphernalia of the blockbuster novel – the cars, suits, palaces, jewellery, hotels, swimming pools and private jets – are methods of asserting power – power over other characters in a text, and over the reader, and over life itself. A fantasy of magic, of magicke in the Western, occult sense – magicke meaning having 'power over' something.

Such glittering objects communicate (embody) romance, magic, mystique, other-worldiness. They say: *this is not your world* to the reader. The objects of luxury connote luxurious, happy lives. This is another lie or fantasy. Opulent materialism does not make one happier, better, or more fulfilled, except in fiction. We all know that! (But we pretend we don't know). This is one of the recurring fantasies or lies of advanced, capitalist societies: that a glitzy surface must mean a glitzy interior. Not so. In this blockbuster fictional world, all that glitters is indeed gold. Surface is everything, because material goods are enough. Marriage, which ends and consummates the romance novel, is not enough. There must be a marriage of money, of great riches.

> There was nothing like having money. No thrill in the world. Even naked ladies standing on table tops with their legs spread. (*Hollywood Husbands*, 45)

Sex is not enough either: it must be sex with $$$$$. A 24-carat kiss. A million-dollar orgasm. The attainments of a personality, of a marriage or a social position, are not enough either: there must be a lot of money involved. Money is sexy, money means power, and is the natural outcome of a journey, a story, based on money.

★

MONEY

As Jackie Collins puts it in *Lovers & Players*:

> Bingo! Everyone was for sale. All you had to do was establish a price. (218)

And in *The Count of Monte Cristo,* Alexander Dumas has the Count lecturing his servants:

> Bertuccio, everything is always for sale when you know the price to put on it.[16]

As Andrea Dworkin notes, money is immensely charismatic. The House of Windsor and the Kennedys are fascinating not only because of their dynastic families, which stretch across and affect history, but also because they are very rich. The names of millionaires are revered worldwide: Aristotle Onassis, Howard Hughes, John Paul Getty, William Randolph Hearst (and more recently, Donald Trump, Bill Gates or Rupert Murdoch). Names such as Rothschild or Rockerfeller have a mystique about them, just as those of expensive objects do: Rolls Royce, Ferrari, Chanel, Gucci, Armani, Rollex – the kind of names one finds in a *James Bond* movie (and a Jackie Collins novel). Millionaires are the divinities of capitalism, the gods of materialism, the ultimate winners in dog-buy-dog consumerism. And there are a large number of very rich people in Collins' fiction. Very, very rich people.

But, to be fair, the novels of Ms Collins do depict the downside of wealth, power and fame. If you were neurotic and depressed b4 you had it all, you will be neurotic and depressed when you get it all (but at least you won't starve!). The ultimate Have-It-All in Collins' moral scheme is not fame or money, but love and romance. When it comes down to it, faced with the choice between the two, a Collins character will always choose love and romance over money and fame (yet her novels do not end with the lovers re-united but destitute, reduced to begging or homeless).

★

---

16 A. Dumas, *The Count of Monte Cristo*, Penguin, 1996, 453.

JOBS

> Where I come from, if there's a buck to be made, you don't ask questions, you go ahead and make it.
>
> James Cagney (1973)

There is 'old money' and 'new money': 'old money' people frown on 'new money' people. Then there is 'funny money' and 'serious money'. 'Easy money' and 'hard money'. All kinds of money.

Old money is revered because it speaks of inheritance, the landed gentry and aristocracy. Money enhanced by the aura of history and heritage (with a prince or queen in the family tree). So some characters never carry anything less than hundred dollar bills. Others who only carry credit cards. Others who talk in terms of Yen, krugerands and deutschmarks. The heroines of the blockbuster novel, especially those of Jackie Collins' world, are winners of new money, and users of plastic money.

> *Cash* was the magic word. Everyone loved it. (*The Santangelos,* 235)

Money is a male domain, a male weapon, a male construct. Mommy looks after the house, while Daddy is the breadwinner, the businessman. In the blockbuster novel, these roles are reversed. The women usurp the male roles and step into their shoes (Lucky Santangelo is the supreme example in Jackie Collins' fiction, the woman who has completely, decisively and flamboyantly *made it*). As Bridget Fowler put it (in *The Alienated Reader: Women and Popular Romantic Literature In the 20th Century*):

> No longer modelled on the Madonna, the heroine in this genre has requisitioned the honorific image of the male entrepreneur as restless, Promethean developer. No longer defined by her family identity, she has become the quintessential self-made woman. (1991, 104)

The jobs women do in the blockbuster novel include movie star, pop singer, magazine editor, fashion designer, movie agent and party hostess (when things aren't so good, they're waiting tables, stripping, hooking and flipping burgers). In Jackie Collins' books women play stereotypical roles, both as characters and in the work they do. There is little transgression of patriarchal and social norms. In Collins' fictive world, male culture is as repressive and regressive as it is anywhere. Her women are assertive certainly, but they play roles defined largely by men. (Don't expect a Marxist/ Maoist/ Militant/ Radical/ Feminist revolution to start anywhere near a Jackie Collins novel).

In the fiction of authors such as Judith Krantz and Fay Weldon, women move outside of received roles; while Weldon is regarded as a feminist writer, Krantz is a quasi-feminist. Her book *Mistral's Daughter* makes all the right noises culturally, with its allusions to the Parisian art world, but the heroine is a stereotype. More committed feminist writers such as Hélène Cixous, Julia Kristeva, Ursula Le Guin, Emma Tennant and Sara Maitland take their women wholly outside patriarchy, into what Elaine Showalter called the 'wild zone' (though they are not blockbuster novel authors, or don't sell as much as blockbuster novel authors – maybe readers, women or men, don't want to go there, to a non-patriarchal, pro-women, pro-feminist space).

The men in the blockbuster book meanwhile do all the usual jobs: music manager, record executive, film director, studio mogul, actor, rock star, chauffeur, etc (and in the criminal underworld, gangster, assassin, drug dealer and pimp). Men are much likelier to have money than women in the blockbuster novel. They also have more influence, socially and economically, if not sexually. It's rare to find a female film director in the real Hollywood industry (you try naming ten major female film directors – after Leni Riefenstahl and Nora Ephron and Kathryn Bigelow and Jane Campion, you start to run out... OK, and now try naming ten major, female film (or TV) producers...).[17] In this, Collins is accurate, tho' she tries to counter the trend by featuring female film executives and directors. Women have economic power largely through their male partners; they are the so-called 'Hollywood Wives' (it was years before a woman became the head of a movie studio, for instance – Sherri Lansing, head of Fox in 1980, aged 35. Yeah, and thirty-plus years later, it's *still* very rare for a woman to hold the top jobs in Hollyweird).

★

---

[17] In Jackie Collins' work, female directors include Cat Harrison in *Hollywood Divorces* and Montana Gray in *Hollywood Wives* (and the sequel).

WORK FOR IT

> 'Here's *my* philosophy,' Madison said. 'If you want something bad enough, you gotta go for it.'
>
> Jackie Collins, *L.A. Connections* (73)

The Queen of the Blockbuster Novel is especially good at depicting people in crummy jobs. Her novels are full of them – and not only when people are young and just starting out. These are the cruddy jobs like parking cars, driving limos, washing dishes, running errands, and flipping hamburgers. Millions have done them. Many of the readers have been there, done that.

Alongside of that is the recurring theme in Collins Fantasy Land of characters being taken advantage of – either they're being paid low wages, or their boss hits on them, or they have to do dodgy things, or they have to work l---o---n---g hours. Jackie Collins doesn't skimp on the significance of hard work. She will put her characters into lengthy episodes of crapola jobs.

And her heroes are often workaholics – Lucky Santangelo gets restless if she's had even one day off. It's not one round of parties, premieres, pampering and poolside layabouting in Collins' fiction. (Many characters in literature don't seem to do much of anything, but we always know what Collins' characters are doing: they're working).

It's part of the Great American Dream: you've got to work for it, *honey*.[18] You've got to put in the hours, *baby*. Not for every character, *darling* – some inherit their wealth, or have rich spouses. Some live off their girlfriends and boyfriends (a recurring motif is guys sponging off women, for years and years. Particularly guys who could easily work if they wanted to).

But for the rags-to-riches characters – which means the main figures in a Jackie Collins tome – hard work can't be avoided.

> "I came to America over eighty years ago, and it's the greatest country on earth. In America you can achieve any dream you want."

So says Gino Santangelo (who else?!) in *Drop Dead Beautiful* (445).

---

[18] 'I write about the American dream: if you set your mind to do something, you can do it'.

AMBITION

> Joey's stomach knotted up, it was shit being nobody. *He* should the star. *He* should have everything Kyle Carson had.
>
> Jackie Collins, *Thrill!* (77)

Jackie Collins' women characters do not lack ambition, however. They can be as ruthless as male characters. The ambition is largely for fame and power and adoration. Getting what they want. *Feed that ego!* Mama's hungry... Everyone wants to be famous, right?: 'everyone wanted to be a movie star. It was the great American dream', as *Hollywood Husbands* puts it (320-1).

The goal is to become a winner, one of the Beautiful People, the glitterati. Peer pressure is as vigorous among Hollywood's players as it is among school kids the world over. Thus, it is crucial always to look good, to be respected, to be seen to win. Nothing less than success will do. Jackie Collins uses a Gore Vidal quote as an epigraph to her book *Hollywood Wives*: 'Nobody is allowed to fail within a two-mile radius of the Beverly Hills Hotel' (5). As Orson Welles pointed out in his wonderful British Broadcasting Corporation *Arena* interview in 1982 (quite possibly the single best TV interview on cinema ever), the *real* currency of Hollywood is not *money* but *egos* (respect, face) – it's about who has the biggest or best deal, or who has the most respect.

A similar scathing view of Hollywood is summed up by the title of producer Julia Phillips' book *You'll Never Eat Lunch In This Town Again* (in this autobiography of her work in the film industry, Phillips didn't hold back from naming names and dishing the dirt on a whole host of real-life Hollywood celebrities and producers and players. Jackie Collins can always hide behind the web of fiction, of course, although if you know something about contemporary Hollywood, the people that Collins is drawing upon are often easy to spot – and Collins satirized Phillips herself in *American Star*, for instance).

Vanity is uppermost: this is the world of face lifts, breast enlargements, wigs and a myriad of nips and tucks. When people sit down their hats fall off. But the glitter must continue to glisten.

Hollywood is presented as both a glitzy paradise and a sleaze pit. It functions as a microcosm of the Western world, a place in which everything found in the capitalist West is exaggerated, blown up, like a Disney cartoon (like the billboards along Sunset, or the movie ads which are plastered across an entire six storey building). Hollywood is the heaven of the Wizard of Oz and stars such as Marilyn Monroe, Clark Gable and James Dean, but it is also the (albeit fancy) hell of Kenneth Anger's gossipy, dirt-dishing book *Hollywood Babylon*, where the stars are shown as drug addicts and idiots, and everyone is a shark.

Wherever the blockbuster novel is set – London, Paris, Venice, New York City – it is always to Hollywood that everything is ultimately related (and even if a blockbuster novel is set in the past, it's often a Hollywood movie template that's employed for the narrative, or the structure, or the imagery, or the themes).

Four

Characters

Montana. Five feet ten inches tall. Waist length black hair. Direct gold-flecked tiger eyes. A wide sensual mouth. An unusual and striking beauty.

Jackie Collins, *Hollywood Wives* (29)

Speed liked money. Only one snag. Money didn't seem to like him. Every time he made a bundle – something happened. He'd win at the track and some big-boobed bimbo would take it all from him.

Jackie Collins, *Rock Star* (10)

CHARACTER TYPES

The character types in Jackie Collins' fiction are easily recognized, as one can see from the brief, punchy portraits in the quotes above from two of her best-known works, *Rock Star* and *Hollywood Wives*. She uses what appear to be cardboard cut-out characters,[1] the stuff of TV sit-coms, 19th century melodrama, TV mini-series and soap operas. Yes, and they are also the characters of Greek tragedy and Elizabethan drama.

Each personality type has a few characteristics, and one or two functions, but little else. Motives and background are sketched in briefly (except for the main character/s, who receive/s longer descriptions). But the motives and the goals are *very strong* – these are the engines that drive the narratives, after all. We are talking motives like: revenge, making it big, having it all. In a word, *succeeding*.

No one could accuse Jackie Collins of creating complex, multi-faceted and subtle characters like those of Fyodor Dostoievsky or John Cowper Powys. Hers is the sledgehammer approach.

But it works. Oh yes, it works.

However, look closer, and, no, these are not 'cardboard cut-out' characters in Jackie Collins' fiction, they are not one-dimensional. The secondary and minor characters might be (and they are in most stories), but the main characters have more layers than that.

★

> I really fall in love with my characters, even the bad ones. I love getting together with them. They tell me what to do; they take me on a wild and wonderful trip.

Each character in the blockbuster novel is concerned about her/ his status, her/ his class, her/ his standing among friends and business partners, her/ his looks, and her/ his power. Each Jackie Collins character is on the make, is planning something or other. The lowliest people have ambitions as big as the wealthiest. Some characters do cross boundaries – Montana Gray, the writer in *Hollywood Wives*,[2] ends up directing her film script (you go, girl!).

More usually, the roles of each character are clearly marked out. It is the same in fairy tales, as Andrea Dworkin noted: 'The heroic

---
1 Well, not cut outta 'cardboard' – more like snipped out of *Vogue* using diamond-edged scissors (the Italian edition, natch).
2 She appears in the 2003 sequel.

prince can never be confused with Cinderella, or Snow-White, or Sleeping Beauty. She could never do what he does at all, let alone better'.[3] (Actually, Dworkin isn't quite right here – because in those fairy tales, Cinders and Snow White are heroines who drive the narrative; as feminists have demonstrated, in their reworkings of traditional fairy tales, and in feminist analyses of fairy tales, heroines are much more pro-active and independent than patriarchal culture would prefer).

Jackie Collins is not a subversive writer, and she uses stereotypes because they function best in her fictional world. She endorses the status quo, she is not radical. She is not going to start a political revolution or usurp the way of life of the Western world. She loves it too much. (But, there *is* some subversion, however, in Collinsland – the idea of a female head of a Hollywood studio, for example, or a woman running a Las Vegas hotel/ casino resort). And, anyway, how many novelists are also ideological firebrands who want to overthrow Western civilization and society?

Jackie Collins' books are one cliché on top of another. It is the same with her characters. We know the Bitch, the Whore, the Stud, the Weirdo, the Drug Addict, the Boss, the Rebellious Teenager, the Workaholic, the Out-of-Control Supermodel, and the Talk Show Host[4] so well. They are comfortingly familiar. We recognize them when we see a soap opera or TV commercial, or watch a movie, or flick through a web page, or hear a pop song.

What Jackie Collins does with each successive book is satisfy the public's craving for something new – new yet the same (that's the trick, the twist, the beauty). The names might be changed, and the locations might be newish (but not often), but there is little that's 'new' in Collins' fiction. Just as manufacturers dress up an old product in new clothing and whoop, 'New formula!' 'Special price!' 'Brand new design!', so Collins, Taylor, Krantz, Cooper, Conran, Holt, Booth Bingham, Susan, James, Shears, Kaye, Crichton, Brown and Archer churn out the same stuff in different disguises (one view of Hollywood movies is that they are 'old stories with new actors'). And if you view storytelling as ancient, then there haven't been any truly 'new' stories for 3,000 years. Or 10,000 years. Or 50,000 years.

---

3 A. Dworkin in *Our Blood*, 55.
4 Collins herself has appeared on most of the main talk shows, including Craig Ferguson (I went to a recording of Craig Ferguson's show in L.A. at CBS; fun, but not a patch on seeing a recording of *Letterman* in New York). In 1998 Collins had her own talk show, *Jackie Collins' Hollywood*

The foundations have been laid down – they come from the culture. Each individual author erects a new building, but always on the same foundations. Facades and faces differ, but it's the same heart inside, the same values, attitudes, morals, characters and situations.

In fact, Jackie Collins has been happy to create stories and characters which replay/ rejig/ rework earlier stories and characters. If you consider Collins' books as relationship stories, you are always gonna be exploring similar relationships with similar characters: the ferociously ambitious young woman or man on their way to the top > the younger woman dating the older man > the plain girl who always gets overlooked by more glamourous girls > the loser boyfriend who exploits/ lives off his girlfriend.

Occasionally, Jackie Collins allows characters from other books to waft in and out of a story, turning her fiction into a narrative 'multi-verse' in the manner of Michael Moorcock or Lawrence Durrell (they often include characters stepping into other stories, or the same characters in new guises).

★

THE VILLAINS

One aspect of Jackie Collins' fiction is very striking – the venality of her villains, the aggression and anger of her bad guys and losers, and the perversity of her psychos.

Altho' Jackie Collins seems like a nice, English girl who went to live in Tinseltown, and is a polite, glamorous guest on chat shows, she can certainly create truly despicable villains. Look at Collins' lovely face – behind it there is a mind inventing abominable weirdos! There are characters who are murderers or psychopaths, yes, and there many more who are simply loathsome people. They lie, they cheat, they steal, they scorn, they bitch, they put people down, they whine and rage about their lives. Some of them pretend to be liberal and caring in public (such as the politicos or the movie stars), but in private they are misogynists and wife-beaters.

There are *so many* truly horrible characters in Jackie Collins' fiction, and one of the obvious reasons is simple: they are mechanical, structural, and functional, engines to drive the machine of the story – because thrillers and thriller-type narratives usually require bad guys to disrupt the status quo. A sicko commits a murder (at the start of a thriller), or a killer plans to nobble a victim (which Collins uses far more often – so that, structurally, the desire for killing bubbles underneath the surface of the story. And often in the end the killer's plans are scuppered or blow up in their face).

★

THE BITCH

The Bitch is, typically, a rival to the Main Heroine. She is frequently a career woman (such as Lucky Santangelo, the 'Lady Boss'; yet Lucky is also a down-to-earth girl, a sort of girl-next-door type). The Bitch uses sex to get her way. Nova Citroen, the society hostess in 1988's *Rock Star,* is summed up like this:

> Everyone loathed Nova Citroen. The Iron Cunt was her nickname. 'She makes Imelda Marcos look like a pussy,' was the general opinion of her loyal staff. (114)

The fairy tale model is of course the step-mother, a schemer up to no good. The Wicked Queen standing in front of the magic mirror in *Snow White* (in the 1937 Walt Disney movie or any other versions, including by the Brothers Grimm), is the key image in fairy tales of the Bitch. Stopping at nothing to get what she wants. And when someone gets in her way, or turns out to be more beautiful, the rival must go.

And Bitches are great fun to write: you'd have to be a terrible writer not to have fun with a Bitch. They are a gift to an author: and readers love them, they love to hate them, as well as to secretly admire them. And everybody enjoys the put-downs, the aggression, the shameless ambition of a Bitch. (And Jackie Collins writes as good a Bitch as any other novelist).

★

CAREER WOMAN

The Career Woman is very often the character the author or narrator sympathizes with most. The Career Woman may be an actress on the up (as in Jackie Collins' *Thrill!*), a journalist (in Collins' *Madison Castelli* novels and *The World is Full of Divorced Women*), a movie agent, a pop singer or a gangster. Or, Collins' most important Career Woman – Lucky Santangelo – a businesswoman. Her clashes with the Bitch are usually over a man. Or a job. Or a rival.

The Career Woman is often married to a loser guy: her task is to either set him right, or to set off without him. Use it or lose it. The women are often moving beyond their men, and their men are expected to catch up or leave.[5] (The view is also found in the fiction of D.H. Lawrence – that it's *men*, not *women,* who're conservative, immovable, and resistant to change).

But the Career Woman is a worker, and thus absorbs the narrator's or author's sympathies (Jackie Collins' books, like the blockbuster novel in general, are founded on the capitalist, Protestant work ethic, and hard work is mandatory, and usually rewarded). The Career Woman is Cinderella or a Princess who's banished to a life of toil, but who eventually makes good. Rags-to-riches – or from Trailer Park Trash to Hollywood St★r.

★

---

[5] 'The trouble with a lot of men was that had no idea to make love, all they knew how to do was fuck', is a common complaint in Collins' world.

Another type of woman that Jackie Collins is terrific at depicting is the young, out-of-control and aggressive woman,[6] like Lola in *Hollywood Divorces*, or Rosarita in *Lethal Seduction*, or Karen Lancaster in *Hollywood Wives*, or Karman Rush in *The World Is Full of Divorced Women*, or Italian supermodel Gianna in *Lovers & Players* (the original model was Claudia Parker in Collins' first book, *The World Is Full of Married Men*). They are women who love danger, being on the edge, going to extremes. They know what they want, and they are trying their hardest to get it. They dress well (i.e., expensively), and expect luxury wherever they go (and guys just have to keep up).

The Wild Women typically live with a disappointing or a downright dull man, and hanker after someone more famous or more erotic or more stylish... in short: more *everything*. They will contem-plate killing their man to leave room for the guy they really want.

They also have the physical attributes to achieve success thru sex and beauty. They are Jackie Collins' panthers and leopards – women as sleek, powerful, dangerous animals. Impossible to ignore, and if you get in the way, watch out!

The Wild Women are some of the characters I enjoy most in Collins Fantasy Land, because it's fun seeing someone who's out of control yet also witty, bitchy, and sexy. The Wild Woman is also unpredictable – it's rare to have a character where you genuinely don't know quite what they're going to do.

★

---

[6] Even a radical feminist such as Andrea Dworkin wrote of wild women, such as in her novel *Mercy*, where Rebecca, a 'ruthless crusher of a dyke', is out on the streets: 'I see her on the street, gold lamé against a window, I see her shimmering, and I go with her for thanks and because she is grand, and I find out you can be free in a gold lamé dress, in jail, whoring, in black skin, in hunger, in pain, in strife, the strife of the streets, perpetual war, gritty, gray, she's the wild one with freedom in her soul, it translates into how you touch, what's in your fingers, the silk in your hands, the freedom you take with who you got under you... and what you give is ambition, the ambition to do it big, do it great, big gestures, free – girls do it big, girls soar, girls burn, girls take big not puny' (108).

MOVIE STAR

There are plenty of Movie Stars in Jackie Collins' glamorous fictional world, and in blockbuster novels in general. Everybody wants to be a movie star, don't they? I know I do! Uhh, not really (or maybe?!...).

> 'Remember – you're a star, too.' (*Vendetta: Lucky's Revenge*, 450)

The male actors are macho womanizers, often ageing, worrying vainly about their looks (and their weight). They are typically shallow and bitter, writhing in menopausal confusion or a mid-life crisis. They enjoy jail bait in their on-set trailers between filming scenes. They are dissatisfied in their marriages. One or two (or is it 100s?) are secretly gay. They have names such as Ross Conti, Steve Magnum, Charlie Dollar and Charlie Brick, and are likened to Warren Beatty, Sean Penn, Kirk Douglas and Robert Redford (what a pity Jackie Collins has never written a novel completely based in reality, or at least using all the real names of real celebrities. So that Elizabeth Taylor, Julia Roberts, Meryl Streep, Madonna, Beyoncé, Jane Fonda, Liza Minnelli, Robert Redford, Paul Newman, Peter O'Toole, Michael Jackson, Steven Spielberg, Mick Jagger, Keef Richards, Rod Stewart, Rupert Murdoch, Bill Gates, Donald Trump and Paul MacCartney would have been named).

Actresses are usually young, eager types, not averse to using sex to gain good roles. They embody raw ambition. If they are older, they are often fading stars like Liz Taylor (or even Jackie's sister Joan Collins), determined to somehow improve their careers. The double standards[7] are alive and well in the real Hollywood of today, where the number of really powerful roles for older women are still rare, where male stars still earn more than women stars, and where far fewer female stars open a movie.

Actors must be masochists, Jackie Collins notes wryly in *Hollywood Wives*. Having done quite a bit of casting myself, I don't know how actors can put themselves through so much rejection in doing the rounds of auditions and casting calls. How many times can you take being turned down b4 you give up?! (However, rejection is the *norm* for actors – well, for any artist).

---

7 One of Madison Castelli's first pieces of journalism is on the double standard – and Cleo James, in *The World Is Full of Divorced Women*, also attacks it.

THE BOSS

Typically a mob leader, nightclub owner, movie studio chief or business person, the Boss's role is the usual one: to lay down laws, to outline the boundaries of power, to issue threats and quests, and to bless the efforts of other characters. When the Boss says jump, everyone jumps. Money talks, and when money talks, everyone listens (no matter how much they might hate the Boss: they know who's paying. So even the charas who wanna quit don't – they need the green).

★

THE AGEING MILLIONAIRE

Some of the Boss characters are corrupt, and ageing: a recurring type in Jackie Collins' world is the ageing millionaire (or billionaire) patriarch, worried about the continuation of their empires after their demise – these are partly satires of real people such as John Paul Getty, Aristotle Onassis, Rupert Murdoch, Michael Eisner and Ted Turner.

Hamilton Heckerling in *Married Lovers* is an archetypal Ageing Millionaire character:

> Hamilton J. Heckerling was big and brash. Loud-mouthed and overbearing. Married five times. A patron of the arts and from all reports a total sonofabitch. (59)

Typically, the Ageing Millionaire is an old, crusty coot fixed in his ways; he's in his seventies; he's still a perv, and has a string of young women (emphasis on young), which infuriates his kids (they hate being older than dad's latest girlfriend); he's been married five times; he lives in luxury in Gotham; he's a control freak; he's obnoxious – but doesn't give a hoot; he's loud – but doesn't care who hears; he has a dark secret which'll be his undoing; and he has a bunch of offspring who continually disappoint him. The Ageing Millionaire embodies the theme of the 'Sins of the Fathers', and the ambiguous relationship that the younger generation have with the older generation.

Typically, there's a big meeting where the Ageing Millionaire plans to make an Important Announcement (another marriage to another babe in her 20s, maybe, or the decision to donate all his wealth to a nobody). His kids're keen to get their hands on the Ageing Millionaire's assets, and he knows that, chuckles, and plans to fox 'em all.

★

THE GANGSTER

Reading *The Godfather* was clearly a life-changing event for Jackie Collins (or maybe it was seeing the movie) – it's one of her favourite novels (and that of her characters). *The Godfather* was published in 1969, just as Collins was starting out herself as a writer. A large slice of Collins' glam-camp fiction is taken up with Italian-American wise guys, as with the movies directed by Francis Coppola, Martin Scorsese, Brian de Palma, Abel Ferrara and others (except, like other writers, including Mario Puzo, Collins doesn't use terms like 'gangster', 'wise guy', 'mafia' or 'cosa nostra')[8]

There's the ageing Don, clearly (and unashamedly) modelled on Don Vito Corleone in *The Godfather* (like Vito Giovanni in *Deadly Embrace*), and also Marlon Brando's performance in the 1972 picture.[9] There's the son-of-a-gun psycho gangster, the twisted offspring of the godfather (like Santino in *Lucky* – Santino (Sonny) is of course the name of Don Corleone's son (and successor) in *The Godfather* – played in the movie by Jimmy Caan). There are guttersnipes and hit-men with dead fish eyes and pockmarked skin. And finally there's the young wise guy, who gets drawn into the crime business gradually. These are Collins' novels' anti-heroes, but they are led astray by the glamour (and cushiness) of the mobster's lifestyle

---

[8] The words 'mafia' and 'cosa nostra' were not employed (or were excised) in the film script of *The Godfather* (and many of the other familiar terms of the genre, such as gangsters, mobsters, crime boss, mob boss and so on were also not included). But they weren't in the screenplay in the first place, remarked Mario Puzo (1972, 63). Instead, the script referred to the 'five families' of the New York and New Jersey regions. One of the reasons for deleting such words was to placate the Italian-American lobbying groups, and also the mafia themselves.

[9] That Collins dated Brando (in the 1950s) no doubt enhances the allure of *The Godfather* movie.

(such as Michael Castelli in the *Madison Castelli* series). And sometimes the young women in the Collinsworld can't help falling for the bad boys.

★

VIRGIN/ INNOCENT

There are a surprising number of Virgins and Innocents in Jackie Collins' fiction. Virgins in more than their sexual identity. They are Virgins to the cut-throat nature of show biz, or to the city, or to infidelity and relationships (i.e., they are also a mechanical function of the narrative, introducing a newcomer to a strange world).

Jackie Collins likes to use Innocents to initiate them into her vision of the bizarre world of the rich and the famous. The Innocents are the Dick Whittingtons or Simple Hans of European fairy tales, who come to the city to find the golden streets (or to fulfill the American Dream). They often end up disillusioned. Eaten away by ambition, they are often actresses or would-be tycoons. *They* are not going to be waiting tables or parking cars for ever. In their eagerness to succeed, they often fall foul of the many sharks. Some Innocents are already wily, however, such as Sunday Simmons in *Sinners*, and can refuse temptation even when it's right in front of them.

★

THE WAYWARD DAUGHTER

An off-shoot of the Virgin or Innocent type is the precocious, spoilt Daughter, on her way to being out-of-control. Rebelling against her parents and their generation, the 15 year-old Wayward Daughter is desperate to have her own car, hang out the coolest people, try out drugs and sex, leave home, and wants grow up fast, and to be Someone (Summer, Nikki's unstable, 15 year-old daughter in *Thrill!*, is a good example). Typically, the Wayward Daughter sinks out of her depth, gets into drugs, or mixes with the wrong people, and has to be rescued. (An insight into how the Wayward Daughter relates to Jackie Collins' own life appears in the *Lucky Santangelo* novels: in the 1990 TV show, Lucky's depicted attending L'Evier, a starchy private school in Switzerland, encountering room-mate Olympia Stanislopoulos who leads her astray with boys, smoking, parties, and staying out all night. It's worth remembering that Collins' own rebellious teen years were spent in the 1950s, not, say the 1970s or the 1980s – by 1960, she was 23).

★

WEIRDOS

No thriller or crime work is complete with a freak or two (as Raymond Chandler knew well). Jackie Collins' blockbuster world has its fair share of creeps, the sort of people who make obscene telephone calls, or send sick letters to stars, or stalk celebrities, or sniff starlets' underwear. The Weirdos and the Freaks are necessary for the form of the stories – to add the threat of violence, and to balance those luscious men with some ugliness. (Typically, Collins will introduce a Sicko early on in her books, then leave them there to smoulder away – so the reader knows that following this character is going to pay off later. In some novels, we follow them for a *long* time – as in *Hollywood Wives*).

Thus, the Weirdos and the Freaks are often little more than functions of the plot, something to push the narrative along, to liven up proceedings, or to give the main characters a jolt or two. Jackie Collins clearly relishes writing about some of these creeps – it's where a writer can go to town on describing twisted behaviour and ideas (without being regarded as sick or weird themselves!). Authors have always enjoyed messing about in the gutter or the slime – they have always done it, for thousands of years. (Collins says she enjoys her characters, and spending time with them – which must, then, include the Sickos and the Freaks. But although critics and fans ponder on how Collins herself relates to the actresses and supermodels in her books, they never regard the psychopaths as reflecting an aspect of Collins' life or personality).

Weirdos never win. *Never*. In Jackie Collins' strictly moral universe, monsters are always punished, and always die.

If there is 'war porn' or 'battle porn', applied to shoot-em-up video games and movies like *Saving Private Ryan* and *We Were Soldiers*, then you could also see Collins' books as 'crime porn' or 'sleaze porn'. Certainly the novels exhibit a sometimes creepy wallowing in the sleazier aspects of being human.

(Who knew that a nice, middle-class, English girl would become so skilled at depicting revolting, sick, base material? The answer is that she was never a nice, middle-class, English girl, but a naughty, middle-class, English girl!)

★

THE WEASEL

The Weasel is a low-life, sell-out, tell-all brother/ sister/ cousin of famous relatives who peddle their stories to the tabloids. The Weasel is a lazy and boring character (and usually male) who leeches off other characters; they're unable to forge their own careers, so they sponge off other people. They wanna Get Rich Quick, but without putting in the work. And for selling their souls and their siblings/ relatives, they are, in the Collinsian moral firmament, punished.

Why? Partly because Weasels have to deal with cynical journalists and the cutthroat media, which'll never pay for a story they can obtain by other means (even tho' journos don't spend their own money, but that of their magazines/ bosses; however, journos love getting stuff for free).

★

THE PROSTITUTE

Not a few women in the blockbuster novel are whores. There's an enormous amount of prostitution in Jackie Collins' novels – indeed, in virtually *every* novel; some are high-class call-girls, but it's prostitution nevertheless.

Sometimes the narrator in Jackie Collins' books is not ambivalent towards these characters: whores are called whores. The narrator makes no apologies. Thus Collins writes: 'Gina Germaine became a star because of her amazing breasts' (*Hollywood Wives*, 109). Several Collins novels feature brothels and call-girl services (brothels in the *Lucky Santangelo* novels, Annabelle's call-girl business in *Poor Little Bitch Girl*).

Women often wield their sexuality like weapons in Blockbuster Land. Some are regarded as hookers by the male characters before they know anything about them; everyone is fair game in Collins Land. The casting couch is a reality. Good head works wonders, Collins tells the reader. Even seemingly minor and mundane characters, such as Stella the make-up girl in *Hollywood Wives: The New Generation*, are treated as prostitutes.

> ...in his time – Ross had had some of the best little cocksuckers in the business. Starlets, whose very livelihood depended on doing a good job. Hookers, who specialized. Bored Beverly Hills housewives who had elevated cocksucking to an art. (*Hollywood Wives*, 11)

In the novel *Rock Star* (1988), groupies are called 'super-cunts': 'luscious lovelies with nothing on their mind except climbing into bed with a rock star' (246-7). And the popular accounts of the supergroup era of the 1970s, of pop acts such as Led Zeppelin, Fleetwood Mac, the Rolling Stones, the Who and countless others, are full of stories about groupies and sex and wild parties and trashing hotel rooms. Nobody wants to hear that the reality of schlepping around the world on a rock tour was exhausting – they want the legends of drug orgies.

As there are supermodels and superbitches, so there are super-whores in blockbuster fiction. Mikki in *Rock Star* is the 'self-titled queen of the groupies... She'd been to bed with all the greats' (248). Pamela Des Barres would be one of the inspirations for this super-groupie character – Des Barres was rumoured to have had relationships with Jim Morrison, Mick Jagger, Jimmy Page, Keith Moon, Noel Redding and Gram Parsons, among others. Other famous groupies included the Hollywood groupies G.T.O (Girls Together Outrageously), 'Sweet Sweet' Connie Hamzy, Cleo Odzer, Bebe Buell, Tura Satana, Chris O'Dell and Anita Pallenberg.

Then there were the rock groupies who took plaster casts of

rock stars' members, led by Cynthia Plaster Caster, a.k.a. Cynthia Albritton. You couldn't make the Plaster Casters up – or you could, but no one would believe you. The sort of rock gods the Plaster Casters aimed to slap wet plaster over were the usual 'cock rock' suspects: Mick Jagger, Iggy Pop, Jim Morrison, Jimi Hendrix, and Robert Plant. Hendrix was one of their long-time goals, which they eventually achieved.

There were the so-called under-age 'baby groupies' centred around Tinseltown such as Sable Starr, Queenie, Kathy Heller, and the 14-year old Lori Maddox (who dated Jimmy Page, Mick Jagger and David Bowie[10]). 'Kiddie decadence',[11] Tony Zanetta dubbed it in his book on Bowie: parties, groupies, Quaaludes, and room service at the Beverly Hills Hotel.

In the music industry in the 1960s and 1970s, women generally played two roles: Groupie (a mixture of fan and whore), or Rock Wife, who stayed at home looking after the children. As George Tremlett pointed out in *Rock Gold: The Music Millionaires*, women in the business (especially on tour) were expected to want sex. 'To be known as a good fuck was no disgrace. Oral sex was almost mandatory' (1990, 104).

Women in Jackie Collins' glitzy world are systematically and endlessly eroticized. Sex is pretty much always mentioned: women must be sexual creatures, her fiction maintains. Some of Collins' characters are only one or two dimensional. One of the dimensions is sex, another is money. One might add power. And vanity.

★

---

10 Lori Maddox claimed she was 'devirginized', as she put it, by Bowie in a hotel room; she was 15 at the time.
11 Zanetta and Edwards: 'Some dressed like Shirley Temple; others wore dominatrix outfits or 'Hollywood underwear', a knee-length skirt, nylon stockings, and garter belts. The star girls streaked their hair chartreuse and liked to lift their skirts to display their bare crotches. As they danced they mimed fellatio and cunnilingus in tribute to David's onstage act with Ronno's guitar' (142).

THE STUD

Men's treatment of women in Jackie Collins' fictive world is sometimes abominable. All men are first class shits, asserts Dindi in *Sinners* (150). True, and the Stud is the worst cad of all, because his function is to have as many women as possible (leaving a trail of broken hearts). He is patriarchy personified, and his emblem is his penis. His ancestor is the Ancient Greek god Zeus, who must take everything in sight (even if it means changing into a swan or a bull; if that's what it takes to Get-the-Girl, Zeus will do it!). It's the phallus doing what it likes to do best, it's men thinking with their members.

As DeVille tells the hero in *American Star*: 'you're just like every other guy – selfish, self-centred, all you care about is your precious dick' (227). As Andrea Dworkin notes in her 1981 book *Pornography*, 'in the male system, sex is the penis, the penis is sexual power, and its use in fucking is manhood' (23).

The Stud is usually a movie star, nightclub owner, gigolo or businessman. John Sessions speaks of the 'great sexy bores like Harrison Ford or Kevin Costner: they do a very good job of looking pained, beautiful, sensitive and blowjobable to half America'[12]

> Sometimes he would reach for the blonde asleep beside him, wake her gently and make love.
> No. Not love. Sex. Just sex.
> Success was great, Money was great, Recognition was great.
> It just wasn't enough.
> Something was missing in his life. (*Lucky*, 221)

Studs in Jackie Collins' books include Jack Python in *Hollywood Husbands*, Al King in *Lovers and Gamblers*, Mike James in *The World Is Full of Divorced Women*, David Cooper in *The World Is Full of Married Men*, Johnny Romano in *Vendetta: Lucky's Revenge*, Steve Magnum in *Sinners*, Nick Angel in *American Star*, Joel Blaine in *Lethal Seduction*, and Bobby Mondella in *Rock Star*. And of course Gino Santangelo in the *Lucky Santangelo* series.

★

---

12 J. Sessions, *Marie Claire*, 50, Oct, 1992, 67.

A gallery of celebrities and stars that inspired the kind of characters that feature in the stories of Jackie Collins (this page and over).

Marlon Brando and Marilyn Monroe.

Liz Taylor. Liza Minnelli.
Anita Pallenberg. Jane Fonda.

Warren Beatty. Robert Redford. Paul Newman.

The Rolling Stones in Hyde Park, 1969 (above).
And still going strong: on the 50 years tour (below).

Madonna

(Photo: Steven Meisel/ Sire Records)

Carmen Electra and Jessica Biel.

Traci Lords

Prince. David Bowie. Al Green (top to bottom).

Christina Aguilera

Beyoncé Knowles
(on stage, London, 2011, above)

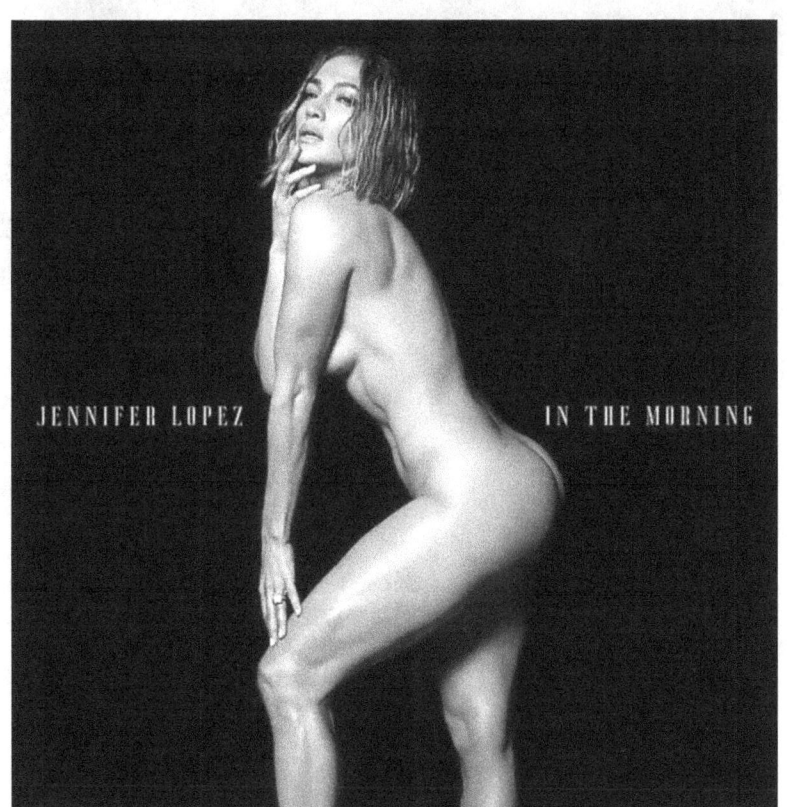

Jennifer Lopez and Britney Spears.

Courtney Love

Five

Language, Form, Structure

He got himself a job slinging hamburgers at a beach hangout, and that gave him just enough money to rent a room. A friend showed him how to play the guitar, and he wasn't bad... The five big Ss remained constant. He was tanned all over, strong from surfing, muscled from working out. He had all the sex he ever wanted, plenty of sleep, and he never once thought of his mother.

Jackie Collins, *Hollywood Wives* (70)

Jackie Collins writes in a knowing, street-wise, world-weary way – the above quote is typical of her prose. She uses short, easy sentences (the opposite of Samuel Beckett's short but complex sentences or Gertrude Stein's apparently simple but meticulously controlled poetic prose). Collins employs an everyday vocabulary. There are no words that present any problems in her work, nothing appears like 'desuetude' or 'hieratic', as in the fiction of Lawrence Durrell. She loves the word 'fuck': Collins' characters use it regularly, as they do in some mainstream movies: 'fuck my husband if you want, but don't take me for an idiot', snarls Cleo in *The World Is Full of Divorced Women* (6); Ross Conti thinks: 'Agents. Fuck 'em and feed 'em to the fish' (*Hollywood Wives,* 83).

Fuck, the Anglo-Saxon term that still makes some puritans squirm, is used by nearly all of Jackie Collins' characters. It is part of the sassy, sussed, street credible attitude in the blockbuster fictional world (but there are Collins characters who consciously avoid using 'bad language' – more of them are female than male, and they're not all prim matrons like Julie Andrews; some carefully control their speech).

Jackie Collins is so successful among readers partly because her books are so easy to read. Little effort is required, other than to turn the pages and hold the book up.[1] Her work is always visual, always describing people visually – the dumb blonde with big boobs or the fat, cigar-smoking producer. Her portraits are concise. She likes slang and vivid verbs ('slinging hamburgers' in the above quote from *Hollywood Wives,* for instance).

An important ingredient of Jackie Collins' style is the North American idiom she uses: although British,[2] Collins writes almost entirely in the American language, using American spelling and phrases. (However, the odd British phrase crops up). That is, after her first books, which are U.S.A.-set (*The World Is Full of Married Men* is based in London, and London continued to feature in novels such as *The World Is Full of Divorced Women* and *The Bitch*).

Jackie Collins assumes the reader knows about the places she's writing about. For instance, she will write that a character has an office in Century City, or gets dropped off on Ventura, instead of saying Ventura Boulevard in Los Angeles. The reader is assumed to know the lay-out of L.A., for instance, or where the Hamptons are in

---

1 Some of us get other people to do that.
2 Collins lived in the U.S.A. for much of her later life, but always kept her English accent.

relation to Gotham. (By the end of a reading a few Collins novels, you do feel like you know L.A. It would be easy to produce a map of Collins' Los Angeles, like the star maps of famous homes for tourists).

Jackie Collins employs short paragraphs. One of her distinctive methods is to use single-sentence paragraphs, to produce a staccato effect:

> On screen she heaved, and panted while he slavered over her.
> Off screen she threw off her negligee, stepped out of her panties and sat astride him.
> One more time.
> The last time.
> He didn't know how right he was. (*Hollywood Wives,* 274)

This short, sharp tactic is part of Jackie Collins' bullet-like prose style. It's a style that is spare and quick because what she is communicating is so world-weary, so easy to understand. Lean and mean. There are no long, complex sentences, with sub-clause after sub-clause, in the whole of Collins' output. They are not part of the blockbuster novel. A blockbuster novel must communicate instantly; beaches do not have dictionaries or libraries on them (though maybe you can google difficult words like *hebetude* on your cel phone or I-Pad – but who the $!&@ would bother?).

And the short, sharp and simple prose style is used *everywhere* in the blockbuster novel – look at the fiction of Peter Benchley and Michael Crichton, for instance, or Dean Koontz and Mario Puzo.

Meanwhile, Judith Krantz comes across as more intellectual – or at least her narrators do. Her vocabulary is rich, but she too is drastically simple in her prose style. 'She looked impatiently out of the train window. They still hadn't reached Lyon and lunch was almost over.' These are typical sentences in *Mistral's Daughter* (343).

Another author who takes the same minimal approach is Stephenie Meyer (b. 1973): the *Twilight Saga*, Meyer's signature work, features a prose style that's so flat it's simply boring (and hopelessly over-written, so that every tedious detail of experience that the heroine li'l Bella Swan goes thru is included).

Dan Brown (b. 1964), famous for *The Da Vinci Code* and other novels (such as *Angels and Demons* and *Digital Fortress*), has a pared-down prose style that's so unadorned and direct it comes across as hebetated. Here's an example from *The Da Vinci Code*:

> Finding the men's room door, Langdon entered and turned on the lights.
> The room was empty.
> Walking to the sink, he splashed cold water on his face and tried to wake up. (97)

While the story of *The Da Vinci Code* (2003) – Jesus's lover Mary Magdalene had kids with the Messiah and the family line's survived into the modern age – was interesting (though largely reworked from *The Holy Blood and the Holy Grail* and other populist religious/ occult/ cosmic mystery books), the structure that Brown chose for his hi-tech thriller was clunky in the extreme (maybe that's why *The Da Vinci Code* made such a terrible movie in 2006).

For instance, *The Da Vinci Code* required a huge amount of explanation and history and back-story to make sense of the plot, so the present-day narrative had to keep stopping. Yet, in the present tense, the author wanted everything to happen within a day and a night. It just didn't work. But the novel seems to have sold by the truckload, so what the hell!

But as a book to read for pleasure, the prose style of *The Da Vinci Code* was so lifeless, it became a struggle. And the characters – particularly Robert Langdon and Sophie Neveu – were truly *boring*. By comparison, Jackie Collins' characters are fantastically alive.

★

ADJECTIVES

The blockbuster novelistic style is almost journalese. It's known as a 'flat' style, an unadorned style, an 'economical' style which goes back to Ernest Hemingway and Raymond Chandler, in which information is punched across at the reader (the prose style is identified as North American). Some writers are brilliant at it (Ursula Le Guin,[3] Chandler and Raymond Carver), some are not always successful (Collins and Michael Crichton), and some attempt the style but fall flat (Dan Brown and Stephenie Meyer).

'Flat', 'workman-like', 'plain' – except in the descriptions, in the adjectives: here comes the lushness. Thus we find words such as *steamy, sexy, glamour, romance, intrigue, passion, sensational,*

---
[3] Tho' Le Guin is not a blockbuster author – and nor is Chandler!

powerful, mysterious, intimate, thrilling, gripping and *beautiful.* These are the buzz words of blockbuster novels. Adam Phipps in Pat Booth's *Big Apple* is described has having 'rakish' hair, 'deep Cambridge-blue eyes', an 'immaculately structured nose', 'snow-white teeth' which flash 'between delicate, full lips' (22). Perfection is possible in the blockbuster world – or something near to it.

Angel in *Hollywood Wives* is described thus: 'She looked particularly beautiful, shining with a very special innocence.' (128) Blockbuster authors limit themselves to a terse, guidebook style, one that includes lists of commodities. But they go over-the-top with the adjectives, because their worlds need to be made as beautiful as possible.

The blockbuster novel's plot is based on *desire*. Desire manifests itself as ambition, a will to succeed. Thus, most blockbuster books involve a quest, a plan, a journey, a struggle to achieve some desire. As *American Star* by La Collins puts it:

> Cyndra had bigger ideas. Somehow she was going to make something out of her life, and nobody was going to stop her. (65)

As with the historical romance, there are often secrets to be revealed, hidden information – such as a bastard child, or childhood incest, or abuse, or murder – which provides some shattering revelation/s at the end of the book. Jackie Collins employs the delayed revelation time after time – and it always works.

Blockbuster fictions are not romances, sagas, or epics (in the literary, technical sense), but they do use many of the devices of the romance or saga (many blockbuster novels are marketed as 'family sagas'). Jackie Collins' books often end with something happy: if not a marriage, then the suggestion of a marriage, as between Kris and Rafaella at the end of *Rock Star*, or Nick and Lauren at the end of *American Star* (Collins likes to evoke a warm, fuzzy feeling at the end).

Jackie Collins employs a lot of main characters (which's one reason for each cast member being given simple, one-dimensional characterizations, so the gentle, sweet reader can follow the ensemble casts. Also, it takes up a lot more wordage to create and develop complex characters). Each character is given a potted history, a habitation, a few of desires and compulsions, and one or two weaknesses. Sex is a popular drive, as is lust for power. (So, actually, they are not 'one-dimensional', but more rounded than that).

Throughout her books, Jackie Collins has to keep each plot strand up to date as the narrative unfolds (a structural challenge). In *Rock Star* she employs a narrative in the present (the chapters are titled 'Saturday, July 11, 1987, Los Angeles'). This plot involves a group of people gathering for a party (a favourite Collins setting), during which a robbery occurs, and the main characters are held hostage. Intercut with this predictable, TV mini-series drama we dip into the lives of the three main characters: we read of Kris Phoenix in 1965, 1973, 1981 and so on, bringing us up to date.

In both *Hollywood Wives* and *Hollywood Husbands,* the past catches up with the characters – the age-old vengeance motif. Vengeance neatly provides the violence, and forces events to a climax. Also, it offers countless possibilities of familial rivalry and emotions. There are the usual excesses to be dealt with – drink, drugs, sex. Careers plummet or rise.

Each character wins out to different degrees of success. The ending of *Hollywood Wives* is typical: each plot strand is tied up neatly. In a jokey/ ironic tone (notice how Jackie Collins' tone lightens in the novels' epilogues, and the bitchiness is put in abeyance), the narrator tells the reader what finally happened to each character. Some get justice, others get their desires gratified. There is a self-righteous sense of fair play winning out over evil and backhandednesss (recalling the addition of morals to traditional fairy tales).

Jackie Collins' fiction is formulaic fiction, just like the Harlequin or Mills and Boon romance, or the John Le Carre or Robert Ludlum spy thriller. It goes from A to B to Z in time-honoured fashion. Collins uses tried and tested formulas for character and plot, for motive and *dénouement.* There are no surprises in the blockbuster novel. Once you've read one and understood the mechanisms, you know them all, as with pornography or the hour-long detective series on TV. The blockbuster novel is a machine-like novel, like a shop assistant ringing up items on a cash till, or a busker churning out cover tunes (Bob Dylan, the Stones, the Kinks, Elton John), or a drug pusher doing another deal. One hears of people having sex by 'going through the motions': it is the same with writing a blockbuster novel.

However, 'formulaic' isn't quite the correct term – rather, Jackie Collins' fiction operates within a set of patterns and parameters, and it employs particular forms, but it doesn't merely follow a 'formula'.

Each novel is actually different – that is, there is a new set of characters, new situations, new relationships, etc. Each novel thus has different challenges, which can only be solved by writing. It's a trial and error process (like editing a movie), even tho' the 'rules', the guidelines, the parameters, the forms, etc, are by now familiar and well-trodden.

Also, Jackie Collins uses different narrative structures: some have *rondo* or flashback forms (present day scenes intercut with flashbacks, which're usually in chronological order), as in *Rock Star* and *Chances*, and some novels have lengthy periods which're left out (and might be summarized), as in *The World Is Full of Divorced Women* and *Lucky*.

★

FORM

The blockbuster novel gleans a feeling of history from the family saga, and the rivalry of siblings and relatives. A sense of dynasty fascinates Westerners, especially North Americans. The Kennedys are called a dynasty: their monolithic imperialism is compared with that of the Roman Emperors. Television shows such as *Dynasty* and *Dallas* and recent shows such as *The Tudors, The Sopranos* and *The Borgias* trade on such things. The blockbuster novel loves a sense of history. Hollywood cinema provides that, in an instant, easily-digested form: Charlie Chaplin, Erich von Stroheim and D.W. Griffith are the Old Testament prophets, the Noahs and Moses-types of the movie world, while Marlene Dietrich, Jane Mansfield and Marilyn Monroe are like the Love Goddesses of ancient times: Cleopatra and Salomé, for instance.

Jackie Collins employs the world of Hollywood and celebrity more than any other, but tends to keep her novels up-to-date, with only a few references to the long and colourful history of Hollywood (that is, her novels trade on the general glamour, celebrity and scandal of Hollywood, but are not historical tomes that explore the rich history of Tinseltown. For instance, Collins could delve into the 1920s – stars such as Rudolph Valentino and Gloria Swanson[4] are

---

[4] Swanson's autobiography is a superb book.

pure Collins characters, and there was plenty of juicy scandal and gossip in Twenties Tinseltown to draw on. I'd love to see Collins exploring the Golden Age of Hollywood). The art world provides a similar sense of history: Judith Krantz's *Mistral's Daughter* features a dynastic trinity of women: daughter, mother and grandmother.

The ambitious blockbuster novel toys with passions sustained over generations. Jackie Collins prefers everything to take place in the present day, with occasional dives into the past. For Collins, the past is only important if it impinges meaningfully on the present (and that usually means within the back-stories of her characters). For writers of the historical romance, such as Victoria Holt and Catherine Cookson, history is to be revered – history is sacred. However, Collins has created her own version of an 'epic' saga – about the Santangelo family.

The blockbuster novel aims for an epic form but is not epic in the true, lit'ry sense of the word, in the sense of Homer's *Illiad* and *Odyssey,* or the Sumerian *Gilgamesh* epic. The blockbuster novel is not epic poetry, either, and only aspires towards the epic mode in the vastness of its global sweep, by taking in cities from Monte Carlo to Tokyo, from New York to Moscow.

In essence, the blockbuster novel veers somewhere between the romance and the soap opera (reconceived recently as the 'family saga'). A soap opera is marked by open-endedness. Soaps never end, they go *on and on.* If there is any narrative closure, it is temporary (maybe a death or a marriage is introduced, but seldom, and it never closes down the soap – only the studio or parent company can do that).

The soap opera centres on the family. The blockbuster novel only does this at times, in a fragmentary fashion. Blockbuster fiction people are not tied down by small children: they are free souls who tup and travel about as they wish. Soap opera people are tied to one place and one family situation.

In Collins Land, for instance, most of the key characters are adults and are usually in couples: some are sons or daughters, and some have sons or daughters. But the majority of the main characters are lovers or husbands and wives, without (young) children getting in the way (tho' Jackie Collins usually includes at least one strong parent-child relationship in each novel, and often there's a seething resentment from the younger generation towards the older generation – it's another 'Sins of the Fathers' motif).[5]

Both blockbuster novels and soap operas feature strong women characters, adultery, rivalry, dark secrets, high profile materialism, career entanglements and claustrophobic peer pressure. When on television, as a mini-series, the blockbuster novel becomes a soap opera (there have been numerous adaptations of blockbuster novels, of course, tho' adaptations of Collins' novels have unfortunately ranged from patchy to terrible).

Like the soap opera, the TV drama and the 'major motion picture',[6] the blockbuster novel uses all the devices of conventional drama. There is always a sense of *performance* in the blockbuster novel, a feeling of playing to a hidden camera, a certain stylized flamboyance (Jackie Collins' charas certainly act like they're conscious of a camera somewhere). Gestures in the blockbuster novel, unlike in the soap opera, are carried off with a flourish. But the soap opera and the blockbuster novel, however, feel the need to update the audience every so often.

Jackie Collins' fiction uses the techniques of magazine fiction (short bursts of information), journalism (stating a case in the first paragraph), soap opera (a large group of characters), television drama (shorthand ways of describing action and character), and cinema (visual descriptions predominate).

Jackie Collins' novels don't linger, and they don't stay with one character or one situation longer than a few pages (often half a page). This is an absolutely vital ingredient in Collins' style: her books are constantly on the move, jumping from one group of characters and plots to another. A Collins novel does not stay with one character alone for long sections,[7] or even for a whole book. No time to get bored, and no need for the author to sustain a major sequence involving just one character (it also encourages short reading spells, like a magazine).

But the blockbuster book is a *novel,* too. For D.H. Lawrence (author of a forerunner of the sex-driven blockbuster novel, *Lady Chatterley's Lover*), the novel was the 'bright book of life'.[8] Lawrence said you could put anything in a novel. In a sense, the blockbuster novel does this. Like *War and Peace,* the blockbuster

---

[5] Occasionally, the viewpoint is with the older generation, disappointed and disgruntled with the younger generation.
[6] Don't you hate that phrase? – nobody says 'motion picture'!
[7] But actually some of Collins' finest moments in fiction are precisely when she stays with a character for a longer period – such as with Lucky Santangelo.
[8] D.H. Lawrence, *A Selection From Phoenix,* 165, 177, 180, 185-8.

novel tends to become a huge ragbag of a book, bursting at the seams with people and situations. Like *War and Peace, Ulysses, U.S.A., The Magic Mountain* or *Remembrance of Times Past,* all big, classic modern novels, the blockbuster novel is intended to be a huge, immensely satisfying read, like a long, debauched meal, or a long, debauched night.9 This applies whether the blockbuster is *Kane and Abel, Lady Boss, Lace, Princess Daisy, A Woman of Substance* or *Polo* (though none of those blockbuster novels are usually placed in the same class as Leo Tolstoy or Marcel Proust).

Publisher: So, what have you got for me?
Author: A big, sprawling, fuck-me-or-die blockbuster novel!
Publisher: Yeah? *(Thinks: 'I've gotta shlepp thru this shit this weekend)* So, Zack... How long is this new book?
Author: 80 pages.
Publisher: Are you nuts?!

Size is crucial – a slim, 80-page blockbuster novel ain't no blockbuster tome at all. *Big is beautiful* in the blockbuster novel world – that applies to wallets, movies, cars, mansions, offices, jets, genitals, lips, eyes and swimming pools as well as the number of pages.

★

BIG BOOKS

Blockbuster novels are usually huge books – four or five hundred pages or more. This is partly because they stretch out the plot into a day-by-day, soap-like story. Like the soap opera, the blockbuster novel features a large number of characters. Such stories require a lot of space to relate them. But even when centred on one or two people, the blockbuster book is still (usually) a long read.

There are other reasons for the long length of the blockbuster novel – 500+, 600+ or 700+ pages: one is economics: not because bigger books are cheaper to manufacture (they don't cost that much more), but because the market (and presumably the reader) wants longer books, books that seem to be 'value for money',

---

9 You start the night in Vegas, but who knows where you'll end up?!

books that seem to have a lot of stuff in them (a lot of story, a lot of characters, a lot of events, a lot of action, a lot of comedy, a lot of sex, a lot of beauty, a lot of magic, whatever).

Actually, publishers use all sorts of dodges for bulking out books that actually aren't so long after all (check out the *Harry Potter* books for a classic example in the contemporary book market): they use short numbers of words per line, larger line spacing (which equals fewer lines per page), and thicker paper. (Jackie Collins' *The Love Killers* was published recently with 28 lines per page (instead of the usual 35), shorter line-lengths, and in 12-point type (this book uses 40 lines per page in 9-point type. However, 9-point size in this font – Lucida Bright– is larger than 9-point in, say, Times Roman: this is 9-point Times Roman). All of which turned a medium-length papercover book into summat resembling a blockbuster book).

(Sidenote: the publishers of *Harry Potter* (Scholastic in the U.S.A., Bloomsbury in G.B.) have used all of the usual tricks – hardcover editions, paperback editions, and audiobook editions[10] (as with Jackie Collins' books). They have also employed marketing tactics such as 'Deluxe Gift Editions' of each *Harry Potter* book (retailing at £42.95/ $64.49), plus 'Boxed Sets' of the first three books (priced £59.95 ($89.99); and the *Harry Potter $pecial Edition Boxed Set*, from Bloomsbury Children's Books (2003), retailed at £115.00 ($172.49).

Publishers Bloomsbury also brought out 'adult' editions of the *Harry Trotter* books (in paperback and hardback), which were aimed at adult readers and shelved in the adult fiction section of bookstores. Then there were further special editions of each book (in hardback). As each *Harry Potter* novel came out, there were new boxed sets, again in paperback and hardback, to incorporate the new books. There were also new 'special' or 'deluxe' boxed sets. And new box sets of the adult editions of the books.

There were large print editions of the *Harry Potter* books. Then there were 'Celebratory Editions' of the books. Plus library editions of the books. And also the usual round of re-issues and re-packaging

---

10 There were audio books on cassette tape. Not just one edition, oh no: there were abridged as well as unabridged editions of each novel on tape. Then there were audio books on CD. And 'collector's editions' of the books on CD (the 'collector's edition' of *Harry Potter and the Sorcerer's $tone*, 2002, cost £49.99/ $74.99). And 'limited editions' of the audio books: the *Harry Potter Quartet Collection (Limited Edition),* from B.B.C. Audiobooks, cost £49.99 ($74.99).

of books, enabling the same products to be sold again and again.)

The same tactics have been applied to Jackie Collins' books - every fan of Collins will have her books in different editions - some in the trade paperbacks of the 1980s (with Jackie in yummy leopardskin on the back), and some of the editions of the 2000s, with their front covers of pale, pastel drawings and paintings (when every new Collins book was first published as a jumbo hardcover edition).

The early books by Jackie Collins were relatively short. My copy of *The Bitch*, for instance (a 1984 Pan trade paperback (size: 4 3/8 x 7 inches), priced £2.99/ $4.49), is a skinny, bulimic book of 156 pages.[11] But with some of the later books, Collins followed the trend in bestselling publishing to compose larger tomes (with her publisher bulking 'em out with thicker paper). *Thrill!*, for example, is 485 pages long (size: 6 x 9 1/2 inches) in hardcover (priced £16.99/ $25.49).[12]

I have copies of Jackie Collins' novels bought in thrift stores on Fairfax and Melrose which are like doorstops - great, big, thick hardcover books the size of hefty *Bibles* (I bought some of my Collins books from thrift stores. You can find Collins' novels in every thrift store in the Western world - along with used copies of all your faves - John Grisham, Stephenie Meyer, J.K. Rowling, E.L. James, Tom Clancy, Stephen King, Dan Brown *et... cet... era...*).

All of this is intended to make the blockbuster novel - and this occurs in *all* publishing not just in blockbuster novels - seem bigger and better value for money. It also justifies charging two or three times the paperback price for a hardback edition (do the math!).

---

[11] And of course *The Bitch* has been republished in later editions as a much bigger book, using the familiar dodges of larger fonts, fewer words per page and thicker paper.

[12] But in *Thrill!* there are the usual publishers' wheezes involved, such as fewer words per page.

Six

★

Sex

They made love standing up until both their bodies were covered with a thin film of sweat. 'You've got to be fit to do it this way,' Butch gasped. Cleo's eyes were shut, a half smile hovered around her lips. 'Hey, baby? What do you think? Together?' Butch asked. Cleo arched back even further. A purely physical fuck. Like Mike she could enjoy it too. 'Any time you're ready.' Together they came, then collapsed on the floor laughing.

Jackie Collins, *The World is Full of Divorced Women*(68)

[Warning: this chapter uses naughty words. If Jackie Collins can use them, I can too]

SIZZLING SEX

> I only know that I prefer writing erotic sex to rude sex, and also, I write great married sex – contrary to popular belief, that does take place!
>
> Jackie Collins (2004)

This chapter will look at sex, sexuality, erotica and porn in the blockbuster novel: if you're too busy having sex to read about it (and who could blame you?), this chapter can be skipped.

Sex in the blockbuster novel is always advertized as being *steamy, hot, sizzling, raunchy, frenetic, over-heated* and *kinky*. In fact, it is the staple diet of erotica – and porn. The encounters, the people involved, the dialogues and the settings, are all straight out of erotica and porn. Sex in the blockbuster novel is chiefly physical, as the above quote shows. It is a conquest, an exercise, a step to success, but rarely a deeply emotional intimacy. It is always heterosexual, except in rare cases, such as Pat Booth's *Big Apple*.

Sex in the blockbuster novel works always within patriarchal norms and contexts. It is not subversive, difficult or dangerous. Rapes occur, but as acts to be avenged, as in Jackie Collins' *Hollywood Husbands*. Abuse is strikingly and disturbingly common in Collins Land (often as something to be forgotten, or to be paid back). Sex is not so much 'sizzling' or 'steamy' in the blockbuster novel, it is more completely ordinary, even at times machine-like (but it's the descriptions of sex that count).

For a negative view of this kind of sex, feminist Andrea Dworkin put it so powerfully in *Pornography*:

> Sex, a word potentially so inclusive and evocative, is whittled down by the male so that, in fact, it means penile intromission. Commonly referred to as 'it,' sex is defined in action only by what the male does with his penis. Fucking – the penis thrusting – is the magical, hidden meaning of 'it,' the reason for sex, the expansive experience through which the male realizes his sexual power. In practice, fucking is an act of possession – simultaneously an act of ownership, taking, force; it is conquering; it expresses in intimacy power over and against, body to body, person to thing. "The sex act" means penile intromission followed by penile thrusting, or fucking. (1984, 23)

The positive view of porn, which's the opposite of Andrea Dworkin's fervent feminist, anti-pornography view (and includes the soft porn and erotica versions of sex in the typical blockbuster novel), is that sex in fiction is pure pleasure and nothing more. It's about having fun, about fantasy, about escapism. It's not meant to be taken seriously. No one is being 'exploited', because we're talking about consenting adults. It's not 'sleazy' or 'creepy' or 'dirty', it's just images or videos or writings of people having sex.

In short, the positive view of porn and erotica is that it's not commercial exploitation of women (or men), it's a fantasy form which everyone knows is fantasy. In the supportive, positive view of porn and erotica, it's just sex - everyone does it (there'd be no human race if they didn't). It's about enhancing life, having some fun. As British comedian Spike Milligan put it, 'people like to fuck'.

★

SEX IN JACKIE COLLINS' BOOKS

> I am still shocking people today, and I don't know why. Is it because I'm a woman talking about sex and men? One magazine said that no one writes sex in the back of a Bentley better than Jackie Collins.
>
> Jackie Collins

There are all the usual situations of erotic fiction in Jackie Collins' novels: women offering themselves on beds, women kneeling to give head,[1] men on top, men deflowering virgins, teens making out in their parents' beds, men eating pussy thru their lunchhour. Few fetishes, few 'perversions'; it's heterosexual sex right down the line, with not much S/M, bondage, violence, anal sex, cross-dressing, transvestism, etc (Lucky Santangelo, Collins' alter ego, prefers straight sex, not kinky or fetishistic sex). If there is fetishism or sadomasochism, or summat outside the heterosexual norm, it's usually the characters depicted in a negative light (the villains or rivals) that perform it. Gay sex - male or female - is seldom depicted. The only very occasional gay sex in Collins' texts is the same as that sanctioned by erotica and pornography: women with women (i.e., one of the recurring fantasies of male-made porn, and newer lesbian porn - lesbian sex).

Very occasionally, a lesbian relationship will be depicted in Jackie Collins' fiction, but, as in *Married Lovers*, only in passing (like the relationship that Anya has with her friend Velma). In *Lucky*, Susan

---
[1] 'Married or not men were all the same. Blowjobs ruled their world' (217).

has an on-off lesbian affair with Paige – and as this is Jackie Collins, Paige is also tupping Gino, Susan's husband. In *Hollywood Wives: The New Generation,* a lesbian scene occurs: but, in true Jackie Collins style, it's in front of 70 people in a film crew (and there's also an irate director husband watching).

There are several lesbians (or closet lesbians) among the female characters in Jackie Collins' fiction. They tend to be portrayed with fewer stereotypical attributes (tho' bitchiness is still to the fore, as always in Collins' stories!). The older women who hire Buddy Hudson for fun and games in their hotel room in *Hollywood Wives*; Brigitte chooses a lesbian lover in *Poor Little Bitch Girl* (after a series of disasters with men); Dallas and Bobbie in *Lovers and Gamblers*; and Paige in the *Lucky Santangelo* series.[2]

Male gay sex is referred to, but not portrayed, although there are gay characters – and many more gay men in the later books, but nearly always in secondary character roles: Jackie Collins very seldom put a gay or lesbian character in the main role. However, one of the 'Hollywood Wives' in the sequel, *Hollywood Wives: The New Generation*, is the homosexual, uptight, snobby Englishman James, who has a troubled relationship with his partner Claude.

And tho' there are some gay characters, male or female, in Jackie Collins' fiction, perhaps not as many as one might expect in stories set in the media and celebrity worlds of Tinseltown, Gotham and London. The gay charas are secondary figures, not the leads; there are more gay male characters in the later works, including some couples. They often conform to stereotypes – so that, yes, they are bitchy, they do gossip, and they are often dancers, or photographers,[3] hairdressers, or designers.

However, there are one or two main characters who're gay: Dario Santangelo is one – the son of Italian tycoon Gino, who's freaked that his son's turned out to be a 'fairy'.

However, there isn't as much sex in Jackie Collins' fiction as one might expect, or as the marketing would suggest (and the press and the media also draw attention to the sex). Far, far more often Collins' novels are about *relationships*, with sex as an occasional expression of the relations between two people. In fact, although detractors of Collins' fiction can draw attention to the superficial treatment of sex and sexuality, most of the time Collins uses sex in

---

2 Lucky has a brief lesbian liaison with Olympia Stanisopoulos, her school chum, in her 'wild child' teen years.,
3 Italian photographers are recurring gay charas.

traditional, literary terms – to define or explore relationships (great sex when a romance starts, for ex, and boring sex when a marriage's in trouble). There's plenty of fooling around in Collins' books, but her books are not porn or erotica.[4]

Jackie Collins has a somewhat ambivalent and prim attitude towards the porn industry: although her novels contain situations out of porn, and also employ the language of porn, Collins in the main demonizes the porn business (and some of her female charas crusade against it, such as Cleo James and Lucky Santangelo). For instance, it's an area of business that the good guys avoid (even the gangsters, such as Gino Santangelo, prefer not to get into porn and prostitution), and the bad guys invest in. Thus, although for many people Collinsworld is a sleazy, low-life kinda place, with its evocations of drugs, hookers, crime and corruption, there are certain areas which're scorned, porn being one of them.

In *The Love Killers* (a.k.a. *Lovehead),* a bizarre sex-death occurs when Mary Ann August kills her lover Claire with a chair leg as she is being sucked (170). Well, I guess a chair leg would do; it's suitably phallic. Far more typical is when Rio and Angelo do the wild thing to James Brown's song 'Sex Machine' (102). Angelo lowers the lights, puts on a James Brown tape, Rio dances to 'Sex Machine', swaying before him:

> 'Show me your stuff, super-stud', she drawled.
> They moved together.
> 'Get up – get on up – get up – get on up – get up – get on up – stay on the scene – get on up – like a sex machine.' Rio sang along with James Brown, while Angelo's grip tightened and he managed to move her over to the bed.

I told you sex in Collins' books was predictable (but that's partly its attraction: if you're going get freaky in a blockbuster novel, it should be to the music of the Godfather of Soul).

Jackie Collins tries to subvert the mechanics of erotica sometimes by having the woman acting powerfully, as a strong and independent character:

> He moved over her breasts with his tongue.
> 'Let's fuck, baby,' she said briskly. 'I'm here for action. We can worry about tongue jobs later.'
> She rolled on her stomach and he entered her from behind. *(The Love*

---

[4] Readers have said they learnt about sex from her books – female readers especially, because Collins' books aren't porn, and young women readers can more legitimately read or buy a Collins novel than porn.

Killers, 103)[5]

Occasionally Jackie Collins' narrator keeps just this side of what might be regarded as respectability, by sometimes calling breasts breasts, instead of tits or boobs, which is the more common language of erotica. But she uses tits and boobs too, often when voicing a character's thoughts or speech – and women call tits tits just as much as men in her fiction (often as bitchy put-downs of rival women when those tits turn out to be plastic). Her characters, though, also speak with the voice of erotica.

Men have big weiners – *of course*,[6] endless energy, permanent hard-ons, and are perpetually horny; women have big breasts, *of course*, trim, athletic bodies (hours in the gym), and they can come and come.

Women are often treated as sex objects by men in Jackie Collins' world (sometimes ruthlessly). If women have large breasts they are to be used for a boob job, as in *Rock Star*. 'He was mesmerized by her thrusting, heaving, heavy tits' (425). If women have large mouths, well of course that's for giving head (always with the 'wide, sensual mouth' in Collins' erotic cosmos). And so on. *And on* (again: the *familiarity* of this kind of writing is part of its appeal: it's like movies showing the familiar scene of two people falling in ❤❤❤ across a crowded room, time after time, or like the Rolling Stones playing 'Satisfaction' at some giant arena for the zillionth time – *Go Mick! Go Keef!*).

Sex is typically introduced very early on in a Jackie Collins novel – then, once it's out of the way, the narrative continues, sometimes only returning to freakiness occasionally. For instance, in *Hollywood Kids*, Collins introduces a scene of a blowjob in a Rolls Royce car driving through the Hollywood Hills – a classic Collins situation on every level – by page six of the 1994 book. Getting head in a Roller cruising thru the Hollywood Hills – are you kidding? But no, it's right there on page 6. How cute is that?!

And in *Thrill!,* Joey and Lara enjoy some head while driving on the P.C.H. – it's gotta be done, right? – I mean, that road was *built* for oral sex! – on the way back from a Sunday power lunch at some

---

5 Rio twists her pelvis, and has Angelo coming too soon; she derides him afterwards (it's part of the revenge plot of *The Love Killers*, of women as *femme fatales*, the praying mantis or spider who shtupps then kills her victims).
6 On a U.S. talk show, Collins said she has a choice, and going bigger is obvious.

Malibu mansion:

> 'Suck it!' he commanded, pushing his hand firmly against the back of her head.
> Oh, God! All he had to do was ask...
> She bent her head, tasting him, enclosing him. And when he came, they were racing along the Pacific Coast Highway at seventy miles an hour and the kick was so potent that she felt herself climaxing herself too. (234)

On the Simon & Schuster website, Jackie Collins said:

> The late great Louis Malle, the famous film director married to Candice Bergen, said of one of my books, 'Jackie Collins is a raunchy moralist.' And I love that description. I know what he meant. The bad guys always get their comeuppance, and the good guys always win. Since we don't always have happy endings in life, I love to create the fantasy, so when people put down one of my books they feel happy, like they've gone on a great trip and had fun! We live in such unromantic times that I like to create great relationships. Chemistry is far more exciting than pornography.

Only a small fraction of the sex in Jackie Collins' work is pervy or violent: there is plenty of sex between lovers who ♥♥♥ each other, sex which is part of love at first sight, sex on a one-night stand which turns into love forever and ever.

Ah, cute, ah, yes, so sweet, so yummy.

Sex in the world of Jackie Collins' fiction is fairly conventional. There's plenty of oral sex – but it's the Great American Blowjob, and men (or women) go down on women less often (much to women's chagrin). And sometimes when they do, they're inept, as in standard porn. Wes Money in *Hollywood Husbands* licks Silver Anderson, but 'eating pussy was not one of his favourite things', and he doesn't usually 'offer this service' (181). Male chauvinist Ross Conti boasts to Karen Lancaster in *Hollywood Wives*, as he eats her out, 'I don't do this for everyone'. Lancaster is right back at him: 'what do you want – an award?' (100) But great lovers, of course, can eat pussy like champions:[7] there's a film producer in *Vendetta: Lucky's Revenge*, who declaims to every woman he meets that he is the greatest pussy-eater. Collins loves to use jokes on getting head – phrases 'you give great party' or 'giving great entourage' are typical, and appear everywhere.

---

[7] 'Men who *really* enjoyed going down on a woman were not thick on the ground', Mandy notes in *Married Lovers* (319).

Cooper's idea of lunch was eating her pussy for a solid half-hour. She'd come so many times she'd lost count. (*Vendetta*, 53)

'At fifteen she'd perfected the art of giving a great blow-job, just so boys would really like her.' (*Married Lovers*, 319) And in *Hollywood Wives: The New Generation* you can even learn 'how to give the perfect blow job', at a party, using 'rubber cocks straight out of the dishwasher!' (18).

A typical sex scene occurs in *Thrill!*:

> He undressed Kimberly slowly. She had on lacy lingerie straight out of a Victoria's Secret catalogue – which really turned him on. First he undid her front-fastening bra – revealing nice tits with chewable nipples. Then he peeled off her thong panties – exposing her shaved bush. Finally he unclipped her garter belt and rolled off her stockings.
> When she was naked he laid her across the outdoor glass table and fucked her quickly – pumping away for only a few minutes before coming. (103)

And in *American Star*, the heroine Lauren Roberts marries a guy forty or so years her senior (older male lovers being a recurring motif in La Collins' fiction): he has a pacemaker and can't get it up, so he goes down on her. It's the first time someone's licked her, and she loves it: 'he devoured her with a passion until she climaxed with a long drawn out cry of ecstasy' (374).

Unfortunately for Lauren R., sex is never more than oral sex in *American Star*, and she wants the whole thing – that is, she wants penetration. (Lesbian sex seems to work just fine without men and penises, though, for lesbians – you've got mouths, lips, tongues and fingers and loads of other bits b4 you get to the sex toys, the dildos, vibes, strap-ons, etc).

But li'l Lauren doesn't feel their marriage has been consummated unless he has been inside her, phallus and all. Through her character Lauren, Jackie Collins voices a common view – that 'full' sex, 'proper' sex, 'complete' sex, and truly satisfying sex, has to include penetration.

So isn't oral sex 'real' sex then? Apparently not. Eh? For many, it is. (It so is!) But for Miss Lauren in *American Star* having oral sex every time with her elderly husband isn't wholly satisfying, and eventually they drift apart.

A few times women are treated as scum. Maxwell Sicily thinks in *Rock Star*: 'They all fuck, and they all lie, and they all spend your money and run out on you.' (60) Oh, boo-hoo, poor guy! Men make women into whores. The women begin to act like whores, having being so thoroughly enculturated like that. Thus this extract from *The World Is Full of Divorced Women*:

> ...he was a bit pissed off that Jon Clapton hadn't warned him this girl would expect to get paid.
> 'Can't you do it for love?' he had asked her.
> 'Fuck love,' Laurie had drawled laconically. 'I don't get no money – you don't get no honey.'
> So he had paid her, laid her, and it had been worth it. (118)

Sex and money are inextricably linked in the sexual politics of Jackie Collins' novels (but the books are simply reflecting what is out there in Western, capitalist societies, in the advanced capitalism of Westernized countries). Money is sexy, and sex is best when there's lots of money involved. Paying prostitutes makes the sex act a business transaction, an ultimate expression of capitalism (like going to war).[8] Men can then assert themselves in two ways: financial and sexual, in the same act, at the same time.

Marriage since earliest times has had an economic element to it, often one that takes precedence over the personal/ emotional elements. Even when women are not paid for sex in Jackie Collins' fictional world, men still treat them like prostitutes: '"Now you can get your clothes on and get out"', Mike tells Erica after sex in *The World Is Full of Divorced Women* (164).

Men like women to be hookers in Collins Land (or to act like hookers), partly because the relationship is based on power, the master-and-slave set-up. A prostitute is anonymous – the anonymity is part of the fascination. Thus anonymous sex occurs frequently. In *The Stud* there is an archetypical encounter between the Stud, Tony, and an air hostess – sex at twenty-six thousand feet (another recurring scenario in porn and erotica, the 8-mile-high club, sex in the restroom, or in the reclining seats, trying to avoid the air stewardesses and the disapproving looks of other passengers). The woman is jokily called 'Tight Skirt' (85).

In *Sinners,* Charlie Brick chooses women that don't talk: 'Her name was Polly Quinn. At least she didn't talk too much.' (29) Talking ruins the fantasy. It is enough that women have big breasts (and can suck well). The look is everything. Anything meaningful, like conversation, is avoided: men prefer to grunt. These are some of the

---

[8] But occasionally, women can get off on the fact that they're paying men for sex – like Venus paying her masseur Rodriguez in *Vendetta: Lucky's Revenge.*

thoughts and attitudes embedded in the blockbuster novel; there are hundreds of others.

★

SEX, SEX, SEX

> 'It was the perfect honeymoon. Sex, sleep, sex, food, and sex, sex, sex!'
>
> Jackie Collins, *Hollywood Husbands* (246)

When sex occurs in a Jackie Collins book, it is often short, intense, sometimes shallow, occasionally loving, and usually by-the-numbers. It is integrated into the whole world-weary style. It is often part of the lassitude, the boredom, the ambition, the desire. People clash for a few days in a sexual stupor then fall apart. Sometimes marriage is the result. Sex is the glue that joins people in wedlock, or it is the problem at the heart of a divorce (*à la* Tennessee Williams). This passage from *Hollywood Wives* is typical:

> And sex, sex, sex. Under the shower. In his dressing room at NBC. On the back seat of a cab. Pressed up against the wall of the hotel elevator. Ross was insatiable, and she loved it. Twenty-six years later she could still feel his hands on her breasts. 'I'm a tit-man,' he used to say. 'And baby, you've got the best.' (275)

There are instances of sex not being tumultuously great, but they are fewer, being for relationships that are on the way out, or relationships that have become problematic or even abusive. But there's also lovemaking out of love – for the successful romantic relationships.

Great sex is the order of the day in the blockbuster novel – of course, we're in Fantasy Land, folks (no menstruation, no menopauses, no impotence, no S.T.D.s, no A.I.D.S., etc. Sometimes safe sex or a condom's mentioned – but not often in Jackie Collins' books). When orgies occur, they are heavenly, like the threesome[9] in *Hollywood Wives* (297). Men and women are driven crazy by bodies: sex is a frenzy, as between Karen Lancaster and Ross Conti in the same novel (ib., 199).

All this is familiar stuff, in Jackie Collins' books, and in

---
9 But Lucky Santangelo, an old-fashioned girl, is *not* into group sex.

blockbuster novels in general: they simply trot out the archetypal situations and characters of erotica.

❤

Let's look at erotica and porn in literature for a moment. Consider the classics of pornography and erotica, in book form, such as *The Secret Life of Walter, Lady Chatterley's Lover, Tropic of Cancer, Fanny Hill, The Story of O, The Story of the Eye, Justine* (and numerous anonymous works, such as *The Pearl* and *The Romance of Lust*) – these works depict sex in similar ways. The books of the Marquis de Sade, Georges Bataille, Henry Miller, Pauline Réage and William Burroughs are celebrated by the intellectual critics and arty bohemians as *avant garde*, experimental, subversive. They are not regarded as pornography, but (defensively) as 'erotica'. However, erotica is simply pornography for intellectuals, for anti-porn feminists like Andrea Dworkin (in *Pornography*):

> erotica is simply high-class pornography, better produced, better conceived, better executed, better packaged, designed for a better class of consumer... Intellectuals, especially, call what they themselves produce or like 'erotica,' which means simply that a very bright person made or likes whatever it is. (1984, 10)

In the Miller-Mailer-Hemingway, North American school of writing, sex tends to be something wholly phallic, aggressive, territorial. Characters make love like guns, going blam, blam, blam. But because it is exalted by (mainly male) critics, it can become (seen as) art. Even when such pornography/ erotica is hacked out by lesser authors, such as Timothy Lea (a.k.a. Christopher Wood, b. 1935) in his *Confessions of* series of the 1970s, the results can be just as silly, crude and for some offensive:

> She has pulled open my trousers like the mouth of a flour sack and has got both hands round my hampton while I am easing her knickers down to knee level with a skill any window dresser would envy[10]

It is humour that saves this from being wholly dumb, as in the works of Henry Miller or John Cleland. Timothy Lea, like Martin Amis in *The Rachel Papers,* is part of the saucy postcard, *Carry On* school of British humour, the nudge-nudge-wink-wink brigade which turn sex into farce; in the U.S.A., authors who send up sex like this would include Terry Southern (see below) and Philip Roth.

There is often a paltry amount of humour in the treatment of

---

10 T. Lea, *Confessions of a Driving Instructor,* Sphere Books, 1972, 90.

sex in the blockbuster novel, however. Humour does not work in erotica, even though some people say that sex is often funny (the most fun I've had without laughing, as Woody Allen put it). Laughter deflates desire, in short.[11]

But in Jackie Collins' work, there is a healthily sceptical view of sex – and it's expressed by the female characters just as much, or maybe more than, the male characters. And there is humour – typically, it comes from the characters' thoughts, ironically commenting upon the sex acts.

In the blockbuster novel, sex must be something awesome, something to be revered. It is elevated above drugs, drink, music, partying and art as a high. On that level, there is hardly any difference between Jackie Collins' books and those made especially for the erotica market, such as the *Emmanuelle* series of the 1970s, or Jan Cremer, or Anaïs Nin, or the tomes written by 'Anonymous' (*You, Me, Her, Him*), which feature on their covers pictures of bits of bodies in close-up.

The *Emmanuelle* books (by Emmanuelle Arsan, a.k.a. Marayat Rollet-Andriane,[12] b. 1932), contain pseudo-intellectual dialogues: they aspire to erotica, like Hubert Selby's *Last Exit to Brooklyn* aspires to Henry Miller and William Burroughs. These books, like *Blue Skies, No Candy* (by Gael Greene), are not dismissed but are discussed enthusiastically by literary critics. Yet they contain many elements that are found in porn, and in many sections are indistinguishable from porn.[13]

The *Emmanuelle* movies led to a highly lucrative franchise, instantly recognizable as classic examples of 1970s softcore porn – or the art film as porn, or the arty porn film. They were marked by exotic locations (like Bangkok in the first movie, the Seychelles or Tibet), glowing soft focus, back-lit cinematography, partial or full nudity, and starred Dutch actress Sylvia Kristel (1952-2012), a terrific screen presence who combined innocence and *joie de vivre* with slinky, European cool.

And the *Emmanuelle* pictures were enormously popular, playing

---

11 Similarly, in lesbian erotica, dildos and strap-ons are taken seriously, and rarely are they called 'a joke, an imitation, or a substitute', according to Lynda Hart in *Between the Body and the Flesh: Performing Sadomasochism*(100).
12 There is some dispute about the authorship.
13 Altho' Andrea Dworkin is known as a passionate hater of porn, critics have noted that her denunciations of porn actually contain lengthy extracts from porn (to illustrate her arguments), and so can be regarded as porn themselves. Also, in her fiction, Dworkin has employed sex scenes and the language of porn.

to packed cinemas. There were a number of sequels (1975, 1977, 1984, 1986, 1988, 1992, 1994, 2000, 2001, 2003, 2004, etc), plus several TV series (such as *Emmanuelle In Space*, 1994), and many imitators and spoofs.

The *Emmanuelle* books were bestsellers, too. This is from *The Further Experiences of Emmanuelle*:

> Then he makes her bend her knees, to move towards him: when the moist cunt touches his prick, he inserts it, using his fingers, then takes hold of her buttocks and makes her envelop it completely.
> He says:
> 'Now ask me to make you come.'[14]

The *Emmanuelle* books were fairly standard, European erotica – and very French, like the movies. (The early *Emmanuelle* movies had the look and heat that the Collins adaptations *The Stud* and *The Bitch* aspired to, but completely lacked).

Erotica, in the form of Anglo-American-European paperback books, are printed (in Britain) by publishers such as Arrow Books, Sphere, Pan, New English Library and Star Books, among others (Pan/ Macmillan are one Jackie Collins' key publishers). In more recent years, publishers, such as Black Lace, Cheek, Nexus and Virgin, have produced erotica aimed at women. These books appear in most bookstores (many are placed on the shelves under 'A' for 'Anonymous', or in an 'Erotica' section).

A typical example of fictional porn with affinities with the blockbuster novel is this extra from Jane Longaway's "Art Gallery":

> I placed one of his hands between my legs and he massaged my clit until I came; then, taking his cock out of my pussy he put it into my mouth and I took his pleasure into me, caressing his hard balls until he groaned and shot the thickest, most salty juice down my throat.[15]

Such paperback porn is churned out hack-like, just like Anaïs Nin wrote pornography for a dollar a page in the 1930s.[16] Many

---

14 E. Arsan, *The Further Experiences of Emmanuelle*, Mayflower, London, 1976, 63.
15 In S. Bright, 142. Another example comes from *The Oyster*, purportedly a reprint of Victorian erotica by Sir Andrew Scott. It is written in a pseudo-archaic style which celebrates anal sex at length as a giggling pastime engaged in by foppish English, snobs (there's often corporal punishment in there, too. Thus: 'Her bottom cheeks wriggled again, so with my free hand, I guided my already stiff cock in between them.' (*The Oyster*, Anonymous, New English Library, 1985, 84.))
16 Anaïs Nin, *Delta of Venus*, Star, 1981; *Little Birds*, Allen, 1980. A terrible movie was made about Nin and her erotic stories in 1994.

authors of erotica (including the 'new women's erotica') don't use their real names. Instead, they give themselves prissy pseudonyms like Monica Belle and Stella Black.

Anaïs Nin's erotic work, though it was also porn, nevertheless contains much finer writing than your average erotica outing. D.H. Lawrence's fiction (one of Nin's models) similarly transcends pornography, partly because it burns with a passion that goes beyond the objectification of women (and men) as sexual beings only (and partly because Lawrence really can write). There is more than sex in the literary fiction of Nin, Lawrence and Henry Miller.

But in the blockbuster novel, sex is typically viewed as the apotheosis of life. Put simply, the blockbuster novel often uses sex as a means to power and wealth. As Bridget Fowler said in *The Alienated Reader*, in these novels, 'economic power at its most concentrated and diversified is linked mythically to sexuality and fecundity'. Consequently, some publishers have referred to the genre as S. 'n' F. (= shopping and fucking). 'These are indeed the fairy tales of modernity.' (1991, 105)

They are also dubbed 'bonkbusters';[17] 'chick lit' was a later term (Lisa Jewell, Danielle Steel, Jodi Piccoult, Jennifer Cruise, Polly Courtney). *Bridget Jones* is a well-known, recent example of 'chick lit' – and how dreary is Helen Fielding's creation Bridget Jones, her loathsome, superificial, bourgeois aspirations, and her dull-as-mud boyfriends and pals compared to Jackie Collins' characters! Give me Jackie Collins any time.

★

WOMEN'S SEX

And we should not forget that women produce or explore erotica, just as men do (for instance, Susie Bright, Pat Calfia, Annie Sprinkle and Nina Hartley). In *Erotic Interludes: Tales Told By Women*, edited by Lonnie Barbach (1986, one of many books of this kind, and one of several edited by Barbach), we find women writing in masculine terms about sex:

---

17 Only Brits would come up with a moronic phrase like 'bonkbuster'!

'I'll fuck you...' I hear my voice crooning the words... I want this man a little more desperately each time we fuck... Anticipating his prick head reaching my cunt makes me curl my ass upward... 'What an ass you've got, you little fucker, the best ass I've ever seen...' I feel his cock hard, jutting into my soft abdomen like a rock. (235)

The above example, by Victoria Starr, is typical of the pieces collected by Lonnie Barbach, and also of the sexual fantasies edited by Susie Bright (*Herotica*) or Nancy Friday (*Women On Top, Men In Love, My Secret Garden,* and *Forbidden Flowers*). They demonstrate that mainstream erotica is a masculinist construction within a patriarchal social system, whoever writes it, and if women get involved they must abide by patriarchal, masculinist rules. For women to write about sex in a non-pornographic way they must go outside of men's/ masculine language, outside of masculinist culture, and outside of patriarchy, which is very difficult (some say, including feminists, that it's impossible). Anaïs Nin said we need to invent a new language of sex. She was right, but she couldn't do it. Many have tried but no one really has done it yet.

In contemporary, Western pornography, the kind produced in *Playboy, Hustler, Penthouse* and *Private* magazines, everything is so simple. Names are bland (Paul, Cherry, Dave), the situations are clichéd (a neighbour sees a woman next door sunbathing ➼ a photo modelling session turns into an orgy ➼ putting on sun lotion on the beach leads to sex ➼ a guy comes home from work to find his wife in bed with her best friend ➼ a neglected wife gets freaky with the U.P.S. delivery guy ➼ a girlfriend returns home to find her man dressing up in her clothes[18] – and A.I.D.S., adultery, divorce, children, jobs, money, illness, bills, unemployment, in-laws and emotional issues are not mentioned.

Porn evokes a fantasy, idealized world in which everyone is permanently available for instant sex. No hang-ups, no complications, no problems. People are reduced to ciphers, to pumping, thrusting, bulging bodies. The emphasis is on physicality – the size, feel and movement of bits of the body. Pornography is a world of mechanical movements as the actors go through the motions, the writers go through the motions, and the consumers go through the motions. All you need is to throw together a few juicy verbs, a few rich adjectives, and you're there:

---

18 Jackie Collins has employed some of those clichéd scenarios.

> Your mouth and free hand teased my nipples, and I felt my body curling into the arc of a brewing orgasm. But my cunt ached, empty. I wanted you to fill me and I gasped: "Oh, fuck me, please!" Your fingers slid easily in[19]

The blockbuster novel is no less formulaic: take a group of people who inhabit the same city, concoct a few rivalries, give them all stupid names like Charlie Brick, Wes Money and Jeff Stoner, make them all hot and seething with ambition – then sit back and watch the story unfold on its own. As one can paint by numbers, so one can write by numbers (there are authors' handbooks which will tell you how to do it). Pop musicians say one can write a Number One hit song to a formula. Movies have formulas: a movie, in the era of high concept postmodernity, should be able to be reduced to a single sentence that can be summed up on a matchbox. In the age of the instant pitch, the hard sell of an idea, sex too has to be easily accessible, instantly accessed on a computer or phone or flat screen, high definition TV.

Except, of course, this is rubbish: 'formulas' are a confection, and the notion that you can simply select a formula or recipe and come up with a perfect work of art is poppycock. If all it took were creating items to formulas, authors, songwriters, musicians, filmmakers and media conglomerates would be churning out songs/ movies/ books/ television using those templates and turning out hits or near-hits every time. Raymond Chandler noted on formulas in a letter of 3.18.1948:

> My whole career is based on the idea that the formula doesn't matter, the thing that counts is what you do with the formula; that is to say, it is a matter of style.

Sex in porn tends to be dead simple: a man gets together with a woman (or another man or maybe a goldfish) and away they go. These are basic desires, like eating and drinking. There is no subtlety involved (who's got time for subtlety?). Similarly, in a children's playground, Mike hates Lisa and Cyndra fancies Petra. Kids understand such emotions: 'I'm your best friend. No, now I'm not your best friend 'cos you dissed me'. Kids' speech is easy to understand. It's the same with erotica, and with the blockbuster novel.

Much of contemporary fiction, too, is this simple. The thriller trades on the simple desires or motifs of chases, money-lusts, and

---

19 From C. Queen, "At Doctor d'Amour's Party", in S. Bright, ed., 1995.

murders.[20] The blockbuster novel is full of school-kid-level hates and loves, and thrives on achieving power. The novels of a host of authors can be reduced to basic desires: fear and thrills (Stephen King, Michael Crichton), mysteries (Dan Brown, Agatha Christie), power (Frederick Forsyth, Tom Clancy and Jeffrey Archer), and desire for wealth and fame (Jackie Collins, Shirley Conran, and Jacqueline Susan).

One might say the same of the works of William Shakespeare, Homer, Dante Alighieri and Johann Wolfgang von Goethe. Somehow, their works are called 'Art' and are regarded as having an Extra Something not found in the books of Dan Brown or Jackie Collins. What is it? It is something mysterious, noble, complex, sublime, tragic, magical, powerful – impossible to define but you know it when you see it or hear it.

Complexity is crucial in 'high art', for the lit'ry crrritics, and Collins, Brown, Archer, Conran *et al* are not complex, and not subtle. They reduce people to a few characteristics. Their people lack a roundedness, a subtlety. This is not the whole reason why Jackie Collins is not regarded as a great artist like William Shakespeare or C.P. Cavafy, but it is part of it. True, the artists called the 'greats' or 'classics' trade on basic human desires – Homer, Catullus, Sappho, and Heinrich von Kleist. But they somehow elevate humanity, they educate it and celebrate it, while Collins, Brown, Koontz, Forsyth and Archer too often merely reflect what they see around them in clichéd, stereotyped, re-hashed ways.

But here I'm simply trotting out the age-old oppositions between 'high art' and 'low art', the snobbish, élitist views, which pigeon-hole art and artists. Which's so dumb – because we love blockbuster novels, just as much as 'high art' novels like *Jude the Obscure* or *The Immoralist*.

The snobbery of intellectuals and critics towards popular fiction is odd when you consider that many other areas of popular culture have been embraced by academia – pop music, action movies, comicbooks, etc. The number of eggheads and academic nerds who've written long, hi-falutin' essays about schlocky, dumb movies like *Alien, Blade Runner* and *The Matrix* is enormous.

Perhaps the only way to describe the complexity of sex is to make fun of it all. No one has yet really communicated the myriad sensations of erotic experience. Many have tried: James Joyce, D.H.

---

20 That's partly why Raymond Chandler chose it, so he could explore other things, like language.

Lawrence, Francesco Petrarch, Catullus, Ovid, and others. But they have all failed.

And perhaps any writing about sex is automatically pornography. Porn is enmeshed in the language at such a deep level, no one has yet found the means to extricate authentic eroticism from pornographic language. D.H. Lawrence tried using the 'forbidden' words (*fuck, cunt, shit*, etc) in *Lady Chatterley's Lover,* but that didn't work either.

Terry Southern and Mason Hoffenberg's *Candy* attempted to subvert pornography with satire. The 1958 book takes its innocent young heroine, Candy, through a variety of humorous situations, in which she becomes initiated into mysticism, sadomasochism, psychoanalysis, incest, and medicine. The authors show how ridiculous porno is by taking its tendency to push physical descriptions to a ludicrous extreme. So Candy's Holy Something is apotheosized as a 'sweet-dripping little fur-pie' and a 'seething thermal pudding'.[21] *Candy* is ten years ahead of its time (it might've been written in 1968), and also it hasn't dated at all (because the humour is solidly constructed – and very funny).

When Candy meets Grindle, a fake, Zen Buddhist guru, he persuades her to try some serious spiritual exercises. These turn out to be just ordinary sex after all. All the hippy *sensei* wants is to shtupp Candy (well, every male character she meets desires that). The descriptions target the hypocrisy of pornography and patriarchy (and send up the po-faced solemnity of teaching):

> 'Now I am inserting the member,' he explained, as he parted the tender quavering lips of the pink honeypot and allowed his stout member to be drawn slowly into the seething thermal pudding of the darling girl. (ib., 208)

When you stand back for a moment, you realize just how silly porn is, how demeaning it can be, but also how fun.

I would recommend the novel *Candy,* and Terry Southern's later satire on Hollywood, *Blue Movie*. Southern's approach is far more critically savage than that of Jackie Collins (except perhaps in her later works, where she could be snarly). Southern's *Blue Movie*, which explored the porn industry in 1970 (nowadays it's a billion-dollar business), is a delightfully witty send-up of making movies (not only porn, but any movie). And *Blue Movie* is a satisfying portrait of

---

21 T. Southern & M. Hoffenberg, *Candy*, 207-8.

contemporary Hollywood, though more irreverent than Collins' *Hollywood Wives* or *Thrill!*.

There's a link, too, between *Candy* and Jackie Collins: in the movie made from the book in 1968, Marlon Brando played the hippy guru, and Collins had an affair with Brando in the 1950s.[22] (Brando's turn as a truly weird religious guide is a satire on the gurudom of the counterculture era, and the Beatles with the Maharishi; he tups Candy in the back of a truck rumbling through the North American desert.)

---

22 However, the movie of *Candy* (Christian Marquand, 1968) is truly dreadful – one of the more bizarre, so-bad-it's-*bad* movies of the 1960s: but worth seeing just for the high calibre of the actors on show wallowing in deep doo-doo Marlon Brando, Richard Burton, Walter Matthau, Charles Aznavour, etc. James Coburn comes out best, getting into the spirit of camp silliness. (But *Candy* is far more enjoyable in its craziness than a later movie adapted from a Terry Southern book, *The Magic Christian* (1970), a truly abysmal outing starring Peter Sellers, Ringo Starr, Christopher Lee, Lawrence Harvey, Yul Brynner, Raquel Welch, etc.)

Seven

Aspects of Jackie Collins' Work

...fucking was his favourite pastime, second only to making money.

Jackie Collins (*The Power Trip*, 119)

THE IMAGE AND THE TEXT

In this chapter I'll look at some of the elements in Jackie Collins' work, beginning with a little more discussion of her media image, because it makes such a strong contribution towards her fiction, and in particular the reception and perception of it.

The image that Jackie Collins projects (or rather, that is projected for her by her publishers, editors and P.R. people), is of a confident, attractive and successful woman. For publishers and P.R. folk, Collins is a dream come true, because she does a great interview (that cute British accent!), and she really does look great (as well as resembling her books and her characters). She is easy to sell as a brand and image, compared to many a writer (let's face it, plenty of authors aren't exactly easy on the eye, many aren't media friendly, many can't do decent interviews, and many have little that's interesting to say).

Maybe being beautiful has nothing to do with literature. Maybe. Who cares what Friedrich Hölderlin or William Shakespeare or Leo Tolstoy looked like? But in the world of advertizing and publishing, beauty goes a long way.

Have a look at the author photos for Jackie Collins' earlier books: in the mid-1980s, Collins was presented to the public in her books as a sophisticated, well-dressed and appealing woman.

I love the photos of Jackie Collins on the back of the British editions of her books: on the cover of *The Bitch* (1984 Pan paperback edition), for instance, Collins wears a denim shirt (undone to the cleavage, *of course*), and a matching, blue necklace. She stares at the viewer intently, trying hard to appear sexy and smouldering. Tons of kohl around the eyes, lip gloss (*de rigeur* in the 1980s), blusher, and very big hair. Wow!

For the cover of *Sinners* (1984 Pan edition), Jackie Collins reclines on leopardskin cushions, wearing – what else?! – a leopard-skin dress! ('My weakness is wearing too much leopard print', Collins has admitted). With the jewellery, the blusher, the eye shadow, the lip gloss and the huge hair, Collins is every inch the power-dressing Eighties woman, oozing confidence, success, and sexiness. A vamp. A model. She looks like she could walk on stage at a rock concert and belt out a Tina Turner or Donna Summer cover. Or like she could slink onto the set of *Dallas* or *Dynasty* and not look out of place.

Collins also likes panther emblems, and wears one as a brooch on the cover of *Lucky*. As well as a leopardskin tie and matching earrings. And what does daddy Gino give his daughter for her birthday in *Lucky*? A panther brooch: 'a pavé diamond panther brooch studded with cabachon rubies and emeralds. It was the most exquisite piece of jewellery she had ever seen' (410). Yes, panthers (also leopards and jaguars) are Collins 'power animals', her totem animals (from shamanism).

The whole Jackie Collins media image is very much part of her novels and the world she writes about. And that sexy, glam image is maintained throughout Collins' writing career, up to the latest published books. There's a strong element of continuity between the Collins' media image and her stories (her brand). Collins gives off the image of a successful author in the publicity created by her publishers, agents and P.R. people. She's an image of the Writer Who's Made Good.

★

THE PAGE-TURNER

Jackie Collins' books definitely have that magic ingredient: the ability to lure the reader on, to make them yearn to find out what happened next. Critics and commercial blurb writers call those books a 'page-turner'. Jackie Collins has it, J.K. Rowling has it, J.R.R. Tolkien has it, Mary Renault has it.

It's a total mystery, how to achieve it, though. If business schools and writing courses and lit'ry classes around the world knew how it was done, it would be the first thing they'd teach. All publishers and media outlets would make it the foundation of their operations.

How *do* you write a book that keep readers panting to know more? It's totally mysterious, impossible to predict or capture or teach. But if you think about the bestselling authors, and about blockbuster novels, it's one of the things they have in common: they are all page-turners.

For this new edition of this study of Jackie Collins' work, I've been reading some of her more recent books. And the magic begins. Despite the stories being hopelessly clichéd, despite the characters and settings and situations being *so* familiar, despite all of that (or maybe *because* of all that?), the magic bites, and you get hooked.

You want to find out what happens next.

And that, folks, is one of the *key* reasons why Jackie Collins – or Jo Rowling, or Judith Krantz, or Harold Robbins, or John Grisham – sells millions of books.

The magic kicks in right after the initial exposition chapters, the passages where characters're introduced, and after the prologue or flashback teaser. We're talking only a few chapters in a Jackie Collins novel. In a movie, it's near the end of the first act, between 20 and 30 minutes (a movie will typically have a first act turning-point after 25-30 minutes, often with a reversal halfway thru each act).[1] (In which case, studying the opening chapters of a Collins book might be profitable, because this is where the seeds of the achievement of selling 500 million books are sown).

If you think it's easy, go ahead and write your own blockbuster novel!

Imagine it: you could spend 2 to 3 months writing it (or two or three days!), and if it's a hit, you can take the rest of the year off and go on vacation in Hawaii!

It's all about confidence.[2]

There are guidebooks on How To Write a Blockbuster Novel, as well as articles online.

Good luck!

★

---

[1] If you want to know more about screenwriting and movies, of all the books out there, I highly recommend Kristin Thompson's wonderful book *Storytelling in the New Hollywood*

[2] 'Confidence is everything', Nick Angelo's acting teacher tells him in *American Star* (313). It's what I keep telling my creative writing students. If you had a magic wand which gave writers and artists total confidence, you wouldn't need anything else – no classes, no learning, no waiting, no worries, no anxieties. You'd just get on with it.

REAL PEOPLE

> I have always stated that real life is way crazier than fiction. In my books, I am inclined to tone things down because otherwise, it doesn't seem believable.
>
> Jackie Collins, *TV Guide*

Jackie Collins includes references to numerous real people, mixing them in with her fictional characters, sometimes in the same sentence, to make the whole thing more convincing. Like when Wes Money meets all the stars at the big party in the middle of *Hollywood Husbands* (with the fake one in the middle):

> Wes tried to maintain an aura of cool as he said hello to Jacqueline Bisset, Whitney Valentine Cable and Angie Dickinson. Three women he had lusted after forever. (248)

Or this list of celebs at Lissa Roman's Las Vegas party in *Hollywood Wives: The New Generation* (the fake ones are 3, 4 and 7):

> The very pretty Britney Spears, James Woods with a young date, singing star Al King, Lucky Santangelo, Dennis Hopper, Lara Flynn Boyle, Nick Angel, Hugh Grant. (399)

Lucky Santangelo has a dinner date with Venus in *Vendetta: Lucky's Revenge* at Morton's restaurant (the fake one is the last one):

> She kissed Arnold Kopelson, the producer, and his smart wife, Anne. She waved at the Marvin Davises, stopped to have a word with Joanna and Sidney Poitier, greeted Mel Gibson, blew a kiss at Charlie Dollar, and finally arrived at her destination. (205)

In *Readers Read* (2004), Jackie Collins said:

> I choose a real life character I find fascinating, then I combine them with other people who are also fascinating to me, and I create a mix. You may recognize some of the people, but you're never quite sure who it actually is.

Among the many recognizable inspirations for some of Jackie Collins' characters are actors such as Charlie Sheen, Sean Penn, Steve McQueen, Paul Newman, Bruce Willis, Brad Pitt, Robert Downey, Jr,

George Clooney, Robert Redford and Warren Beatty, and actresses like Elizabeth Taylor, Sophia Loren, Nicole Kidman, Jennifer Lopez, Angelina Jolie, Carmen Electra and Julia Roberts. And the supermodels: Naomi Campbell, Claudia Schiffer, Christy Turlington, Kate Moss, Tatjana Patitz, Linda Evangelista and Cindy Crawford. Photographers/ artists such as David Bailey and David Hockney. And pop stars such as Madonna, Prince, Mick Jagger, Elton John, Whitney Houston, Beyoncé, David Bowie, Michael Jackson, etc.

> I have this theory that people in Hollywood don't read. They read *Vanity Fair* and then consider themselves terribly well read. I think I can basically write about anybody without getting caught.

The 'bespectacled filmmaker', a 'genius, an autocrat and an egomaniac' who's been ten years in analysis, and appears on Jack Python's talk show in *Hollywood Husbands* is clearly modelled on Woody Allen (though Steven Spielberg and one or two others might also be inspirations).

Many Hollywood couples are fodder for Jackie Collins: Madonna and Sean Penn, Brad Pitt and Angelina Jolie, Jack Nicholson and Angelica Huston, Kim Basinger and Alec Baldwin, Paul Newman and Joanne Woodward, Tom Cruise and Nicole Kidman, etc.

Some other possible inspirations for Jackie Collins' characters would include Don Simpson, the infamous, debauched film producer, who went on to make high concept blockbusters such as *Beverly Hills Cop, Top Gun, The Rock* and *Crimson Tide*. And producers Joel Silver (*The Matrix*), and Joe Levine (1905-1987), famous for his straight-talking attitude towards filmmaking, which included plenty of swearing.[3] Flash, the British lead singer of the Layabouts in *Lucky*, is clearly drawn on the wonderful John Lydon (his rotting teeth being one of many clues).[4] Porn stars such as Traci Lords are real-life Collins characters.

One story of recent times is so perfectly a Jackie Collins story you couldn't make it up – and that's the story of Princess Diana, which includes glam and glitz in spades, and fame, an Egyptian playboy as a lover and an extraordinary demise (pursued by

---

[3] Thru his Embassy Pictures company, Levine's production credits included: *The Graduate, A Bridge Too Far, The Lion in Winter, Magic, Long Day's Journey Into Night, Carnal Knowledge, The Producers* and *Zulu*.

[4] John Lydon's another Brit who lives in L.A. He loves it. Better weather than England, more laid-back, and great for taking his boat out onto the sea.

paparazzi in Paris). But nobody needs to write that particular novel, because the story has been reworked in thousands of news and TV and radio items. Indeed, years after Princess Diana's death the media still manages to put the story or Diana on the front page. (Collins very rarely refers to Princess Di)[5]

A *paparazzo* in *Goddess of Vengeance* has a history of nailing celebrities:

> He shadowed Jackie O. Captured Elvis fat and thin. Michael Jackson in his pjs. O.J. on the run. Diana and Dodi. (418)

From time to time Jackie Collins will provide a list of celebrities for some party or function: the bitchy list reads like a litany of Collins' characters: this's from *Hollywood Wives: The New Generation*:

> There was the big action star, who'd spent his entire life pretending to be straight. The innocent-looking *ingénue*, who was into whips and chains. The TV executive, who screwed around on his wife with the stars of his shows. The mother-daughter combination, who'd double-teamed their way to the top by blackmailing certain studio executives. The hot young actor hopelessly addicted to crack cocaine. The skinny TV actress with an even worse case of anorexia. And the madam, whose little black book was worth more than anybody would care to guess. (397)

Often Jackie Collins will create a character who's clearly based on a particular real person – like the female producer with a drug habit, cropped hair and an anorexic body in *American Star*, called Julia somebody or other, who is clearly drawn on film producer Julia Phillips, who produced movies like *Close Encounters of the Third Kind*[6] and *Taxi Driver*, and who famously spilled the beans on Hollywood big time in her tell-all autobiography *You'll Never Eat Lunch In This Town Again*, one of the must-read books on contemporary Hollywood (if you like Jackie Collins' books, you will *love* Julia Phillips' book. It's like a Jackie Collins book, but the names and people are real). Collins satirizes Phillips nastily by giving her bad breath and a bad temper, and she's desperate for a fuck (266).

---

[5] There's a reference in *Goddess of Vengeance* (418).
[6] Producer Julia Phillips fell out with Steven Spielberg, as she relates bitterly in her autobiography *You'll Never Eat Lunch in This Town Again*, she was thrown off *Close Encounters of the Third Kind* by Columbia apparently because of her drug-taking (Phillips' autobiography is full of drugs, in particular the cocaine that was prevalent in the entertainment world of the 1970s).

Another essential book on Hollywood – Robert Evans' autobiography (*The Kid Stays In the Picture,* 1994) – is cited in *L.A. Connections* (Madison, the heroine, is listening to it on audio tape). *The Kid Stays In the Picture* was turned into a fascinating documentary in 2002 by Nanette Burstein and Brett Morgan. And Bob Evans is a Collins character and Hollywood player if ever there was one (Evans was the producer at Paramount of mega-hits[7] as well as flops (he produced a movie beloved in Collins Land – *The Godfather*), dated stars like Ali McGraw, fell out famously with Francis Coppola[8] (among others), had run-ins with the law, and was linked to a Hollywood murder case).

Some fans have hungered for a Jackie Collins novel which uses real people. Maybe in 70 years after the last surviving relatives die, or when copyright runs out! Because the entertainment industry (especially in the U.S.A.) is incredibly litigious.

The familiar legal notice is printed on the imprint page of each Jackie Collins book:

> This book is a work of fiction. Names, characters, places and incidents are either a product of the author's imagination or are used fictitiously. Any resemblance to actual people living or dead, events or locales is entirely coincidental.

If you *really* wanna know who Jackie Collins is basing her characters on, she often gives a clue the first time they're introduced. In *Hollywood Wives: The New Generation*, for instance, the film director Larry Singer (note the Jewish surname) is placed alongside Steven Spielberg, so he's probably partly drawn on Spielberg (Singer also has an actress wife, like both of Spielberg's wives). The brother film directors in the same 2001 book're compared to the Farrelly brothers, which gives you an idea of where Collins is coming from (the Coen brothers might be another inspiration).

---

[7] Robert Evans was a very successful film producer: *Love Story, Rosemary's Baby, The Odd Couple* and, after *The Godfather, Chinatown.* Evans later produced the turkeys *Black Sunday, Players* and *Urban Cowboy.*

[8] Francis Coppola fell out with Robert Evans big time during *The Godfather.* Their professional dislike of each other became one of Hollywood's long-running disputes. Coppola hated that credit for the success of *The Godfather* was given to Evans. Coppola stressed that Evans had nothing to do with it, and went on to prove his assertion by making the Oscar-winning *The Godfather 2* without Evans. Meanwhile, Evans insisted that his influence was crucial to the movie (such as demanding a re-cut).

HUMOUR

Humour is an ingredient in the Jackie Collins novel that shouldn't be under-estimated. In fact, it's essential to the mix. Although there's plenty of romance and family saga stuff in these rags-to-riches stories (plus all the bad times), Collins deploys humour all the way through. She can write some crackling one-liners and ripostes (most of the humour derives from witty dialogue, rather than situation comedy). The later works feature much more humour. Particularly enjoyable are the put-downs and super-cynical bitchiness – often lines which can only come from thinking for a moment about what would be cool to say:

- By the time he split, she had divorced her husband and returned to her old ways. Hooking suited her better than cooking. (*Hollywood Husbands*, 37)
- Wes couldn't help noticing that when Whitney Valentine got angry her tits swelled like a couple of melons, and her nipples headed straight for the entire male population's eyeballs. (*Hollywood Husbands*, 272)
- Freddie's demeanour was as cold as an Eskimo dick. (*L.A. Connections*, 19)
- 'Honey, the truth is the truth. Wake up and smell the hard-on.' (*Thrill!*, 44)

Sometimes Jackie Collins' writing is really bad taste, as in this example from *Thrill!* in which a fashion model's body is compared to victims of the Holocaust: 'an anorexic English model who appeared to be no more than fourteen with her waif-like face and concentration camp body' (105).

At times, Jackie Collins' novels read like a good, 1930s screwball comedy, when the dialogue was rapid-fire (compared with the s-l-o-w line readings of some contemporary N. American and European TV and movie dramas). I'm not suggesting that Jackie Collins is on the level of comic wits like the Algonquin 'vicious circle' (George S. Kaufman, Alexander Woolcott, Robert Benchley, Dorothy Parker and Harold Ross), or S.J. Perelman, or the Marx Brothers, but her humour does have an earthy, sexy wit that Groucho Marx would appreciate. (But, you know what?, some of Collins' work *is* of the quality of the famed Algonquin Table wits).

The humour serves to lighten the proceedings, yes, which can be bleak at times. But humour is also part of Jackie Collins' innate style – and worldview, I would say (and Collins in interviews certainly comes across as a friendly and humorous person – at least compared to the out-and-out grouchs that some writers can be! She must be a joy to interview compared to some authors – well, you know who I'm talking about!!).

Humour also inevitably sometimes breaks the fourth wall, and brings the reader out of the secondary world of the novel. It's a reminder that this is all a story, a confection.

★

DIALOGUE

When characters talk, it's in short sentences, and the dialogue zips back and forth rapidly. Jackie Collins is especially good at witty one-liners, and occasionally comes up with a killer metaphor:

- He 'dumped his first wife quicker than a hooker gives head' (*The Bitch*, 20).
- 'The problem with Phil was that he had no taste: he'd fuck a plant if it looked at him sideways' (*Married Lovers*, 139).
- 'Everyone *knows* she's waiting for him to drop so she can inherit his millions an' start bumpin' and grindin' with cabana boys.' (*Married Lovers*, 20).

Jackie Collins is terrific at reproducing casual speech, which not every author can do. The use of the word 'like' among young Californians, for instance, is spot-on, because sometimes when you're, like, on the West Coast, everyone, like, seems to, like, speak like that. If you, like, took the word *like* out of the speech of Californians it'd, like, be totally weird and, like, so short.

The casual speech, combined with occasional swearing, is a really important ingredient in Jackie Collins' prose style: look at any page of a Jackie Collins novel, and there's dialogue everywhere. Indeed, the story and content of Collins' work is largely embedded in her dialogue, and is a product of the dialogue. Sometimes Collins' novels read like film scripts with the stage directions taken out. Nothing wrong with that.9

And Jackie Collins likes to include 'bad language' for many of her characters (including Lucky Santangelo). Collins is an author like Henry Miller; swearing is simply embedded in the Collins style (her narrators swear as well as her characters!).

★

MORE BITCHING: 'DISH IT, GIRL!'

There are so many easy targets for Jackie Collins' poison pen in Hollywood and the media circus in Europe and North America. Alcoholics, drug addicts, neurotics, sex perverts – and that's just a small dinner party in Laurel Canyon. Ageing stars who try to halt time with plastic surgery. Starlets with silicone boobs. Actors with a squeaky-clean image who're kinky weirdos behind the scenes in Vegas hotel rooms. The film producer with an out-of-control cocaine addiction.

Bitch, bitch, bitch – dish the gossip, girl!

And characters in Collins Crazy Land snipe and gossip all the time.

> Antonio [a gay, Italian photographer] had commandeered his own table, and he proceeded to point people out as they boogied past. He had a line of gossip on everyone. '*She* take the heroin.' '*He's* a bigamist.' '*She* in the porno films.' '*He* only like two women.' (*Hollywood Husbands*, 101)

And we love it. Jackie Collins can do gossip and bitching as good as *anyone* in pop culture, including prize bitches like Dorothy Parker or Mae West.

Journalists are fair game for any novelist, and in *Hollywood Husbands* Jackie Collins provides a vicious portrait of a bitch who interviews the 'bitch-goddess' herself, Silver Anderson:

> She was a middle-aged woman with brittle looks and dyed yellow hair. She was a failed actress, a failed singer, and a failed writer of novels. Finally she had made her mark with a weekly page in a London daily newspaper,

---

9 A script, as William Goldman and countless others have pointed out, is only a template, a guide, for the filmmakers. It's not meant to be a finished piece of literature. Collins has written scripts.

and was now known for her vitriolic dislike of successful actresses, singers, and novelists. (111)

Ouch! And Collins gives her a 'phoney smile' and body odour too! *Meowww!*

★

FLASHBACKS

Back-story is typically introduced by Jackie Collins (and other bestselling authors) with short chapters (often printed in italics), as one or two characters (always the chief characters) are given some background history (typically involving some lowly beginnings or some 'dark secret' from their past, such as violence or abuse).

Back-story in Jackie Collins' work acts exactly like the flashbacks in movies: to provide motivation and justification, and to flesh out characters. The flashbacks are there to provide the viewer or reader with information on the chief characters which can explain their behaviour and motivations (and also their goals and ambitions).

Such flashbacks clarify the characters for the reader/ viewer: in a movie, they are used sparingly, because screen time is so precious. In a novel, there's more time to stretch out and explore the past. However, Jackie Collins typically does *not* indulge herself in the flashbacks, but sticks to short bursts of information, and usually features only one really important piece of information in each flashback. (And yet, some of Collins' finest writing are when she constructs a narrative of lengthy flashbacks – as in the *Lucky Santangelo* series, when we delve into the pasts of Gino Santangelo, Costa Zennocotti, Carrie Berkeley *et al*).

Also, Jackie Collins allows herself a number of flashbacks (while a typical Hollywood flick only has time for one or maybe two flashbacks). But Collins spaces them out, so they are sprinkled throughout her narratives; thus, information is revealed at carefully-judged moments, putting the author way ahead of the reader most of the time (however, the reader of a Jackie Collins book knows how the story will end – at least as far as the main characters are concerned. Justice will be meted out, and morals will be upheld).

An example of how back-story operates in Jackie Collins' work is the use of troubled childhoods and the past in the 1998 novel *Thrill!* The narrative moves forward, involving the usual combination of relationships, ambitions, changing partners, and divorces, against a background of Hollywood and making movies. The central love relationship in *Thrill!*, between Lara Ivory and Joey Lorenzo, is consummated by halfway through the novel. It's a rapid, intense love affair, with great sex.

So far, so expected.

The lovers are crazy about each other, so what can go wrong? The *past*: both have troubled pasts, which have been presented to the reader as snapshot flashbacks in italic type. So the key tension in the narrative of *Thrill!* is: *when* will they find out about their dark secrets from the past? And will that information disrupt their new relationship?

If you wanted to, you could apply literary critical analysis to this use of flashbacks, and give Jackie Collins' books the sort of solemn, critical treatment accorded to Fyodor Dostoievsky or Charlotte Brontë or Daniel Defoe. That is, you could bring in hi-falutin' themes and issues. You could say, for instance, that Collins is asking serious questions: such as, does the past and upbringing define a person? Is someone the sum of what's happened to them? Can people start afresh? At what age is an individual defined for life? Are people always changing with each new experience? Or more general questions: who defines and controls history? What is the relation between history and social agency? What is the relation between history and the present day in society and politics?

★

SHORT CHAPTERS

Another ingredient of Jackie Collins' style is the short chapter. It's a common feature of bestselling novels, and has a number of functions. For the writer, it means short bursts of information; for the reader it means easy-to-digest chapters, a few minutes to consume each one. For the writer, it means keeping up with a host of characters or simultaneous events, by switching rapidly from one to another. For the reader, it means something like the parallel action or cross-cutting of a movie, and it means the reader is constantly being updated with each story, and their new developments. For the writer, it means collating the novel structurally into short episodes, rather than lengthy sequences which might run on in traditional novels to 30 or 40 pages or more. For the reader, it means bestselling novels are snacks, and don't overwhelm them with masses of information.

For the writer, short chapters means the story has to be kept in line carefully, and each story strand has to be pretty clear (and different from the others). For the reader, it means that ambiguity and confusion is kept to a minimum, because each short chapter usually has a clear and strong line.

There are other functions: short chapters can be extracted for publicity purposes; digressions and meandering narratives are curtailed, because writers have to concentrate on jumping from one plot strand to another. Short chapters have obvious links to magazine publishing (the so-called 'blip' publishing, dissecting information into short bites), and television news, entertainment shows, lifestyle shows, etc.

Nothing new here, though: short chapters were *de rigeur* in the 19th century, when authors such as Charles Dickens and Thomas Hardy wrote for magazines, and novels were broken down into weekly installments (typically ending on a cliffhanger). And the 'penny dreadfuls' and the 'bloods' worked in short serial form. Indeed, nearly all narratives in history have been short – long-form stories are much rarer. Stone Age folk didn't carve out stories on blocks of granite in caves in 26 weekly installments! (This week, the new fur-lined bikini! Next week, how to cook for a whole dinner party using only two clumps of grass and three handfuls of mud!).

In fact, when writing was invented in Mesopotamia, between 3,400 and 3,200 B.C. (as cuneiform script), the clay tablets were only concerned with who paid for what and how many. (Not stories, not mythologies, not religions, but money and property).

Also, look at any page of any Jackie Collins book, and you'll see short sentences and short paragraphs. Collins doesn't let her characters go in for lengthy speeches (no Shakespearean monologues here). And she doesn't go in for lengthy descriptive passages (compare with any page of Charles Dickens or Leo Tolstoy).

Jackie Collins says that she writes her books in longhand (with a diamond-encrusted fountain pen from Cartier, I hope). That might have some bearing on the form her novels take.

★

NARRATION

Technically, Jackie Collins tends to stick to two traditional narrative viewpoints – the third person, God-like narrator, and the first person, subjective viewpoint. Typically, her books are composed from a third person, past tense narration, with the narrator always ahead of the reader. Sometimes the narrator allows the reader into a character's thoughts and feelings, but more often allows the action and dialogue to tell the reader how a character is thinking and feeling. In Collins' fictional world, action is character, uh-huh, but it's often *dialogue* that is the action (or, more correctly, the *interaction* between characters). In this respect, Collins resembles Jane Austen, who composed whole chapters consisting of conversations flowing back and forth between characters.

Jackie Collins will shift into first-person narration typically for the flashbacks, or when she wants to let the reader directly into her main characters' heads. This can be very amusing when Collins has her characters debate with themselves, in short, italicized sentences, along the lines of:

> *You really want this guy, don't you?*
> *No I don't, shut up!*
> *Then why are getting all flustered just talking to him on the phone?*
> *I'm not!*
> *Quit kidding yourself, you like this guy A LOT.*
> *No, I do NOT!*

One aspect of Jackie Collins' glam romance fiction that few fans or critics note much is the *structure*. These are *ensemble* pieces, involving groups of inter-connected characters. That takes more than a little working out – not only connecting the characters, not only creating a variety of characters (and goals and desires and flaws and obstacles), not only starting at 'A' and ending at 'Z', but also manufacturing the numerous dramatic developments along the way – the 'B', 'C', 'D', 'E', 'F', 'G', 'H', 'I', 'J', 'K', 'L', 'M', 'N', 'O', 'P',

'Q', 'R', 'S', 'T', 'U', 'V', 'W', 'X' to 'Y' segments.

★

JACKIE COLLINS IN ANCIENT ROME

One thing that Jackie Collins has done is to limit herself to a very narrow kind of novel. She writes stories set in the present day about similar groups of characters in three cities: L.A., New York and Las Vegas (mainly). As Collins puts it, somehow her characters always gravitate towards Los Angeles and Las Vegas. Her most ambitious work by far is the *Lucky Santangelo* series, which goes back to earlier periods, such as the 1930s. I for one would love to see Collins have a go at more historical fiction – the era of Ancient Rome is the most obvious historical era, perhaps, for a Collinsian work-over. Ancient Rome has everything and then some for a blockbuster novel: betrayal, vengeance, intrigue, ambition, sex, debauchery, violence, you name it.

Hollywood cinema exploited the ancient world to the max in the 1950s and 1960s, with self-consciously OTT epics that featured sex, death, action, violence, romance, beauty and spectacle (building, of course, on the example of the King of Ancient World Hollywood Schlock, Cecil B. DeMille). Going back to Ancient Rome might free Jackie Collins up for a grander vision of families and relationships (Ancient Rome was certainly another inspiration for the *Godfather* movies, for example, and other movies set in the modern era).

But maybe Jackie Collins is too attached to breakfast in New York, sexy flings in the Beverly Hills Hotel, and walks along Malibu beach – in present day U.S.A. In fiction, you can go *anywhere*, you can be *anybody*, you can do *anything*. But I guess that Collins doesn't want to stray too far from one of Steve Wynn's luxury hotels and casinos in Vegas, or where you can't get a pedicure or hail a cab.

> This was New York, and here you could get away with anything. (*Vendetta: Lucky's Revenge*, 25)

★

DON'T LECTURE ME!

Jackie Collins *doesn't do* some things which can be irritating about some authors: she doesn't, for example, lecture the audience, like D.H. Lawrence[10] and Thomas Hardy (and many others) can't help doing, and she doesn't rant and rave, as some writers do, like Henry Miller. She doesn't wander off the point into lengthy discursions, as John Cowper Powys does (but we love him for it). She doesn't alter the tone of her writing into something self-consciously churchy and hi-falutin', like J.R.R. Tolkien in the second half of *The Lord of the Rings*. She doesn't show off as a writer with complicated sentences or unusual words (as Lawrence Durrell does). She doesn't introduce idiosyncratic theories or ideas which can disrupt a novel (as Aldous Huxley does).

★

FICTION AND REALITY

For some readers and critics[11] and fans of Jackie Collins' books, her stories and characters are just too exaggerated, too out there, too unbelievable. Maybe. This *is* fiction, after all. We are talking about *stories*. About stuff that's *made up*.

Yeah.

But if you know anything about the Hollywood movie industry, about Hollywood stars, about how the media circus works, about Broadway theatre, about television, and P.R., and fashion, and modelling, and photography, and magazine publishing, and big business, you'll also know that what goes on in those areas of contemporary life can be *very* crazy. And there are some pretty out-there people in those regions of the modern world. Oh yeah.[12]

So, as Jackie Collins has often pointed out, real life and real people are *way* more extraordinary than what she puts in her books

---

10 D.H. Lawrence, bless him, could go on and on to the point where it's painful. Lawrence is one of those authors who have ten million things to rant about, and when he's on one of his rants, he won't stop until he's dead certain the reader gets it. Unfortunately, that can be a major flaw when it consumes so much air.
11 'The biggest critics of my books are people who never read them'.
12 Scandals continue to pile up: Harvey Weinstein, Bill Cosby, Heidi Fleiss, etc.

(director Ken Russell has said the same thing - reality is much stranger than movies). If you put these people into a novel, no one would believe you: Andy Warhol. Michael Jackson. Madonna. Liz Taylor. Traci Lords. Elvis Presley. David Bowie. Mick Jagger. Richard Pryor. Whitney Houston.

What probably makes it unbelievable in Jackie Collins' works and in blockbuster novels in general, is the *form* of the stories, and how the stories are told, with all those coincidences, sudden miracles and turnarounds, and how events unfold.

But it's also a *mistake* on the part of the reader to expect or demand 'realism' - or any relation to reality. Despite Jackie Collins stating that her novels give us 'the truth', or that she bases her characters on 'real people', she is writing *stories*. If you want 'real' dirt, go to a documentary, a historical or factual account of Hollywood stars.

★

THOMAS HARDY AND JACKIE COLLINS

Thomas Hardy (1840-1928) is a useful comparison in the realm of clichés. Oh, Hardy is *so* clichéd it's not true! His novels are regarded as some of the finest written in the English language, and are analyzed in countless scholarly tomes and academic conferences,[13] but if you've read all of Hardy's works many times and have studied them at length, like I have, you quickly discover just how repetitive and clichéd Hardy's books are.

Take young love.

How many times has Thomas Hardy trotted out the same situations, the same characters, the same romances and break-ups. Again and again *and again,* Hardy goes over the same depictions of young love, the poor guy and the rich lady, and comes out with the same settings, the same looks, the same misunderstandings.

But Thomas Hardy knew what worked - with readers if not with krrrritiks.

We could compare Jackie Collins with pretty much any of the major, celebrated novelists and discover that those guys (they are

---

[13] Yes, people really do gather in Dorset and elsewhere to discuss Hardy's work!

mainly guys) could be just as sensational and corny and hokey and unbelievable and silly as any blockbuster author.

Presentation, context, advertizing, publicity, perception, etc, have a lot to do with it. Say if you published a Jackie Collins novel in a sombre book jacket (a moody, black-and-white photo of a windswept moor), with no glammed-up author photo (her name would be J.J. Collins), and included serious pull-quotes from the *New Yorker* or the *Times Ed*. And you knew nothing about Collins or her other books. Would the book still be received in the same manner? Probably – because Collins' prose is a giveaway: item: 'What a bullshit artist Nico was. The absolute best. The original fuck-and-run merchant' (*The Bitch*, 28); item: 'Venus could elicit a hard-on from a stone statue!' (*Vendetta: Lucky's Revenge*, 73). It's true you don't find sentences like that in the novels of George Eliot or William Faulkner.

However, there *are* a whole slew of modern novelists who employ 'bad language' and sleazy settings and lowlife characters but who're regarded with awe by some literary critics: Tom Wolfe, Gore Vidal, Philip Roth, Jim Thompson and Elmore Leonard.

And there's one aspect of the critical reception of Jackie Collins' books that's inescapable: *she's a woman*. In short, male authors can write books with sex and sleaze and violence and gangsters and be regarded highly critically: Henry Miller, Jean Genet, even Mario Puzo. But women authors are simply not viewed in the same way.

★

OBSTACLES

Jackie Collins certainly likes to pile up obstacles for her characters. In *Thrill!*, the main character, super-beautiful Hollywood star Lara Ivory, has a very troubled past: at the age of five her family is slaughtered in front of her by her father, who then blows his brains out after calling her an ugly, little slut (talk about OTT! And yet there *are* real incidents like that). Lara gets shunted off to some nasty relatives, and continues to have an unhappy childhood (well, this *is* a novel!). At fifteen she falls for a Z-rate musician, whom she worships and marries, aged 16. This guy, much older than Lara, doesn't believe in any kind of sex other than Lara giving him blowjobs. Of course he treats her like dirt, and drinks, etc.

Then, when Lara hits Hollywood, and finds someone who'll look after her a little - a gay guy called Tommy - he dies after 10 months! And so it goes on and on for Lara, from one terrible experience to the next.

★

YOU ONLY LIVE ONCE

One of the great things about Jackie Collins' books is that you don't have to read them twice: you get everything first time round (I've never heard of someone re-reading a Collins book. I have re-read one or two of the novels for this study). Everything is on the surface and easy to understand and absorb. No hidden meanings here, no subtle shifts in subtext or theme or point-of-view, no convoluted plots or a cast of 100s of characters to keep track of (actually, the plots can become a little complicated in Collinsiana - or maybe it's keeping track of ensembles of characters. But the beauty of Collins' novels is that she uses the same types again and again, so you always kinda know where you are. And *all* writers use the same character types).

★

RELATIONSHIPS

I've mentioned elements such as glamorous lifestyles, and consumerism, and shopping, and beautiful people, and Hollywood, and the media circus, and sex, but one element is more important in Jackie Collins' books than any of those ingredients: *relationships*. More than sex, glitter, violence, ambition, dark secrets, revenge, fame, movies, music, and celebrities, Collins' books are about *relationships,* and they chiefly concern *relationships*. We're talking emotional stuff between people - and although it's true that sex is often the means or chemistry or discourse between people, it's actually the relationships themselves that're really important.

In short, Jackie Collins' novels are about people getting on with each other (or not), falling in love (or out of love), getting married (or getting divorced/ separated), being friends (or falling apart), being good parents (or bad parents), being good children (or bad kids), and so on and on and on and *onnnnnnnnnnn*.

I've drawn attention to sex in Jackie Collins' work (and it's part of the P.R. – it's a hook), but there's far more *talking* about sex than *having* sex: sex is simply one expression of the state of (a) relationship in Collins' books. Eating and drinking might be others, or walking on the beach, or going for a drive, or flying to New York, or whatever.

But it's all about *relationships* – with finding one's way in the world (a.k.a. rags-to-riches) as a theme close behind. That can mean a job, or money, or professional relationships, and it's tied in with ambition, goals, and the discovery of murky secrets from the past.

And sprinkled over the two elements – relationships and finding one's place in the world – is the glittery, glamorous, gorgeous world of Hollywood, high finance, rock music, Las Vegas, gangsters, gambling, stardom, etc. But if you take away the emotional elements – between husbands and wives, between lovers, between parents and children – you have absolutely nothing. Well, you have some shiny materialism, some jewellery from Cartier or Tiffany,[14] some luxurious houses in Malibu or Vegas, some jumbo jets and Gulfstream jets, and some stretch limos and Ferraris. And you have one or two action set-pieces. But little else. (Some would take all the shiny stuff and forget about relationships).

❤

You'll notice the high volume of older-younger sexual relationships in Jackie Collins' work right away. There are so many one wonders if there is some personal significance for it (Collins' husband Oscar Leman was older, and Collins dated Brando when he was 29 and she was 15). Usually it's older men preferring younger women – like Nico Constantine in *The Bitch* or Richard Barry in *Thrill!* or Michel Guy in *Vendetta: Lucky's Revenge*). Occasionally it's older women preferring younger men – like the Bitch herself, Fontaine Khaled:

---

[14] Jackie Collins is big on jewellery, and is always referring to women dripping with diamonds and rubies. And she describes jewellery like an expert from Tiffany.

old was not what Fontaine needed. She needed youth – she enjoyed youth – she revelled in the male body beautiful and an eight- or nine-inch solid cock. (20-21)

But the problem with youth is that it hasn't made it yet. It doesn't have money, resources, contacts. It has sex, a great body, but no cents. So the older folk support the younger ones, and they resent that.

♥

In relationships, from a woman's perspective, Jackie Collins is particularly good at wives who've long out-grown their husbands: the guys are happy to stay at home and watch sport on TV, drinking beer, but the women *want to go out and party!* There are many scenes in Collins' fiction of:

♠ Women trying to talk to their men while the guy stares at the television and barely acknowledges them.

♠ Young women who find solace with *much* older men (sometimes even the sex is better).

♠ Young women who become fascinated (sometimes fatally) with bad boys (they can't help it – these guys are just toooooo sexy and toooooo much fun to be around).

♠ Teenage women who out-grow their teenage boyfriends (their ambitions stretch far beyond getting laid occasionally and watching TV).

★

BIG BOOBS

Jackie Collins' narrators bitchily draw attention to plastic surgery and silicone breasts, which're everywhere in her novels. If a character doesn't point them out, the narrator will ('a vapid blonde with huge boobs and a serious overbite', snarks the narrator of *L.A. Connections* [12]). There are numerous references to perfect 36B's, and perfect boobs only seem to exist if they're artificially enhanced (everybody's body is a cyborg-body here, with artificial augmentations). And if the narrator moves from someone's face to describe their body, their boobs will be described, especially if they're plastic tits.

> She had it down, moving to the music like the seasoned veteran she was, big tits swaying to the beat of Mariah Carey's 'Butterfly'. (*Lethal Seduction*, 162)

Indeed, Jackie Collins draws attention to breasts more than *any* writer I've ever read, more than any writer you can think of – including all the usual suspects among literary, macho writers, and all of the erotica/ porn authors.

Is this sexist? Maybe. Probably. Yes… Maybe.

I don't know: this is a female writer talking about female characters in books read by millions of women (you can bet that the readership of Ms Collins' novels is mainly women).

'Perkily waiting were a perfect pair of 36B tits. *His* tits. He had paid for them' (*Hollywood Husbands*, 212). Yes, that's the ultimate in capitalist ownership – you don't just own your wife legally, thru marriage, you own her actual body, because you paid for those wobbly augmentations.

And Jackie Collins refers to breasts more than anything else when her narrators are eroticizing the female characters; sometimes long legs or a slim waist are cited. The mound, the bush, occasionally, but only rarely the clitoris. (However, in *Chances*, horny teen Gino Santangelo discovers that massaging the 'magic button' produces amazing results in girls: in *Chances*, he's 'feeling for the magic button. Susie gave a little sigh. He had found it' (18). Gino, rapidly gaining the moniker of 'Gino the Ram', decides not to tell his buddies about the magic button.)

★

RAGS-TO-RICHES

Jackie Collins has remarked that rags-to-riches narratives are very appealing: certainly *Cinderella* or *Great Expectations* stories appear in most of her books. She has also cited *Cinderella* directly in relation to her characters: 'sometimes Lara Ivory felt like Cinderella,' she wrote in *Thrill!* (316). And in the running flashback in *Married Lovers*, the waif Anya even works like a slave for a neighbourhood family, scrubbing the floor, and sleeping in the kitchen amongst the mice, rats and cockroaches (2).

Even when some of the main characters are already successful, there are always other characters who are on the up. Someone is always climbing up from the gutter, from the ghetto, from the suburbs, to attain Hollywood stardom, or success at the tables in Vegas or the businesses on Wall Street.

Nico Constantine, the Greek, self-made man in *The Bitch*, drags himself up from nowhere to learn the tricks and trades of the wealthy lifestyle. No, not secretarial skills, or engineering, or real estate: it involves learning about wine, food, gambling, skiing, racing cars, horses, polo, etc (11). Yeah, and by the time he's hits Hollywood, Nico has the lifestyle of the rich and famous down to a 'T':

> The bachelors of the Beverly Hills community flocked around to be his friend. He had everything they all wanted. Class. Style. Panache. The Money wasn't so impressive, they all had money, but he had that indefinable quality – a charm that was inborn.
> For ten idyllic years Nico lived the good life. He played tennis, swam, messed around on the stock market, gambled with his friends, invested in the occasional deal, made love to beautiful girls, sunbathed, saunaed, hot bathed, went to the best parties, movies, restaurants. (14)

★

LOS ANGELES, LAS VEGAS AND NEW YORK

> I love Los Angeles. I love Hollywood. They're beautiful.
> Everybody's plastic, but I love plastic. I want to be plastic.
>
> Andy Warhol

It's the characters and the stories, I think, that contribute most towards making Jackie Collins' books so successful. For me too, it's also the settings – I adore Los Angeles, New York and Las Vegas, and never tire of living in them or reading about them.

> Las Vegas. The heat. The special smell. The hustle.
> Las Vegas. Home. From birth to seventeen.
> Las Vegas. Youthful memories crowding his head. The first time he got laid, drunk, stoned, busted. The first time he fell in love, ran away from home, stole his parents' car.
> (Jackie Collins, *Lucky* [22])

Bobby waxes lyrical about Las Vegas in *The Santangelos*:

'The first time I saw Vegas at night, I was a kid asleep in the back of my mom's Ferrari', Bobby reminisced. 'Lucky pulled over to the side of the road and woke me up. 'Take a look, kiddo. It's a sight you'll never forget,' she told me. And yeah – she was so right' (410)

Las Vegas is certainly one of the great cities of the world, an 'only in America' place, a Party Town so over-the-top you can't believe it when you first visit it. And yet, after a few days, it's all so obvious, you get it, it all fits.

The Las Vegas of the classic, Rat Pack era was based around Fremont Street and the surrounding area, but that is now the *old* part of Las Vegas, where the older casinos and resorts are found. These days, Las Vegas has spread out across the Strip to become one of the most extraordinary cities in the world. (In 1900, the white population of Las Vegas was just 20 people; when gambling was legalized in 1931, the State had 91,000 citizens. By 1960, it grew to 64,000 in Vegas and 285,000 in Nevada. Today there are 2.6 million in Nevada and 600,000 in Vegas).

Now it looks like movies such as *One From the Heart* was tame by comparison in creating a neon-drenched Las Vegas: if you visit Vegas today, you'll find mind-boggling recreations of Venice and Paris, *indoors* (plus all of the familiar landmarks, like the Eiffel Tower, the Opera, St Mark's Square, the Venetian canals, etc). Oh, and New York City. And an Arthurian castle (Excalibur). And the enormous, orchestrated fountains at Bellagio.[15] A battle at sea between pirate ships at Treasure Island casino (with the 'Sirens of T.I.'). The erupting volcano outside the Mirage. The lions at the MGM Grand.

The casinos, hotels and resorts in Las Vegas have become entire theme parks on their own, each one containing theme park rides and attractions, zoos, gardens, plus a range of restaurants, stores, cafés, bars and hotels. Las Vegas has become its own movie, its own theme park, and its own vast tie-in merchandizing operation. Las Vegas is also not just one movie, but many movies (and not all of them are Italian-American gangster flicks!). Some are rags-to-riches musicals with showgirls and playboys, some are honeymoon comedies, and, yes, some are gross-out, bachelor night comedies.

Las Vegas is, like Disneyland, a movie in three-dimensions, a theme park on a colossal scale to itself. Las Vegas isn't simply

---

[15] The dancing fountains in the lake in front of Bellagio, lit by coloured lights, are accompanied by Frank Sinatra or Italian opera.

'postmodern', in Jean Baudrillard's notion of Disneyland as postmodern America personified; Las Vegas is way beyond that.[16]

Visiting Las Vegas is not only like being in a movie, it's like being in a Jackie Collins' novel, a thousand Hollywood thrillers, 500 wacky comedies, and a Living History of Entertainment in the U.S.A.

The world of Jackie Collins is not all North America, it's a particular part of the U.S.A. – California. And California means Los Angeles pretty much, with occasional jaunts to Malibu and other spots up the Pacific Coast Highway[17] (but not Frisco, no sirree, not the Central Valley, not Eureka, not Napa Valley or wine country and not Palm Springs).[18]

Like so many other Brits, Jackie Collins and her novels take to the West Coast like people starved of sunshine and good living (for the same reason, 4 million Britons flock to Spain each year). In *L.A. Connections*, Collins writes of artist David Hockney, one of many Brits who've embraced Californication: Madison 'found Hockney's work arresting and very Californian – which was interesting considering he was from England' (366).

New York. His city. His territory. His *home*. (9)

Many of Jackie Collins' books are set in New York (at least partially), but you wouldn't class them among the Great New York Novels. For a start, Collins' books don't capture the most distinctive aspect of New York City life – the street-life, the intense, in-your-face hustle and bustle of the streets. I'm writing these lines in New York, and Collins' New York simply doesn't nail what it feels like to be living in Gotham. (Of course, New York is among the most written about cities of recent times). But Collins got better at writing about N.Y.C., especially in the later novels.

However, Jackie Collins definitely does nail elements of life in the City of Lost Angels, from the car culture and the homes behind guarded gates, to the shopping on Rodeo and Melrose and the mesmerizing vista of the millions of glittering lights viewed from the Hollywood Hills, a view I never get tired of – the glimpses from

---

16 As David Thomson put it in *The Big Screen*, 'as Hollywood's own glamour began to decline, and feel the beginnings of shame, Las Vegas offered a remake, a parody, and then a pastiche of it' (267).

17 Maybe a spin up P.C.H. in a Porsche for breakfast in Santa Barbara, as in *Hollywood Wives: The New Generation* (But jeez, why bother going all the way to boring Santa Barbara, when you've got Malibu?).

18 However, there are visits to Palm Springs in the *Lucky Santangelo* series, because Gino Santangelo retires out there.

Mulholland Drive, or the awe-inspiring visions from atop Griffith Park (and one or two of Collins' characters stop for a moment to drink in that stupendous view).

★

As well as setting most of her books in modern North America, most of Jackie Collins' characters are North American. The novels are set in the present day of when they were written (or a few years earlier). And when Collins explores the pasts of the main characters, it is ten or twenty years before the present – so in the 1980s novels, Collins is writing about the 1960s and 1970s in N. America, and in the 1990s novels it's the 1970s again, and the 1980s. However, Collins' own youth was spent in London and England in the 1940s-50s – *very* different from America in the Seventies! Well, let's just put it this way: Britain in the postwar Fifties was nowhere near as sexy and glam and wealthy as the U.S.A. in the 1970s!

> America. She was in America.
> The thought made her weak with excitement.
> (*Dangerous Kiss,* 327)

Indeed, Jackie Collins is of the generation in Britain that fell in love with all things North American when it hit Albion big time in the mid-1950s – the music, the movies, the fashions, the places, the whole mythology of it. (Collins was 18 in 1955, the period when the U.S.A. began its cultural colonization of Europe).

America or England?

Dreary, foggy, suburban Britain or glitzy, out-size America?

Many folk in Britain opted for the Great American Dream – British pop musicians, for instance, like the Rolling Stones, the Beatles, the Who, Eric Clapton, David Bowie and everybody else, and plenty of filmmakers. As Paul McCartney put it, Route 66 and the American South in the blues music that he and John Lennon loved sounded so much more glamourous than dear, old England:

> We know about the Cast-Iron Shore and the East Lancs Motorway but they never sounded as good to us, because we were in awe of the Americans. Even their Birmingham, Alabama, sounded better than our Birmingham.[19]

The music and the culture of rock and pop music is North American, and black, as numerous commentators have noted. Altho'

---

19 B. Miles, *Paul McCartney*, Secker & Warburg, London, 1997, 201.

some Brits argue otherwise, pop music, like jazz, and blues, and rhythm & blues, is an *American* cultural form (with roots going back to African American culture, and Africa itself).

Movies were crucial in the Americanization of Britain: many British pop musicians have noted how significant it was when they first saw *The Girl Can't Help It* (Frank Tashlin, 1956) or *Blackboard Jungle, Don't Knock the Rock, Rebel Without a Cause* and *East of Eden* (both blues and rock 'n' roll, like the movies, and the fashions, were *American*: whether it was jazz, blues, rock 'n' roll or r 'n' b, it was all North American. In the 1950s, British youth was Americanized to a profound degree, and it hasn't recovered since: from the 1950s onwards, British culture (and society) has been thoroughly Americanized).

★

MUSIC

A key component of the blockbuster novel *à la* Jackie Collins is music. Pop music. Rock music. Music is cited numerous times in Collins' books, and Collins is a big music fan, talking enthusiastically in interviews about many acts:

> I'm crazy about music – I love everyone from Jay-Z to John Maher to Jason Mraz to Mariah. I'm also very fond of rap and soul and latin music.

Thus, Jackie Collins in 2010. Pop musicians feature in many of Collins' novels, and of course one of her books is called *Rock Star* (no relation to the 2001 movie starring Mark Wahlberg and Jennifer Anniston – not a bad movie, really, but not as good as Collins' novel! Although Walhberg is a classic Collins type of actor/ star).

In the books by Jackie Collins set in the 1960s, the music was the Beatles and the Stones (naturally), plus James Brown, Marvin Gaye and Smokey Robinson. In the Seventies it might be Al Green, the Bee Gees, Elton John, Bobby Womack, Santana and Rod Stewart. In the Eighties novels: Sade, Lionel Richie, Annie Lennox and Bruce Springsteen ('Springsteen always cheered her up; he could do no wrong' [*Hollywood Husbands*, 202]). In the 1990s novels: All Saints, Mötley Crüe, N.W.A., Sting, and Mariah Carey. In the 2000s,

50 Cent, Eminem, R. Kelly, L.L. Cool J, Black-Eyed Peas, and Nora Jones.

> Love had snuck up, taking her completely by surprise. And the amazing thing was that love had nothing to do with sex – the sex would be the final prize, because she knew it was going to be sensational.
> Putting in a tape she sang along to the upbeat sounds of Salt 'N Pepa sexily mouthing off on 'Whatta Man'. Then she shoved her foot down hard on the accelerator, zooming her Porsche home as fast as possible.
> (*Lovers & Players*, 477)

If you want a soundtrack to Jackie Collins' novels (which she provides herself in the stories),[20] it would be anything by the Rolling Stones or James Brown. Soul divas like Tina Turner, Diana Ross, Donna Summer and Aretha Franklin. One song out of millions hits the spot in evoking the decadent, narcissistic and rich bitch days of the 1970s, and that's Carly Simon's 'You're So Vain' (hell, it even has Mick Jagger on backing vocals!). 'You're So Vain' is a whole Jackie Collins book in 3 minutes.[21]

> You walked into the party
> Like you were walking onto a yacht,
> Your hat strategically tipped below one eye
> Your scarf, it was apricot;
> You had one eye in the mirror as
> You watched yourself gavotte,
> And all the girls dreamed that they'd be your partner,
> They'd be your partner, and…
>
> You're so vain
> You probably think this song is about you.
> You're so vain,
> I'll bet you think this song is about you,
> Don't you?
> Don't you?[22]
> (Carly Simon)

Yeah, and the one song that might be referenced more than any other in Collins Music Land is 'Satisfaction' by the Rolling Stones.[23] It's got everything: sex, raunchy rock, a great chorus and hook, and of course Mick, Keef and the boys at their finest (the image of the

---

[20] Stephenie Meyer has provided detailed playlists to accompany her *Twilight Saga* novels.
[21] Even down to the many rumours about the subject of the song – was it Warren Beatty? Or Mick Jagger?
[22] © BMG Rights Management US, LLC.
[23] It first appears in *The World Is Full of Married Men,* when Claudia puts it on: 'a very loud Rolling Stones 'Satisfaction' was turned up full volume' (50).

Stones of course fits perfectly, too – the one-time 'bad boys' of rock 'n' roll, with Jagger as the sexy star singer). 'Satisfaction' was also about escape and fulfilment – about getting material as much as sexual gratification. 'Satisfaction' is the song that blasts out during the photo modelling sessions in Collins' novels.

> I can't get no satisfaction,
> I can't get no girl reaction,
> 'Cause I try and I try and I try and I try,
> I can't get no, I can't get no.
>
> When I'm ridin' round the world,
> And I'm doin' this and I'm signing that,
> And I'm tryin' to make some girl,
> Who tells me baby better come back later next week,
> 'Cause you see I'm on losing streak.
>
> I can't get no, oh no no no,
> Hey hey hey, that's what I say,
> I can't get no, I can't get no,
> I can't get no satisfaction.
> (Mick Jagger and Keith Richards)

And the Rolling Stones're still going strong 50 years later! As Collins' characters note in *Drop Dead Beautiful*:

> "The Stones must be as old as this kid's grandfather," Ace said...
> "Thing is, they're still rockin'," Max pointed out. "Saw their last concert in L.A. They rule!" (313)

★

MODELLING AND FASHION

Hollywood is at the centre of Jackie Collins' fantasy world, but the worlds of music and fashion are close behind. I have already drawn attention to the significance of pop and rock music in Collins' work, but fashion and photographic modelling are vital, too. Some of Collins' major characters are models – such as Lauren Roberts in *American Star*, or Jade Johnson in *Hollywood Husbands*, or Muffin in *The World Is Full of Divorced Women*, or Brigette Brown in *Vendetta: Lucky's Revenge*. And there are a bunch of minor characters who're models. Plus the usual selection of photographers (like Antonio or Luke), and supporting players like make-up artists, hairdressers, clothes designers and advertizing executives.

Jackie Collins portrays the world of modelling and fashion as a chaotic, commercial business, where vanity and egotism are primary. Models, too, are more examples of Collins' powerful women, like her actresses, her agents, and her producers. They are women who're hopelessly neurotic and narcissistic, but also in charge of their lives.

It would be difficult to exaggerate the already crazy world of fashion and modelling, and Jackie Collins' depiction of that world of money, drugs, sex, music and the all-important image is not over-the-top at all. Supermodels make headlines, and are a regular ingredient in the celebrity culture of the Western world, featuring in 100s of magazines, chat shows, TV shows, billboards, and commercials.

★

ACTORS

Having been an actor in loads of TV shows, known many actors and actresses (and dated for many people the Best Screen Actor of them all, Marlon Brando),[24] Jackie Collins can write about actors and acting with sympathy and insight and humour. In books like *Thrill!*, *American Star* and *Hollywood Husbands*, Collins relates the long slog from doing the rounds of auditions and acting classes, finding an agent, to the lucky break, doing bit parts and commercials, and finally to stardom. It's not all fairy tales: Collins also shows the actors who didn't make it, as well as the actors who crash and burn. And there are actors who've been strippers or call-girls.

Many of Jackie Collins' actor characters (particularly the guys) are drug users, or sexist bores, or violent, or assholes in some way or other.[25] Many of the older male actors are threatened by younger actors. All are vain. All are neurotic. Most are insecure. Many are insensitive and selfish. Some are very stupid. All have an insatiable desire to be admired.

---

24 Brando was 29 at the time. Collins' sister Joan opined of Brando: 'fascinating and scary. Not somebody I'd want to get involved with for one second.'
25 Cleo on men: 'Give, and they would take. Run, and they would follow' (*Divorced Women*, 48).

> Everybody wanted to be a star. (*Vendetta: Lucky's Revenge*, 166)

Is there some resentment that she didn't become a big star as an actress, as her sister Joan Collins did? Maybe – certainly J.J. Collins can be as bitchy about actresses as about actors: this's from *Married Lovers*:

> Mandy couldn't stand actresses, they were all so dull. The poor dears harbored nothing but thoughts about themselves – their acting classes, their Pilates lessons, their diets, their yoga, their strength training, their psychics, their perfect little bodies, their designer gowns chosen for special events, and their borrowed jewelry. Borrowed jewelry indeed! How crass was that! (61-62)

One of Jackie Collins' recurring types is the handsome, attractive and confident young actor: they dress in dirty jeans and denim jackets and all the women want them. They fool around with plenty of women. They know they're going to make it BIG, and have a ruthless desire to do so. They know they are good. The model for this character type is a young Marlon Brando or a young James Dean.

But these young, cocky, super-cool guys have it too easy: being the main characters, they always get the girl, and they always get the lucky break that catapults them to stardom. By contrast, the young women characters have to struggle that much harder to reach the top. And the obstacles the young women face seem tougher – like all those fat, smelly slobs who hit on them or try to rape them.

★

SICK, NASTY, VIOLENT

There is a surprising amount of abuse in Jackie Collins' books. Physical abuse, sexual abuse, verbal abuse. The sheer amount of sexual abuse and child abuse is striking (usually it's under-age women being molested by pervy, old men, but sometimes men preying upon under-age boys).[26] At the artistic level, introducing abuse is another way of creating obstacles for your characters for them to overcome, and for generating conflicts. But Collins employs child

---
[26] In the *Lucky Santangelo* series, the villain Santino Bonnatti is about to sodomize the 4 1/2 year-old Bobby when Lucky intervenes, shooting him.

abuse in almost every story she's published.

Plenty of Jackie Collins' fiction contains some sick and nasty moments. Oh, maybe not the sickest and goriest and bloodiest stuff you might find in the 'real world' or in history – the Nazis and the Holocaust have got that covered. But some pretty vile stuff, stuff you *won't* find in the books of Jane Austen, George Eliot, or ten million romantic novels.

Indeed, when it comes to portraying violent deaths, child abuse, rapes, murders and tortures, Jackie Collins happily, gleefully and joyfully out-does many male novelists known for depicting some hateful things.

Some places in the stories of Jackie Collins on the following pages, starting with Hollywood (above).

Hollywood Boulevard

On the road in L.A.: Hollywood Freeway; downtown; Wilshire Blvd; Santa Monica Blvd (top to bottom)

Rodeo Drive in L.A., a key locale for shopping in Collins Land.

Los Angeles – including the view that Jackie Collins loved, from up at Griffith Observatory (above).

Malibu Beach (top).
Venice Beach (above and left).

One of the three key cities in the fiction of Jackie Collins, Las Vegas.

Hotels and resorts in Vegas – Caesar's Palace (top) and Excalibur (above).

Another night in Vegas.

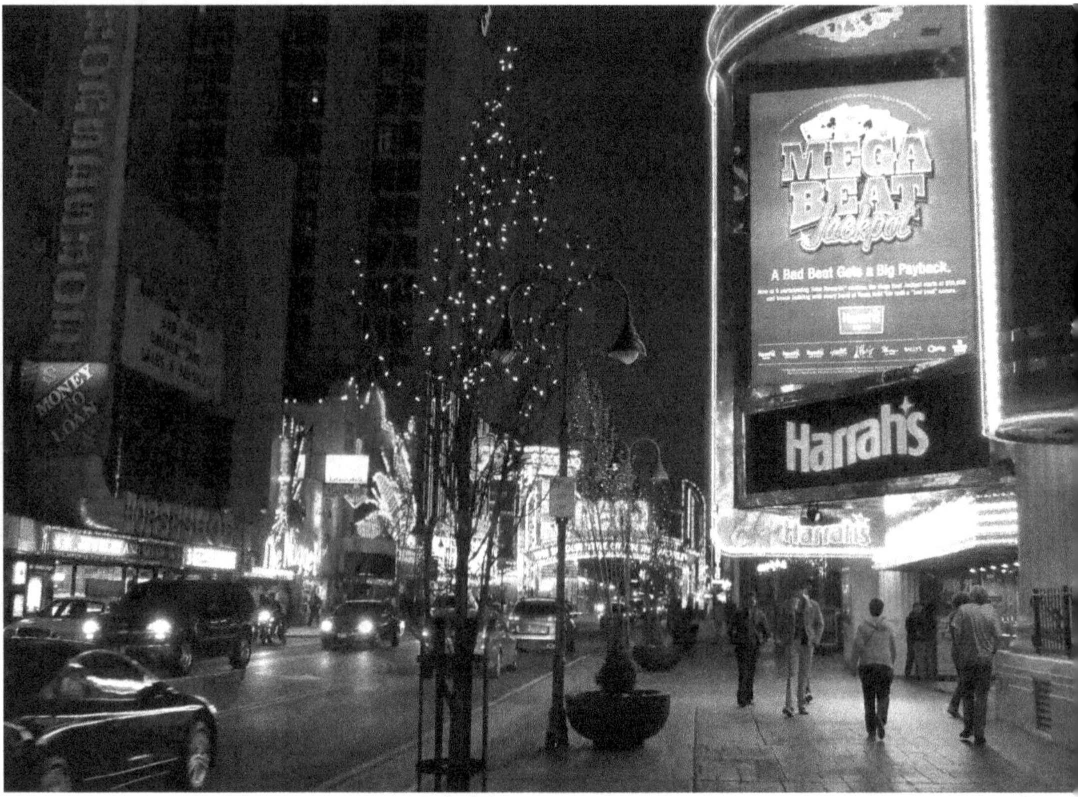
MONEY TO LOAN
MEGA BEAT Jackpot
A Bad Beat Gets a Big Payback.
Harrah's

Paris

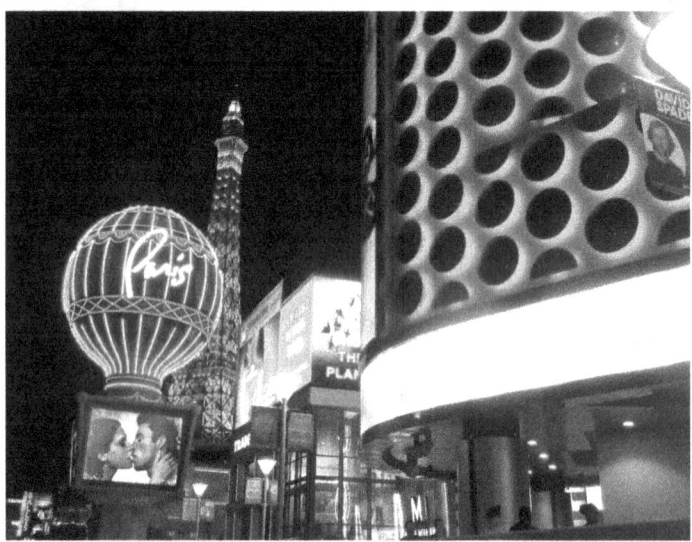

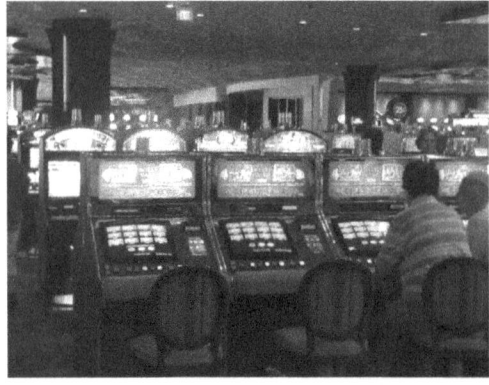

New York City, a popular location in Jackie Collins' later books.

Eight

Manners and Morals

'You know what?' Buddy announced excitedly, the day after their wedding, 'We're headin' back to Hollywood. You and I kid – that's where we're both gonna make it so big they won't even know what's hit 'em!'

Jackie Collins, *Hollywood Wives* (48)

GOALS

The goals of the blockbuster novel character are, to sum up: to achieve maximum success. Success can mean fame, as in the above quote, not the fame of a small-town crook, but the huge, media fame of a movie star (the American Dream). Success means power – being able to wield power. Power means attaining a superior position over other people. Thus a mob boss is a typical role beloved of blockbuster people. Or a millionaire. To be able to light cigarettes with twenty dollar bills. To lunch at the best restaurants (snagging the best table), and drive the priciest cars. And to be seen exerting power, to be acknowledged.

Power is embodied and summed up in certain symbols or trophies: the 'trophy wife', flashy cars, luxurious houses, Olympic-size swimming pools, homes in the country and apartments in Paris and New York. Power means great sex, too, and the symbols of power – cars, houses, yachts, etc – are sexy.

Cars are called huge phallic symbols by critics of the Freudian persuasion. Characters relate to cars like lovers – as in *The Rich and the Beautiful*, 'her touch on the accelerator was the touch of a lover' (24) (Oh, gimme a break!). And 15 year-old Summer in Jackie Collins' *Thrill!* thinks: 'in a couple of months she'd be able to drive legally. How radical would that be!'

Cars feature a lot in erotica too – sex in cars, on top of cars, beside cars. Getting head while driving combines two male fantasies – escaping from the family and responsibilities on the open road at high speed, and great sex (and the technofetishism of the vehicle. There are many blowjob scenes in cars in Jackie Collins' fiction). Cars are part of masculinist fantasy: they are sold in countless magazines, hoardings and TV ads as gleaming, sleek animals, sex machines that respond ecstatically to every touch (no blockbuster novel character would ever be without a car – or a cel phone. *You're in L.A. without a car?! Don't expect me to* walk *from here to La Cienga! It's three blocks! Are you nuts?!*).

The goal is to achieve a fantasy lifestyle. Total capitalism – every part of your life becomes commodified, turned into a commodity. The theory is that if you are surrounded by beautiful objects, then the parts of your life underneath – the emotions, relationships, anxieties – must also be (or will become) beautiful. Beauty is more than skin-deep in a blockbuster novel, it is everything. This is a world built on vanity, on looking good in the eyes of other people, especially one's peers. Thus, big breasts, botoxed lips, chunky jewellery, diamonds, black party dresses and blow-waved hair are signs of achievement. The hard body. Working out in the gym.

If you can look like Sophia Loren or Raquel Welch (in the 1970s), or Scarlett Johansson, Paris Hilton or J. Lo in the 2010s), you're made. Glamorous people hang on desperately to a glossy, ritzy self-image: they try to look young and sexy. Extra layers of foundation and blusher are piled on to cover wrinkles (plus being photographed from the correct angle). And then comes the cosmetic surgery, the nips and tucks, the liposuction.[1] Think of how many fading stars look as they age: Joan Collins, Barbara Cartland, Zsa Zsa Gabor and Jane Fonda. Many younger stars are similarly concerned with their looks: in the 1980s and 1990s it was: Jerry Hall, Nastassja Kinski, Brooke Shields, Cher, Demi Moore, Bianca Jagger, Pamela Anderson, Daryl Hannah and Kim Basinger (all of them Jackie Collins types). In the 2000s-10s, it's: Britney Spears, Monica Bellucci, Charlize Theron, Liv Tyler, Jessica Biel, Angelina Jolie, Beyoncé and Halle Berry. The look of a celebrity is the star's livelihood, which has to be maintained with make-up artists, hairdressers, trainers, etc (the era of the entourage).

Men of course simply grow old and become 'distinguished' (and Jackie Collins' novels are full of such ageing, male characters, some of whom fret about their looks): women turn into hags or whores or frumps. Women can't win, because men set the rules in the beauty game. Men are not scrutinized as ruthlessly as women are (although they are no less vain – liposuction is used by many men,[2] and men have always been anxious about hair loss, penis size, muscles, weight, exercise and fitness).

The body must be a well-groomed and luxurious object in the ruthlessly materialistic world of the blockbuster novel. The body must gleam just as much as those cars, houses, jewels and suits. The glistening, toned, tanned, honed body means a glitterized, toned self, a new personality, a self-transcendence into all-round, wall-to-wall, 24-carat richness.[3]

The morals of the blockbuster novel are simply those of the

---

[1] 'Charlene was an ode to Botox, Juvena, silicone, collagen, and any other facial fillers on the market. Lipo-suction was her best friend', Collins' narrator bitches in *Married Lovers* (23-24).
[2] C. Bowen-Jones, "Men as Sex Objects", *Marie Claire*, 50, Oct, 1992.
[3] Toned and gym-honed bodies have increasingly been part of Hollywood movies, too, since the 1980s.

Western world: swinging Sixties liberalism pepped up with Eighties dog-eat-dog capitalism, Nineties caring/ sharing liberalism swept aside by the return to superficial capitalism in the 2000s/ 2010s. Oh yeah!

In all blockbuster novels, money talks. Sex, money, fame, power, beauty and pleasure are the goals. Pleasure is the end-point of the long slog towards fame. The desire stems from lacks, such as the lack of wealth. The desire is to attain all those things one was deprived of in youth. To achieve that legendary adoration because one was ignored as a school kid. To become a beautiful swan because one was always the ugly duckling as a teenager, or beaten up, or abused ('this'll show 'em! I'll become *beautiful!*'). And so on. Cleo James sums it up in *The World Is Full of Divorced Women*:

> Where has all my women's lib good sense gone to?
> Live and let live.
> Fuck and let fuck. (6)

In the 1960s the attitude was 'let it all hang out... anything goes... whatever turns you on... free love... turn on, tune in and drop out,' etc. In the 1970s and 1980s this ethic (a liberal form of the bad boy magician Aleister Crowley's 'do what you will'), became compressed, into 'do anything, but get out of my way'.[4]

The moral of our era became hard-edged, money-driven, pushy, nervy, cocaine-fuelled as it moved from the 1960s to the 1970s. Instead, of 'I'm all right, Jack', it was 'fuck you, I'm all right, Jack'.

The thing to do was to get away with anything. There are no responsibilities, no moral or social guilts, no regrets, no looking back. Even with A.I.D.S. there is no moral responsibility. If you can get away with doing something, then do it (it's the morals of all gangsters, with *The Godfather* – the book and the movie – as the bible. And even in the age of 'safe sex' warnings printed in erotic fiction, and other A.I.D.S.-related public announcements, Jackie Collins' books have sometimes avoided both A.I.D.S. and warnings about the disease, altho' it is mentioned more in the later novels, such as *Vendetta: Lucky's Revenge* and *The Power Trip*).

In the 1970s Erica Jong had pinpointed this attitude with her notion of the 'zipless fuck', the anonymous fast food sex act:

---

[4] Aleister Crowley is a perfect Jackie Collins character thirty years b4 the time! Indeed, if Crowley had been created by a blockbuster novel author, nobody would have believed them.

> The zipless fuck was more than a fuck. It was a platonic ideal. Zipless because when you came together zippers fell away like rose petals, underwear blew off in one breath like dandelion fluff. Tongues intertwined and turned liquid. Your whole soul flowed out through your tongue and into the mouth of your lover. For the true, ultimate zipless A-1 fuck, it was necessary that you never get to know the man very well... another condition for the zipless fuck was brevity. And anonymity made it even better... The zipless fuck is absolutely pure. It is free of ulterior motives. There is no power game. The man is not 'taking' and the woman is not 'giving'.[5]

The zipless fuck is pure sex with no strings attached, no diseases, no questions asked, no problems, no consequences. It is the idealized sexual encounter of pornography, in which people are always available for instant, quick sex. This is the sex of the blockbuster novel. It's even better if you can combine sex with money with improving your career prospects, or with a vengeance ritual ('revenge fucks' are common in Jackie Collins' fiction).

Sex is a weapon: if a chance presents itself for attacking someone by using sex, then it should be taken. Bobby Mondella does just that in *Rock Star* by Jackie Collins, when his boss's wife starts sucking him:

> 'Now!', she said urgently. 'Turn around now.'
> He did as she asked, plunging deep inside that elegant mouth, ready and waiting to taste and tease him with feathery jabs of her tongue and a low animal groaning sound.
> *Eat your heart out, Marcus,* he thought, *I'm getting my own back for Sharleen.*
> He surrendered to sensation. There was really nothing else he could do, except lean back and enjoy it. (203)

When they're not pushing for fame and success, the blockbuster novel character lies back and enjoys it. Drugs, sex, music, and sunbathing are typical pastimes. Lazing around, eating chocolates, taking drugs and drinking are cool. Pleasure is a major discourse. Other people are valued for the amount of pleasure they can offer. Not just in sex, but in career, money, fame and power. Sex, however, is an instant judge of a character. Thus, in *Big Apple* by Pat Booth, people are evaluated in sexual terms, as if they are sex toys, sexual commodities:

> The bottom line was that in bed Mariel was extraordinarily good, a virtuoso performer. For that alone he was happy to overlook the fact that in other respects she was a very bad girl indeed. (24)

---

[5] E. Jong, *Fear of Flying*, 19-20.

And yet, in Jackie Collins' fiction, *work* is never far away – Lucky Santangelo, Collins' signature chara, is not one to sit by the pool and spend hours texting her friends. She wants to be in the centre of the action. Which means working.

★

ATTITUDES

Some of the attitudes in the super-cool, super-trashy, super-capitalist blockbuster novel are found in all literature: making money is good, and legitimizes and valorizes *any* kind of life, and any kind of behaviour. Having many sexual partners is good, and gives a person charisma – as Kris puts it in Jackie Collins'*Rock Star.* 'all those assholes jerkin' off over your picture probably don't like it either. Single is sexy. I learned that one a long time ago' (240). He's talking to Cybil, a 'highly paid, extremely visible commercial model' (1).

Power relations must be maintained at all costs – people must be put in their place. Ass-licking is essential. Looks are prime – an ugly person has never made it.[6] Intimacy is to be avoided, especially during sex. History, education, politics, creativity, depth, subtlety and being serious are unnecessary. Cute if you got 'em or can do it, but not essential.

Another recurring attitude: if men are adulterous, they are shits. But they'll do it anyway; they can't help it, poor dears. This view is found in much of world literature. Certainly in the plays of William Shakespeare or Molière or in Classical Greece. Monogamy is clung onto by female characters in literature: it is OK for men to tup anything, of course, that's from men's point of view.

The morals and attitudes of the blockbuster novel are those of idealists, fantasists and dreamers – all them with the emotional age of children. The blockbuster novel world is not the real world. It is a world of fantasy, in which dreams can come true if only you believe in them deeply enough: it's Walt Disney's wishing upon a star time, it's the *Rocky Horror Show*'s 'don't dream it, *be it*', it's the American Dream as a trip to Oz and back.

At Oscar award ceremonies breathless, tanned movie stars thank

---
6 Unless they're already rich.

their agents/ producers/ children/ friends/ gods and say, 'folks, anyone can succeed. All you gotta do is to really believe in yourself. Just go for it!' This is a particularly North American attitude; the idea that anything is possible in the real world if you aim high enough (Collins' charas believe this, too). Those who live in the real world know that some things are just not possible. Such as ending world poverty overnight, or saving the world like a North American action hero in a blockbuster movie. Solutions to such problems exist in brains and in language, for the doubters and cynics, but not in a few simple actions in the real, physical world (the blockbuster novel, we need to remember, is not a real, physical object – only the book is, and even then books are moving towards e-books, books online and books in a digital form. The blockbuster novel is *culture*, it is something that exists only in people, in their minds and thoughts and memories – and dreams).

The blockbuster novel can be reduced to a series of fundamental human desires – for contact, recognition, power, sex, pleasure – which are treated in a childish, playground fashion. These basic urges, the stuff of Freudian psychoanalysis, are given sophisticated glosses, smooth, slick and colourful surfaces and contours which hide the infantile needs seething underneath.

The blockbuster novel can be reduced to a sequence of desires which achieve differing degrees of gratification. Like little children, blockbuster novel people stomp about, pouting when they're abused, sulking when they're criticized, clinging onto old hopes or old boyfriends, and flinching when their looks slip. Buddy Hudson in *Hollywood Wives* is absolutely typical: he storms out of an orgy that goes wrong: he fumes: 'he was Buddy Hudson. He was going to be a star, and nothing would stop him.' (74)

The desire is to be a Somebody, to escape being a Nobody. Not to help others, or be useful socially or even personally, but to satisfy one's own desires. The mythology of materialism is a selfish one. All popular magazines, TV shows, radio stations, movies and websites proclaim the cult of the individual, the self-satisfied self: *Vogue, Hello, Glamour, Rolling Stone, Access Hollywood, Entertainment Tonight, Pretty Woman, Titanic, Billboard, Variety* and the Sunday newspapers. The global media exalts the glittering, sequined starlet and her partner, the bronzed, muscular movie star or movie producer. These people are the rich and the famous, the role models of this epoch, of the Western world.

Naturally, these are the people that populate the literature of this era. Instead of the kings, queens, heroes and villains of old mythologies and romances, we have movie stars, presidents, millionaires, oil sheiks, pop stars, serial killers, TV chat show hosts, politicians, terrorists and bimbos.

Don't you just love it?!

Nine

The Blockbuster Novel
In Literature

Maybe he could fake it. Fake an erection? What an ace trick that would be. Wow! No more money problems. Patent the scam and watch the big bucks roll. He could see the book title now. HOW TO GET A HARD-ON WHEN YOU'RE NOT IN THE MOOD FOR SEX. A *sure* best seller.

Jackie Collins, *Hollywood Wives* (167)

THE BLOCKBUSTER: ART?

No, the blockbuster novel is not art. At least, not in the tradition (or definition) of 'great writers' such as William Shakespeare, Euripedes, Emily Brontë or Alexander Pushkin. According to the crrritics, the blockbuster novel simply does not have the same depth, mystery, insight, weight and passion. But then, the block-buster novels' aims are not exactly those of great art. The blockbuster book aims to entertain, to provide escapist fodder for hungry minds intent on dreaming. But then Thomas Hardy, Charles Dickens and Anaïs Nin wrote popular pieces, aimed at a wide audience. And as Michael Moorcock says, aiming to entertain is a high, noble aspiration, and not easy to achieve.[7] Film director Hayao Miyazaki says the same: it's very difficult to entertain people.

> Those who join in the work of animation are people who dream more than others and who wish to convey those dreams to others. After a while they realize how incredibly difficult it is to entertain others[8]

But of course, the blockbuster novel *is* art. The only difference is one of degree.

One thing the blockbuster novel does is entertain. Jackie Collins' work is immensely readable. She writes books that are consumed swiftly: the reader gorges on them, has a reading binge. The reviews concentrate on the compulsive nature of reading a blockbuster novel:

✳ 'I was compelled to read every page',
✳ 'a genuine page-turner',
✳ 'impossible to put down',
✳ 'this pacy paperback is extremely entertaining',
✳ 'you'll probably stay up all night reading *Hollywood Wives* eagerly flipping the pages',
✳ 'a book so addictive it's worth staying in for'.

(Sources: *Los Angeles Herald-Examiner* on *Rock Star*; *Wall Street Journal* on Collins; *19* magazine and *Cosmopolitan* on *Hollywood Wives*; *M* Magazine (*Mirror*) on *Hollywood Wives: The New Generation.*)

(There is even a book called *The Page-turner*). A 'page-turner' is what readers are looking for, and a 'page-turner' is what publishers

---
7 M. Moorcock, *Death Is No Obstacle*, 1992.
8 Hayao Miyazaki, *Starting Point, 1979-1996*, tr. B. Cary & F. Schodt, Viz Media/ Shogakukan, San Francisco, CA, 2009, 25.

are *desperate* to find.

Jean Rook in the *Daily Express* (a British newspaper) sums it up neatly: Jackie Collins 'characters are racy as Ferraris. Her plots fast-moving as Porsches... *Hollywood Husbands* is like a box of chocolates. You feel a bit guilty but, God, you enjoy it.'[9]

★

It's difficult to remember any particular character or incident or insight in a blockbuster novel: all the characters, events and ideas (tend to) blur together. Life becomes one fast, orgiastic party, a stupor of bitching, lust, hatred, sex, drugs, fame and disillusionment. There is little else that one recalls in the blockbuster novel. After the glitter, the gore, the bitchdom and the self-adoration has faded away, precious little remains. Blockbuster books do not leave vivid afterglows, like, say, the haunting passion of Cathy and Heathcliff (*Wuthering Heights*), or the melancholy magic of Prospero (*The Tempest*), or the tragic terror of Oedipus (Sophocles).

Or is that being snobbish again? Maybe blockbuster novels really are full of memorable characters and incidents. Maybe. Some are, but many are not.

But in Jackie Collins' novels, although the plots and the characters are somewhat interchangeable, afterwards you do retain the feeling and atmosphere of the fantasy land she creates, some of the action scenes, some of the witty, barbed dialogue, some of the jokes, etc. And definitely some of the entertaining characters. And we have to remember that Collins herself has no illusions that she's writing Great Art.

The blockbuster novel's place within world literature is like a one-night stand is a sea of eternal love-affairs and decades-long marriages. In the archetypal one-night stand, people have drunken, quick, bad sex (or maybe a fantastic fling in the back of a Cadillac), and wake up with hangovers wondering who the hell is snoring next to them in bed. Indulgence followed by guilt. It's the same with a blockbuster novel. (Collins has used that scenario many times).

★

---

[9] J. Rook reviewing *Hollywood Husbands*.

THE BLOCKBUSTER NOVELIST

What is the literary standing of Jackie Collins? She is one of the popular authors who sell millions of copies. One thinks of Collins next to Virginia Andrews, Jilly Cooper, Robert Ludlum, Harold Robbins, Wilbur Smith, Stephen King, J.K. Rowling, Dan Brown and Danielle Steel. The big name authors who fill the racks in supermarkets, news stands, K-Mart, C.V.S. and Target.

Among female authors, Jackie Collins is part of a group of blockbuster writers: they include Judith Krantz, Shirley Conran, Catherine Cookson, Jilly Cooper, Jodi Piccoult, Virginia Andrews, Marion Zimmer Bradley and Maeve Binchley. Collins does not write, say, historical blockbusters like Catherine Cookson or Victoria Holt, or family sagas like James Michener or Barbara Taylor Bradford, but she is marketed and consumed in the same fashion.[10]

Jackie Collins' contribution to women's writing is to create strong women characters. 'I enjoy writing strong, beautiful, sexy females', she says (*Rock Star*, 461). But she is certainly a different author from much-celebrated female authors such as Jane Austen, Doris Lessing, George Eliot, Gertrude Stein, Mary Renault, Ursula Le Guin, Virginia Woolf or the two Emilys (Brontë and Dickinson). In high art terms, Collins would not be placed in the same company (but all of those writers are quite individual, too). Yet in terms of the sheer pleasure of reading, of culture, of engaging with stories and characters and texts, Collins can be placed beside any author.

★

IS JACKIE COLLINS A FEMINIST?

Jackie Collins is no feminist. The term 'feminist' rarely appears in Collins' work,[11] and if it does, it is usually disparagingly, as when Matt Traynor's ex-wife in *Lucky* is referred to as a 'retarded feminist' (79).[12] Despite writing about strong women, all her characters uphold

---

10 To be picky, Collins' books *are* historical novels – to the degree that Collins sets them in particular years (1985, say), even tho' she's writing them only a few years later.
11 Lucky is described as the 'original feminist', tho'.
12 However, in *Lady Boss* there is a strong feminist character, Mona Sykes.

patriarchal values, norms, forms, myths, and lies. Collins' women aspire to be just as men want them: 'strong, beautiful, sexy females', as Collins puts it herself (she seems to prefer the term 'women's lib' to feminism). Collins' writing is not subversive. Not in the slightest. She does not question society, she merely reflects it, including its worst aspects. Collins is far from the pro-feminist works of Hélène Cixous, Ursula Le Guin, Isabel Allende, Margaret Atwood, Elizabeth Bishop, or Gertrude Stein. Liberation and equality are her political projects.

Much of Jackie Collins' output, seen *from a feminist perspective*, is ultimately disappointing, depressing and at times disgusting (indeed, it's dangerous being a feminist in Collinsland: Margaret Brown is shot in the opening pages of *The Love Killers* at a feminist rally in Central Park. This is also one of the very few times in Collins' fiction that someone takes to public action). Collins panders to every whim of patriarchal society and culture. She exploits her texts for all they can offer. Her fictions, if you look thru second wave feminist eyes, perpetuate a host of lies, falsehoods and misinformation about sexuality, identity, desire, politics, lifestyle and society. At times she is no better than writers such as Jack Higgins or James Herbert, authors who go for the cheapest thrills and the sickest special effects. Although blockbuster writers are not usually blood and gore merchants, like stalk 'n' slash movie directors or horror genre hacks, their view of humanity is often as degraded and degrading.

What a pity that many blockbuster authors don't aim sometimes for that area of experience which Elaine Showalter (in *The New Feminist Criticism*) calls the 'wild zone':

> The 'wild zone' stands for aspects of female experience exclusive to women (there's also a corresponding male area which is outside women's experience). Women know what the male territory is like, although they have not seen it, because it 'becomes the subject of legend', but men do not know what is in the female 'wild zone', because the general circulation of ideas has been controlled by men, and men either think that female experience lacks value, or else they simply do not recognize that it exists. (1986, 248)

However, Jackie Collins' books are highly critical of men – and women. *All* of Collins' characters are given a critical treatment. Nobody's perfect. Many male characters are regarded as cheats, as liars, as jerks, as only after one thing (sex), or they want their ego exalted, to be told how wonderful they are. They are the creeps who pick up women without really thinking about it, and who continually sell women the corny lines about their wives not really being interested in sex any more.

Men trotting out the same cheap pick-up lines again and again is a recurring motif in Collins Fantasy Land; her female characters have heard it all before, and it exasperates them. Sometimes they go along with men's cheap tricks, out of boredom or loneliness, or because there is something they want.

In fact, Jackie Collins' treatment of male characters is among the most savage I can think of in contemporary, Western literature. In fact, it's tough to think of a major author, male or female, who has created so many despicable men, or put men down so often (well, there *are* some authors, but Collins certainly sticks the knife in deep).

Jackie Collins isn't merely critical, she portrays many men as truly revolting people. Not only the psychos and the brutes, but even the guys who're s'posed to be sympathetic or decent. If Collins isn't a feminist, she does put down many men in a ruthless fashion. So vigorous is Collins' denunciation of some of her male characters that lesbian separatists and radical lesbians might warm to her work. (Lesbian separatists are feminist lesbian women who would prefer a world without men, or at least a world in which men are allowed nowhere near them. It's an ideal and a utopian dream that's very compelling, but almost impossible to achieve in practical, social, political terms. I'd got for it, but millions would oppose a world without men, including millions of women).

It can seem as if women are stronger than men in Jackie Collins' fiction: they can appear more practical and pragmatic, quicker to see the flaws in a situation. They know what men are after, and occasionally they'll let them have it. And Collins, thru her female charas, has questioned notions of equality,[13] and the double standards of patriarchy. But certainly Collins' female characters are far more assertive in the social sphere than their counterparts in 19th century literature, for instance. The social mobility of women in the era of the 1960s to the present day is celebrated at length and in detail in Collins' fiction. Some of her female characters are still dependent on men, some still see their identity in relation to the

---

[13] In *The World is Full of Divorced Women*, Cleo complains: 'Women were still the second classes of the world. Judged by their looks. Judged by their morals' (91-92).

men in their lives, some still regard themselves as victims, and many are suppressed by the patriarchal realm. But there are many women who are independent, who are assertive and decisive, who are going after what they want. When you compare the women characters in Collins' fiction to those of George Eliot, Edith Wharton, Jane Austen and Emily Brontë, you can see just much how things have changed.

Lucky Santangelo is Jackie Collins' most switched-on, pro-woman character, yet even Lucky enjoys being home with her family, and appreciates her kids, in the traditional, conservative, non-feminist manner (and she is devoted to one guy, Lennie Golden). The feminist philosopher Julia Kristeva noted that women might be feminists but one of their deepest desires was to bear children.

For Julia Kristeva, rejecting motherhood is not a serious option for most women; indeed, for many women fulfilment can be found in bringing a child into the world. Kristeva exalts the mother-child bond, and love – not love for herself, not for an identical being, and not love as erotic fusion with another. No ma'am; Kristeva means 'love for an other... the slow, difficult and delightful apprenticeship in attentiveness, gentleness, forgetting oneself' (*The Kristeva Reader*, 206).

Jackie Collins' texts are thoroughly masculinist and patriarchal. But then, almost *all* texts are patriarchal, according to French feminists such as Hélène Cixous. For feminists such as Cixous, Julia Kristeva, Luce Irigaray and Monique Wittig, it is immensely difficult to produce a fully *feminine* text, an authentically and properly *feminine* or *female* or even *feminist* text, partly because, as feminists such as Mary Daly and Dale Spender note, language is firmly entrenched in patriarchal values and attitudes. Collins' books are simply populist pieces of entertainment that reflect the dominant, patriarchal culture of the Western world.

If you want an author who is going criticize and re-order the Western capitalist world, you need to read someone else (you know who the revolutionary authors are).

But I would guess that the aim of Jackie Collins with her books is to produce an entertaining reading experience for her readers. Not political revolution. Not usurping the Western, capitalist world. Not radical feminism, and not second wave feminism or third wave (postmodern) feminism.

Do you expect the books of Jackie Collins to revolutionize Western society? Why? That is not their intent! No popular novelist of recent times has done that, have they? Jackie Collins is not a radical, political leader, a revolutionary firebrand! She isn't Che Guevara or Malcolm X! And she doesn't want to be!

Seen from the viewpoint of entertainment and pleasure, the works of Jackie Collins are supremely successful, and enjoyable. If it's a 'guilty' pleasure, if it's 'trashy' fiction, it doesn't matter: Collins' books deliver the goods, certainly: she is very, very good, kind of unstoppable in terms of success in her field – like the Walt Disney corporation with its theme parks, or MacDonald's with its hamburgers. (If you feel 'guilty', go read something else. If you think Collins' books are 'trashy', go read summat else. There are probably two thousand novels regarded as classics. Go read them).

Ten

The Novels of Jackie Collins

She couldn't keep her eyes off his penis – it gave 'big' a whole new meaning. Rich *and* well-hung, what more could a girl ask for?

Jackie Collins, *Lethal Seduction* (109)

THE WORLD IS FULL OF MARRIED MEN

If *The World Is Full of Married Men* is the first Jackie Collins novel you read, you might think, *eh? I don't get it! What's all the fuss about?* And if like me you got round to reading *The World Is Full of Married Men* later, after reading many of Collins' other books, you may find it very tame. (So how it became a 'best-seller' is a bit of a mystery, even accounting for the cultural era of its publication – the late 1960s – and the differences to today.)

The World Is Full of Married Men was the first novel that Jackie Collins published, in 1968. It concerns a married couple in London, David and Linda Cooper, who fall apart and have other relationships. David is a businessman who's been having affairs for years; he's the classic womanizer in Collins' fiction, selfish and egotistical (the forerunner of 100s of similar guys). Linda meanwhile is of course kind, gentle, well-meaning, shy, and unloved (and there's a genuine melancholy about Linda – she recalls the clichéd 'bored housewives' in songs by the Rolling Stones of the period).[1]

Unfortunately, both characters in *The World Is Full of Married Men* are fairly dull, and the narrative is also very pedestrian compared to Jackie Collins' finest works, like *Lucky* or *American Star* (we return to these character types many times in Collins' subsequent work). David gets involved with Claudia Parker, a young, sexy photographic model (and former porn star), and Linda has a fling with a young politico and art student, Paul (they join a Ban the Bomb demo[2] in London's Trafalgar Square, and attend a house party in Hampstead full of counter-culture/ hippy types). There are (dinner) parties, hotels, bars, and penthouse apartments. Some romantic fooling around and partner swapping, all as expected (such as Claudia with David Baileyesque photographer Giles, and David with his shy, mousey secretary, Miss Field).

The World Is Full of Married Men is set in London in the late 1960s, and occasionally evokes a quaint Englishness, but this is not a Great London Novel, nor a Great Swinging Sixties Novel; London clearly doesn't inspire Jackie Collins like Los Angeles or New York or

---

1 These are the women who take tranquillizers – pills and drugs crop up as references in the lyrics of a few late 1960s songs by the Rolling Stones. Pills that help busy moms get thru the day ('Mother's Little Helper'). Women that get their kicks in dodgy Stepney instead of well-heeled Knightsbridge. And people on the edge of nervous breakdowns ('19th Nervous Breakdown').
2 About the only time a Collins character has manned the barricades.

Las Vegas (or it didn't at the time).3 *The World Is Full of Married Men* limps along with a join-the-dots, A-B-C plot and themes and characters (and too many of the characters are samey and tend to be interchangeable).

The only spark of vintage Jackie Collins is the young, wannabe starlet Claudia Parker, one of Collins' out-of-control, young women. It's Claudia who utters the first words of Collins' very first book:

> 'When I was fifteen, I was amazing – absolutely amazing! Dear Mummy was terrified to let me out on my own, she felt I was bound to come home pregnant, or something silly like that.' (7)

Claudia Parker is the first in a long line of Collinsian 'wild child' characters: she is 'a very beautiful girl' with 'long, shiny ash-blond hair', 'enormous, slanty green eyes', a 'perfect' face with 'a small, straight nose' and – of course – 'luscious, full lips' (always with the 'full, sensual mouths' in Collins' work!). Collins will repeat this same characterization (and appearance) many times (such as with Lucky Santangelo) – Claudia even has 'a pantherlike grace', one of Collins' favourite descriptions.

Claudia Parker is the first of Jackie Collins' independent career women – a forerunner of Lucky Santangelo and the film directors, photographers and business women that populate the later Collins books. Claudia tells David Cooper early on in *The World Is Full of Married Men* when he makes possessive moves on her:

> 'I don't bug you about things, so just forget it. You don't own me, and I don't own you, and that's the way it should be.' (10)

Ultimately, you just don't care about the characters in *The World Is Full of Married Men*, and that can be fatal to the kind of relationship-and-romance-based fiction that Collins writes. (There are usually other elements to enjoy in any novel, but not so much in this one).

It's hard to believe that *The World Is Full of Married Men* was a best-seller; if it was submitted to a publisher today, it would be returned with a standard rejection letter. Is that being cruel? Maybe. Or realistic.

Put it this way: look at the leap in juice and heat between *The World Is Full of Married Men* and *Sinners* (a.k.a. *Hollywood Zoo*,

---

3 Even tho', by some accounts, London was a very 'happening' city in the late Sixties.

a.ka. *Sunday Simmons and Charlie Brick*), published in 1972. If Collins had carried on writing books like *The World Is Full of Married Men,* we wouldn't be here today discussing her work (perhaps we would, but the greatness was yet to come). Maybe it was North America that did it: because when Collins went to the U.S.A., or when she started to write about it, her work began to sparkle.

★

SINNERS

Let's move on to *Sinners* (also titled *Hollywood Zoo*, a.ka. *Sunday Simmons and Charlie Brick*),[4] an early (1972) Jackie Collins novel. Well, it contains all the usual Collins elements, such as the large group of characters, the multiple plots, the Hollywood setting, the movie-making situations, a bit of sex, a creepy psycho, and so on.

Easily the most memorable character in *Sinners* is Sunday Simmons – one of J. Collins' impossibly beautiful but oddly restrained and withdrawn actress characters. Sunday has the chance to have just about any man (and some women), but turns them all down, withholding herself for most of the narrative. And, yes, she does have the troubled background, which contributes towards her introspective and wary personality. (Characters who are very attractive and full of desire yet consciously withhold themselves and distance themselves from others in Collinsworld include Brigitte Stanisopoulos in the *Lucky Santangelo* series, and Lauren in *American Star*).

Sinners, though, has a rather flat prose style: workmanlike, it does the job, but it's not a patch on Jackie Collins' later works, which have far better jokes, slicker bitchiness, and a more cynical and all-knowing view of the film industry, and Hollywood, and celebrity, and relationships. Collins' writing definitely improved the further along her career she went, so that the books of the 1980s are Collins at her best.

Thus, *Sinners* isn't vintage Jackie Collins, like *Hollywood Wives* or *Thrill!* or *American Star.* But it is an easy and enjoyable read.

---

4 Collins was advised to change the title for the U.S.A., and then again.

Charlie Brick, Steve Magnum, Dindi, Carey St Martin, Jack Milan and Marshall K. Marshall are all typical if not classic Collins characters. And Collins does create an impressive psycho in Herbert Lincoln Jefferson, the chauffeur and Stalker From Hell (as well as the coven of guys who gather at a next door neighbour's house to tup Herbert's fat, needy wife Marge for money. This's one of the strangest and creepiest episodes that Collins has created).

★

THE LOVE KILLERS

...So, hi, we're back after the commercial break with *Lovehead* (1974): re-titled *The Love Killers*, it was Jackie Collins' fourth novel (the third, *The Stud*, is discussed later). *The Love Killers* opens with the assassination of a feminist and political activist, mid-speech, in Central Park: Margaret Lawrence Brown is shot in the middle of a passionate anti-prostitution meeting.

Thus, the narrative spine of *The Love Killers* is a revenge story, as the sisterhood surrounding the murder victim, Margaret Brown, decide to wreak revenge on the Italian-American mobster who ordered the hit: Enzio Bassalino (because Brown's proselytizing was bad for business). Instead of attempting to nobble Bassalino himself, they go after his sons. Just *how* they're gonna get vengeance by seducing the Bassalino studs isn't revealed at first. (It seems to consist of the women romancing the guys then leaving them, as if that would psychologically devastate connected men who have several girlfriends/ mistresses, and who can take their pic of women. Lara admits to herself that Brown wouldn't have approved of what they are trying to do [154]).

In keeping with *The Love Killers* presenting a revenge plot, there are few romances, and few characters seem to be having a good time – with all of the focus on wreaking vengeance on the Bassalino dynasty. Which makes for a rather downbeat reading experience, compared to some of Jackie Collins' other novels. Indeed, the only really fulfilling time is in the past, when the sisters recall their encounters with the political firebrand Margaret Lawrence Brown. If you're looking for laughs, or Collins' one-line zingers, go elsewhere!

(Only Lara and Nick get the happy ending – pretty much everybody else winds up dead).

Indeed – *The Love Killers* is a sleazepit of a novel, in the sense that the narrative coalesces around a group of women using their womanly wiles to seduce and entrap some men who killed their guru. But Margaret L. Brown was a firebrand feminist, and the last thing she would've endorsed would be women reducing themselves to sexual predators, pandering to the lowest desires, in order to enact revenge. For a feminist, the sisterhood acts like reactionary *femme fatales,* indulging patriarchy with a silly scheme that paints them as sex objects. The ruse goes against Jackie Collins' dictum that 'girls can do anything'.

★

So, among the characters, we have Enzio Bassalino, the vicious, 69 year-old gangster; Mary Ann August, his current mistress (the latest in a long line of women); soul singer Dukey K. Williams; Margaret Lawrence Brown, the activist feminist; Lara Crichton, the bored but gorgeous jet-setter; Beth Lawrence Brown, a shy, young woman who wants to do her bit in the revenge scheme, but is out of her depth; and Rio Java, the feisty, black woman who chews up men for breakfast. Plus assorted hit men, lackeys, and exes.[5]

Enzio Bassalino demonstrates his bastardness when he has a hapless suitor for his wife Rose carved up with knives right in front of her by four of his lieutenants. Nope, do *not* ask for a divorce from an Italian-American gangster! Even better, don't marry him in the first place! (Taking her cue from *Jane Eyre,* Jackie Collins has Bassalino keeping his wife, now seemingly mentally ill from the experience of seeing her lover chopped up, imprisoned in his house).

So *The Love Killers* reaches a finale by having the issue of making the Bassalinos pay side-stepped: Frank is blown up in a limo at a funeral for his wife (whom he abused, his beatings leading to her demise). Angelo is killed running a red light (as he hurries over to his mistress Rio Java for another perv session), and the godfather himself, Enzio Bassalino, is shot by spurned mistress Mary Ann August, as she clambers over him with her breasts in his mouth (and she has also beaten Claire to death with a chair leg. Who'd thought cute, bubbly Mary Ann would turn out to be a ruthless psycho?). Then his mad, reclusive wife Rose knifes Mary, and then her husband.

---

[5] The same charas with the same names crop up in later novels: Enzio, Lara, Angelo, Nick, etc (as if Collins has a pool of her favourite character names, and insists on using them in each novel).

Then the whole manse blows up! (Several others charas meet sticky ends, including assassin Leroy, chewed by dawgs, and Rio Java is shot on stage preaching about feminism, just like Margaret Lawrence Brown in chapter one).

Does some of this sensational, melodramatic material sound familiar? *The Love Killers* was published in 1974, and the shadow of *The Godfather* and Mario Puzo looms large over it. Collins continued to mine *The Godfather* throughout her career.

★

THE WORLD IS FULL OF DIVORCED WOMEN

The World is Full of Divorced Women (1975) was Jackie Collins' fifth novel, and her follow-up to 1968's *The World Is Full Married Men* (something that Collins would do occasionally, such as in the *Lucky Santangelo* series). *The World is Full of Divorced Women* is, once again, a relationship story, about men and women and their love lives and ambitions. The format is also classic Collins: short chapters, containing brief sections visiting each character/ group of characters. As with some of Collins' other Seventies works, there is a weariness, a cynicism, a defeatism bubbling underneath *The World is Full of Divorced Women* – happiness is always just out of reach.

The characters in *The World is Full of Divorced Women* are cut from the Collins Cookie Cutter: Cleo James is the principal character, the Collins Wife and independent woman: she possesses the familiar Collinsian physical attributes ('slim girl with long straight dark hair, big eyes, a wide mouth'), wears the familiar Collinsian garb (Biba boots, Gucci belt, Oliver Goldsmith sun glasses), has the familiar Collinsian job (she's a journo for the Gotham magazine *Image*), and experiences the familiar Collins dissatisfactions (adulterous husband, men hitting on her), and the familiar Collinsian desires (children, a family, the keys to Heaven).

Other charas in *The World is Full of Divorced Women* include Muffin ('Sweet. Adorable. Gorgeous. Sexy. Muffin!'), the working class, English supermodel who also does pin-up assignments and nudie calendars (she's the earthy model found in numerous Collins books); her boyfriend Jon Clapton, a trendy, London photographer in the David Bailey/ *Blow Up* mold (but he won't leave his wife Jane and marry Muffin); Cleo's hubby, record executive Mike James; Muffin's modelling chums; Little Marty Pearl, a teenybooper idol in the manner of Donny Osmond or David Cassidy; his manager, Jackson;, movie star Butch Kaufman; Ramo Kaliffe, an 'Arabian film star'; Stella, Cleo's distant, self-absorbed and aggressively narcissistic mother who belittles Cleo at every opportunity; Russell Hayes, her magazine boss who fancies her; and Cleo's friends (Ginny, Susan, Dominique, etc).

So Cleo James is searching for fulfilment following the break-up of her 4-year marriage (Cleo discovers her spouse fooling around with her so-called friend Susan in his office). She flees to London (where most of the first half of *The World is Full of Divorced Women* takes place). Where can a nice, smart, attractive and newly-single woman like Cleo find a decent, non-weird, non-chauvinistic guy? One man rubs himself to climax on top of her in his suit; another wiggles his John Thomas in front of her and pleads for some head; Ramo Kaliffe lechs over her; and several others try to pick her up.

Mike James, one of the few sympathetically portrayed guys in *The World is Full of Divorced Women* (though not positively – he can't keep it zipped up, and continues to dally around), is having a crisis of conscience, and wants to make up with Cleo. He pursues her to London, but she doesn't wanna know.

Meanwhile, *Sun* newspaper/ Page Three model Muffin is trying to persuade Jon Clapton to leave his miserable wife Jane and get a divorce; when he drags his feet (as men always do in the world of Jackie Collins about leaving their spouses/ family), she has a fling with teen heartthrob Marty Pearl (he in turn is attempting to shake off his possessive, over-protective mom, who insists on joining him on tour). Marty and Muffin, like other couples in *The World is Full of Divorced Women*, decide they're madly in love and havta marry instantly (instantly but also secretly). It doesn't work out: the *paparazzi* discover it, and surround the register office; Jackson, Marty's manager, is furious when he finds out (Clapton is disconsolate).

Being a 1975 novel, *The World is Full of Divorced Women* reads

---

6 'John Thomas' is Muffin's phrase – well, this *is* a novel written in the mid-1970s (talking about bawdy British humour, there's a send-up of the *Confessions of a Window Cleaner* books/ films – Muffin's ex-boyfriend Geoff is a window cleaner).

like a historical work, a piece of history, because its cultural references seem so, well, *old*: Bobby Womack, Barry White, John Wayne, Andy Williams, Twiggy and Justin de Villeneuve (and Jon Clapton's alimony amounts to £50 (= $75) a week). Clapton feels caught in the middle, between Muffin and Jane, but all he seems to really care about is making $$$$ (he has his eye on molding Muffin into an all-round performer, and taking her to the U.S.A.).

Some of the charas from Jackie Collins' other stories pop up in *The World is Full of Divorced Women*, such as Al King and Doris Andrews from *Lovers and Gamblers*.

In *The World is Full of Divorced Women*, no one's happy, and everyone's chasing their desires/ dreams – which, this being a relationship novel, are to be fulfilled in relationships (Cleo has 'problems that might be eased if there as only someone who cared enough to listen' [67]). *The World is Full of Divorced Women* is a modern update and flipside of a Jane Austen novel: in *Pride and Prejudice*, marriage is the goal, and the battleground (with the economics of marriage and matchmaking never far away). In *The World is Full of Divorced Women*, the charas have gone thru marriage (sometimes several), and emerged worn-out and disillusioned. It's the divorce/ separated version of a 19th romance story (instead of the build-up to a marriage, it's the aftermath, the disillusion, and the separation). And yet these characters, these women, continue to search for a mate and a date.

There are several subplots of mental instability in *The World is Full of Divorced Women* – Daniel Odel is a manic depressive, Mike James falls apart when his wife Cleo leaves him, and one of Cleo's friends, Dominique, commits suicide (so the stakes are upped in *The World is Full of Divorced Women* – Cleo/ the narrator relates Dominique's death to her treatment by some of the men in her life (such as Shep, who forced himself upon Cleo).)

Following repeated attempts by her husband Mike to make up with her in *The World is Full of Divorced Women* (he still can't stop fooling around), our heroine, Cleo James, leaves him for good: divorced, she plumps to go to California and shack up with Hollywood movie star Butch Kaufman. Unfortunately, like a Woody Allen character taken out of New York City, she finds her brain is turning to mush in the Californian lifestyle of sitting around getting a sun tan, yoga, BBQs, and talking with Butch's vacuous friends. It's not enough for a Collins heroine – as Collins asserts in her note on

The World is Full of Divorced Women in the front of one of the reprints, 'sex and cooking' are not enough for her women.

Yes, *The World is Full of Divorced Women* takes the inevitable Pan Am flight West – to Tinseltown, Jackie Collins' home-from-home. Here, the final straw for Cleo is the arrival Butch's 13 year-old, out-of-control daughter Vinnie, another of Collins' wild children ('Vinnie was the classic case of too much too soon' [268]).[7] Cleo walks. Conveniently, Cleo falls straight into the arms of Jack Nicholson-ish actor Daniel Odel, an object of fascination for Cleo (he's a great actor, but is odd, demanding, controlling,[8] and suffers from depression[9]). Collins gives Cleo and Daniel the biggest sex scene in *The World is Full of Divorced Women* – when they make out in his Benedict Canyon digs:

> 'every beautiful minute' [...] 'it was goddam *marvellous*. A heightened sensation of sexual energy and power' [...] 'an uncontrollable orgasm that swept over her in exhausting waves of intense delight' [...] 'when she reached orgasm for the third time it was incredibly gentle and beautiful and totally draining'

Poor Muffin, meanwhile, our British, working class photo model, has descended into doing porno (where she's 'exhibiting her snatch in a bunch of filthy magazines' [250], which she loathes). She misses Dear, Old England, and slides into drug-taking, while her husband Jon Clapton desperately tries to keep them both from losing the rental Cadillac and the rental home by angling for any job going in La-La Land. Muffin drifts into a lesbian liaison with the famous Karmen Rush (in private, she's a dominatrix, her bedroom is all-black, and she has C.C.T.V. peeping into the rest of the house).[10]

Pornography beckons again, with a *Deep Throat* rip-off (*The Girl With the Golden Snatch*), which stars Muffin and is filmed mostly at Rush's home (it's a spoof on the *James Bond* movie released in 1975, *The Man With the Golden Gun*). Muffin gets to snub her ex-boyfriend Jon Clapton royally – Muffin's the second of the divorced women in the novel who triumphs.

---

7 Later, Cleo warms to Vinnie.
8 'And if one of his old movies was on television the only time you could breathe was in the commercial' (269).
9 Daniel Odel suffers from depression, which leaves Cleo James perplexed, curious, sympathetic and then angry (Collins' first husband committed suicide).
10 At a party, Karmen and Muffin retire to her chamber, and, like the Great Gatsby or Howard Hughes, she watches the party on the TV monitors; it's the best way to attend a party, she says.

The Girl with the Golden Snatch is, in Karmen Rush's opinion, a masterpiece of porn: as she puts in Collins' inimitable style: 'It had comedy and humour, an interesting story, and the best looking cunt in Hollywood' (284).

★

And so *The World is Full of Divorced Women* closes with Cleo James in the ascendant – as a career woman, pursuing her love of journalism with her own TV chat show.[11] *The World is Full of Divorced Women* is about breaking out of marriage, about pursuing your own goals, about establishing a social identity outside of marriage, men and relationships. *The World is Full of Divorced Women* doesn't end with a Grand Romance, or a Big Reunion of Lovers, or the Solving of a Mystery or Murder: those issues have been dealt with in the chapters running up to the final pages. For ex, Cleo meets up with Daniel Odel, the man she's fascinated by above all other offers, but their encounter ends with fragmentation (Daniel already has a girlfriend, a 20 year-old English girl who's devoted to him). Besides, Odel had rapidly married a Swedish woman, Ingmar, while Cleo was A.W.O.L.,[12] but that marriage soon foundered. Poor Daniel is too jealous, too petty, and too controlling for Cleo (he hates the idea that she wants to have a career).

Meanwhile, Mike James pops up for one last time (having followed Cleo onto a flight): Mike is the ex-lover you can't rid of, the man who keeps hanging on, hoping for a reconciliation (or at least some skin action). No dice: Cleo cuts him off by telling him she's secretly getting married (she isn't – she is the main 'divorced woman' of the book's title). And Russell Hayes, her magazine boss, resigns himself to being placed in the 'friend' category (i.e., not the 'lover' category). And the last possibility in the relationship stakes for Cleo, Butch Kaufman, plays the hurt, lost boy (which Hollywood actors are great at in Collinsland): nope, Cleo ain't coming back to him (she left him and his Malibu mansion after 6 months).

> Annie was no longer a good thing. Talk about demanding! Equal orgasms wasn't in it. She wanted equal everything, including a drive of his Ferrari. *Never.* (222)

---

11 Her first guest is, appropriately, Muffin – however, Cleo is now a born-again feminist, and she's about to lay into the pornography industry, which's was a big deal in L.A. in the 1970s (and still is).
12 She thought she might be pregnant with Daniel's child, but it turns out she wasn't.

LOVERS AND GAMBLERS

One of the intriguing narrative elements in *Lovers and Gamblers* (1977 - great title) is that the two main protagonists, Dallas Lunde and Al King, have become jaded with sex. Which begins the story in the opposite direction from most Jackie Collins' characters, who're driven by impulses such as greed (money/ fame) and sex/ drugs (pleasure). When we first meet Al King, rock/ soul superstar, he's with two women who, despite their best efforts going down on him, are soon sent away. 'With all his success he had nothing, no one. Plenty of everything. But what did that mean when you were alone in bed at night.' (148). So, success... and emptiness.

Meanwhile, Dallas Lunde starts out as a sheltered girl who, after discovering sex (usually with older men), soon sees it merely as means of achieving her goals. (We know, from the outset, that these two are meant for each other, even tho' Dallas remains aloof to Al's advances for a long time - which provides the mandatory obstacle in a romantic plot).

Dallas Lunde is one of Jackie Collins' young women with a shady past: she's a hooker, she has a vaguely sadomasochistic relationship with an aggressive, black prostitute, Bobbie, and she is involved with some very sleazy scenes. But Dallas wins a 'Coast To Coast' beauty queen contest (by shtupping some of the judges and using blackmail - establishing her as (1) fiercely ambitious, and (2) corrupt). From beauty queen, Dallas moves up to actress, winning an agent, and the road to legitimate success. (She is very aspiring - but later that evaporates in disinterest).

> She was not interested in dating the Hollywood rota of known studs - a rather boring group of pseudo-sophisticated macho-hams who liked to notch up every new famous female on an imaginary fuckbelt. (280)

By this time, tho', Dallas is already a cynical, jaded, and weary soul in *Lovers and Gamblers* who regards relationships as exploitation, and sex as joyless. Dallas is a great beauty, but inside she's empty as a cardboard box thrown on a trash heap. 'Men didn't understand her. She was young and beautiful, why wasn't she out fucking her brains out?' (109)

Dallas L. is fated to be the victim of choice of ageing sexual predators - often they're business tycoons with too much money and no commonsense (like Aarron, who wants her as the face for his perfume brand, or motor mogul Ed Kurlnik). Meanwhile, her colleague and occasional lover in the prostitution game, Bobbie, turns against her following a date with a client that goes wrong (the old coot expires, and Bobbie reckons they should flee instead of reporting it).

Al King, meanwhile, is similarly bored and jaded, despite being incredibly successful (think: a pop/ soul star like Tom Jones or Rod Stewart or Al Green or Elton John). He embarks on a U.S. tour which, despite its setbacks (ticket touts, injuries in the audience), is a hit. King is a Brit with a brother (Paul) who devotes his life to doing whatever Al wishes (and in his personal life, Paul keeps promising his girlfriend Linda that he'll leave his wife Melanie for her, but of course, he never does). Like many another successful guy in Jackie Collins' world, King is a stud who works his way thru women like candy, immediately discarding them. He has a surly, resentful, spotty son (Evan), and an understanding but shy, retiring, dull wife (Edna).

Wives and girlfriends usually remain at home on rock music tours (and certainly in the male chauvinist Seventies, when wives were unwelcome), but in *Lovers and Gamblers* they decide to join their husbands Al and Paul King (with predictably calamitous results – Edna walks in on Al ejaculating inside a hooker's mouth while another one's draped around his legs, and Melanie discovers Linda in Paul's bed – his long-time photographer girlfriend).

For this reason, *Lovers and Gamblers* has a desperate, melancholy atmosphere – like other Jackie Collins books of the 1970s (such as *Sinners* and *The World Is Full of Divorced Women*). Even tho' many of the plotlines and the characters're the same as Collins' later fiction, there's something very sad and hollow about Collins' Seventies books.

Al King tours with a support act called the Promises, comprising three black women (evoking acts such the Three Degrees, the Ronettes, the Ikettes and Diana Ross and the Supremes). Little Nellie is hopelessly in love with Al King.

So the Al King tour of the United States of North America rolls on, leaving casualties in its wake: the wives who visit from Blighty, to find their hubbies less than amenable; the wayward son (Evan) who goes A.W.O.L. with a coupla no-hoper, teenage groupies, who teach him the thrills of pill-popping and bad sex in a sleeping bag outdoors; Bernie the tour manager, fat and sweating and perpetually harassed (Bernie's every line of dialogue starts with the phrase, 'what the fuck –'); the Promises (the support act) add aggravations; Nellie from the Promises slashes her wrists when Al leaves her for another woman – who's also in the Promises (Nellie dies); and brother/manager Paul King tries to keep everything together.

❤

Meanwhile, in the Dallas Lunde side of the story of *Lovers and Gamblers*, things aren't going well, either: she's got hitched to her eager, hustling, nice guy, Jewish agent, Cody Hills (it was a wham-bam-Las Vegas-two-in-the-morning wedding), the studio boss who's signed her for a million bucks (Lew Margolis) knows that she was a hooker (he used to have her dress up for him and play games – sex games such as: *I'll be the Jackie Collins-type author and you be the haggard publicist*, that sort of thing), and her former lover/ enemy/ hooker friend Bobbie keeps popping up demanding $$$$ to feed her heroin habit.

Poor Dallas Lunde just doesn't seem to enjoy life much at all anymore – especially when Bobbie expires, and her scheme of blackmailing Lew Margolis backfires. Then there's Doris Andrews, the film star with the clean, virginal image (like Doris Day or Julie Andrews), who turns out to be a predatory lesbian (with her sights set on Dallas and, later, Evita, Jorge's wife).

We know that Dallas and Al King're going to get together in *Lovers and Gamblers* – it's the standard Jackie Collins ploy of having your lovers bickering, falling out, being snooty (or overly druggy and drunk), but finding each other fascinating all the while. Yes, Dallas knows that Al is a wham-bam stud who enjoys big-boobed hookers, but, somehow or other, he's about the only guy who raises more'n a glimmer of erotic desire for her. And Al, despite being the superstar on a rockin' tour, finds Dallas intriguing (partly, of course, because she's repeatedly turned him down. He only wants the woman who doesn't want him).

Halfway thru *Lovers and Gamblers*, I guess Jackie Collins decided, you know what?, this baby needs a little intensification. A little livening up. A little *heat*. Because, after all, the 1977 novel could burble along to its inevitable ending: the corporate, psychological, financial, social and sexual unification of Dallas Lunde and Al King (the lovers of the book's title).

So the Queen of Hollywood adds one of her thriller plots: there's a total shift of time and place, and Jackie Collins introduces a trio of new charas (plus their parents) – the Gamblers of the title:

the well-meaning, quiet but curious teen girl (Cristina), the bad boy she falls for (Nino), and the nice, polite boy her folks would prefer her to hitch up with (Louis).

We're in South America for this section of *Lovers and Gamblers*, the land of Sao Paulo and Rio, an alternative to the N.Y.C.<>L.A.<>L.V. triangle that Jackie Collins usually uses. The plot? A teen romance plot (so Cristina is initiated into sex by the older Nino), plus a kidnap plot (Nino is a would-be Che Guevara, a member of an anti-capitalist organization). Nino sort of blackmails Cristina (she's under his sexual spell); but when Cristina discovers that some of Nino's methods are dodgy or downright violent, she gravitates towards the calmer, nicer Louis.

Jackie Collins brings the two halves of *Lovers and Gamblers* together by having Nino using Cristina for funds (knocking off the rich friends of her family for jewellery), and in the kidnap plot. This being a novel of the 1970s, with disaster movies big news (*The Towering Inferno, Earthquake, The Poseidon Adventure* and of course *Airport*), Jackie Collins employs a 100% guaranteed plot device: a plane crash.

The recipe is simple: (A) gather all of your principal characters in a plane,[13] and (B) have them getting hijacked. Then (C) the aircraft crashes. In (D) the Amazon jungle. Works every time; it plays into your every neurosis and fear; it kills off some of the secondary charas; it brings the major charas closer together; everyone else is fretting about them; and it provides a suitably spectacular finish to your story. (As in: if this won't get the lovers together, nothing will).

You'd have to be terrible writer not to be able to write a good plane crash narrative – it's a scenario that gives you everything as an author (highs, lows, intense emotion, life-and-death decisions, etc). A plane crash is an intensification of what we're all doing every day: surviving.

So Jackie Collins delves into disaster movie territory, into enduring against all odds, with all of the expected scenes: nasty bugs and critters (mosquitoes, ants, spiders, snakes and jaguars), no food, crash victims who're expiring due to lack of medical attention, bickering survivors, etc. When Collins allows herself a full-on action episode, it's exciting. This is the first of the big action set-pieces in Collins' fiction.

---

13 This takes quite a bit of finagling by Collins to achieve. Because some of the characters, such as Cristina and Nino, don't have a legitimate reason for being on the jet.

Everybody is amazed by Al King, who turns out to be a Boy Scout Supreme, plus he's eternally optimistic. Who knew the selfish stud (and mere musician), who thought about no one but himself, would prove to be such a dependable, resourceful 38 year-old guy?

Dallas L., too, doesn't sink into whingeing or sickness, and rallies the troops. Her early life living and working in a zoo stands her in good stead for dealing with the rigours of the Amazon jungle. (Incredibly, the now-committed lovers have the strength to tup in the jungle, while everybody else is on their last legs and nearly dead. Well, this *is* a Jackie Collins novel, and her characters always have the energy for some shtupping – especially if they are the chief couple).

The group of plane crash survivors thins, inevitably, as supplies run out, injuries aren't treated, and illness runs unchecked (rescue missions are conspicuously absent). Thus, Cathy the stewardess dies (and is torn apart by jaguars). And fat Bernie, the tour manager, is dragged into a river by alligators (despite Al King having a gun, which he's just used to shoot a monkey for food. But he doesn't think to use it to save his loyal publicity man). Even Evan, Al's spotty, forlorn and rather hopeless son, comes a cropper (again of jaguars, when he goes off hunting for food alone). It's one of the few times when Collins' totem animal, the jaguar (or panther), slinks into the foreground of a story, and acts as a real animal.

Lovers and Gamblers ends as expected: the survivors make it back to civilization; there's a media frenzy; Al and Dallas hole up in Beverly Hills and do nothing for 6 months (apart from enjoying Being In Love); Linda leaves Paul; Edna wants to forget that she was ever married to Al (she now lives with a boring, safe guy and his mom); Paul gives up being Al's manager; and Cody Hills becomes the agent for both Al and Dallas, now two of the hottest stars in the celebrity firmament (*Lovers and Gamblers* ends with them coming out of retirement, to face the press for the first time). And, unable to resist extra sweeteners if they're available (fattening, but sooo nice!), Jackie Collins adds the possibility for romance btn Linda and Cody.

★

THE BITCH

The Bitch (1979) is a follow-up to *The Stud* (1969). 1979 was a busy year for Jackie Collins' output: not only *The Bitch* novel, but also the film adaptation of *The Bitch*, plus a movie of *The World Is Full of Married Men* and *Yesterday's Hero* (with *The Stud* movie released a year earlier).

Fontaine Khaled is the main character of *The Bitch*, a rich, middle-aged jet-setter whose millionaire husband has died. She owns a nightclub in London called *Hobo* which's not doing so well. Much of the book takes place in London and Las Vegas. Like many of Jackie Collins' books, *The Bitch* is split narratively across two main characters, who come together romantically for a while.

The other main character is the ageing wise guy and all-round, super-cool dude Nico Constantine, a self-made Greek who lived with a successful opera singer for years before she died. Presumably this is a reference to the diva and superstar of the music world, Maria Callas, the famous singer who dated the Greek tycoon Aristotle Onassis, and died two years before *The Bitch* was published. (So many of Jackie Collins' characters live off other people – of course, it's partly a dramatic device, to enable those people to have money – and also for them to have wealth without having to be bothered with minor irritations like work). Nico gambles in Vegas (including betting his house), loses badly, and winds up owing a lot of dough to the Italian mobsters who run the casino.

This narrative strand of *The Bitch* is routine thriller stuff, and it reads like a comicbook, right down to Nico C. stealing a precious ring from an old woman (after jumping her bones, of course), and hurrying off to Blighty to cash it in for his markers. It's an Ealing comedy or a schoolkids' version of what crooks in Las Vegas might get up to. In the 1960s, a softer version (minus the sex and swearing) might be one of those caper movies starring Cary Grant, Audrey Heburn and Grace Kelly (*To Catch a Thief* or *Charade*. And of course Omar Shariff would play Nico – as he should've done in the movie version of *The Bitch*).

The Bitch is partly a Las Vegas novel. Not the greatest book set in Las Vegas, and not Jackie Collins' best Vegas outing, but it's got the mob (*of course* – they built Vegas), and it's got gambling and casinos (seemingly impossible to avoid in a Vegas story), and it's got goodtime girls ('they only come here to develop their cunts and their bankrolls!' as head mafioso Joseph Fonicetti puts it [90]). Yes, and there's even a crooner clearly modelled on Frank Sinatra (well, if it was OK for *The Godfather* (book and film), to do that with its Johnny Fontane character, why not?).

The Bitch and *The Stud* are also discussed in the chapter on Jackie Collins' movies.

★

The novels of the 1970s develop over the decade towards the highpoints of Collins' career artistically: the first *Lucky Santangelo* book in 1981, *Chances*, and her biggest success, *Hollywood Wives*, in 1983. Each of the 1970s novels is fascinating – *Sinners*, *The Love Killers*, *The World Is Full Of Divorced Women*, *Lovers & Gamblers* and the movie tie-in *The Bitch* – but we probably wouldn't be talking about Collins' fiction today on the basis on those Seventies works (they also appear greater in retrospect in the reflected heat from the later works, in particular the *Santangelo* series and the *Hollywood* series).

Chronologically, *Chances* (1981) is the next book in Collins' writing career: it's discussed in a separate chapter, as is *Hollywood Wives* (1983) and its sequels. Instead, we jump ahead to 1993:

★

AMERICAN ST★R

So for this new edition of this study of Jackie Collins and the bestselling novel I've been reading some of Collins' more recent works. After reading *Thrill!*, published in 1998, I picked up *American Star* (great title), published in 1993.

Déja vu.

Or something.

Because in the first pages of *American St★r* there's

(1) A young, cocky kid, who's

(2) Swooningly attractive to the girls,

(3) With trailer park origins, called Nick Angelo[14]

(4) And he's a wannabe actor.

(5) And he's shunted onto relatives.

---

14 No, not *Sant*angelo!

(6) And has an Italian name.

It's Joey Lorenzo from *Thrill!* all over again!

And guess what? The other main character in *American Star* is

(1) A young, highly attractive girl, who's

(2) Rather prim (she doesn't swear),

(3) And she wants to be an actress, and

(4) She even has the same name: Lara in *Thrill!*, and Lauren in *American Star*.

Doesn't matter a bit, of course – every author repeats the same sort of characters from book to book, poem to poem, play to play, from opera to opera. It's OK for William Shakespeare to do it, or William Thackeray, or Edith Wharton. (But these novels were published only five years apart – cutting it a bit fine, perhaps).

★

American St★r (1993) was the first Jackie Collins book I felt emotionally involved with – her books are hugely entertaining, but rarely on a deeply emotional level. Or, to put it another way, you don't much care about Collins' characters. You follow their lives like actors in a loud, glossy Hollywood movie, but they don't move you much (or at least, at a deeper level).

American Star does, though. It packs an emotional punch, and I found myself really rooting for Lauren Roberts and Nick Angelo to get together. It's a love story first and foremost – maybe the finest in Jackie Collins' work. Collins is using classic structures and situations here – by creating two soul mates, giving them a brief interlude of idyllic togetherness, then pulling them apart. But constantly reminding the gentle, candy-pink reader that the lovers are yearning for each other, despite the numerous other relationships they have.

It's a classic scenario, and it works like gangbusters in *American Star*. It is also fabulously, hopelessly *romantic*. Oh, *soooooo* romantic! ❤ ❤ ❤ Uh-huh, there's only one girl for Nick Angelo, and that's Lauren Roberts. And there's only one guy for Lauren Roberts, and that's Nick Angelo.

It appeals to romantics, idealists and dreamers, like me. Life *should* be like this, shouldn't it? Well, in a book it *can be*. In a novel, you can order life however you like. (Which's one of the greatest appeals of art, of course).

★

American Star is fun structurally, because for once Jackie Collins doesn't pepper the present-tense narrative with flashbacks for each character. Well, not so much. OK, all right, there *are* flashbacks, but there is also a lengthy section of *American Star* which concerns the early days of the two main characters, Lauren R. and Nick A. In other words, the Goddess Collins doesn't bring the narrative into the present day for a long stretch (the novel is set in 1992), but allows herself a lengthy and continuous sojourn in the past. We're talking the 1970s. Remember them? Collins takes the gorgeous, meticulously-attentive reader on a journey through the Seventies for a pizza slice of Middle Americana.

This part of *American Star* comes across like 1970s shows/movies such as *American Graffiti,* or *The Last Picture Show,* or *Grease,* or an episode of *Happy Days*... But a bit more savage. With more alcohol and beatings. With abortions. And a bit of sex.

Yes, the setting in *American Star* – a small town called Bosewell in Kansas (yes, we're back in Kansas, Dorothy) – is classic Middle America. It's Teen Romance time, it's Teen Soap Opera time, it's every high school drama or romantic comedy you've ever seen. There's the High School Jock, the Football Star, complete with blue eyes and crew cut, name of Stock. There's the cool James Dean-a-like Drifter from outta town, Nick Angelo – all the gurrrls *lerrrv* him, naturally (he is directly compared with Dean a coupla times).

Nick Angelo would probably be one of Jackie Collins' many insufferable, asshole actor characters, if he'd been introduced as he is aged 35, in the prologue of *American Star*, and in the latter section of the novel. Because by then he's a superstar movie actor who has it all. But as the honey-sweet reader has followed Nick throughout the narrative, right from his lowly beginnings in a trailer park in Bosewell, Kansas, he is treated quite differently. Indeed, Collins gives him a drink problem when he's a star, but few other flaws. Because this is a love story, and he's the hero. And you don't want your heroine finding true love with a creep.

There's Little Miss Pretty-and-Prim (dubbed 'Miss Thighs Together Roberts' by Dawn [107]), our Cinderella, our heroine, Lauren Roberts. And her over-weight, over-eager Sidekick School-mate, Meg (also a quivering virgin, of course). There's Nick's Deadbeat Dad, Primo, a fat, violent, alcoholic layabout (sound familiar?). There's Nick's Step-mom, Aretha Mae, who works as a maid for the rich family that owns half the town, the Brownings (and, what a surprise, she was molested by the Big Boss White Man, Benjamin Browning – *Gone*

With the Wind with rape).

And so it goes on.

Want more? You got it:

✖ There's an engagement party (cue rowdy kids, including the local no-goods, the bikers).

✖ There's boys trying to get to second base with girls in cars at the make-out spot at night.

✖ The bad boy works in a garage (he's John Travolta in *Grease*).

✖ There's a New Year's party where the jock punches out the hero after his girl's thrown his engagement ring back at him.

✖ Hell, there's even a school play in which our two heroes play the leads in *Cat On a Hot Tin Roof*.

✖ And the old drama teacher Joy Byron[15] is a goddam ageing hippy, with jangly bangles and beads!!! (She appeared in *Hollywood Wives*).

What's not to like in this utterly, completely, totally, like, clichéd narrative? It's extraordinary that Jackie Collins can, like, write such material, but also that people, like, buy it. But the global media of course churns out TV shows and movies like this by the dozen. Why not novelists?

Clichés *work*.

Oh, they do. They so do.

And Jackie Collins can handle a cliché as deftly as anybody. And she can make them do the job of unfolding a narrative. And of course, *every major writer* – from Homer 3,000 years ago through the troubadours and the Renaissance and Christopher Marlowe and the Elizabethan Age to Victor Hugo and the Romantics up to the present day – uses clichés.

Some disguise them. Some pretend they're hi-falutin' literary art. But look at the great writing in the history of the world and you or I could point out a hundred clichés in every single work.

So when you read the first third of 1993's *American Star,* you soon realize you've been here a million times before. Maybe it's the familiarity that's so comforting. But it works, because *American Star* tells a story in a confident manner and draws you along. Somehow, La Collins manages to deliver a series of clichés and seen-it-all-before situations and characters and make it all appealing. It's not 'new', but, hell, *what is*? It's not 'new', but it is fun, and it is entertaining.

You can't go wrong with certain fundamental emotions and

---

[15] Joy Byron is a spoof, I would suggest, of the famous acting coach Stella Adler, who taught Marlon Brando.

characters and situations. Well, you can if you're a bad writer, but Jackie Collins is certainly a highly skilled, perceptive and clear writer.

She can *write*. Yes, Jackie Collins can *really* write.[16]

★

Classic ingredients:
(A) The bad boy from the wrong side of the tracks. Man, he just happens to be a talented actor and handsome and great in the sack.
(B) The do-gooder, bee-oot-ee-fool Cinderella who's waiting for her prince to come along and wake her up sexually and socially.
(C) The repressive, controlling parents.
(D) The deadbeat, perpetually drunk slob of a fat ass dad.

OK, so there's not too much complexity or ambiguity to these characters or situations in *American Star*. Or originality – we've all met these characters thousands of times before. Nick Angelo and Lauren Roberts are every kid, every young lover, every hero and heroine you've ever met.

And no one would pretend that *American Star* is Great Art or the highest form of literature. But no one is fooling anybody here: the author, the reader, the publisher, and the book itself isn't lying or faking. (Only the P.R., marketing and hype does that. It's their job).

Sure, *American Star* isn't *The Adventures of Tom Sawyer* or *To Kill a Mockingbird*. But it isn't trying to be the Great American Novel. But who knows? Maybe Jackie Collins' books will be regarded as classics in the future. Maybe her books will have solemn, academic books written about them, or become study texts in colleges.

Yeah, you can take a class in *English Literature From 1840-1900*, or *Women Writers of the 20th Century*. Maybe Ms Collins will be included in a course at Yale like: *Blockbuster Novels From 1980-2010* or there'll be a conference at Harvard called: *Oral Sex In the Bestselling American Novel*.

(I'd love to start up a Jackie Collins Conference – it would be based in Las Vegas (where else?!), in a plush resort, with the usual talks, movies, previews, guests, etc, plus plenty of games, gambling, drinking, carousing, and of course cosplay – dressing up as Lucky Santangelo or your favourite Bitch-Goddess from Collins' fiction).

---

16 So what if she uses a diamond-encrusted fountain pen custom-made by Cartier on handmade paper? Sitting by the pool in a Bev. Hills mansion? She can *write!*

★

Jackie Collins closes Book One of *American Star* with an outrageous *deus ex machina* event. Yes, we definitely are in Kansas, Dorothy – because the Wizard of Oz (or should that be Collins the Author-as-Wicked-Witch?), has sent an almighty tornado which tears apart li'l, ol' Bosewell, KS. Handily, the Twister From Hell performs an important narrative function: it dispenses with both of Lauren's parents and Nick Angelo's no-good dad. And just in time, too: because slimy, lecherous Primo was starting in on Lauren when she'd visited the trailer park looking for Nick (there's a little bit of a cliffhanger here, as Lauren was about to defend herself with a knife from being raped by Primo).

Silly? Unbelievable? *Who the* @¢$! *cares?!* This is a Jackie Collins novel! This is what she does! (She likes natural disasters – there's a biggie at the end of *Thrill!*).

If the twister stretches belief in *American Star*, the results of it also require some big suspensions of disbelief. For instance: in a love story (*American Star* is sold as 'a love story for the Nineties'), you have to invent good and strong reasons for the lovers to be apart (and enduring ones, in a story running over many years). It's Rule One of composing romantic stories. Obstacles, conflicts, differences, arguments – all that stuff (warring households in the most celebrated love story in literature, for instance – *Romeo and Juliet*). And *American Star* keeps the lovers apart for a good, long time – but always mentions that they still think about each other (well, *duh, of course* they do!).

★

American St★r leaps forward from the mid-1970s to the end of the 1970s, with Nick Angelo now living in Chicago. Yet although he thinks about Lauren Roberts all the time (despite living with a new girlfriend), he hasn't seen her in five years. The reader has to go along with all this – it's part of the overall structure of the 1993 novel and the author's intent. But we know that Nick is a go-ahead kinda guy: after all, when he arrived in the Windy City he got himself a job on his first day out looking for one (while his two buddies, Joey and Cyndra, take days to find somthing). So the reader has to believe that Nick wouldn't track down Lauren (she's gone to live with relatives in Philly – that old Jackie Collins stand-by. Always with the hero/ine scurrying back to relatives, and always with the aunts and uncles being not very welcoming and it's all just a stop-gap).

Oh, Nick writes to li'l Lauren and calls her (but of course she's left, and her folks are dead). But there are loads of ways you can reach someone if you really want to – yes, even in the golden days of the Seventies, without cel phones and e-mails and texts and the internet and the like. And Nick would know other people in Bosewell who could get a message to Lauren, or tell him she's upped and left for the city of brotherly love. (And of course, Lucky Santangelo would hire Boogie or a private detective to track 'em down).

Jackie Collins employs a device that Thomas Hardy used so effectively in *Tess of the d'Urbervilles* – the crucially important letter that goes astray. In *American Star*, Louise doesn't seem to bother getting the letter Nick sends to Lauren until it's too late.

So the climactic ending of Book One of *American Star* – with its near-rape of the heroine Lauren and the tornado that demolishes the Mid-West town and kills the heroes' parents – has plenty in it to separate our two lovers. However, when five years swing by without a peep from either one to find the other, it does stretch credulity a little. Or a lot.

At the same time, the reader knows it's a tease. Because Jackie Collins writes fairy tales. Oh yeah, there might be drug abuse, child abuse, sleazy nightclubs and some fucking, but these are still fairy tales. And fairy tales must have happy endings. Indeed, happy endings are *the single most important element in a fairy tale.*

Here's the ending of *American Star*, with Nick and Lauren literally flying off into the sunset, in a plane bound for Canada:

> They stared into each other's eyes and smiled.
> The dream was finally coming true.
> They were together and they both knew without a doubt that this time nothing would ever spilt them apart again. (568)

So we know all will end well. And we also know that the author won't have spent two hundred pages relating the small-town life of the two key characters and then forgotten all about them.

We also know that Nick Angelo survives, because *American Star* opens with that favourite Jackie Collins device, the prologue (set in 1992).

★

In *American Star*, Jackie Collins is orchestrating her characters back and forth across the U.S. of A. Well, not everywhere: it's Chicago, New York, Vegas and Tinseltown, primarily (the cities that feature in most of Collins' books, tho' Chicago not so much). The lovers – Nick Angelo and Lauren Roberts – are kept apart for a long time, years and years. In between, *American Star*'s filled with new relationships and developments:

- there's an accidental murder in Las Vegas, which's covered up;
- Cyndra gets rid of total asshole Reece Webster;
- a new guy appears for Lauren (Oliver; he's old enough to be her grandfather – but he does give great head);
- a near-rape from rock star Emerson Burn (the third, no less, for poor Lauren);
- Emerson pursuing Lauren in Gotham;
- Cyndra finally on her way with a record deal;
- Nick having several girlfriends (DeVille, Annie, Carlysle, and movie producers);
- more acting classes for Nick;
- and a break in Nick's first movie role (plus an improbable promotion from a minor role to the lead. Sure, it *could* happen, but experienced film producers would go through a long list of more well-known actors before opting for an unknown, no matter how good he is).

And so on. Uh-huh.

★

One thing's for sure, Jackie Collins' books don't hang around. No waffle here. No meandering. No fucking around with philosophical pontifications about Third World debt, or left-liberal laments for the demise of global Marxism, or postmodern whinges about the imperialist, monopolistic materialism of Starbucks, Disney, Amazon, E-bay and MacDonald's.

Nope. None of that. Not a jot.

Instead: endless relationships and permutations on existing relationships, new characters introduced with a flourish of a few adjectives and adverbs, plus more marriages, more break-ups, more dinner parties, more blowjobs in the back of limos, etc.

It's a carousel.

It's cute, really.

It's a Jackie Collins novel.

★

...So when Lauren Roberts and Nick Angelo finally encounter each other, it's at a dinner party in New York, New York where

Lauren is working as a caterer.

Hm-mmm. Uh-huh.

Nick's there with sex-mad Carlysle (she's got her hand in his pants under the table), and Lauren's brought out from the kitchen by the host, to be shown off. Grandfather Oliver, her fiancé, is there too.

It's not the meeting of the should-be-lovers that the reader expects in *American Star*, and it doesn't have the flash-bang-wallop consequences one might anticipate. No hugs, no kisses, none of that. No. Lauren flees.

And by this time, Jackie Collins has been teasing the tender, luscious reader for quite some time. Collins knows all the tricks by now (*American Star* was her fourteenth novel, in a career going back 25 years, to 1968). It's like delaying orgasm – the longer the better. There's a lot of narrative foreplay in *American Star*, you might say (and Collins' women tend to like *lots* of foreplay).

★

At another meeting, at another dinner party, the lovers can't stop going for it:

> The only person she really cared about was Nick. In fact, she loved him just as much as she always had. He was in her heart and in her soul, but she was trapped in an impossible situation, and there was nothing she could do about it.
> 'What's going on, Lauren?' Nick walked in, startling her.
> 'Uh... nothing.'
> 'Can I see you?' he asked, urgently.
> 'You are seeing me.'
> His green eyes captured her attention. 'You know what I mean.'
> She knew exactly what he meant.
> He walked over and stood very close, pulling her to her feet.
> She was melting inside. Falling... falling... And when he began to kiss her it was like time stood perfectly still and nothing else mattered. They kissed feverishly. His hands touched her face. 'Oh God, Lauren, I missed you so much.' (479)

But it's also significant – and part of the dramatic structure – that neither Nick Angelo nor Lauren Roberts are completely happy throughout their many years apart. Between 1979 (in Book Two) and 1988 (in Book Three), 9 years have gone by, and both Lauren and Nick reap huge successes in their careers: Nick's become a superstar movie actor, and Lauren's a supermodel with a swathe of *Vogue* covers covering the walls of her Park Avenue office.

Book Two of *American Star* charts the rise to success, and

Book Three the complications of that success. But throughout *American Star*, neither Lauren or Nick are wholly fulfilled (jeez, who is?!). They have achieved all of the outward manifestations of success, including money and fame and social power. But the heart of the American Dream is not fulfilled.

This is a key element of this kind of romantic/ relationship novel: that the outer life of a person may be shiny and golden, but inside these people are still dissatisfied. The morals? Oh, the usual ones, that:

(1) money can't buy happiness,
(2) money can't buy you love, and
(3) fame is no substitute for a loving relationship.

Yes, in a romantic novel, love is the all-conquering experience that everybody wants, and is hankering after. L♥O♥V♥E. Love is the only thing that melts everything into a pink goo, that solves all ills, and that will make the characters *truly* happy.

So Nick is married to Annie, partly to prevent her from going to the cops about the accidental death that occurred in Las Vegas. But he sure ain't fulfilled and he's taken to the bottle. The fame and the success in the world of Hollywood has become taken for granted, and is not what he expected.

Lauren meanwhile has married a workaholic and very old husband, forty years older than herself. And she becomes a workaholic herself, as she manages her modelling career.

Jackie Collins is fully aware of the soapy quality of this novel. She features a conversation between Nick and his sister Cyndra:

> 'I've always loved her, and I guess I always will.'
> 'Don't go getting romantic on me, Nick. I can't stand it.'
> 'There'll never be another girl like Lauren.'
> 'Listen to you – it's pure soap opera.' (450)

The Mid-West setting of *American Star* is unusual for a Jackie Collins novel – or, rather, it's unusual for Collins to spend so much time in a novel in the Mid-West. However, the narrative does inevitably to shift to the Big City – in this case, the Big Three of Chicago, Gotham and L.A.

It's the Mid-West for a reason (not the Pacific North-West, for example, or the Deep South). It's Small-Town America, it's Suburban America, with all the prejudices and interests of Middle America. It might be anywhere, but it's not: it's the Mid-West in a particular time and place.

It's the Mid-West partly because of the narrative of rags-to-riches. So the journey of the characters in the novel – from Kansas to Chicago then L.A. and New York is meant to echo that of the North American Dream. That anybody can make it. It's about get-up-and-go... it's about having a dream and living it... it's about hustling and working hard and reaping the rewards...

You can see the story in other American folk from the Mid-West who made good, such as Walt Disney or Orson Welles. Nick Angelo is a classic Mid-Westerner in this respect: he's a hard worker but also has a vision. He wants to make something more of his life. Like Lauren. Like Cyndra.

★

In the middle of *American Star* you can see the author searching around for where the story is going to go. Often these are the most interesting parts of a novel. The writer's got their characters, put them out there, doing things, with a rough idea of how the narrative is going to unfold. The details are worked out in the composition. Nick Angel's story has a clear line – he's in Los Angeles, struggling to become an actor, taking acting classes, driving limos, etc. Lauren Roberts' narrative through-line is a little more diffuse or uncertain: she's gone to New York, has a rapid romance with a photographer (but is jilted at the altar), and works as an unappreciated, do-anything assistant for a modelling agency.

In this part of *American Star*, the two main characters (and the subsidiary characters around them), are struggling to find their way in the world. It's the middle section of the rags-to-riches story. The 1993 novel is working through its inter-related issues of love, sex, money, jobs, ambitions, goals, friends, the past, etc.

And the novelist herself is developing the characters and the situations and the themes of *American Star* right in front of the reader. For instance, one can easily see how the character of Nature, the British, six-foot tall, Cockney fashion model, begins to absorb the author – especially in her speech, which Collins writes brilliantly.

Nature is a loud, earthy, out-spoken woman, highly successful but neurotic and vain with it. Nature becomes an influence on the heroine's life, when Lauren decides to leave Samm's modelling agency, get married, and also set up her own company with Pia.

After being jilted on her wedding day by Jimmy Cassady (who turns out to be gay – and not just gay, but positively festive!, as

Samm puts it), Lauren stays with Nature, and becomes *her* assistant. Nature assumes importance in Lauren's story by the sheer force of her personality – she's a character you can't say 'no' to. She leads the author as much as she leads Lauren. And that's fun to watch (especially as Nature and rock star Emerson Burn are a volatile and chaotic couple, with the usual bust-ups and partying).

★

The introduction of Lauren's thoughts are amusing – Lauren talks to herself (don't we all?), and has conversations with herself about the current dilemmas in her life. Presented in italics, on separate lines. Thus:

> *Well, Roberts,* she thought. *What are you going to do?*
> *I don't know.*
> *You'd better decide.*
> *I can't.*
> *Why?*
> Good question. Why couldn't she decide?
> The answer came out of nowhere.
> *Because I still love Nick Angelo* (279)

Of *course* Lauren Roberts still loves Nick Angelo! That's what the book's about – long-lasting love! Long-suffering love! Love that never dies! *Bluurrrgh!*

★

The conclusion of *American Star* unites the lovers in a fairy tale ending, up in a plane flying to Canada (linking up with the prologue). All of the loose ends have been tied up neatly. A little *too* neatly, really: the plot creaks towards the end of *American Star*. For instance, Jackie Collins simply dispenses with Nick's wife Annie by killing her off in a car crash: 'It was the last time he saw either of them again. Their car was in a head-on collision. Neither Lissa nor Annie survived' (533). But it's not a simple get-out clause for Nick, who's embroiled in an acrimonious split with his wife Annie, because he also loses the light of his life, his daughter Lissa. Freedom has a price.

A few pages later on, near the end of *American Star*, Oliver, Lauren's ageing husband, sends her a letter setting her free of him – he's now in the South of France, having hooked up with a widow closer to his age. So that sets Lauren free to re-unite with Nick. And right after she's read the letter, in the lobby, she's jumping into Nick's red Ferrari and zooming off into the sunset.

Meanwhile, the Cyndra plot-line in *American Star* is resolved in an equally far-fetched manner: her first husband, Reece Webster, the con-man from the past, turns up wanting a large hand-out to stay silent about the death in Las Vegas which was covered up. Cyndra plans to finish him off with a gun her bodyguard gave her. But she doesn't have to: a hooker hurls a glass ashtray at Reece, injuring him so badly he dies.

We're in fantasy land in *American Star*. But sometimes the characters wake up and tell the author that real life is more important:

'Samm, sometimes life comes before fantasy. Making a movie is fantasy, being with my husband is real life.' (522)

The secondary characters grouped around the two main characters in *American Star* parallel their stories: Cyndra is the sister of Nick, and becomes a mega-star in the world of pop music. Her rise to fame and fortune echoes that of Lauren and Nick, but Cyndra has unfinished business: she is the product of her black mother Aretha Mae being raped by the wealthy white guy Benjamin Browning. Cyndra gets her own back in a suitably OTT manner, denouncing Browning at a public luncheon and on national television.

Joey, one of the three friends who run away from Bosewell, KS to Chicago, is less fortunate, turning to drugs. With ambitions of being a stand-up comedian, he is one of the casualties of *American Star*, despite Nick trying to help him out, getting him into a drug rehab clinic. Joey eventually OD's.

Meanwhile Stock, the muscle-bound football jock type, at one time engaged to Lauren, stays put in small-town Bosewell, and marries Lauren's one-time best friend, Meg. Scott and Meg are ridiculed by Cyndra and Nick when they return to Bosewell for being phonies (and fat).

In fact, the 1993 novel is pretty damning of the people who stayed in Bosewell, Kansas, and didn't try to pursue the Great American Dream. Aretha Mae falls ill with pneumonia; Harlan, Nick's kid brother, becomes, improbably, a transvestite selling tricks (but is rescued by Nick and eventually works for him); and characters such as Dave and Louise fall on bad times.

★

American Star is a love story, and in this Hollywood-style love story set largely in Hollywood, everyone is waiting, as Lawrence

Durrell said once, to hear those three magic words: *I L♥VE YOU*. Everyone wants to hear it, wants to hear the other person say it. When Nick is inside Lauren, they play around with saying it:

> ...they made love fast and passionately. He teased her – taking her almost there and then making her wait until she begged for more.
> 'Tell me what I want to hear,' he said, urgently. 'Tell me – I want to hear you say it.'
> She couldn't stop herself. 'I love you, Nick – I always have.' (510)

★

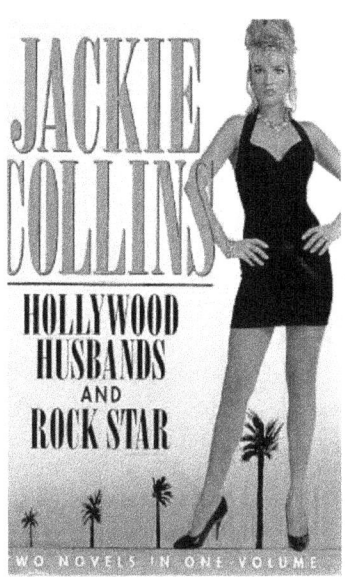

Jackie Collins' books (this page and over).

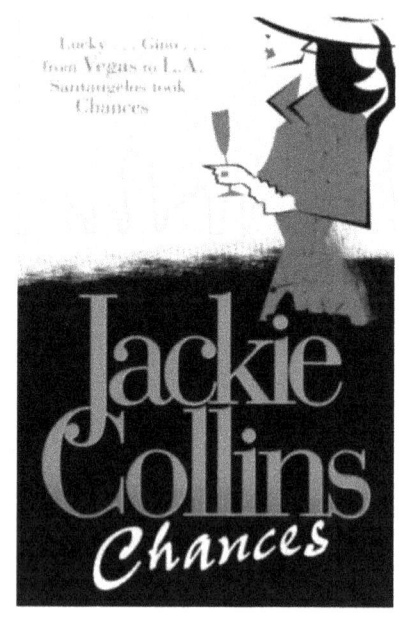
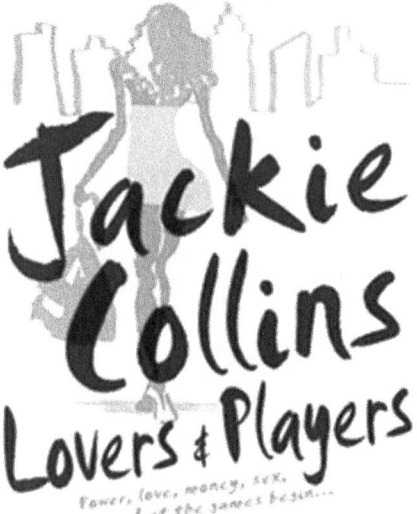

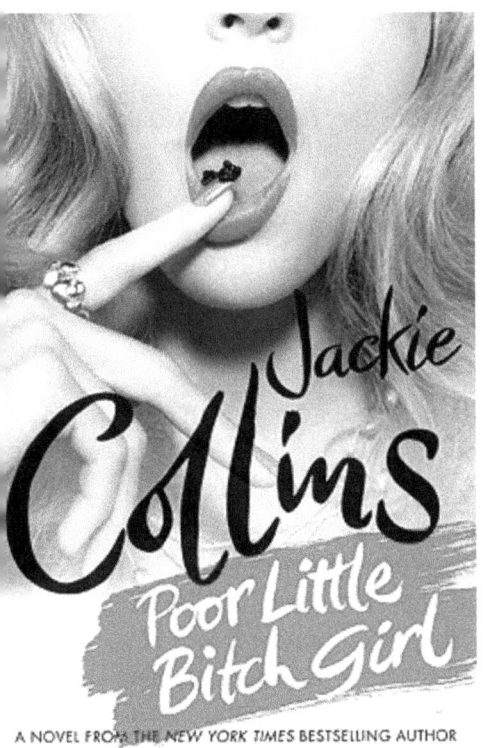

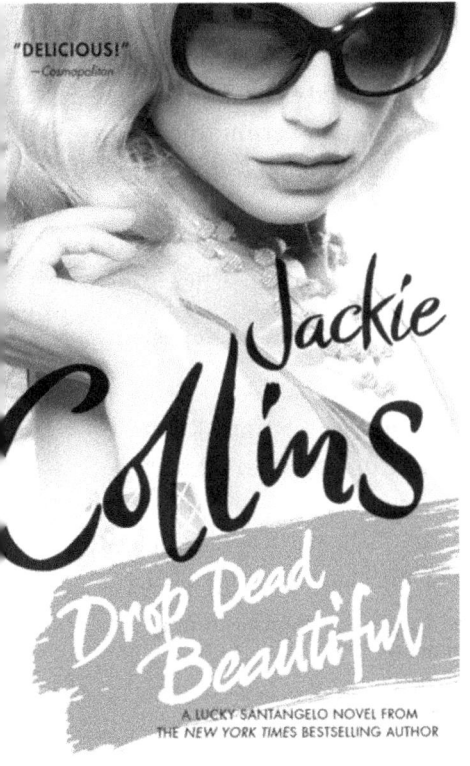
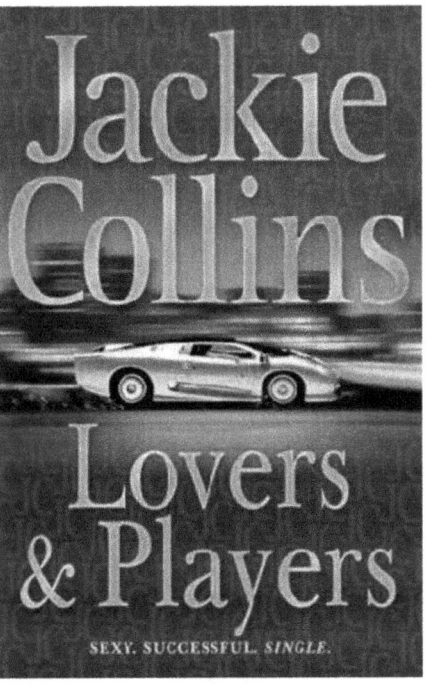

THRILL!

> I always write about that rags-to-riches dream. They come to Hollywood and if they get everything, then it's just too much for them to absorb.
>
> Jackie Collins on *The Advocate* (TV)

Let's have a look at *Thrill!*, a 1998 novel written by Jackie Collins (in some ways, it's a rewrite of *American Star* – and to a shameless degree, as noted above). I really enjoyed this book. It's got the whole Jackie Collins number, from beginning to end.

Check out the cover first, and see how *Thrill!* fits in with other bestselling books on the bookstore shelf:

The British hardback (published by Macmillan) costs $28.00 (£16.99). No photo on the cover, instead, it's a fab leopardskin pattern. Jackie Collins' name's in huge, white letters (embossed, of course), with the title below. There's a white silhouette of a panther at the bottom (with a gold collar – it might've wandered out of a Las Vegas floorshow – a panther with a collar or on a chain – taming a wild animal, a feral beast as a pet – that's *so* Jackie Collins!). The panther emblem crops up in other Collins' books (there's a Panther Studios in Hollywood, for instance, run by Lucky Santangelo in *Lady Boss*).

Why panthers and leopards? Oh, probably because they are sleek, sexy, independent and dangerous – suitable totem animals or pets for a sleek, sexy and dangerous character.[1] For example, Beverly D'Amo, the tall, black model in *Hollywood Husbands* partly based on Grace Jones, is described as 'a panther in the old sackerooney! Je-*sus*!' (320). Lucky Santangelo moves like a panther. And in *Lethal Seduction* we read:

> 'Oh, my God,' she said. 'I *love* cheetahs. They are *the* most beautiful animals.'
> 'You should watch them running. It has to be the most powerful sight you've ever witnessed.' (135)

And *Thrill!* has its own tag-line, like a movie: 'Kiss me! Kill me! Thrill me!' (The phrase has been used many times – even U2 have a song like that – 'Worship Me! Adore me! Pay me!').

The blurb for *Thrill!*, on the inside flap of the hardcover edition, summarizes the plot, and offers a list of the characters: Lara Ivory,

---

1 If Jackie Collins has a 'power animal' or spirit guide *à la* shamanism, or a dæmon *à la* Philip Pullman, you can bet it's a panther.

Nikki Barry, Joey Lorenzo, Aiden Sean, etc.

And *Thrill!* is sold like this:

> Sexy and suspenseful, filled with compelling characters and passionate relationships, *Thrill!* is Jackie Collins at her unputdownable best.

And on the back of *Thrill!* is a colour photo of Her Royal Highness: still glam, still attractive, but looking older (aren't we all? She was 61). She sits at a desk cluttered with glass and shiny oddments, her pen poised over a notebook, and addressing the viewer with a slight smile. She is recognizably the glamorous Jackie Collins of her novels: a fitted, black jacket, a necklace, a low neckline, gold earrings, plenty of lip gloss, blusher, eye shadow and of course she has big hair. She might be a business woman in her office before heading off to a power lunch or a meeting with the board of executives (i.e., she's Lucky Santangelo!).

★

Everything is familiar and in place in *Thrill!*:

✔ a contemporary, North American setting, as usual (chiefly L.A. and New York, as usual);

✔ an ensemble cast, as usual;

✔ short chapters, as usual;

✔ snappy, casual dialogue, as usual;

✔ numerous relationships, as usual;

✔ falling in and out of love, as usual;

✔ ex-lovers from Hell, as usual;

✔ allusions to contemporary popular culture (with many to the Hollywood industry), as usual;

✔ shopping sprees, as usual;

✔ dark secrets in the past, as usual;

✔ romance, ambition, envy, lust, sex, betrayal, and jeopardy, as usual;

✔ and the familiar situations of movie-making, parties, beach houses in Malibu, eating in restaurants, staying in hotels, all as usual.

★

What's *Thrill!* really about? The usual two main themes and narratives of Collinsland:

(1) emotional and erotic relationships;

(2) making it in the Western world – pursuing the American Dream. Rags-to-riches, baby! ('I write about the American dream: if

you set your mind to do something, you can do it. My fans know they're getting the real thing', Jackie Collins remarked).

Thrill! is essentially a love story, or the love story element is perhaps the key narrative component. Lara Ivory is at the centre of *Thrill!*: she is impossibly beautiful, a thirtysomething Hollywood star with a troubled past. She is somewhat prim and buttoned-down (never swears), neurotic and self-assured, surrounded by assistants, hairdressers, make-up girls, and overly-protective friends. She's put up a defensive bubble to block out the nightmares, as you do. She's also a one-man woman, faithful and true, who abandons her husband film director Richard Barry when she walks in on him getting head in his trailer.

Joey Lorenzo is the bad boy of the 1998 book – again, highly attractive, but he's spent much of his life mooching off other women. He's a drifter, self-assured but also insecure. He steals 7,000 bucks from his girlfriend, Madeleine Francis, to help his mom. Eventually, he does time for an ugly scene where his mom's wise guy boyfriend Danny gets shot, and comes outta jail wanting to be an actor.

Much of the back-story flashbacks in *Thrill!* concern both Lara Ivory and Joey Lorenzo, with each flashback dipping into their backgrounds, structured chronologically, bringing the story closer to the present tense of the narrative (the same structure is used in many Collins books, including the *Lucky Santangelo* series).

However, *Thrill!* is also an ensemble piece, and there are a host of characters grouped around the central couple of Lara Ivory and Joey Lorenzo, including Lara's friend and producer Nikki Barry; Lara's ex-husband, now married to Nikki, successful, big budget, Hollywood director Richard Barry; Summer, Nikki's wayward, 15 year-old daughter; Summer's father and Nikki's ex, Chicago shrink Sheldon; Summer's pal Tina; Madeleine Francis, a New York agent and Joey's ex; Aiden Sean, an actor with a drug and drink problem who just happens to be brilliant (and steps in to make love to Nikki when Richard drifts away from her); and psycho photographer Alison Sewell, who's obsessed with Lara.

Some of the minor characters in *Thrill!* are fun – Roxy, the earthy, punky hairdresser, and Yoko, the make-up girl. In the early part of the 1998 novel, Roxy comes out with some humorous lines – 'yeah, that's what my date said the other night – right after I told him to screw off on account of the fact he came all over my new

Anne Klein skirt' (42) – so it's a pity when Roxy and Yoko fade from view in the second half of the book.

The setting of *Thrill!* – of movies and Los Angeles and New York – contributes a huge amount to this novel. Jackie Collins refers to real places and people and imaginary places and people without explaining too much – it's assumed that the reader knows plenty about contemporary celebrities and their lifestyles. It's taken for granted that the reader knows all about celebrity culture and magazines like *Hello!, National Enquirer, People* and *OK*, about the lifestyles of the rich and famous, about contemporary movies and movie stars, and about life in Los Angeles and New York City.

Thrill! presents a satirical portrait of a celebrity photographer or *paparazzo* – the unloved Alison Sewell. Jackie Collins combines the *paparazzo* with the celebrity stalker: Sewell is obsessed by Lara Ivory and follows her around. The allusion to Princess Diana and her pursuit by *paparazzi* is clear (*Thrill!* was published a year after Diana's death in 1997). In short, Collins evokes celebrity photographers as vultures, feeding off the stars, and links them to stalkers by fusing them into one character. It certainly isn't flattering. However, Collins is a Super-Class-A Vampire, as rapacious as the *paparazzi* – she's been feeding off the stars and celebrities for her entire career.

The satire is particularly blunt in *Thrill!*, and it's possible that Jackie Collins herself, like J.K. Rowling and other famous authors, has been the subject of celebrity photographers (and Rowling has also spoofed celebrity culture in the *Harry Potter* books).[2]

★

The climax of *Thrill!* involves an action sequence comprising multiple chases towards two locations: Nikki Barry, Aiden Sean and her ex-husband Sheldon racing to find poor, little Summer, who's having a nightmare time in Los Angeles, and Richard Barry, Cassie, Alison Sewell and Joey Lorenzo hurrying to Lara Ivory in the remote beach house North of Malibu. (OK, so credibility goes out of the window here, but, hey, it's the climax of a Jackie Collins novel!).

---

[2] The *Harry Potter* books contain satirical attacks on journalists and tabloid journalism (ruthlessly parodied in the gross caricature of Rita Skeeter, the *Daily Prophet* and *The Quibbler*); and the cult of celebrity (Gilderoy Lockhart, and Harry himself). Jo Rowling's biggest gob of bile is saved for the repulsive journalist Rita Skeeter, who writes for the *Daily Prophet* (and later does a hatchet job on Albus Dumbledore). Skeeter's a stereotypical gossip columnist: aggressive, sly, dishonest, unctuous, who twists everything anyone says. Rowling makes it clear that she regards some journalists as nothing better than (dung) beetles, like flies and parasites who swarm around trash and fæces.

Of course it's raining hard and there's a storm. *Of cours*e there's a car crash (Cassie's injured but the guy in the Porsche dies). *Of course* there's a rockslide[3] and Barry's killed. *Of course* evil psycho Sewell attacks Lara in the dark house, but *of course* Joey's there, coming to the rescue and nearly dying in the process (*of course* he's saved by a tree branch on the cliff in a fall, and *of course* the stalker-*paparazzo*-psycho plunges to her death in the Pacific Ocean).

You'd have to admit that big-scale action is not always Jackie Collins' strong point (but I always prefer it when she goes for action, and some of her action sequences are superb), but it doesn't matter, because the basic structure of the climax is all worked out according to the goals and rewards of this hyped-up, North American fairy tale. So each character gets what's coming to them, pretty much, with no surprises among the winners and losers.

Thrill!'s fairy tale ending occurs in the epilogue, which shifts forward to 'a year later', and ties up some of the plot lines, with the major one – the Lara-Joey romance – coming last, in the privileged position (the equivalent in a movie of the close-up on the lovers' clinch). The compressed format of the epilogue in *Thrill!* also sidesteps the need for the author to stage the key scene, which's the disclosure scene, when Lara and Joey tell each other their darkest secrets. The 1998 novel has been building up to this moment, but doesn't, in the end, show it. Again, that doesn't matter too much, because this fairy story can have only one ending for the two lovers.

And that is: ❤ ❤ ❤ ❤ ❤ ❤ ❤

★

---

3 L.A. had experienced an earthquake in 1994.

LOVERS & PLAYERS

2005's *Lovers & Players* was another of Jackie Collins' more recent novels set in New York, New York. It contains the usual retinue of Collinsian characters, from the wild boy, male model Jett ❧ and his crazy, Italian, supermodel girlfriend Gianna ❧ to the author-identifying character, Amy ❧ the young, black musician trying to make it, Liberty[4] ❧ and the familiar cast of cutthroats, dodgy music managers, rap music honchos, modelling agents, entertainment lawyers, and pervy billionaires.

Although *Lovers & Players* is writing by following familiar patterns, it works. All of the elements are duly ticked off:

* Dark secrets and revelations from the past. *TICK.*
* Young wannabes desperate to make it. *TICK.*
* A murder plus mystery plus resolution. *TICK.*
* High-class settings, consumerism and clothes. *TICK.*
* New York City, Los Angeles and Las Vegas. *TICK.*
* Suffering and poverty and kids rising from the gutter. *TICK.*
* Sex – straight or boring or kinky. *TICK.*
* Inter-woven storylines. Short chapters. *TICK.*
* Bad deeds are punished; the good guys win out. *TICK.*

The ending of *Lovers & Players* is just too upbeat and pat, though – Amy and Jett get together, Chris and Gianna become a couple, Liberty's reunited with her mom, Diahann re-connects with old flame Leon, Red Diamond's arrested, and on the last page, Liberty hooks up with Damon (after he shows her the papers proving his divorce from his wife – she's been holding out on him).

As you read the final pages of *Lovers & Players,* giant pink hearts ❤ ❤ ❤ float up from the text and pop over you head, emitting soft puffs of Chanel perfume. It's cute (and expensive), but it works.[5]

But *Lovers & Players* is a solid piece of work, and it's certainly entertaining. Yes, we've all been here b4, whether it's in Jackie Collins' fiction – or *anyone's else's fiction.* Hmm, because even the

---

[4] 'I have considered rap music stars, and there is one in my new book, Lovers and Players, and there is also a hip-hop music mogul who I think you will like a lot.'

[5] One copy in a thousand of *Lovers Players* was sold with exploding Chanel perfume bubbles. I got the one-in-a-thousand; lucky me!

works of the greatest of them all – Dante Alighieri or Homer or Bill Shakespeare – get repetitive after a while.

What makes Shakespeare and Dante 'high art', and Jackie Collins 'low art' or 'popular art'? And does it matter any more? Not really. That argument was bogus from the start.

Yes, *Lovers & Players* is another fairy tale – with sex and cel phones added. The clarity of Jackie Collins' prose is undeniable – there is no confusion about what she is writing about, and what she is trying to say. No, scratch that – she isn't 'trying', she's *saying it*!

Yes, *Lovers & Players* is a genre piece – and the genre is Collins Fantasy Land, her own version of blockbuster fiction. Part family saga, part chick lit, part murder mystery, part city novel, part airport kitsch – it's Collins' vision of life in the contemporary world of the West, of North America, of New York and Los Angeles, that really pulls it together.

Memorable lines in *Lovers & Payers*:

'Men. They were either gay, into kinky sex, cheating on their wives, momma's boys, jerks, drug users, cheats, pimps, or actors – the worst kind' (9).
★
In school we never got into who had the best grades, it was always whose father had the biggest grossing movie and whose mother was on the cover of *People*. (433)

I love that idea – in the school playground, the kids are saying to each other: 'my dad's crude comedy *Kiss My Ass!* grossed 14 mil Friday night, so you can bite my butt!'

MARRIED LOVERS

Married Lovers (2008) – it has the dedication: 'For my three daughters – Tracy, Tiffany and Rory. My greatest achievements' – was a middling Jackie Collins outing. As you know by now, I prefer my Jackie Collins bitchy and full of energy, with plenty of electrical crackle arcing between the characters (what Collins calls 'heat'). Lashings of barbed one-liners, and sex, and comedy.

Married Lovers didn't have that: because apart from the running back-story of child prostitute Anya and her voyage of agony and vengeance from Russia thru Amsterdam to the New World, this was almost exclusively a *relationship* novel. That is, *Married Lovers* was all about romantic, erotic relationships among the inter-connected denizens of dear, old Los Angeles. X fancies Y but Y prefers Z. You know the score.

Married Lovers was centred around Cameron Paradise, the main author-identification figure, a personal trainer in her mid-20s. Do I need to tell you she's gorgeous, independent, practical, ambitious, has 2 dogs, and left her abusive husband in Hawaii to start a new life in the City of Angels? Let Collins tell ya:

> Cameron was a stunningly beautiful woman in a sporty casual way. Five feet eight inches tall with a well-toned body, flawless skin, high cheekbones [6] and dirty blonde hair worn short and spiky with long bangs that drifted sexily above her pale green eyes. (6)

All of the other characters in *Married Lovers* are cookie-cutter Collinsians, ranging from cute and charismatic to weird and dangerous. Oh mama, can anyone find happiness and true lerrrve in this crazy old city?

The central section of *Married Lovers* largely concerns Cameron Paradise being split emotionally between two guys, Don Verona, the Craig Fergusonesque talk show host, and Ryan Richards, the unhappily married film director. Verona seems much more fun to me – wealthy, smart, witty, a Hollywood player – but although both 39 year-old men are attractive, and basically good people (i.e., they don't have any of the warning signals that Collins attaches to unsuitable suitors), it's with Richards that Cameron experiences the authentic 'love at first sight' connection, when she sees him for the first time and looks into those baby blues (though she hardly knows him). So it's the Paradise-Richards relationship in *Married Lovers* that turns out to be the longed-for romance that rounds off the book (in pride of place in the last pages).[7]

Married Lovers contained the usual Collinsian settings: big houses in Bel Air, a gym, a Malibu retreat, countless restaurants and hotels. And the regular group of characters: hot-shot screenwriters,

---

6 Wait, where's the 'wide, sensual mouth'!?
7 It does seem a little lame that it takes a year and a half for Richards and Paradise to finally get together. Her reason doesn't quite fly, either: 'Just lazy, I guess'. But who wants a lazy-ass heroine?

independent film directors, talk show hosts, a dull, spurned soap star, an ageing actress desperate to make a comeback, a U.C.L.A. screenwriter, and plenty of Hollywood wives. And not one but two abusive husbands intent on revenge.

Nobody would call *Married Lovers* Jackie Collins' finest novel, or her most memorable, but it does move along pretty well, if slower and more dialogue-heavy than some of her other books (too much of the dialogue is low wattage, and about nothing in particular). Yet *Married Lovers* does possess the secret ingredient of popular fiction: that magic Page-Turner element which every publisher wants to put in a bottle and sprinkle like Disney Fairy Dust over every book they put out.

Yes, even low-power books like *Married Lovers* keep you reading on to find out what happens. But part of the problem with *Married Lovers* is that altho' Cameron Paradise is appealing and attractive, with a healthy suspicion of (and disinterest in) celebrity culture (and a vehement dislike of *paparazzi* and attention), she doesn't have a single flaw. The biggest issue she has to deal with is her Husband From Hell, Gregg, who tracks her down to L.A.

So if there's a theme to *Married Lovers* it's about finding love, about women finding a guy who's decent, about women trusting men. Because Anya the Russian prostitute's trajectory echoes Cameron's, except it's on a whole other level of abuse and horror. Anya's had one of the worst times any character in Collins Land has undergone, and she's on a trail of revenge. Cameron, meanwhile, fled her violent schlub and wants to start over and forget all about it (except she can't). In Jackie Collins' *œuvre*, the past always catches up with you, and in due course the abusive pig Gregg returns (though quite late in the piece).

★

One element in *Married Lovers* rankles with me: that it's Anya, the Russian prostitute who's undergone unspeakable misery as an under-age hooker, and been exploited to the max, who is killed by the psycho husband Gregg in the climactic siege scene. Anya has been the subject of the continuous flashback sequence in italics in *Married Lovers* – and in a Jackie Collins book, that means Bad Stuff Is Happening, and the outcome will not be good. It's true that Anya does swear revenge on men in general for the horrific way she's been treated. But although she works her way socially upscale, from one relationship/ marriage to another, until she snags the ageing billionaire Hamilton Heckerling, she doesn't hurt or kill anyone. She isn't the stalker psycho of the usual flashback narrative in Collins' books. But she's murdered, and everybody else walks free.

★

THE POWER TRIP

In 2012, Jackie Collins published *The Power Trip,* a stand-alone novel about a group of couples on a luxury cruise in Mexico aboard a luxury yacht. This made a change from the usual settings of Collinsland, of L.A. or Gotham; actually, of course Collins used those settings once again (plus London, Miami, and Paris), drawing vignettes of the charas before the trip.

The Power Trip featured the usual retinue of Collinsesque characters: supermodels (Bianca),[8] Russian business tycoons (Aleksandr Kasianenko), soccer stars and their wives (Taye and Ashley, very much evoking Britain's boring Beckhams), high power journos (Flynn and Xuan), famous film stars (Cliff Baxter, in the George Clooney/ Jack Nicholson mold), former waitresses/ wannabe actresses (Lori), bratty teenagers, Russian gangsters (Sergei Zukov), etc. (Some aspects of *The Power Trip* seemed to draw on the 2010 *Paris Connections* film – there's a Russian tycoon called Aleksandr, for instance, plus fashion models, etc, though not tying in directly like *The Stud* and *The Bitch* did with their films).

There were the usual thriller/ murder plots in *The Power Trip* (Sergei Zukov wants revenge for the death of his brother Boris). A bunch of rich and famous people on a boat is a perfect stage for murder, of course.

The Power Trip is again composed in very short sections – typically a page and a half. And, again, the same scenarios are used as in many previous Jackie Collins outings (packed off to a Swiss boarding school, for ex, and the same names: Venus, Sierra, Hudson, etc). Well, *The Power Trip* was Collins' 29th novel, so repetitions seem inevitable.

The Power Trip was another relationship story – it's essentially a portrait of several couples. No marriage or relationship, needless to

---
[8] Bianca is one of 'the most famous women of colour in the modelling world', alongside Tyra Banks, Beverly Johnson and Naomi Campbell (64).

say, is 'happy' or fulfilled or without its flaws.

❧ So 24 year-old Lori is pissed that middle-aged, mega-star Cliff Baxter is planning to dump her (Baxter tells everybody in every interview that he's not the marrying kind, and never will be);

❧ So Russian oligarch Aleksandr Kasianenko is trying to wrest himself free from his wife Rushana so he can propose to moody, headstrong model Bianca;

❧ So Taye is devoted to his wife Ashley but she seems perpetually grumpy;

❧ So Senator Hammond Patterson seems to have the perfect marriage with Sierra Snow, but she's deeply unhappy, and he's a mean S.O.B. underneath the smooth, liberal exterior;

❧ So tall, thin, grouchy, ambitious, social climber, English designer Jeromy is jealous of his younger, blonde, Mexican, superstar boyfriend Luca Perez;

❧ So Flynn discovers that the love of his life, Sierra, is also on the cruise...

In *The Power Trip*, the relationships become entangled, as everyone seems to lust after anyone but their significant others. Thus, Ashley's smitten by Mr Movie Star, Cliff Baxter, but her husband Taye remains devoted to her (after all, she's allowing him sex every night on their vacation); Baxter wonders if settling down with Lori might be a good thing after all; Bianca works herself up into a jealous rage because her Russian tycoon boyfriend is spending too much time with 'Miss Intensity' (as Bianca dubs her), the do-gooder, Chinese journo, Xuan; Jeromy seethes with resentment because he can feel his blond, Mexican superstar is slipping out of his grasp; so Flynn and Sierra, the would-be golden couple of *The Power Trip*, finally get to meet and talk, realizing that Hammond (one of the nastiest of Collins' villains) callously split them up years ago (with some faked photographs); and Hammond meanwhile is hitting on anything with a pulse.[9]

As usual, Jackie Collins adds a thriller plot to the relationship-romance witch's cauldron: in *The Power Trip*, it concerns a kidnap scheme by Sergei Zukov, hoping to nab Aleksandr Kasianenko, who supposedly dispatched his brother Boris. Sergei has hired a bunch of Somali pirates, no less, led by Cruz. His daughter, Mercedes,[10] is a feisty, independent, young woman who's the spy on the yacht, the

---

[9] So maybe a trout would do.
[10] Mercedes is a very enjoyable character, and you wish there was more of her in *The Power Trip*.

Bianca. Mercedes is busy setting up the raid (seducing the Russian bodyguard Kyril for instance, confiscating ammunition, and scoping out the cash and jewellery she's gonna lift when the operation's over).

The kidnap/ pirate plot in *The Power Trip* is kept simmering in the background, as Jackie Collins cuts from the yacht and the visits to islands in the Sea of Cortez to the Russian gangster Sergei Zukov (and also an accusation of sexual assault against Hammond Patterson in the Bill Clinton vein).

The pirate raid provides the climactic set-piece for *The Power Trip*, and it's certainly one of Jackie Collins' finer episodes. She's done the research about hostage scenarios, kidnappings, ransoms and the rest. Sure it reads like a Hollywood action movie – that's the whole point! This is *Jackie Collins* we're talking about! But when Collins gets down and dirty with the boys (the macho novelists), and creates an action-filled sequence, it's exciting and convincing. Collins has included the essential bits about cutting communications, the heroes taking an assailant hostage, the hurrying to and fro around the dark ship, and of course the mandatory storm at sea. (Plus Collinsian touches, like Mercedes and Cashoo having a flying fuck in the midst of the raid – there's always time for a flying fuck in a Jackie Collins novel).

During the pirate attack, Flynn, the macho journalist, proves his mettle (I mean, his *cojones*, as Miz. Collins likes to say), and assumes the role of leader as the heroes fight back (making sure the women're led to the safe room, for instance, and grabbing one of the Somali pirates, Amin). A pity, tho', that the girls don't get to burst out of the panic room to tackle the Mexican firecracker Mercedes, when Bianca spots her robbing Aleksandr's safe (Bianca is all for taking on Mercedes, but the other women prefer to stay out of harm's way in the safe room). Happily, Collins *doesn't* portray the women being reduced to quivering wrecks in the face of danger, and they're able to climb the ropes up to Aleksandr's stateroom (tho' Ashley, the British wimp, does get close to losing it).

Who's gonna die in the pirate raid in *The Power Trip*? We know someone is! After all, Sergei Zukov is determined to make Aleksandr Kasianenko pay dearly for killing his brother Boris, and Hammond Patterson has been threatening his wife Sierra Snow with the death of her former boyfriend Flynn.

In the end, it's the ultra-sleazy politico Hammond who's killed (and it's another of Jackie Collins orgasm-and-death scenarios: just as the Senator tups Renee, an Australian maid, taking her virginity, he's shot in the back). Killed by the Somali Basra, Hammond's demise of course leaves the way clear for Flynn and Sierra to get together with the loves of their lives – each other (but poor Renee is catatonic with shock).

At the end of *The Power Trip*, in the epilogue (three months later), Jackie Collins decides *not* to play out the plots as expected. Thus, altho' Flynn and Sierra get pride of place as the last entry in the epilogue, they *don't* wind up together – and this's after Collins has laid the groundwork, by portraying Hammond Patterson as a vile sleazebag, the guy who split them up years ago, and who issues death threats, by killing Hammond,[11] and by making sure there's plenty of sizzle and heat between Flynn and Sierra in the present day. But no, the happy ending doesn't occur for them.

The rest of *The Power Trip*'s epilogue plays out pretty much as expected, except that several loose ends are left dangling: Cruz and Mercedes get away, and Sergei Zukov doesn't nab his prey, Aleksandr Kasianenko (nor is Sergei caught). Cliff Baxter decides to marry Lori, Ashley gets pregnant, Luca and Jeromy split up (Luca re-unites with Suga, as well as finding a new boyfriend), Bianca and Aleksandr go their separate ways (Aleksandr invites Xuan to join him in Moscow). And so on.

★

---

[11] The sexual assault case against Hammond (exploited in the press by his out-of-control daughter who goes by the name of 'Radical' (!)), is swiftly forgotten, and now Hammond's deemed a hero who protected a young woman from the Somali pirates.

THE *MADISON CASTELLI* SERIES

L.A. CONNECTIONS

L.A. Connections (1999) was initially published as four short stories: *Power, Obsession, Murder* and *Revenge*. A new lead character, Madison Castelli, is introduced to the glamorous and sleazy world of – where else? – Los Angeles. L.A.... always L.A., the City of Angels (and why not? It's a fantastic city). Castelli is an appealing character: late twenties, incredibly attractive (*duh, of course*), tall, smart, independent. She's a major babe (she's Lucky Santangelo all over again – note the Italiano name, Castelli), but chooses to disguise it:

> try as she might, nothing could disguise her almond-shaped eyes, sharply defined cheekbones, seductive lips, smooth olive skin, and black unruly hair, which she usually wore pulled back in a severe ponytail. Not to mention her lithe, five-foot-eight inch body, with full breasts, narrow waist and long legs. (12)

Madison Castelli's a Gotham journalist who's recently been jilted by her two-year lover David. So she's out on her own, visiting L.A. to do a story for the magazine she works for, *Manhattan Style*.[12]

So far so good.

L.A. Connections is a mystery or thriller story, a who-dunnit. Unfortunately, Jackie Collins is not the most accomplished mystery or detective writer in the business (or not here, at least). She is not Raymond Chandler (one of her childhood idols), and I found *L.A. Connections* a little too routine and straight and uninspired. The witty, bitchy humour and sarcasm is there, but not as successfully delivered as in books like *Hollywood Wives* or *American Star*. In short, *L.A. Connections* is not vintage Jackie Collins.

Another problem with *L.A. Connections* is that the characters are just not that fascinating. We have all of the usual Collins people here:

❖ Natalie, Madison's friend, a TV presenter of entertainment news.

❖ Her co-anchor on the show, Jimmy, who's handsome and doing better than Natalie.

---

[12] Collins covered similar territory in 1975's *The World is Full of Divorced Women*, where Cleo James is a New York journalist who's sent to London for an assignment.

♣ A photographer, Jake Sica (Jimmy's brother), who falls for Kristin Carr the call-girl, that Madison also likes.
♣ The super-agent Freddie Leon who's a workaholic and cold as a dead shark (clearly modelled, like Zeppo White in *Hollywood Husbands*, on super-agents in L.A. such as Mike Ovitz and Bryan Lourd – a reference to Ovitz is included, including his famous run-in with the Walt Disney corporation).
♣ Leon's long-suffering wife (he's having an affair with his secretary, Ria Santiago).
♣ Leon's partner at the agency Max Steele, the multiple womanizer of every Collins novel.
♣ There's Mr X, the serial killer who's killing call-girls.
♣ Salli Turner is the voluptuous bimbo and TV presenter who turns out to have a sweet personality, but is brutally murdered.
♣ There's Salli's rough boyfriends, Eddie Stoner and Bobby Skorch (who's an Evil Knievel daredevil).
♣ And Howie, the playboy son of rich parents, who turns out to be the psycho killer, Mr X.

Madison Castelli, at least in this 1999 book, is not Jackie Collins' most successful characterization. Making her a journalist instead of a detective gives her some of the same functions – a journalist can investigate crimes and move in a variety of social circles, like a detective, and is on a quest (for a story) like a 'tec (and a journalist is of course a common stand-in for the author themselves).

The sleazy aspect of *L.A. Connections* is the high-class call-girl circuit, with Kristin Carr as the call-girl who becomes a victim of Mr X, and Darlene as the madam partly inspired by Heidi Fleiss. There's a nasty, vindictive side to *L.A. Connections* which I found off-putting and disturbing. That's always been a part of Jackie Collins' fictional world, but because *L.A. Connections* is a thriller, the brutal murders are part of the central narrative. They are not one of the sub-plots.

Towards the end of *L.A. Connections*, Madison Castelli takes on much more of a private detective role than a journalist, as the plot thickens and works towards the climax and the death of the bad guy, Mr X. Part of the problem with Madison as a central character is that she doesn't have any major flaws. She's kinda great at everything.

Structurally, *L.A. Connections* is a murder mystery like a million other murder mysteries: it opens with a killing which's solved at the end of the book. Along the way, a host of possible suspects are set up, keeping the reader guessing. Many elements of this book were recycled for the movie *Paris Connections* (alongside *The Power Trip*).

★

LETHAL SEDUCTION

Madison Castelli became the star of her own series, with Jackie Collins writing follow-up books, such as *Lethal Seduction* and *Deadly Embrace*.

The sequel to *L.A. Connections* is *Lethal Seduction* (2000). It's a novel with Ms Collins writing well below her talents. Oh, it contains many of the elements we know and love in Collins Fantasy Land, but it's not a patch on, say, *Hollywood Husbands* or *Thrill!* Part of the issue with *Lethal Seduction* is that the narrative elements aren't particularly engaging. Instead of the murder mystery of *L.A. Connections*, the secret to be solved in *Lethal Seduction* is the true identity of Madison Castelli's father, Michael. Turns out he was a hit-man for the mafia (sound familiar? Been here before? We all have, kiddo!).

Apart from that, much of *Lethal Seduction* is about relationships, including Madison C.'s on-off affair with cute but distant photographer Jake Sica. The mystery about Madison's father fades from view, and is only called in late in the narrative (to help clean-up a death in a Vegas hotel – shades of the *Lucky Santangelo* books). Instead, Collins concentrates on getting her characters to a climactic sequence set in Vegas, for a boxing match.

The rest of the characters in *Lethal Seduction* are familiar Jackie Collins types: Dexter Falcon the soap star, Joel Blaine the playboy stud son of a millionaire, Jamie Nova the gorgeous model and designer, and Carrie Hanlon, a supermodel. And there's Rosarita Falcon, easily the most fun character in *Lethal Seduction* – a super-bitch, eternally dissatisfied with everything, she has some great, catty dialogue. The ditzy, blonde stripper from Vegas, called Varoomba (on account of her enormous bust), is another enjoyable character (particularly in the exchanges with Chas, the wise-guy father of Rosarita and her dull, straight sister, Venice). And some of the characters from *L.A. Connections* return, such as Jake Sica and Michael Castelli.

Rosarita Falcon's kookoo plans to murder her husband Dexter Falcon by poisoning him absorb some of the narrative of *Lethal Seduction*, as do her assignations with bad boy Joel Blaine (he's into exhibitionism, and likes to shtupp Rosarita with half of New York City watching thru the windows of a skyscraper). Another sub-plot is Jamie's suspicions about her husband's infidelity. Turns out he's gay, and has taken up with another guy.

Characters from Jackie Collins' past novels breeze into *Lethal Seduction* – such as Silver Anderson, now an ageing soap actress, who gives Dexter a blowjob in her dressing room, and veteran rocker Kris Phoenix (from *Rock Star*), who has a near-fling with Jamie. And the locations in *Lethal Seduction* are New York and Las Vegas, with a stop-over in L.A. (naturally – it's not a Jackie Collins novel unless we are checking in to the Beverly Hills Hotel).

★

DEADLY EMBRACE

Deadly Embrace (2002) is the third *Madison Castelli* book, except this time it's very much about Madison's father, Michael Castelli. *Deadly Embrace* could be better titled as 'Michael Castelli and his women and his children', because that's what it's all about. Madison herself features only a hostage in an over-the-top kidnapping scenario in L.A.

Deadly Embrace is another of Jackie Collins' voyages into the past, this time going back not only to the youth of Madison Castelli's daddy Michael, but also to his parents, Vinny and Anna Maria. And it's another revenge narrative, with Michael haunted by the death of his mother and the crippling of his father by the local hoods (Mame, Bone and Roy). The vengeance theme plays out across the generations (like the Santangelo<->Bonnatti feud in the *Lucky Santangelo* books), with Madison's mother Beth being killed after Michael murders Roy, the cousin of Mame (and Mame's married to the neighbourhood mob boss Vito Giovanni).

Deadly Embrace is also a post-9/11 novel: the dedication at the front of the book is to the people involved in the terrorist attacks of September 11, 2001. Thus, the hostage scenario which occurs in the present day of *Deadly Embrace*, involving Madison and her friends Natalie and Cole, consciously alludes to the terrorists taking control of the planes on 9/11 (how the kidnappers don't seem to care if they kill anyone, for instance. And notice that Collins sets the present day action on July, 10-11, 2001, two months exactly before 9/11).

You have to admit that the narrative structure that Jackie Collins opted for in *Deadly Embrace* is clunky and not wholly successful. It employs the familiar strategy of having events in the present day intercut with an on-going dip into the past (in the usual *rondo* musical form). Thus, each chapter has titles such as '1975' or '1982', and explores a different stage in two people's lives: Dani Livingston and Michael Castelli, and the people surrounding them. Additionally, in the present day scenes, there are other narratives apart from Madison & co. being taken hostage (they include Michael's offspring, Vincent in Las Vegas (plus his friends), and Sofia, travelling in Europe).

The structure of *Deadly Embrace* is thus not only fragmented, it's bitty and confusing. Ultimately, *Deadly Embrace* is a familiar mixture of Collinsian ingredients – not a feast, like the *Lucky Santangelo* books or the *Hollywood* series – more like room service in a Vegas suite, where you eat the fries and ice cream and leave everything else. Nothing wrong with that, of course – *Deadly Embrace* does feel like a night out in Las Vegas. And *what happens in Vegas, stays in Vegas* – because after reading a Jackie Collins book, you experience the razzle and the dazzle, the high romance and the high octane, but you can leave it all behind.

Like the best fantasy literature, a Jackie Collins novel is a self-enclosed and self-perpetuating world, a realm with its own rules and codes of behaviour. Like Las Vegas, you *know* you're gonna have a good time. There's simply no question about it, Collins *delivers*. You see a blackjack table you like, a dealer who's pretty cute in a cowboy hat and black-and-white vest, with plenty of skin on display, and off you go. In a Collins book, you turn the page, the dialogue hits with short, crisp statements, and you're sucked in.

Deadly Embrace is also another of those love affairs over decades which Jackie Collins likes to depict, with numerous obstacles and set-backs preventing the lovers – Dani and Michael

– from being together. It's true love, deep love, eternal love – 'he was the love of her life, and he always would be' (402) – and the reader knows it's all going to turn out well, but the author piles on the impediments, right up to the final chapters.

Yes, and *Deadly Embrace* is also a novel set in the Big Three Cities – 1. Gotham (i.e., New York), 2. 'the Meadows' (i.e., Las Vegas), and 3. the Angels (i.e., Los Angeles):

> As they neared the bright lights of Vegas, she went into shock. 'It's – it's like fairyland,' she gasped, darting her head this way and that.
>   'Just you wait,' Sam said, chuckling. 'You got the good stuff to come.'
>   'I do?'
>   'Bet on it.'
>   And sure enough, the moment they hit the Strip she could barely speak. 'Oh, my Lord!' she exclaimed. 'Look at all these people.' (42)

★

THE NUMBER ONE BESTSELLER

Jackie Collins

Wild, notorious, trouble . . . she's . . .

LUCKY

Eleven

'Never Fuck With a Santangelo': The Lucky Santangelo Series

Never fuck with a Santangelo.

Jackie Collins, *Vendetta: Lucky's Revenge* (265)

'BET ON IT': INTRO TO THE *LUCKY SANTANGELO* SERIES

I have said that Jackie Collins hasn't explored historical fiction much, but she has: in the ten *Lucky Santangelo*[1] novels (1981, 1985, 1990, 1996, 1999, 2007, 2009, 2011, 2014 and 2015), Collins has attempted a history of modern America, no less, via the form of the melodramatic thriller, the relationship novel and the gangster genre. But perhaps I am thinking of Collins' model, *The Godfather* (the movie much more than the novel). It was the 1972 film adaptation of the Mario Puzo book that attempted a history of modern America, and succeeded (tho' Collins is a fan of the novel, and her characters are too!). In the fourth *Santangelo* book, the ageing don, Gino Santangelo, tells Lucky:

> 'Paige an' I are sittin' here watchin' *The Godfather*. I take a look at it once a year. *Godfather One* and *Two* – forget *Three*.'
> 'Getting in touch with old friends, huh?' Lucky joked.
> 'One of these days I'll tell you my real life story, kiddo.' He chuckled. 'Gino, the early years. What a movie it'd make!'[2]

The ambition of the *Lucky Santangelo* series is not quite up there with the *Godfather* franchise, but it does cover much of the same ground, from the 1920s, thru the founding of Las Vegas, to the recent era. And the ten *Lucky Santangelo* novels pile up across time, so you need a family tree to keep up with it all (and handily *Drop Dead Beautiful* includes one).

Real-life mafiosi dons who were models for *The Godfather* included Carlo Gambino, and the flamboyant John Gotti (he was played by Armand Assante in an H.B.O. movie). Meanwhile, Lucky takes her name from 'Lucky' Luciano (*Goddess of Vengeance*, 223), a famous figure in the criminal underworld, also the subject of movies (Jackie Collins quotes Luciano as an epigraph for the first *Santangelo* book, *Chances* – along with Al Capone and Vincent Teresa. And Gino Santangelo is likened to Bugsy Siegel and Lucky Luciano).

But the *Lucky Santangelo* series isn't wholly a *Godfather*/ Mario Puzo clone (or tribute) – actually, much of the series is Jackie Collins' usual stamping ground of – you guessed it – New York and Hollywood. Indeed, Lucky Santangelo becomes the head of a film

---
1 Does the name 'Santangelo' come from Giorgio di Sant'Angelo (1936-89), an Italian fashion designer (best-known for his work with lycra)?
2 There *was* a movie made of Gino Santangelo's early years – in the *Lucky Chances* mini-series of 1990. But it wasn't *The Godfather* (however, what gangster epic movie is? No movie has touched *The Godfather*).

studio (Panther Studios), so she's dealing with actors, directors, and film shoots (and her husband Lennie Golden is a comedian turned actor turned director; Lennie is a comedian in the Billy Crystal and Robin Williams mold [*Lady Boss*, 73]). The *Lucky Santangelo* series also includes the familiar fashion models, wannabe starlets, lawyers, agents, photographers, and the like, plus plenty of rivals and villains.

The ten *Lucky Santangelo* novels are:

1. *Chances* (1981)
2. *Lucky* (1985)
3. *Lady Boss* (1990)
4. *Vendetta: Lucky's Revenge* (1996)
5. *Dangerous Kiss* (1999)
6. *Drop Dead Beautiful* (2007)
7. *Poor Little Bitch Girl* (2009)
8. *Goddess of Vengeance* (2011)
9. *Confessions of a Wild Child* (2014)
10. *The Santangelos* (2015)

The *Lucky Santangelo* series was clearly important for Jackie Collins - she began it back in 1981, with *Chances,* her 8th novel (published when Collins was 44). The first three *Lucky Santangelo* books are probably the finest, as stories and prose. It's significant that three of Collins' final books were *Lucky Santangelo* books - *Confessions of a Wild Child,* which explored Lucky's origins, and *The Santangelos* (her last novel), plus *The Lucky Santangelo Cookbook* (the cookbook is a little ironic, because Lucky is well-known for not being interested in cooking, or being a great cook. However, restaurants and eating out are recurring elements of the jet-setting lifestyle of Collins' characters).

The *Lucky Santangelo* series centres around Lucky Santangelo Richmond Stanislopoulos Golden, Jackie Collins' ultimate successful, modern woman, but the series is actually often another of Collins' sagas and relationship stories, involving a large cast of characters. The *Lucky Santangelo* books, for instance, explore Gino Santangelo in the early installments, and, along the way, many other charas, such as Dimitri, Olympia, Paige, Lennie, Brigette, etc.

And, as with Jackie Collins' other books, the same character types crop up in each *Lucky Santangelo* novel - and when one has been killed off, Collins simply invents a new one (often using family/

dynasty motifs – so there is 'son of', or 'sister of'). Hollywood cinema does this with sequels all the time (with its 'old stories with new faces' routine. Hollywood is cranking out movies today that're basically the same as movies of the 1920s. The same sorta charas, the same sorta stories, the same sorta themes, and the same sorta celebrity culture).

Similarly, there are new charas introduced in each *Lucky Santangelo* book – new lovers for Lucky Santangelo, as well as new friends, and of course new opponents or rivals (typically they have a connection to the arch rivalss of the Santangelo family, the Bonnatti clan). Thus, in book four, *Vendetta: Lucky's Revenge*, Donatella Bonnatti is the main villain, keen to pay Lucky back for killing her husband, and in book six, 2007's *Drop Dead Beautiful*, the Bonnattis're resurrected again (the *Godfather* movies did this: in *The Godfather 3*, Vincent was Sonny Corleone's bastard son, and Michael's nephew).

Each *Lucky Santangelo* novel is sort of a 'stand alone' work, but of course the reader benefits if they've read the previous installments. Jackie Collins does provide plenty of plot summaries, tho', and also flashbacks. (These are essential, because Collins' plots do tend to blur together, like her characters, so you need these reminders of the previous storylines).

Each *Lucky Santangelo* book is set a few years earlier than when it was published. Thus, *Chances* was published in 1981 and was set in 1977. *Lady Boss* (1990) is set in the mid-1980s. Jackie Collins has not written one *Lucky Santangelo* book after another, but has returned to the series after publishing other, stand-alone stories, and some stories in her other book series, the *Hollywood* novels. In the later *Lucky Santangelo* books, years are not noted, perhaps because that could negatively date the stories. (However, you can work out roughly when each novel is set by internal evidence). Anyway, it doesn't matter much – a book set in 1986 ain't much different from one set in 2006 or 2016.[3] (Gino was born in 1906 and Lucky in 1950).

MEET LUCKY SANTANGELO.

In each *Lucky Santangelo* book, Lucky Santangelo Richmond Stanislopoulos Golden is described in this manner:

---

[3] Detractors complain that some of Collins' books are not up-to-date, or that Collins hasn't kept up with contemporary culture. But in the world of Collins' fiction, it doesn't matter.

> darkly, exotically beautiful, with a tangle of wild jet curls, dangerous black eyes, smooth olive skin, a full sensual mouth, and a slim body. 7)

This description of Jackie Collins' chief female character is from *Lady Boss*, when the *Lucky Santangelo* series was revving into its highest gear.

In *Vendetta: Lucky's Revenge*, Lucky is described thus:

> Lucky was a wildly beautiful woman in her late thirties with a mass of tangled jet curls, deep olive skin, a full, sensual mouth, black opal eyes and a slender well-toned body. (7)

And in *Goddess of Vengeance:*

> Lucky Santangelo was a lethal force. A woman with a dangerous and powerful past. A strong intelligent woman who seemed able to achieve anything she set her mind on. And a beauty too. (228)

But many Jackie Collins heroines are portrayed thus: Montana in *Hollywood Wives*, for ex, is tall, with black hair, 'gold-flecked tiger eyes' and – *hey!* – 'a wide sensual mouth' (*Hollywood Wives*, 29). Oh man, you just *gotta* have that 'wide sensual mouth'! (And what is a 'wide sensual mouth' used for in Collinsland?! Dishin' the dirt, of course!).

Lucky Santangelo is a go-getter, a jet-setter, a winner against all the odds, a fighter, an achiever:

> She was a fiercely independent, strong-willed woman who never compromised and always took chances. (*Vendetta: Lucky's Revenge*, 7)
> ★
> Wherever she went Lucky brought a room to a standstill, for not only was she wildly beautiful, she was also a powerhouse – a woman to be reckoned with – a force of nature. Street smart and forever savvy – Lucky Santangelo had it all. (*Drop Dead Beautiful*, 4)
> ★
> Lucky was unique, a one-of-a-kind woman who possessed the three Bs in abundance: brains, Beauty and Balls. (*Drop Dead Beautiful*, 106)

In short, Lucky S. is a female version of Gino S., as the narrator (and other charas) remark from time to time: 'she was him in a dress. What a girl!' (*Dangerous Kiss*, 34). 'You're exactly like your father', Paige tells Lucky, 'You look like him, you sound like him, you *are* him' (ib., 312). Gino in turn is of course fiercely proud of her (altho' they have their differences): 'His daughter, Miss Balls of Fire, the original feminist' (ib., 35).

> What was she going to do now? Cry?
> No fucking way. She was a Santangelo. Santangelos didn't cry. (*Dangerous Kiss*, 156)

Never get in Lucky's way! She is a woman on the rise. Or, as the Santangelo family motto has it: '*Never fuck with a Santangelo*'. We wouldn't dare! We know better'n that!

> She was a true star, an incredibly smart businesswoman who could achieve anything she set her mind to. The thing about Lucky was that she needed to be collaborative, but she also needed to be in control. Nobody told Lucky Santangelo what to do. (*The Santangelos*, 8)

According to Jackie Collins' daughter Rory:

> no character captured her heart more than her beloved and immortal Lucky Santangelo. Mum used to say: 'Lucky is who every woman wants to be'. What I do know is that Lucky is exactly who my mother wanted to be – and in many ways she was. (R. Green, 2016)

Lucky admits, and Jackie Collins knows well, that she could not have achieved so much without her father Gino in the *very* patriarchal, *very* masculine, *very* boysy world of gangsters, mobs, syndicates and the like. Well, not in *this* particular world of North America in the 1960s and 1970s, which has stuck quite close to history and reality.

As well as '*never fuck with a Santangelo*', another key mantra of Lucky's, and of Jackie Collins', is: '*girls can do anything*' (it's the dedication in *Lady Boss*, for Collins' daughters). This is *utterly crucial* to Collins' fiction, and Lucky is the embodiment of it. (As Lucky says often, 'bet on it').

Lucky Santangelo is Jackie Collins' Ultimate Survivor – despite all of the set-backs, despite rivals killing people around her, or making attempts on her life, our Lucky wins thru and survives. Nothing, in the end, can hold her back.

And yet, altho' Lucky Santangelo is a successful, ambitious and driven personality, a business woman who's also a workaholic and likes to be in the centre of the action, she is also quite a conventional girl. In terms of love and sex, for instance, Lucky is old-fashioned and traditional. She believes in romance and love, and marriage, and trust, and loyalty. (She has been married several times – to Craven Richmond, Dimitri Stanisopoulos and Lennie Golden).

Lucky Santangelo is an old-school girl when it comes to sex:

good, old heterosexual lovemaking is enough for her. In *Vendetta: Lucky's Revenge*, Lucky thinks:

> She knew some people could only get off by indulging their fantasies, but as far as she was concerned it was kind of a sick obsession. What was wrong with normal sex? Who needed fantasies and props? (365)

Later, tho', Jackie Collins' narrator notes that Lucky was into role-playing with her husband Lennie, and even Tantric sex, which Lennie indulges in (*Goddess of Vengeance*, 278).

Lucky Santangelo also has old-style morals. She isn't one of Jackie Collins' promiscuous characters. Altho' she is a female equivalent of the male characters in many respects, she is conventional, and believes in monogamy. For instance, following Lennie Golden's apparent death in *Vendetta: Lucky's Revenge* (he's been kidnapped, but Lucky doesn't know that, she thinks he's dead), she feels guilty about dating Alex Woods (only the once), even months later.

Jackie Collins' heroines, and the characters portrayed in a mainly positive light, are not drug addicts. Lucky Santangelo, for example, Collins' premier heroine, drinks and smokes when she's at her lowest, and takes an occasional joint. But she is not a regular drug user. Instead, addictions are allotted to the loser charas, to the lazy, out-of-work actors, and the insensitive, egotistical film directors.

Thus, curiously, Jackie Collins doesn't have Lucky Santangelo tupping 100s of men. Well, in her wild child youth she does, but, actually, she is, for much of the *Lucky Santangelo* series, a happily married woman. Or, if not 'happy', then at least a One Man Woman. The man? Lennie Golden, the comedian-turned-film-director. Indeed, Lucky gets hitched to Lennie at the end of the novel *Lucky* – and then remains with him, on and off, for much of the series. So instead of allowing Lucky to have liaisons all over the place in the novels *Lady Boss, Vendetta, Dangerous Kiss, Drop Dead Beautiful, Goddess of Vengeance,* etc, Jackie Collins has Lucky sticking with one guy.

As Lucky Santangelo is rather old-fashioned, and believes in monogamy, the romantic relationship angle in the *Lucky Santangelo* series for the title character is about maintaining a marriage, when it's threatened by arguments, rifts, splits, misunder-standings, adultery, and the appearance of love childs. But Lucky and Lennie survive, becoming one of Hollywood's success stories in marriage. (It's not about Finding True Love, then, as in the romantic fiction genre, but about protecting it once you've found it, and working to keep it alive).

Lucky Santangelo is a mom. Hell, yeah – but she's not a stay-at-home mom: she has a nanny (CeeCee) for the kids, and leaves for work every day (in the novels where she's running Panther Studios). But she *is* a mother, and Jackie Collins repeatedly has Lucky thinking about her kids. They are her solace often. But Lucky is also a panther:

> She wondered if that's what she should do – buy a house in Santa Barbara and forget about the film business, just veg out and be with her kids.
> No way. She'd be bored within days. She needed action, and plenty of it.
> (*Vendetta*, 211)

Lucky Santangelo is a soul music freak (like her creator) – she loves Marvin Gaye, Ottis Redding, Luther Vandross and Smoky Robinson (who doesn't?): 'Old movies and soul music are my two passions', Lucky remarks (*Vendetta: Lucky's Revenge*, 321). 'I'm in the mood for Luther, Bobby Womack, Teddy P., Marvin and Isaac', she purrs in *Lady Boss*, as she sends Boogie (her long-suffering gofer) down to Tower Records on Sunset to buy her some sounds (160). In *Chances*, Lucky trades soul faves with her half-brother, Steven Berkely: Donna Summer, Stevie Wonder, Isaac Hayes, Michael Jackson, Marvin Gaye, Al Green, Otis Redding, Nina Simone, Bille Holiday,[4] etc (300-1).

★

CHANCES

OK, time to jump in the Ferrari and roar off down the Pacific Coast Highway as we consider *Chances*[5] (1981), the first *Lucky Santangelo* novel (and you could argue that it's the First Great Jackie Collins novel; it was her 8th book). *Chances* is set in 1977 (on July 14 and 15), during a black-out in New York City, which brings together the major players: Lucky Santangelo (aged 27), her father Gino (age 71),

---

[4] Collins has her black hooker Carrie working in a brothel with the young Holiday.
[5] Not an original title – one of Joseph Conrad's bestsellers was titled *Chance*.

Gino's colleague Costa Zennocotti, her brother Dario, her black half-brother Steven Berkeley, and Carrie Berkeley (Berkeley's mother).

Chances employs a flashback structure in a *rondo* form: that is, we cut to the past from the present tense in New York (the musical *rondo* structure is A-B-A-C-A-D-A-E, etc). Each chapter is given a date and a name: 'Gino 1928', 'Carrie 1943', etc. When we cut back to the present, we follow the story of Lucky and Steven, trapped in an elevator in between floors in a skyscraper; Dario defending himself from a gay pick-up who's turned violent in his apartment; Carrie venturing up to Harlem to meet a blackmailer during the rioting on the streets in the black-out; and Gino flying back to the U.S.A. after a long absence in Israel (for tax evasion).

The present-day chapters in *Chances* are short, with the bulk of the novel exploring the pasts of Carrie and Gino. *Chances* is very much a New York novel: not only is the present tense set in New York, but many of the flashbacks are too.

> New York. His city. His territory. His *home*. (9)

As with other *Lucky Santangelo* books, *Chances* isn't all about Lucky Santangelo. It is not a *Bildungsroman*, a growing up story, all about a single individual. Several characters, not only Lucky, are given the flashback treatment, as well as the present day scenes: Gino Santangelo, Steven Berkeley, Dario, Costa Zennocotti and Carrie Berkeley. These characters crop up throughout the *Lucky Santangelo* series: Lucky and Gino (father and daughter) are the people who act as the focus, along with Carrie and her son Steven (actually, it's Gino and Carrie would take up more pages and chapters in *Chances* than any other character, particularly in the first half of the novel).

Wow! How sleazy and sensational are the opening chapters of 1981's *Chances*?! Jackie Collins piles on the excessive storytelling: she includes sodomy (between Dario and a pick-up), under-age rape and prostitution, a priest raping a boy, a house fire, a knife fight, racism, under-age pregnancy, theft, minor crime and organized crime, and near-murder (and that's all by page two! Well, it feels like that!).

And in subsequent chapters of *Chances* – particularly those about Carrie Berkeley, the under-age prostitute – we read about gang rape, rape of under-age boys and girls, girls being hooked on heroin and kept like slaves, child abuse, battery of women, etc. (Carrie has perhaps the most painful upbringing of any Jackie Collins character (altho' she has some strong competition!) – add to this that she's black).

This is savage stuff, the law of the city streets where it's dog eat dog (dog rape dog, dog kill dog), and everybody is out to exploit everybody else (hell, that's capitalism, folks!). In this view of early 20th century life, when people get off the boat at Ellis Island, they first try honest trades (cleaning, cooking, laundry), before swiftly being sucked into the underworld of prostitution and crime. Mugging, robbery and coercion is only a hair's-breadth away, and New York City turns out to be one helluva tough place (as in Frank Sinatra's croon – if you can make it here, you can make it anywhere).

It's a grim view of life, it's the underbelly of the Great American Dream. It's extreme, but then, Charles Dickens and Elizabeth Gaskell also explored the under-life of Britain in the 19th century. Jackie Collins' vision is more explicit, in terms of the 'bad language' and some details of graphic sex, but the portrayals of crime and prostitution aren't so much different from Dickens or Gaskell.

In which case, the overriding theme or goal in *Chances* is: *survival*. Whatever it takes, you've gotta survive (Lucky S. is one of the great survivors in Jackie Collins's fiction). But there is a gender split here, where the dice are loaded in favour of men and masculinity and patriarchy: young women like the 13 year-old Carrie are put to work on the streets or in brothels, with little means of choosing their own destiny.

Carrie Berkeley experiences one of Jackie Collins' toughest fictional lives. She's a young, black woman who is forced to become a whore at the age of thirteen; she is hooked on heroin and drugs by a pimp (Whitejack); she is beaten; she slaves away later as a maid (and other menial jobs); she is forced to dance and strip for money; she is raped several times; she is put in a mental institution for years; she has her child kidnapped – and more.

Certainly the *Lucky Santangelo* series is about an important issue: the price of being alive. It's about the costs of success, about the flaws in the Great American Dream. In short, of the will to life.

Using characters who're movie moguls, film stars, lawyers, rock stars, and other achievers, as well as those dwelling in the underbelly of Western society – the gangsters, the hookers, the pimps and the drug lords – acts as a glitzy, flashy, sexy hook.

But the issue is the still the same, whether it's about jet-setting high rollers or down-home farmers in Iowa: it's the Faustian pact of life: are you going to survive? Are you going to pay the price of life, for the pains as well as the pleasures of being alive?

Thus, Jackie Collins is also a moralist, to the extent that her stories are clear that the higher you reach, the more ambitious you are, the costs can be greater.

GINO SANTANGELO.

Chances delves into the back-story of Gino Santangelo in depth, as well as Carrie Berkeley. Gino's story might well have come directly from Mario Puzo's book *The Godfather*. Many elements are very familiar, as if the gangster's way of life is the alternative history of the North American Dream.[6]

So we read about Gino Santangelo's journey from street kid (born in 1906 in Italy) and car mechanic to small-time hood, from his childhood in the Bronx and Harlem (putting up with his useless father Paulo, who beats his hooker girlfriend Vera), to moving out into the wide, wide world. First he does the occasional job for local gangsters (as a car driver), then sets up his own theft and bootlegging business, with Aldo, Pinky Banana (yes, he's called Pinky Banana for *exactly* that reason!),[7] and some hand-picked cronies.

> He wanted money. He wanted all the good things that money could buy. (73)

Five-foot six-inch Gino Santangelo is a confident, cocky Italian-American, a would-be wise guy, a gangster-in-the-making. Gino is given the prerequisite tough childhood (a violent, loser father Paulo, who's in and out of jail), where the struggle to survive is all-encompassing. Gino is a stereotype, sure: he hangs out with the boys, he chases after girls,[8] he tries several low-paid jobs before drifting into the criminal underworld. The newspapers dub Gino 'Infamous Bootlegger', 'Violent Criminal', 'Numbers Racketeer' and

---

[6] The novel goes back to 1909, when it relates the story of Gino Santangelo's folks, Paulo and Mira, coming to North America.
[7] Pinky has a typical Collinsian relationship with women: 'Piranha sat up in bed. She was naked and sported the most pneumatic breasts in the whole of Philadelphia. Sometimes Pinky thought he hadn't married a woman, he had married a pair of tits.' (471)
[8] 'Gino the Ram', as he's known, is a skirt chaser *par excellence*. His secret technique is to touch the clitoris (the 'magic button').

'Notorious Gangster' (640).

One of Gino Santangelo's mantras is:

> 'You've always gotta have a plan, an' you always gotta stick to it' (75)

And Jackie Collins uses that word, *plan*, many times: 'sounds like a plan' is one of Lucky's mantras.

Gino Santangelo is also duped by others as a mug – he stays celibate for a year or so, after falling in love with Leonara, the daughter of Costa's foster parents in San Francisco. He goes back East, and vows to work until he has enough green to marry her. To do the right thing, as they say. At this point, even super-stud 'Gino the Ram' (his nickname) hasn't had Leonara. No, and he steers clear of women for a year, too (and he's just outta jail!). Turns out that Gino's been played for a sap (*Chances* is full of such lingo), and Leonora has already been dating other guys (and gets pregnant, and then married).

Gino Santangelo's rackets, in his small gang, comprise bootlegging (of liquor), and other small crimes. Gino is aligned with 'good' gangsters and conscientious criminals: he draws the line at prostitutionanddrug-running[9] (later he gets into gambling). Stealing, cheating and coercion are OK, but not drugs. So it's the 'bad' gangsters, like the Bonnattis, who deal in narcotics and prostitution (yet Gino works with the Bonnattis). The moral hypocrisy of this outlook is spoofed in the 1998 film *Jane Austen's Mafia!*, where the Don laments the old days: 'we steal things, we kill and dismember people. Now it's all drugs. Where's the honour?'

Jackie Collins has got the underworld of gangsters, hookers, speakeasies, thefts, tenements, bars, restaurants and brothels down pat. *Chances* isn't a Great Novel in the sense of classics like *Anna Karenina* or *U.S.A.* or *The Great Gatsby*. But so what? It reads well, it's entertaining, and it also contemplates Major Themes like Death, Love, Loss, Ambition, Crime and Survival.

> He *knew* there was a better life out there somewhere. And he *knew* the only way to get it was with money. (76)

The film directors of gangster movies are fêted by critics: Tsui Hark, 'Beat' Kitano, John Woo, Francis Coppola, Martin Scorsese,

---

[9] 'Gambling, loansharking, the numbers racket. He refused to touch prostitution and drugs in spite of pressure from Enzio' (246).

Abel Ferrara, Ringo Lam, Brian de Palma, Quentin Tarantino, etc. Why not Jackie Collins too? *Chances*, and other *Lucky Santangelo* novels, are as entertaining as the great gangster movies, and finer-crafted than many of them, too (and certainly *far* more explicit than any 'R' rated movie).

Chances explores a famous chapter in North American gangsterdom – the creation of Las Vegas. Jackie Collins refers to real-life mobsters such as Bugsy Siegel, who was in at Las Vegas at the beginning (and was killed soon after for his corruption). So Gino Santangelo founds a syndicate to build a hotel in Vegas, the Mirage (aided by Jacob Cohen, the Boy).

> Lucky walked to the very edge of her terrace and leaned over. The view was staggering – a shimmering city of lights – a neon paradise. (672)

☆

Gino Santangelo is the successful son with a loser father – Paulo disappoints Gino in every respect, to the point where he doesn't want to see him anymore. Unfortunately, Gino's step-mom, Vera (yet another hooker), is too fond of Paulo (allowing him to beat her repeatedly). This particular relationship reaches a climax halfway thru *Chances*, when Gino discovers Paulo punching Vera one more time, and Vera holding a gun and shooting him. Unfortunately, Gino takes the rap for this murder, and goes to prison for seven years (this isn't Gino's only time inside).

In jail, incredibly, Gino Santangelo discovers books. Yes, *books!*

> *The Great Gatsby* from cover to cover. And then again. Reading wasn't half bad. He wondered why he'd never tried it before. (319)

As Sam Goldwyn put it, 'I read part of the book right the way through'.

In the course of his career, Gino Santangelo kills – Senator Richmond asks him to deal with a young, black kid who's blackmailing him (the old man wrote silly, incriminating love letters). Gino takes care of it, and kills two people in the process (when they attack him). Meanwhile, Gino's wife Cindy and Sam Lawson (a private detective) suffer unexplained deaths (these were contracts, not murders that Gino performed himself), and Cindy's toyboy Henry Moufflin had a bad car accident. .

Later in *Chances*, Gino Santangelo orders a hit on 'the Boy', Jacob Cohen, who's been stealing from the Mirage hotel business in

Las Vegas. There is a war over the control of the Las Vegas operation – Enzio Bonnatti, with Gino's agreement, goes after Pinky Banana, but in the event his wife is killed (in a car explosion straight out of *The Godfather*). In retaliation, Pinky murders Gino's wife Maria. The reprisals continue (Gino deals with Pinky, who's been a rival since their days in Gotham, personally).

Gino Santangelo's life is filled with women in Jackie Collins' version on the gangster genre. By the time he's successful, he can take his pick. Some women prove to be trouble – like Cindy, his first wife (altho' he would've preferred to have married Leonora). When Gino falls for socialite Clementine Duke, Cindy, jealous, has him followed by private detectives. Thinking she's got the better of Gino, and demanding a divorce (she already has another guy lined up), she threatens him with exposing his business enterprises. Astonished, Gino can't believe that *she* is threatening *him*. So Cindy duly takes an accidental tumble from their high-rise apartment (and the private detective Sam Lawson and the Henry Mouffin are also taken care of).

Clementine Duke is one of Jackie Collins' older, sophisticated women who fall for younger, rougher guys: Gino Santangelo is fascinated by Clementine (he even names his club, Clemmies, after her), and they conduct a passionate affair. Clementine's husband, Senator Richmond, advises Gino on his business interests. Richmond is partial to (often black) teenage boys, and has Gino clean up the occasional blackmailer (it's a pretty boy who threatens to blackmail the Senator).

Another of Gino Santangelo's women in *Chances* is Bee, a loving and – unusually – regular woman, very different from the showgirls, film starlets and hookers he sometimes fools around with. Unfortunately, altho' Bee waits for Gino for the entire seven years he spends in the penitentiary (after taking the rap for Vera shooting his father, Paulo), and visits him every week, he ends up being bored by life with her and her child in New York. One day, he simply walks out.

And there's sex in *Chances*: with Cindy:

> He turned her over and entered her from behind and rode her like they were two dogs in the street. They were both in a frenzy when the third orgasm hit them. It was short, hot and wild. And only then did Gino feel at peace. (177)

With Clementine:

> 'Bend over the table. I won't disturb a thing.'
> She did as she was told, anticipation flooding her whole body. He entered her from behind. Slowly, luxuriously, as though they had all the time in the world.
> 'Ooooh…' her breath fluttered, 'you certainly learned your lesson well.' (252)

And with Bee:

> He grabbed her by the cheeks of her ass as they lolled in bed.
> 'Gino! Not again!'
> He grunted and eased himself in from behind.
> She raised her big white bottom and he pumped easily in and out. It was the third time, but the pleasure was still as sharp. (368)

Maria, the daughter of the Love of His Life That Never Was (Leonora), becomes the One for Gino Santangelo. He is crazy about her, and she becomes the mother of Lucky Santangelo and his son Dario. Leonora develops into a hard-bitten, cynical alcoholic, who loathes Gino with a vengeance. Maria, her spitting image, is twenty when she and Gino get together (in the late 1940s).

But this is the period of the war over Las Vegas, the hotels, resorts and gambling, and it's Maria who's the major victim. One day Lucky, aged five, discovers her mother floating in the swimming pool, dead, in 1955 (an event which haunts Lucky for the rest of her life, and is reprised in every *Lucky Santangelo* entry).

For Gino Santangelo, Marie's murder is the cost of survival, and of making it big, in the Great American Dream. You can have all you want, but you'll have to pay for it – sometimes with the most precious thing in your life.

Yet another slice of North American celebrity legend that Jackie Collins uses in the 1981 novel *Chances* is Marilyn Monroe. So Collins creates Marabelle Blue, a wayward film star suffering from low self-esteem and depression who's seeing a Senator in Washington. Inevitably, Marabelle attaches herself to Gino Santangelo who, for a time, is besotted with her (this is a woman that half of the United States of America would give their right ball to sleep with, as Collins' narrator puts it). But in the end the sloth and the depression prove too much (plus the suicide attempts), so Gino and Costa arrange the removal of Marabelle to a house in Mulholland Drive (by bringing back her estranged stunt-man husband).

★

LUCKY.

The 1981 novel *Chances* also relates the teen years of Lucky Santangelo, which includes being sent to boarding school in Switzerland by Gino Santangelo, and playing the rebellious daughter (along with her friend Olympia Stanislopoulos) - hanging out in the South of France in a villa, and sneaking out of boarding school with Olympia, where Lucky discovers the joys of boys (fooling around with kids like Ursi. When she touches Ursi's weiner for the first time, Lucky is impressed: "Oh my!' she said in awe. 'Wow!" Soon, Ursi is 'coming in a series of triumphant spurts' over her hand, and Lucky is excited: 'Lucky grinned. She felt the power. She wanted more' [507]).

Jackie Collins portrays Lucky Santangelo in *Chances* as a 'wild child': she had already written of wild girls, a favourite character type, but Lucky is the premier 'wild child'. Indeed, Collins went back to Lucky's youth in one of her last books, *Confessions of a Wild Child* (2013). However, most of the significant areas of Lucky's teen years had already been explored in *Chances* - *Confessions of a Wild Child* is simply a (tamer) reworking of the same material, with slight variations (writing in the first person, for instance).

★

Anyway, back to our Ferrari sportscar dash through *Chances*: the novel builds towards the merging of the present day stories (July, 1977) with the flashbacks. So that, as we follow the lives of Carrie, Steven, Lucky, Dario and Gino in the past, we reach a coupla years before 1977.

The finale of *Chances* focusses on the new hotel being built in Las Vegas, the Magiriano (a combination of the names Gino and Maria). This is Lucky's Big Project, which she has lavished her attention on (the motif is reprised later, in *Drop Dead Beautiful*, with the Keys resort). Unfortunately, Enzio Bonnatti and his organization have set their sights on the Marigiano, too (Bonnatti has a stake in the Mirage, but he wants the Marigiano). Things reach meltdown when, after a single night of passion with her schoolgirl crush, Marco (Gino's man in Vegas), is gunned down by the Kassarri twins (they were also responsible for the murder of Lucky's mother, Maria, in 1955).

That's one climactic sequence in *Chances*; the other is the arrival from Israel of Gino Santangelo in New York City in the present day

(1977). As usual in a Jackie Collins yarn, nothing goes according to the schedule. Gino might be back, but his kids have been rebelling! Lucky doesn't want to be treated like a girl anymore, and wants part of the action of running several businesses (including the Vegas hotels and casinos). Gino doesn't see it like that – at all! So they agree to disagree.

Meanwhile, Dario has been playing the role of the Wayward Son like a movie star – diving into the sleazy underworld of gay New York, holding riotous parties (in Gino Santangelo's apartment), and begrudging his sister, Lucky, for the amount of power she holds within the family.

Marco[10] being shot dead outside the Magiriano is over-the-top, and it's replayed outside the hotel in New York, with Gino, Costa and Lucky upstairs. Who's behind it all? Gino knows: Enzio Bonnatti.

To put the focus on Lucky Santangelo and away from her father, Jackie Collins has Gino Santangelo suffer a heart attack on hearing the news that his son Dario has been shot. Collins does this because she wants Lucky to take up reins of the Santangelo empire, to become a true gangster by – what else? – killing someone (the macho initiation ritual). Trouble is, Gino is far too strong a guy to have a heart attack! Gino is a true survivor, built like a bull, who lives to nearly a hundred!

★

LUCKY

Lucky (1985) is the second installment in the *Lucky Santangelo* series, J.C.'s Hollywood version of a *Godfather* or Mario Puzo-style narrative. In Jackie Collins' career *Lucky* follows her biggest success, 1983's *Hollywood Wives,* and comes before the first *Hollywood* series sequel, *Hollywood Husbands* (1986). Meanwhile, in 1985 the TV series *Hollywood Wives* aired (so, it was a busy period in Collinsiana).

Lucky Santangelo (born in 1950) is another of Jackie Collins' many strong career women.[11] She's independent, confident,

---

10 In *Drop Dead Beautiful,* Collins refers to Marco as Lucky's fiancé (5), which must be a mistake.
11 And Lucky's a casual girl, preferring Tee shirts and jeans to high fashion – Rodeo Drive ain't her style.

ambitious, determined, strong-willed... Oh, let Collins tell us:

> Lucky Santangelo.
> Dangerous.
> Stubborn.
> Strong.
> Crazy.
> Sensual.
> Everything. (637)

And of course li'l Lucky's fabulously sexy and attractive:

> She looked, at 33, sensational. The years only heightened her darkly exotic beauty – made her more intriguing and mysterious. She was staggeringly beautiful in an erotic and unusual way. (482)

Jackie Collins wanted a female mob boss, but she had to do quite a bit of narrative work behind the scenes in order to create one. Because although you might have a female studio head for the first time in Hollywood history (Sherry Lansing,[12] in 1980), a woman running an Italian-American crime family is something else ('Lucky had grabbed what she had wanted in a man's world' [270]). If you thought the U.S. government was conservative (Democrat or Republican), and the liberal media was also conservative, a crime organization is even more reactionary and traditional (and thoroughly patriarchal and masculinist). As Gino Santangelo (her father) tells Lucky, *you're a woman.*[13]

But with *Chances* and then *Lucky,* Jackie Collins pulls it off. When I say Collins had to do a lot of narrative work, I meant that the ground had to be prepared to enable the reader to be persuaded that such a thing were possible. Making Lucky Santangelo an independent, determined, ambitious and smart person was a no brainer. Making her the daughter of a mob boss was vital (blood and family ties are fundamental in this kind of story and world, which is founded on traditional, familial, conservative politics). Lucky's love-hate relationship with her father Gino Santangelo is essential. Giving Lucky added motivation to learn the ropes of the business by having Gino marry her off to Mr Dull-and-Conservative was one of many elements (Lucky's resentment at her dad fuels her ambition). And of course, a narrative development like Gino having to stay abroad (in Israel) for tax evasion, and then falling ill, was necessary

---

[12] Lansing is cited in the *Lucky Santangelo* novels (*Dangerous Kiss* 46).
[13] Lucky is a liberal, like her dad: 'He blamed religion and people's differences for all the troubles in the world. Lucky agreed with him' (465).

so that Lucky could have a clearer run of the operation. (In short, Lucky couldn't have done it without stepping into the businesses and operations that Gino had already established: Lucky could not have started from scratch as a would-be mob boss in the fiercely patriarchal and reactionary world of Italian-American organized crime).

You can see Jackie Collins having fun with the gangster genre in the novels *Lucky* and *Chances*: apart from placing a woman at the top of a criminal organization, she makes Gino's son Dario gay! His only son! (Again, you could see that as another instance of Collins making it more acceptable that Lucky would take over from her father.)

Some of the narrative turns in *Lucky* were unexpected. I didn't think that Lucky would marry the ageing billionaire Dimitri Stanislopoulos, for instance. Take him, yes, but not marry him. Or have a child.

'Course, the *Lucky Santangelo* novels aren't all about Lucky and her efforts to embroider the perfect cushion cover. They are ensemble pieces again. So it's Lucky plus Gino plus Matt plus Dimitri plus Olympia plus Lennie plus Jess plus numerous other characters in the *Lucky* novel. And these characters aren't depicted solely in relation to Lucky – they have their own chapters, episodes and trajectories. So the stories of Olympia Stanislopoulos, the millionaire's daughter with too much money and spare time, and her on-off relationships with Flash (the Brit rock star) and Vito (the Spanish crooner) or Lennie Golden (the comedian on his way up the ladder, who hankers after lost love Eden Antonio), take up plenty of the 1985 novel (Lucky thus inherits Lennie from spoilt, rich girl Olympia).

The fundamental relationship in *Lucky*, and many of the *Lucky Santangelo* novels, is not the usual one of a man and woman, but a father and a daughter. It's the fiery love-hate relationship between Lucky and Gino Santangelo that forms the foundation of the *Lucky Santangelo* series.

> She loved him. She hated him. Goddam it, she *missed* him. (270)

Lucky Santangelo is a daddy's girl, a father complex girl, to the point where she has some of her most satisfying relationships with father surrogates, such as Costa Zennocotti (Gino Santangelo's 'brother' and long-time adviser) and Dimitri Stanislopoulos (Olympia's pa).14 Indeed, Lucky is a female version of Gino (as several charas point out).

Once again, the predominance of the young-woman-and-older-man relationship in a novel by Ms Collins is striking. Fathers, in Collins' world, are admired and resented; for their offspring (and particularly their daughters), they are frustrating, incorrigible, controlling, jealous, ignorant, loving and the focus of so much attention.

The biggest impediment to Gino Santangelo marrying gold-digger widow Susan is not the fact that she's gonna marry him and fleece him, but Lucky's jealousy. Indeed, so strong are Lucky's feelings for her beloved daddy, she leaves Las Vegas when she can't get through to him, and finds herself ignored as he whiles away weeks then months with Susan in Beverly Hills.

But it all comes out well in the end: *Lucky* closes with a wedding, between Lucky and comedian Lennie Golden, a pure fairy tale ending ('It was the perfect wedding' [639]). This becomes the central romantic relationship in Lucky's life for the most of the rest of the *Lucky Santangelo* series. However, in the final pages, it's the father-daughter relationship that is the emotional focus:

> 'Y'know somethin'?'
> 'What?'
> 'I kinda always forgot t'tell you this – an' I guess it's not important – ' cos you know anyway.'
> 'Yes?'
> 'I love you, kid. I *really* love you. And I'm proud of you. Real proud.'
> She blinked away tears – because it wouldn't do to cry on her wedding day, and fell into his arms. 'I love you too, daddy.' (638)

♥

I have said that Jackie Collins' New York City novels aren't as satisfying as other fictions set in or about Gotham, and that Collins doesn't quite capture the white-hot, electrical intensity of the City That Never Sleeps, but you gotta admit that Las-Vegas-and-Jackie-Collins is a perfect fit, just like Jackie Collins-and-Hollywood (tho' in her later books, Collins nails parts of Gotham).

Thus, *Lucky* is a terrific Las Vegas novel.15

---

14 But Lucky's doesn't like it when Uncle Costa points out that Dimitri Stanislopoulos is an old man and a father figure: 'Fuck you – Costa', is her response (265).

15 There you go – it's been a while since we had a single-sentence paragraph, one of the staples of the blockbuster novel.

What's not to like? Las Vegas has everything an author could possibly want: gangsters, mobs, showgirls, hookers, big shows, gambling, crime, sleaze, scandal, and a city ruthlessly dedicated to hedonism like nowhere else on Earth. In Vegas, stories writes themselves – you just sit back by the pool and watch those characters burn themselves up in fires hotter than demons dancing round the rim of the biggest pit of agonized souls in Hell.

And in *Lucky,* Jackie Collins exploits Las Vegas to the max. Because in Las Vegas there's no need for excuses for over-the-topness: Las Vegas *embodies* excess. A Jackie Collins novel simply can't take place in a quaint, sleepy village in rural England or Bolivia or Iowa. Or it can *start* there, but it sure as sh¡t has to end up in Vegas, L.A. or Gotham.

Lucky Santangelo muses on why she's attracted to Las Vegas in *Drop Dead Beautiful*:

> She often wondered why felt such close to ties to Vegas, although deep down she knew why. It was the place it had all begun for her when she'd taken over from Gino and finished building the Magiriano. It was the place she'd become a woman of substance, a woman capable of doing anything. (467)

♥

To clear the decks and jump-start the narrative of *Lucky* about two-thirds of the way thru, Jackie Collins employs one of her tried and tested devices – the catastrophe. In this case, it's a plane crash, which polishes off horse-faced actress Fern (and most of the crew), but not Olympia Stanislopoulos, the super-rich heiress. The repercussions of the crash, however, force apart the lovers that we know're gonna get together at the end, Lucky and Lennie Golden (we know that Lennie is destined to be with Lucky from the moment they meet in Las Vegas, and Lennie turns down Lucky's invitation for free love. Waaaa? Lucky Santangelo spurned by a guy she hits on? Unheard-of!).

Lucky Santangelo retreats into sombre 'it was meant to be' fatalism after the crash, going back to Dimitri Stanislopoulos on his island, where the elderly billionaire becomes a recluse in perpetual mourning over his beloved wife Fern. Lennie Golden, meanwhile, does the noble thing and stays with Olympia Stanislopoulos while she recovers from the accident.

Olympia Stanislopoulos is an enjoyable character, but you have little sympathy for her: spoilt, lazy, insensitive, exasperating, needy, clingy, shallow, and rude to everyone (basically, she's a rich bitch). Out of control on coke (and whatever she can lay her hands on), and pathetically devoted to British rock singer Flash, Olympia goes thru life like a clumsy, blonde baby elephant, expecting everybody to jump when she yells, *jump!*

The model in the latter part of the *Lucky* novel is probably the doomed, obsessive love affair between Sid Vicious (of the Sex Pistols) and his North American girlfriend Nancy Spungen (though there are other rock 'n' roll relationships like that which have spiralled into oblivion). Olympia and Flash're found dead in their hotel room in New York, echoing the fate of Spungen and Vicious in 1978. (Vicious and Spungen come across as very sad personalities: Vicious was a lost soul, bored, lazy, disaffected, resentful, and increasingly out of control, and Spungen was a mean and squalid figure who exploited Vicious ruthlessly.)[16]

☆

The climax of *Lucky* is a full-on, kidnapping scenario, one of the most successful in Jackie Collins' work (indeed, for some fans, *Lucky* is the best of the *Lucky Santangelo* novels). All roads lead to Blue Jay Way[17] in the Hollywood Hills above Sunset Boulevard. In order for this to be Lucky's moment of action, daddy Gino Santangelo has to be someplace else, so Collins rather obviously puts him in a Porsche heading along the P.C.H. for a naughty weekend in 'Frisco with curvy, compact Paige (yes, Gino is back with Paige). Uncle Costa turns out to be not so useful in a crisis, and nobody can get hold of Lennie or Lucky, or anyone else (these were the days – 1983, in this part of *Lucky* – before cel phones).

Here the cross-cutting technique Jackie Collins employs in *Lucky*, combined with short passages (like a million other blockbuster novelists), works wonders. It's *exactly* like the parallel action in an action-adventure movie, flitting from one scene to another during the climactic final act. Thus, while the suspense escalates as the kidnapping develops further, the narrator cuts back to Gino and Paige happily cruising up the coast: and Gino is the one person who'd be able to act decisively and Save The Day (Gino remains a

---

16 Sid Vicious (John Beverly) more than met his match with his North American girlfriend Nancy Spungen, whom John Lydon (and others in the Sex Pistols camp) utterly loathed. For Lydon, Spungen ruined Vicious with heroin and a sordid and bitter dive into drug addiction. When he was with Spungen, Vicious was impossible to deal with, according to Lydon. For Chrissie Hynde, Spungen 'turned Sid into a sex slave' (J. Lydon, 1993, 139).

17 A Beatles reference, perhaps? (To the George Harrison song).

very connected guy – with a single phone call, he can take care of business, including getting rid of people permanently).

The climax of *Lucky* is far more satisfying than 1,000s of similar movies and TV shows. Yet it does follow the formulas laid down by (principally North American) television and cinema from the 1910s onwards. Cross-cutting, a multiple race to a destination (pure D.W. Griffith), a powerful threat (Santino Bonnatti is an out-of-control, psycho gangster),[18] and the heroine in a key position of action and decision. Notice, though, that Lucky Santangelo doesn't carry a gun, and doesn't get to finish off Santino (she follows her colleague Boogie into the house; in the event, it's Brigitte Stanislopoulos who pulls the trigger).

And at the climactic point in *Lucky*, Jackie Collins does something which no North American movie or television show would ever do: she calmly whisks the reader away from the scene! It's the equivalent of cutting away from the moment in *The Godfather* when Michael shoots Solozzo and the police chief, after that astonishing build-up of suspense. Michael would come out of the restroom, sit at the table, listen to the conversation, with the filmmakers skilfully building up the tension, then cut away to Clemenza making pasta in the kitchen!

But Jackie Collins does just that, and *Lucky* shifts to eight months later. Collins loves to dig out that big black hole of What Ifs? and allow the reader to fall into it. But once you get into the epilogue chapters of *Lucky*, the tensions and suspense are worked out with a methodical poetry. Lucky doesn't kill Santino Bonnatti, and the author doesn't want to have her heroine a killer, even if it's totally justified, by the moral scales of this kind of novel (however, Lucky had already killed Enzio at the end of *Chances*). So it's fitting that it's Brigette who does the deed (although Eden's threatened to do it many times, and Eden would be a more satisfying choice after the years and years of abuse she's undergone).

---

18 Santino Bonnatti is one of the ugliest sons-of-bitches that Jackie Collins has created, a terminally abusive and violent gangster. When oh when is he going to have lungs ripped out of his chest, the reader wonders? (Santino is re-surrected in the character of Anthony Bonar/ Bonnatti in *Drop Dead Beautiful*. The book is more explicit than any movie or TV show, too, in depicting Santino as a child molester, undressing Lucky's 4 1/2 year-old son Bobby and just about to abuse him (along with Brigitte Stanislopoulos).

LADY BOSS

> They both knew what they wanted, and were determined to get it. Stardom and fame.
>
> Jackie Collins, *Lady Boss* (287)

This is vintage Jackie Collins (does that mean as much as vintage Wolfe? Or vintage Faulkner? Or vintage Dickinson? To some people, yes it does). In 1990's *Lady Boss* (the third *Lucky Santangelo* entry, dedicated to Collins' daughters Tiffany, Tracy and Rory – 'girls can do anything!'), the *Lucky Santangelo* series is in full flight. *Lady Boss* is set in 1985 and 1986. In *Lady Boss*, Lucky Santangelo sets her sights on running a Hollywood film studio (Panther[1] Studios), partly because she is married to actor Lennie Golden (at the start of *Lady Boss*, Lucky and Lennie are still madly in love, but are living separate lives – Lennie's making movies in Tinsel Town, and Lucky's running her businesses in Gotham):

> 'Chinese food, Marvin Gaye music, and great sex. What do you want?'
> 'Indian food, Billie Holiday, and great sex.' (340)

One of the primary plots in *Lady Boss* has ageing movie mogul Abe Panther demanding that Lucky Santangelo go undercover at Panther Studios to find out what's going on behind the scenes at his studio before he'll sell it to her. Thus, Lucky dons a wig, glasses and shabby clothes, and works as a secretary at Panther (she *hates* the clothes, but enjoys the freedom of a new identity).

Panther Studios is owned by the 88 year-old Abe Panther, one of the last of the old school, Hollywood moguls (such as Sam Goldwyn, Harry Cohn, and Louis B. Mayer). Like Gino Santangelo, old Abe is a grouchy, vain, proud but lovable guy, who's seen everything, but gave up control of Panther Studios when he had a stroke. (Panther is really a Hollywood mogul version of Gino – they both shack up with younger women, both enjoy being powerful (and ordering people about), and both demand respect and deference. Abe's inamorata is Inga, a sullen, plain Swede who resents the fact that she never became a big star after being in movies). Thus, Lucky doesn't found a film studio, like the founding fathers of Hollywood – she buys one.

Jackie Collins presented Panther Studios as one of the mini-

---
[1] What else could it be called?

majors – similar studios of the 1980s and 1990s would include Orion, Vestron and Dino de Laurentiis's studio (D.E.G. – De Laurentiis Entertainment Group). The legendary film producer de Laurentiis is another very Collinsian character and possible inspiratiion for Panther (see appendix).

The dodgy dealings of head honchos Mickey Stolli, Eddie Kane and Ben Harrison at Panther Studios in *Lady Boss* draw on scandals such as David Begelman at Columbia in the 1970s (no need for Jackie Collins to invent financial corruption in La-La Land when there are scandals like that (and many more) to draw upon!)[2]

Before Panther Studios is taken over by Lucky S., its bread and butter is T. & A. flicks. Buck Graham, head of marketing, goes straight for the common denominator:

> Whatever the content of the film, Buck sold it with a strong dose of tits and ass. As far as he was concerned, America had a permanent hard-on. (394)

Yet for some readers, Collin's own books could be regarded as porn, and violent sleaze, just like the movies that Panther Studios produce.

Jackie Collins portrays Hollywood as a man's club:

> The boys were gathered. No girls.
> *Shame.*
> *That's Hollywood.* (185)

In *Lady Boss*, Jackie Collins spoofs the kind of foul-mouthed, violent action movies which Hollywood is churning out (in 1990, sure, but still today): this is a sample from a screening:

> 'You motherfuckers,' sneered Johnny Romano in full closeup, his handsome face filling the screen.
> 'Who you callin' "motherfucker"?' answered the actor playing opposite him.
> 'Don't fuck with me, man,' said Johnny menacingly. 'Don't do it.'
> 'Listen, motherfucker, I fuck with anyone I want,' replied the other actor. (307)

Lady Boss is perhaps Jackie Collins' most sustained attack on pornography. Maybe Collins had read some of the feminist anti-porn polemics (such as Andrea Dworkin, Catherine MacKinnon, and Susans Griffin and Brownmiller), whose work was at its height in the 1980s

---

2 Indeed, lawsuits fly about all over Tinseltown.

(with the Dworkin-MacKinnon bills designed to ban or suppress porn).[3]

So when Jackie Collins has her main character, Lucky Santangelo, taking over a Hollywood film studio, a number of issues are tackled: one is the exploitation of women in movies (the portrayal of women as hookers, or housewives, or victims of violence). Another is equal pay for actresses (it's still unequal today). And another is porn: Panther Studios produces schlocky movies where women are second class citizens, and, via executive Eddie Kane, it is helping the Bonnatti syndicate to transport their porn into Europe (hiding the shipments in amongst Panther Studios' product). Thus, Collins also manages to squeeze in another appearance by the Santangelos' arch enemies, the Bonnatti clan from Sicily.

Lucky Santangelo vows to change all of that when she is made head of Panther Studios: much of the plot of *Lady Boss* concerns Lucky's adventures undercover at the studio, doing some detective work to expose the dodgy dealings of the studio executives (which include charging bottles of Cristal champagne to the studio, all the way up to trading in porn and fiddling the prices of film scripts). Lucky's challenge is: 'how to make movies without exploiting women' (201).

Once again, altho' some of these plots are exaggerated for dramatic purposes, if you know anything about Tinseltown, much of this material is familiar and grounded in real events. The links between organized crime have been proven in Hollywood (and also in the Hong Kong film industry). Alas, precious little of this juicy material made it into the *Lady Boss* TV mini-series.

❤

In *Lady Boss,* it's Venus Maria (a.k.a. Virginia Venus Maria Sierra) who gets the back-story treatment (with short flashbacks printed in italics). Jackie Collins has drawn heavily on the life story of Madonna Louise Ciccione Ritchie (b. 1958, Bay City, Michigan),[4] down to her Italian-American upbringing, liaisons with gay dancers, co-writing with male songwriters, her visits to Manhattan, her controversial pop

---

[3] In the 1980s, Andrea Dworkin and Catherine MacKinnon pushed their legal anti-porn bill in North America, a move that created a lot of comment among feminists, because versions were suggested for the cities of Minneapolis, Boston, LA and Indianapolis, where it became law for a while (Gillan Rodgerson & Linda Semple: "Who Watches the Watchwomen?: Feminists Against Censorship", in F. Bonner *et al*, eds., 268). For Dworkin and MacKinnon, the very existence of pornography was an infringement of women's civil rights.
[4] *Lady Boss* cites Madonna – Venus Maria 'left Madonna, Pfeiffer and Basinger trailing in her wake' (72). And later on, Cher.

promos (featuring lots of dancing), etc.

Venus Maria grows up in Brooklyn: American-born, Italian parentage, mother dead, four sexist pig brothers and a deadbeat father, whom she looks after (cooking, cleaning, washing, shopping, ironing (68-69)). For Venus Maria, 'her brothers considered women were put on the earth to clean, cook, fuck and shut up. Charming monsters' (377).

Venus Maria is one of Jackie Collins' tough and ambitious wannabe stars, a young woman who wields her sexual magnetism like a weapon (in *Lady Boss*, she snags a big prize, Mr New York, no less – business tycoon Martin Swanson, who's also going after owning a Hollywood studio). Later, Venus has liaisons with movie stars Cooper Turner and Billy Milena (but Venus, like Lucky, is a faithful woman, devoted to her man).

> As far as her fans were concerned Venus Maria could do no wrong. She was their video queen. Their princess. She was everything they aspired to be. Dangerous Stylish. A woman unafraid in a world run by men. A "fuck you" woman. (346-7)

Tabloid journalism and celebrity culture are big parts of *Lady Boss* – Venus Maria's loser brother Emilio sells her secrets to the gutter press, and the *paparazzi* duly stake out her home. Emilio doesn't want to work – he reckons he can score some green from $elling $tories about his sister Venus to the media (this's a recurring motif in Collins' fiction, as well as deadbeat men who leech off women). Meanwhile, her boyfriend, 'Mister New York', Martin Swanson, loathes the negative publicity (his wife Deena is talking about divorce, and decides to take her own revenge, planning to kill Venus Maria).

A Hollywood brothel, up in the Hollywood Hills, run by Madame Loretta, is another ingredient in *Lady Boss* (again, as reality shows, Jackie Collins isn't exaggerating much about Hollywood madames and brothels here). Several actresses work for the brothel, including Leslie Kane. (From Hooker-To-Hollywood-star is a trip that Collins' characters have undertaken several times).

❤

Lucky Santangelo's love life can't run on straight tracks, from bliss to bliss, or mundaneity to mundaneity: when it's going well, it sounds like this:

> 'OK, this is what I'd like to do,' she decided. 'Go to a movie. Eat popcorn

and spill it all over myself. Feel sick, have one of those horrible fizzy orange drinks. And then I want to go home and make love all night long. Can we do that?'

'You know something? That's why I'm crazy about you. We have exactly the same tastes.' He took a beat. 'Woody Allen?'

She answered instantly. 'But of course.'

They lined up for a Woody Allen film. Saw it. Loved it. And talked about it all the way home. (340)

When it ain't going so well, Lucky and her beloved Lennie Golden have a huge argument about her leaving for Japan for 6 weeks (really she's going under-cover at Panther Studios). Lennie, furious, is having a bad time filming on location in Acapulco (Acapulco? yeah, it's tough being a star!); he walks off the movie and goes into seclusion in Gotham, and then on the Riviera (yes, it's *really* tough being a star! Acapulco? South France? New York? Well, that's how I justify my travels: if you're going to be miserable, you might as well be miserable somewhere fabulous).

(Cooper Turner, another Collinsian Hollywood super-stud, is wheeled in as a possible alternative to Lennie for Lucky, but in the event Lennie returns, and Cooper marries Venus Maria, and they become 'the darlings of the tabloids. What an explosive mix!' [559]).

Lennie Golden's beef with Lucky Santangelo – that buying a film studio attacked his manhood, seems to have been forgotten, when, on the final page of *Lady Boss* (559), they are talking about working in movies together. (In the next book, *Vendetta: Lucky's Revenge*, it becomes an issue again).

❤

There're two big set-pieces that round off *Lady Boss*: the first one sees Lucky Santangelo orchestrating the take-over of Panther Studios. After going under-cover, and digging up the dirt on the dodgy dealings among the producers and the executives (such as coke-addled Eddie Kane, and the sleazy producer duo who turn out tits and ass dreck), Lucky is able to wrest away control of Panther Studios. Old Abe Panther makes a rare visit to the studio (after ten years away), gleefully scuppering the hopes of his offspring (who're desperate for a slice of his $$$$).

Thus, in *Lady Boss*, Jackie Collins revels in placing a woman at the top of a film studio: her chief heroine, Lucky Santangelo, gets to stick it to the patriarchal, masculinist Hollywood industry. She tells the two sleazoid producers where to go, gets the better of industry veteran and studio head Mickey Stolli (taking over his office), and vows to produce intelligent movies which don't exploit women.

The second set-piece in *Lady Boss* is that Jackie Collins staple, the grand, Hollywood party. This time it's a surprise birthday bash for Venus Maria, the second, main heroine of *Lady Boss*. Everyone in Hollywood seems to be there, including Hollywood Royalty: Clint Eastwood, Roger Moore, Michael Caine, Billy Wilder, the Bacharachs, Lionel Richie, Luther Vandross, etc.

The birthday party brings together pretty much every character in *Lady Boss* (as usual in a Collinsian finale), and the events play out pretty much as expected: Venus Maria's scuzzy brother Emilio (much to Venus's dismay), arrives to gloat (along with his wannabe actress date, Rita, who dresses like a Hollywood Boulevard hooker); Abigaile brings Saxon, her long-haired, bisexual hairdresser (to get back at her husband, Mickey Stolli); Gino Santangelo, complaining to his daughter Lucky that he's getting old (he's 79), has his spirits revived when Paige turns up at the party (they exit for the Beverly Wiltshire); loser producer Eddie Kane regrets being a S.O.B. to his wife Leslie (who's there as one of Madame Loretta's girls); Warner Franklin arrives with the film star Johnny Romano (afterwards he jumps her bones in the limo along Sunset).

❤

Lady Boss ends with the plots being tied up as usual. There are two murder plots: one is the gangster plot, as the hated Bonnattis re-surface to cause trouble for Lucky Santangelo. Santino Bonnatti turns up at the film studio demanding the million bucks he's owed (Mickey Stolli cleverly weasels out of making himself or Eddie Kane liable, as he ankles his job). Bonnatti decides to put out a contract on Lucky: happily, the hit-man Link is an idiot, and the murder – by drowning in the Pacific Ocean – is bungled, enabling Lennie Golden to rush to the rescue to save his princess. (The coda relates that Gino Santangelo makes one phone call and both Bonnatti and his hit-man Link are taken care of, mafia-style).

The second murder plot is part of the opening tease at the start of *Lady Boss*, when Deena Swanson, fiercely jealous of her husband's philandering, decides to kill the Bitch (her name for Venus Maria). Deena reckons that her spouse is more serious about this woman than usual (the more we learn about super-rich Martin Swanson, tho', the less the Venus-Swanson match seems a good one). Deena, another daddy's girl (who goes hunting with him and happens to be great with guns), shoots herself when confronted with Venus and Swanson making love after the birthday party (a flashback to Deena's teen years sort of explains/ expiates Deena, when the 14 year-old girl stumbles upon her pa tupping a hitchhiker, and takes a shotgun and blows her away).

As to the other plots in *Lady Boss*: well, Lucky S. gets back together with Lennie G. (of course!), and all is forgiven (plus they have two kids in rapid succession). Mickey Stolli moves back in with Abigaile (and of course is soon back to his old, Hollywood mogul ways). Eddie Kane slams his Ferrari car into a concrete wall and expires. Gino marries Paige. Johnny Romano makes a 'heart-warming comedy' and doesn't say motherfucker once (echoing stars like Arnold Schwarzenegger who went from action flicks to comedy in the late 1980s/ early 1990s). Emilio Sierra shacks up with a Contessa (Rita left after a furious argument). Abe Panther marries Inga, his long-suffering partner. Ron, after his lover has left him for Antonio the photographer, snags the older, richer sugar daddy of his dreams. Martin Swanson's fortunes take a dive (for a while), and he moves to Spain. Leslie Kane is discovered by Abigaile, and becomes a huge star within a year. And finally, Venus and Cooper Turner get married.

♥

Some memorable lines in *Lady Boss*:

> She looked down at him like a mother who'd just caught her son jacking off over a naked picture of Hitler. (190)

> She had a pair of legs on her that could strangle a giraffe! (217)

★

VENDETTA: LUCKY'S REVENGE

1996's novel *Vendetta: Lucky's Revenge* features Lucky Santangelo in full power as the head of Panther Studios in the heart of Hollywoodland (the book begins in 1987). Forgotten who Lucky is already? Jacqueline Jill Collins reminds ya:

> Tough exterior. Soft interior. Drop-dead gorgeous. Strong, stubborn, sensual, street smart, vulnerable and crazy. The package that was Lucky was really something. (14)

The novel includes several plots: the chief villain/ revenge plot concerns Donatella Bonnatti planning to pay Lucky back for shooting her husband Enzio. So Lucky's husband Lennie Golden is kidnapped (by the Bonnattis), and her business, Panther Studios, is taken over when the board votes her out (after Lucky had put in a lot of effort in winning the studio away from Mickey Stolli and his regime).

One of the romantic plots in *Vendetta: Lucky's Revenge* involves Lucky and film director Alex Woods; he's making his new movie *Gangsters* at Panther Studios (from the one time they had sex, Woods holds a flame for Lucky throughout the rest of the *Lucky Santangelo* series). Woods is one of those quirky, upcoming directors of violent, dramatic pictures in the Quentin Tarantino/ Oliver Stone[5] mold.[6] Collins gives Woods a ridiculously over-cooked back-story: Vietnam War, a film student at U.S.C. (University of Southern California, one of the centres of the 'New Hollywood' generation – George Lucas, John Milius, Walter Murch, Randall Kleiser, etc), and a series of dead-end jobs in Gotham (as he tells his mom in an interior monologue):

> *Hustled my ass for a couple of months so I could eat. Kept door at a low-class strip joint. Ran interference for a busy hooker. Cut up carcasses in a meat factory. Drove a cab. Chauffeured a car for a degenerate theater director. Bodyguarded a criminal. Lived with a rich older woman who reminded me of you. Procured drugs for her friends. Managed an after-hours gambling club. Worked as an assistant editor on a series of cheapo slash/ horror stories. And finally the big break – wrote and directed a porno movie for a lecherous old Mafia Capo. Tight pussies. Big cocks. Erotic porno. The kind that really turns people on. And a story. Next thing Hollywood beckons. They know good pornography when they see it.*(17-18)

Meanwhile, there's yet another rags-to-riches plot in *Vendetta: Lucky's Revenge*, and yet another supermodel plot, as Brigette Stanislopoulos tries to re-invent herself as Brigette Brown, a 19 year-old, wannabe fashion model in Gotham. Along the way she encounters egotistical photographers (Luke), rival supermodels (like the British Robertson, seemingly partially modelled on Kate Moss), and pervy fashion agents (Michel Guy).

---

[5] Oliver Stone is one of the inspirations for Woods – the clue is that Stone is cited in relation to Woods (along with Martin Scorsese), on page 270. Stone also fought in Vietnam.

[6] There's also some Martin Scorsese/ James Toback/ John Milius in Woods' characterization. And of course he has the surname of the incredible actor James Woods.

And there's Venus Maria, the Madonna/ Whitney Huston/ Cher type introduced in *Lady Boss*, a mega-star with a strong youth fan-base who's hoping to move into features. Venus

> managed to look vulnerable, smart and incredibly slutty all at the same time. It was an irresistible combination. Women admired her strength and men couldn't wait to fuck her. (34)

There's the weirdo – this time is Donatella's teenage son Santo,[7] who's obsessed with Venus Maria (he writes her pervy letters). Santo is fat, very spoilt, and resents everybody (he plays a key role in the finale of *Vendetta: Lucky's Revenge*).

There's the ageing actor Cooper Turner, who splits from his wife Venus Maria, and dates Leslie Kane, a famous actress (Venus dumps him publicly at a dinner party, when she finds out about his affair/s. But she can't get him out of her mind, and by the end of the book they are re-united.)

And the minor characters of *Vendetta: Lucky's Revenge*, who pop up elsewhere in Jackie Collins' glitterverse, such as Charlie Dollar (the stoned, goofy actor), macho star Johnny Romano, and Freddie Leon (the ice-cold talent agent).

Heavily in debt, but with two movies making money, Panther Studios is the beloved home of old Abe Panther, another of Lucky's mentors and patriarchs. (The symbol of the panther is a favourite Collins emblem: 'M.G.M. had its lion – but Panther Studios had the *real* power symbol' [*Lady Boss*, 75]).

Jackie Collins has fun with putting a woman at the head of a movie studio, to upset the old boys' network of the Hollywood movie industry (which's still in place today, of course). For instance, Lucky Santangelo insists on paying Panther's female stars the same as the male stars.

> 'In my kind of movies women are smart. They are not relegated to the kitchen, bedroom or whore house. They're strong, well-rounded women with careers and lives of their own who do live their life through a man. *That's* what intelligent women want to see.' (37)

Oh why didn't Jackie Collins get to run a film studio for real for a year or two?! Lucky Santangelo also asserts that there will be male

---

[7] Santo Bonnatti attends a school in L.A. where the kids are so connected you can buy anything – 'the schoolyard was a virtual bazaar of drugs, weapons, porno magazines and videos' (245). There;s a joke in *The Naked Gun 3* where a school playground in L.A. is full of kids with guns.

nudity as well as the usual female nudity in her pictures (much to the outrage of the filmmakers, who claim that women don't wanta see naked, male butts. Lucky retorts: wrong, women loved seeing Richard Gere waggle his bits in the nuddy in *Looking For Mr Goodbar*): 'If we get to see tits an' ass, we get to see dick too' (14). And Venus Maria tells head honcho Mickey Stolli, 'women get off on seeing guys with it all hanging out', but they don't get to see that because men run the industry and 'men can't handle the competition, so they don't want us getting an eyeful' (*Lady Boss*, 245).

The equal pay for women, the equality of nudity, the smashing of the old boys' network and the patriarchal hierarchy of the film business – none of that has occurred in the decades after *Lady Boss* and *Vendetta*.

The hostile takeover plot reflects the era of the 1980s and the 1990s (*Vendetta: Lucky's Revenge* is set in the late 1980s), in particular the buying and selling of film studios such as M.G.M. and United Artists (Kirk Kerkorian bought and sold M.G.M. several times, it seemed).[8]

Among the enjoyable sections of *Vendetta: Lucky's Revenge* is a lengthy set-piece involving Lucky Santangelo having a wild night on the way to Palm Springs with film director Alex Woods. He can't keep up with her, of course – because Lucky is Jackie Collins' original 'wild child'. Collins is great when she allows herself the luxury of pursuing a single event for more than a page or two. So they stop off at a sleazy roadhouse in the middle of nowhere, where there's strippers and lotsa drinking, threatening hillbilly locals, and fights're barely avoided. Lucky is an entertaining date for a night out, and she's way ahead of the guys (in every way!).

★

One of the amusing subplots of *Vendetta: Lucky's Revenge* is Lucky Santangelo showing film director Alex Woods what it's *really* like to live in the world of crime and the mafia. Lucky is the real thing, while Woods is merely a guy who writes stories about that criminal world.

Yes – let's not forget that by now Lucky Santangelo is a killer:

---

[8] Kirk Kerkorian bought out M.G.M. (in 1969). Transamerica sold United Artists to M.G.M. and Kirk Kerkorian in 1981 for $380 million, where it became the M.G.M./ U.A. Entertainment Company. Ted Turner bought M.G.M./ U.A. in 1985, sold U.A. and then M.G.M. back to Kerkorian (but kept hold of M.G.M.'s film library).

she shoots Enzio Bonnatti dead, and orders the death of the Kassarri twins (in *Chances*).

★

Meanwhile in *Vendetta: Lucky's Revenge*, over in Sicily, Lennie Golden is surviving, chained to the rock wall of some sea caves below the cliffs. He's being kept alive for the Happy Ever After ending, of course (as Lucky's most beloved partner in all of the *Lucky Santangelo* series, Golden isn't going to be sacrificed just yet). And it's not all *Count of Monte Cristo* dungeons and hardship and cruelty for Lennie, too: this is *The Count of Monte Cristo* Jackie Collins-style! – his captors send along their daughter, who just happens to be voluptuous, like a young Sophia Loren (out of the movie *Two Women* (Vittorio De Sica, 1960), the narrator notes [377]).9 So that Lennie imagines he's in some old, Italian picture.

> Sometime he felt he was in the middle of an Italian movie acting out scenes. Beautiful peasant girl with incredible voluptuous breasts and sturdy thighs rescues handsome American stranger from a life in captivity. Shit! Universal would make it in a minute! (377)

Of course, Claudia is going to help Lennie escape, and to seal the deal, of course Lennie and Claudia get down and dirty (inevitably, Claudia gets pregnant – tho' we don't find that out until the next book, *Dangerous Kiss*, when Claudia turns up in Malibu trailing Lennie's love child behind her).

★

The set-piece in the finale of *Vendetta: Lucky's Revenge* is a Hollywood dinner party. Well, we've been here before, lads and lasses, and it is rather uninspired, but it does offer a legitimate reason for all of the major characters to be brought together. The characters and the plots include the thriller/ crime/ mafia plot and plenty of relationships plots:

▼ Lucky Santangelo getting closer to nailing Donatella Bonnatti as her chief opponent;
▼ Alex Woods taking Lucky as his date instead of the sweet but out-of-her-league Tin Lee (Woods remains keen on Lucky);
▼ the ex-lovers Cooper Turner and Leslie Kane who've split up acrimoniously (Leslie is determined to win him back);
▼ Mickey Stolli, newly (re-)installed at Panther Studios, is an old

---
9 Sophia Loren and Gina Lollobrigida were known as the *maggiorata*, the 'curvy girl', a stereotype of Italian women.

rival of Lucky's (she ousted him from the studio);

▼ Venus Maria creates waves with her sexual magnetism (Mickey's hoping for head in return for casting Venus in Woods' movie *Gangsters*);

▼ Johnny Romano turns up with Daniella (the French, high-class call-gir);

▼ Santo, Donatella's fat, 16 year-old son is there (he obsesses over Venus), as is Abigaile's wild child daughter Tabitha;

▼ and the professional Hollywood Wife, hostess Abigaile, goes into meltdown as her precious dinner party threatens to implode under the impact of seething jealousies/ resentments/ desires.

It all plays out as expected in *Vendetta: Lucky's Revenge*: Tin Lee turns up to embarrass Alex Woods (who's still crazy about Lucky Santangelo – yes, as we all are!); Abigaile tries to remain calm; Lucky finds out more about Donatella (and enjoys causing trouble for the Stollis); and the teens Tabitha and Santo share a joint (then some heroin), and fuck at Donatella's home (including on Santo's mom's bed).

For the finale of *Vendetta: Lucky's Revenge*, Jackie Collins ladles on the sugar and the honey, enhancing the Happy Ever After ending with some hugs and kisses and smiles all-round. So Brigette's modelling career goes into overdrive (hoardings for Rock and Roll jeans go up in Times Square); Michel Guy gets his come-uppance (with a threatening visit from Lucky in Gotham); Johnny Romano hooks up with Daniella; Venus Maria and Cooper Turner are re-united in orgasmic bliss; Leslie Kane nabs Charlie Dollar as her next conquest (the tabloids love it, 'a front-page sensation'); Tabitha transforms from Bratty Punk into Bratty, Hollywood Princess; and Alex Woods' new movie *Gangsters* receives a red carpet premiere at Mann's Chinese Theater (where else?), which's the setting for many of the *dénouement* scenes.

As for Lucky Santangelo? – well, she gets her man back, when Lennie Golden, aided by Sophia Loren-lookalike Claudia, manages to flee captivity in the Sicilian caves, making his way to Palermo then Naples and Rome, and all the way back to Lucky's arms.

> 'You're the most special woman in the world, and I love you more than I can ever put into words.'
> 'Love you, too, Lennie,' she said softly. 'And I always will.'

> They smiled at each other and squeezed hands, and it was as if they'd never been apart. (455)

Thus *Vendetta: Lucky's Revenge* ends with these lines. As for the thriller/ revenge plot – well, of course, once Lucky Santangelo is in the ascendant, feeling as if she can accomplish anything, she is unstoppable. She wrests back control of her studio, Panther, ousting Mickey Stolli and Donna Landsman (a.k.a. Donatella Bonnatti). Now all Lucky has to do is to deal with Donatella herself: so she grabs her gun, puts on her blackest clothes (Lucky becomes a ninja assassin!), and heads over to the Landsman abode in Bel Air.

Remember that spoilt, 16 year-old brat Santo, the teenage Bonnatti? His mom, Donatella, furious with the way that Lucky Santangelo has turned the tables on her, rounds on him. The screaming match at home escalates, until Santo takes out the shotgun he bought from a kid at school and kills both his mom and his step-father, the hapless George. Lucky arrives soon afterwards, and finds her job already done. So Jackie Collins neatly excuses her heroine from killing (or, rather, killing again).

The crazy evening in *Vendetta: Lucky's Revenge* is brought to a close when Santo Bonnatti, high on a Clint Eastwood/ Chuck Norris killing spree, hurries over to Venus Maria's place, to punish her for all her sins – and his sins, everyone's sins. Venus is enjoying multiple orgasms with Cooper as he eats her – 'transporting her to the land of ecstasy, giving her orgasms the like of which she'd never experienced before' (442-3) – and it seems as if Jackie Collins is going to stage another sex-and-death bloodbath. But then the guard dogs that Venus has hired sink their teeth into Santo's tubby frame. End game.

★

Vendetta: Lucky's Revenge has the usual Chanel handbag of Collinsian one-liners:

> Venus could elicit a hard-on from a stone statue! (73)

> What was it with men?
> Obviously brains and a hard-on did not mix. (308)

> The man was in his nineties, and he still hung onto his money like a hooker on a bad night. (448)

Dangerous Kiss (1999) was the fifth novel in the *Lucky Santangelo* series (and Jackie Collins's nineteenth novel). It was business as usual in Collinsland: relationships, romance, marriage, soap opera, sex, sleaze, murder, fashion, and of course Hollywood.

So in *Dangerous Kiss*, we have the usual group of Collinsian characters, with Lucky Santangelo at the centre, tho' by no means the only star on the block (Lucky's Big News is that she's stepping down from running Panther Studios, to spend time with her family).[10] There's Lucky's husband Lennie Golden, for instance, who spirals into depression[11] after being the victim of a car jacking on Wilshire; poor Mary Lou, Steve Berkeley's beloved actress wife, is shot dead in the car next to Lennie[12] (thus, Steven has also fallen into the psychological abyss); there's Brigitte, the Stanisopoulos heiress, who is drugged and date raped by a 31 year-old, Italian Count, Carlo (and gets pregnant) – he's after her money; there're several supermodel chums of Brigitte's (new characters such as Lina, Suzi, Didi and Kyra Kattleman);[13] and Price Washington, another new character, a black superstar comedian (in the mold of Eddie Murphy, Chris Rock, Will Smith and Martin Lawrence), who's having trouble with his surly, teenage son Teddy (who's involved in the robbery/ murder); meanwhile, Price's live-in help, Irena Kopistani, is sort of in a relationship with Price (well, she thinks of herself as his 'sex slave'); and Kopistani's daughter, Mila, is the obligatory Collinsian, out-of-control teenager who pulled the trigger and killed Mary Lou Berkeley.

Popping in and out of *Dangerous Kiss* are familiar faces like Charlie Dollar (film star), Venus Maria (superstar), Cooper Turner (film star), Alex Woods (film director) and Freddie Leon (talent agent).

Cockernee supermodel Lina ('an incredibly exotic-looking black girl from the East End of London', 10) has her sights set on Steve Berkeley, the Denzel Washington-lookalike lawyer, and half-brother of Lucky S. Gino Santangelo wisely spends much of *Dangerous Kiss* taking it easy in Palm Springs with Paige (well, he is 87 now!).

Much of *Dangerous Kiss* is concerned not with the two

---

10 Collins having presumably squeezed all of the juice out of the notion of a woman – yes, a woman! – running a Hollywood film studio.
11 Collins' first husband, Wallace Austin, suffered from depression, and committed suicide in 1964.
12 Lennie blames himself for not being able to prevent it.
13 The usual loud, brash, black supermodels in Collins' Glamland.

Santangelos, Lucky or Gino, but with the sad tale of Brigitte Stanisopoulos, the 25 year-old, Greek heiress: when she's thirty, she'll inherit billions (in a similar fashion, *Poor Little Bitch Girl* was a *Lucky Santangelo* novel focussing on Lucky's son Bobby). Hence, Brigitte's a prime target for gold-diggers, such as Carlo, the Italian Count. Unfortunately, Carlo is a major prick[14] (shallow, promiscuous, lazy and violent): he drugs Brigitte so he can have his wicked way with her. Then he beats her. Repeatedly. Then he gets her hooked on heroin,[15] making her malleable enough to whisk away to Italy for a shotgun marriage. Carlo is bad news all-round – a jealous, controlling Italian guy (the worst kind! Lucky thinks). And then, to wean her off heroin, Carlo simply abandons Brigitte in the family's hunting lodge, deep in the Roman *campagna*. She loses her premature baby, and tries to make for civilization (only to be knocked unconscious while riding a bike).

Meanwhile, Lucky Santangelo falls out with Lennie, fed up with his long-lasting depression (a recurring motif in Collins' fiction): he prefers to take long walks on Malibu beach rather than be the Family Man and Loving Husband. They have a short (one night) separation, after which they make up (in the usual Jackie Collins manner – with s♥x. Isn't it always the way?!).

Further complications emerge in the Lucky-Lennie relationship in *Dangerous Kiss* when Lennie sulks because Lucky is planning to produce a movie with Alex Woods at the helm (Woods has a huge crush on Lucky – well, who wouldn't?). And then, at a party for Brigitte Stanislopoulos at Lucky's Malibu home, the Sophia Loren-lookalike from Italy, Claudia. turns up – a ghost from the past, from the time when Lennie was held captive in a cave in Sicily (in the previous novel), and was helped to freedom by Claudia. Claudia has a child in tow – Lennie's son (Leonardo), from that one night stand. That sends Lucky into the expected emotional spiral, and once again their marriage is on the rocks (Lennie takes Claudia and his son to the Chateau Marmont Hotel for a spell). But of course it all ends well, and the Lennie-Lucky marriage endures.

And there's sex – as naughty Mila Kopistani exploits the clueless Teddy:

> 'Wanna touch my tits?' Mila whispered seductively in his ear.

---
14 A technical term for a not very nice person.
15 Which happened to her mom, Olympia Stanislopoulos, and to Carrie Berkeley, Stephen's mom.

'Wh-what?' he stammered, sure he hadn't heard correctly.
'Do you?' she encouraged, moving even closer.
'C-can I?'
'Christ, Teddy,' she said forcefully. 'You're such a loser. For God's sake, go for it.' And with that, she grabbed his hand and shoved it up her T-shirt.
Feeling her hard, pointed nipples, he nearly came in his pants. Her tits were the best thing he'd ever felt. (130-1)

The murder plot in *Dangerous Kiss*, involving teens-on-the-loose, Mila Kopistani and Teddy, culminates in an exciting trial sequence, with the press in a feeding frenzy over the participants – comedian Price Washington, his son Teddy, Lennie Golden, and Lucky S. (they drag up the salacious details from Lucky's past).

Jackie Collins is a conservative moralist, as we know, and so the killers receive their comeuppance – Mila is diced in jail by her roomie Maybelline Browning, and Maybelline's brother Duke is shot by none other than Lucky (in another sleazy episode, where Duke has Lennie strung up from a beam naked in Malibu, while he takes Claudia over a chair, until Lucky saves the day, arriving at just the right time, and rescues her husband).

Only one aspect of the ending of *Dangerous Kiss* rankles: Claudia dives in front of Lennie, to save him from being shot, and she dies! Waaa? Not only did Claudia help Lennie escape from the caves in Sicily, and not only does she have his son and bring him up without asking for help, she also hurls herself in front of him! Her reward? Only to die! Come on, Jackie, that's too harsh! (Oh, we know that it clears Claudia out of the way so that Lucky can enjoy her beloved Lennie without a woman looking like young Sophia Loren bothering their marriage).

★

Memorable lines in *Dangerous Kiss*:

'Get your mind out of my pants,' he joked.
'Why? I like it there!' (236)

★

DROP DEAD BEAUTIFUL

Drop Dead Beautiful (2007) was the sixth *Lucky Santangelo* novel. As in *Dangerous Kiss*, Lucky Santangelo is only one member of an ensemble piece. For instance, it's her out-of-control, 16 year-old daughter Max (a.k.a. Maria) who's in one of the chief plotlines (she's kidnapped by the wannabe actor Henry Whitfield-Simmons, whom she met on the internet (Max is given two chums – Cookie, the black daughter of 'forty-nine year-old smooth soul-singing icon' Gerald M., and Harry, who's pale, Goth and gay – i.e., unthreatening for a teen girl. Cookie and Harry are both spoilt, Hollywood kids, like Max, with successful parents). Whitfield-Simmons resents Lucky for passing him over for actor Billy Melina, and uses capturing her daughter Max to get back at her. It all goes wrong for psycho loser Whitfield-Simmons, tho', when Max hooks up with a guy, Ace, and he holds them both captive in his dad's log cabin up in the wilds beyond Big Bear).

So upcoming movie star Billy Milena[16] is now dating superstar Venus Maria, who, at 41, is tired of being branded the older woman with a younger lover (Cooper Turner has left her and is seeing a teenager, in the usual manner of the ageing, Hollywood celeb who prefers women young enough to be their grand-daughters).

In *Drop Dead Beautiful*, Jackie Collins resurrects the Bonnatti versus Santangelo blood feud yet again. This time it's drug lord Anthony Bonnatti (now 'Bonar'), a 'son of', 'adopted child of' character, who's determined to bring down Lucky Santangelo and her new Keys resort in Las Vegas (Bonar has Francesca, the crabby, ageing widow of Enzio Bonnatti, on his case to defend the Bonnatti name and wreak revenge on the Santangelos. Francesca brought up Bonar as a kind of grandson). Yes, Lucky, who stood down from running Panther Studios (and producing a movie, *Seduction*), is moving back into the hotel industry in Vegas (Keys will be her third hotel in Sin City, a giant, plush, and exclusive resort for high rollers who have more $$$$ than Howard Hughes).

Anthony Bonar/ Bonnatti is a son-of-a-bitch in the Scarface/ Al Pacino mold (he's basically Santino Bonnatti Mark II): super-rich, super-arrogant, and super-mean. His wife, Irma, poor thing, is kept cooped up like a bird in a mansion-as-cage in Mexico City (Bonar has several mistresses stationed around the globe, in Miami, Gotham,

---

[16] *'Leonardo, Taylor, Rob, take a backseat. Billy Milena is the hottest dude in town – any town'* (*Goddess of Vengeance*, 161).

etc), and her children are elsewhere, so she starts up an erotic liaison with – who else? – the young, Mexican gardener, Luis (who has a pregnant wife she doesn't know about):

> Luis had stroked her nipples, fingered her crotch, then dropped to his knees and started going down on her, his tongue forcing its way through her wiry pubic hair, darting into her most secret place – a place that Anthony had *never* visited with his tongue.
> After a few minutes of indescribable ecstasy, she'd shuddered to an earth-shattering climax, moaning with passion as Luis stood up. He'd then gathered her into his strong arms and carried her over to the bed, whereupon he'd laid her down, once more spread her legs, and mounted her, slowly and surely moving and forth inside her. (97)

We know that Anthony Bonar is going to go ballistic when he finds out. (Early on in *Drop Dead Beautiful*, to demonstrate what a lethal wretch Bonar is, there's a scene where Bonar sort of accidentally kills his date Tamsin[17] in the middle of a sex session that gets out of control; Tamsin, for instance, demands that Bonar go down on her and he, the original Italian, chauvinist pig, never does that!).

Meanwhile, big, bad, old Gino Santangelo is celebrating his 95th birthday with a big family-and-friends bash at his daughter Lucky's Bel Air home (the Malibu house is being rebuilt following landslides).

> He was a true survivor and let no one forget it. He'd outlived them all – Enzio Bonnatti, Pinky Banana, Jake the Boy, all the old crew. He'd weathered jail, a heart-attack, the death of a child, a couple of assassination attempts, the murder of his beloved first wife. Jeez! And a thousand other things. (*Drop Dead Beautiful*, 86)

Lucky's son Bobby is crowing about running his successful club in Gotham (and cracking wise with mom Lucky incessantly). Acclaimed director Alex Woods stills holds a flame (and an erection) for Lucky (that one night they shared way back in *Vendetta: Lucky's Revenge* has haunted him ever since, and the procession of Asian girlfriends thru his life haven't made him forget, not even his current squeeze, the long-suffering lawyer Ling, who is especially envious of Lucky – or Alex's attraction to Lucky). But Lucky, as we know, is a One Man Girl, and it's Lennie-Lennie-Lennie all the way for her (Lennie Golden spends most of *Drop Dead Beautiful* glued to his computer, writing another film script. Well, after a car-jacking and murder in one book, and the kidnapping earlier, it's time for Lennie to have a more

---

[17] Unfortunately, Tamsin is one of the bank managers who oversees the payroll of the Santangelo hotels in Vegas.

relaxing time in the *Lucky Santangelo* series!).

Other familiar charas make an appearance in *Drop Dead Beautiful* – Brigitte Stanislopoulos, Lina, Charlie Dollar, Cooper Turner, and Cole (the personal trainer from the *Madison Castelli* books), tho' some of them are only cameos.

Certainly, *Drop Dead Beautiful* is, like *Dangerous Kiss*, not the finest or most engrossing of the *Lucky Santangelo* novels. Part of the problem for Jackie Collins is clearly that Lucky Santangelo has by now faced numerous threats and challenges, including kidnapping and murder. Lucky's also so successful – in movies, in Las Vegas, in business – that there are fewer goals in her life (yet she remains restless). Thus, devising new and interesting scenarios to place Lucky in is a tall order. Because by this point in the *Lucky Santangelo* series, Lucky is virtually a superhero (with the same lack of suspense found in superhero narratives, because we know that the superhero will always triumph, no matter *what* the obstacles are, and no matter *how* venal the villain is).

One aspect of the challenge of the later *Lucky Santangelo* books is that Collins had created a narrow set of narrative parameters for her characters and her series. Collins wanted to keep the stories with certain contexts, settings, and themes. Thus, many of the possibilities for plots for Lucky, Gino, Lennie and co. were not available.

The set-pieces in *Drop Dead Beautiful* include the kidnapping of Max (and Ace) by inept maniac Henry Whitfield-Simmons; Gino Santangelo's 95th birthday celebrations in Bel Air; and the opening night of the Keys resort in Las Vegas (which provides the climax of the novel. Yes, we *have* been here before in Collins Land, with the opening of a hotel! But, hell, it's not a chore, is it, when we're staying in a five-star penthouse with a spectacular view from the balcony of the 'shimmering city').

So, the finale of *Drop Dead Beautiful* takes place during the splashy opening of the Keys resort in Las Vegas. Everybody's here: the psycho (Henry), the Bonnatti rivals (Anthony and Francesca), the Santangelos (Lucky and Gino), the stars/ celebs (Venus Maria, Billy Milena, Charlie Dollar *et al*), the cops (Franklin), plus their entourages/ extended families/ friends/ mistresses/ assistants/ bodyguards.

The thriller plot's resolved in *Drop Dead Beautiful* in a very silly manner, when Irma snatches up a gun that falls out of Ling's handbag[18] and uses it to shoot her hated husband Anthony Bonar in the front row of the lingerie show (Bonar's been so nasty to her (as only men can be in Collins' moral universe), including cutting the balls off her lover Luis, and humiliating her in front of everybody, bringing along his grandmother Francesca and one of his mistresses, Emmanuelle, to the opening night). Meanwhile, Renee wisely calls off blowing up the Keys resort with explosives (which would've meant the end of several people precious to Lucky, and maybe even Lucky herself).

Meanwhile, the other thriller plot in *Drop Dead Beautiful*, involving rich kid psycho and failed actor Henry Whitfield-Simmons and his twisted ambition to whisk Maria/ Max Santangelo away, is rapidly brought to a close: Henry turns up at the Keys resort, tricks Max downstairs to the empty spa, where luckily homeboy Ace is nearby to come to Max's rescue. (Whitfield-Simmons is arrested later for the murder of his supercillious dragon of a mom).

Among the upbeat endings in *Drop Dead Beautiful* (some included in the months-later epilogue), are Venus and Billy getting hitched, Irma moving back home (to Omaha) with her kids, and Keys being a roaring success.

★

Memorable lines in *Drop Dead Beautiful*:

Getting old was a bitch, but it was better than the alternative. (515)

Falling in love was a bitch. Getting over it was even worse. (321)

★

---

18 It turns out that Ling, Alex Woods' Chinese lawyer girlfriend, has been sending Lucky the 'drop dead beautiful' cards, and hopes to nobble Lucky, because she's jealous of Alex carrying a torch for Lucky.

Poor Little Bitch Girl (2009) - great title! - it comes from a 1936 Shirley Temple musical movie - was a *Lucky Santangelo* novel in which neither Lucky nor Gino Santangelo feature much. Instead, the Santangelo link is Bobby Santangelo, Lucky's first-born son (from her marriage with Dimitri Stanisopoulos, the Greek shipping magnate). So it's a sort of side-story *Lucky Santangelo* book (like *Drop Dead Beautiful*). However, many of the charas in *Poor Little Bitch Girl* appear in subsequent *Lucky Santangelo* novels: Frankie Romano, Denver Jones, Carolyn, Annabelle Maestro, Ralph Maestro, and M.J. Plus the usual retinue of secondary charas: Zeena, Chip, Kerri, Nellie, Sam, Mario, Rosa, Benito, Ramirez, etc. And Lucky does appear in several phone conversations (and the *Lucky Santangelo* books are ensemble pieces anyway).

The chapters in *Poor Little Bitch Girl* are headed up with the charas' names: 'Denver', 'Bobby', etc. The characters who get chapters named after them include Denver, Bobby, Annabelle and Carolyn. The chapters run in a cycle, which repeats. (Also, the 'Denver' chapters are written in the first person).

The settings in *Poor Little Bitch Girl* are, as ever, L.A. — N.Y. — L.V. (tho', for the down-and-out section of Los Angeles, Jackie Collins is vague, and doesn't like to name streets or areas, as if she's wary of irritating readers who live there - even tho' we are told it's in the South-East of L.A. - i.e., Inglewood, Watts, Compton, and South Central).

As to when *Poor Little Bitch Girl* is set - well, Gino Santangelo is stated as being 97, so you can work it out: it's 2003 (Gino was born in 1906). However, Madonna is cited as being over fifty - so it must be 2008 or later (because Madonna Louise Ciccione Ritchie was born in 1958). Timelines are fudged in Collins' work - it's fiction.

Apparently, *Poor Little Bitch Girl* re-used material that Jackie Collins had prepared for a TV show about heiresses which wasn't made. Characters inheriting money is a recurring motif in Collins' work (partly, perhaps, because it's a legitimate and quick way of people having lotsa $$$$).

☆

A story takes its time to emerge in *Poor Little Bitch Girl,* as the Goddess of Hollywood spends a while introducing the charas. So Ralph Maestro, Annabelle's old school, chauvinist, movie star pa, is involved in the murder of his actress wife Gemma Summer; Denver Jones is embroiled in the case as Maestro's legal defence (aided by cynical, shark lawyer Felix); Bobby and M.J. are developing their chain of nightclubs across North America; Carolyn is pregnant and hoping that the middle-aged senator (Gregory Stoneman) she's dating will leave his wife Evelyn (no hope there!); and Annabelle, who runs a high-class call-girl service with her boyfriend Frankie Romano, endures an ugly experience with an aggressive client (another of Collins' unflattering portraits of a Middle Eastern guy who bullies women). Annabelle is the 'poor little bitch girl' of the title (321).

The thriller stories in *Poor Little Bitch Girl* comprise: (1) a murder story, a gift for the tabloids, when Ralph Maestro's wife Gemma Summer is killed in her bedroom; and (2) a kidnap scenario, when senator Gregory Stoneman decides he doesn't want to deal with his pregnant lover, Carolyn.

The Ralph Maestro murder plot is a not-especially-gripping did-he?-didn't-he? outing.[1] Not compelling because *Poor Little Bitch Girl* doesn't seem interested in it; rather the interst lies in how it affects the people linked to it – such as his out-of-control, estranged daughter Annabelle (who'd rather be shopping in Saks or Gucci than dealing with her father or thinking about her dead mother). And Maestro, the ageing action star, is another of those egotistical, unsympathetic actors that we don't care much about (and there's a hint that he molested his daughter Annabelle).

And then the kidnapping plot: we *have* been here before in Collinsville: in *Poor Little Bitch Girl,* the senator Gregory Stoneman isn't going to leave his social gadfly (and richer) wife Evelyn (because of his political career in D.C.), and decides that he can't deal with Carolyn being pregnant and making demands on him. So he hires a couple of (ineffective) Chicano no-goods to sort of bounce her around in the trunk of a car, so she'll lose the baby. What a sleazebag! Of course, Jackie Collins (remember, *she's* in control here, not her characters!) *won't* sacrifice a baby, so the ruse back-fires on Stoneman. Carolyn manages to escape, after undergoing a grungey ordeal on the mean streets of L.A., before she's rescued by Denver.

Author surrogate (and a candidate for the perfect *Cosmopolitan* reader – she's smart, economically independent, down-to-earth and for once not a size 8), Denver Jones spends much of *Poor*

---

[1] The murder mystery is teased by Jackie Collins several times – she introduces a character, Hank Montero, who is boldly called 'the wild card'.

Little Bitch Girl having affairs with one guy or another: there's Mario, a cool, Hispanic super-stud who stupidly involves Denver in a three-way sex scene unannounced (no, Denver doesn't like that stuff at all! What a douche!); a relationship with Gotham screenwriter Sam (this continues into later *Lucky Santangelo* novels); and an uneasy time with her ex-boyfriend, Josh (they argue over who keeps their dawg, called Amy Winehouse; he wants to make up, but he's put on weight, and, anyhow, *he* left *her*, and Collins Girls *never* go back). Denver ends up with the prize she idolized in her teen years at school, Bobby Santangelo (but at the end of *The Santangelos*, the final book in the series, Denver is back with Sam). Like the relationship films of Woody Allen, and like many a romance novel, many of Collins' stories are simply romantic musical chairs.

> There's something totally addictive about sex [thinks Denver]. When you haven't had it in a while, a girl can definitely live without it. But when you're back in action – watch out! (242)

Among the other relationship-based plots in *Poor Little Bitch Girl* are: Annabelle deciding that her coke-addled, star-struck boyfriend Frankie Romano has got to go (even tho' he can play the Concerned Boyfriend role quite well when he's sober); Brigitte Stanislopoulos has chosen a lesbian lifestyle, and takes up with an Ozzie, Kris; M.J. hooks up (no, *marries*, Vegas-style) an 18 year-old, Carrie (much to Bobby's disgust); and Bobby has an uncomfortable infatuation with superstar Zeena (who's into S/M, and treats him like a dog), tho' he ends up pursuing Denver.

Poor Bobby is set upon by Zeena in the shower:

> Basically Zeena had molested him, and his dick had happily gone along with it.
> Goddam it! Why hadn't he locked the hotel door? Or at least the bathroom door?
> But then again – knowing Zeena, locks would present no deterrent. Miz Superstar could probably spring a lock with her snatch! (312)

☆

There isn't really a big set-piece at the end of *Poor Little Bitch Girl* – well, there *is* a Hollywood Funeral, with all the trimmings (as the narrator puts it). Unfortunately, Jackie Collins doesn't get her manicured nails into the funeral, so it soon passes by without much incident (apart from Annabelle's image coming out well, as she milks the role of the Sorrowful Daughter – on the advice of Fanny Bernstein, of course. Oh, and Ralph Maestro's arrest, which's almost an after-thought).

Turns out that Ralph M. likely did hire Hank Montero (a dim-witted stunt guy) to kill his wife Gemma Summer, when he found out she was fooling around. Jackie Collins mentions famous murder cases like O.J. Simpson and Phil Spector. But of course, this being Hollywood, Maestro gets away with it (for now).

Poor Little Bitch Girl ends with a sex scene, as Denver Jones and Bobby Santangelo get freaky on the final page (in pride of place as the novel's Golden Couple). Denver is another of Jackie Collins' 'you can do it' girls, living proof that 'women can do anything' ('can' - and 'should'). Starting out as a lawyer for a law firm of sharks, Denver becomes an Assistant D.A. - prosecuting the bad guys, instead of defending corrupt Hollywood stars who float above the legal system due to their elevated status. (No one is above the law in Collins' ethical cosmos, and definitely not mere actors).

☆

In sum, *Poor Little Bitch Girl* is something of a missed opportunity: it has many of ingredients we've come to expect from a Jackie Collins tale, but somehow the piece doesn't catch fire. Is it because the characters lack passion? Intensity? Ambition? (Or that Collinsian term, *heat*). Somehow, we don't root for them as much as in Collins' better stories. Also, it has to acknowledged that two of the four main charas in *Poor Little Bitch Girl* - Carolyn and Denver - are a little dull, and their predicaments don't move us as much as they might. Even including Caroyln's horrible experience of being kidnapped (the kidnapping and hostage scenarios in Collins' books such as *The Power Trip, Vendetta: Lucky's Revenge* and *Lucky* are far more engrossing).

Indeed, the kidnap plot - no, the whole of *Poor Little Bitch Girl* - needs some of Gino Santangelo's cocky flash and Italian passion to heat it up. Part of the problem is the structure - because no one we root for knows that Carolyn's been kidnapped (and it takes Denver a *lot* of time to get round to following up her friend's text messages).[2] Thus, the kidnap plot pivots around Gregory Stoneman's guilty conscience (but this was the guy who wanted to rough up his lover so she'd lose their child! - so the plot doesn't really deliver the necessary dramatic juice), and then there's the sheer hell that Carolyn undergoes.

The charas aren't quite as scathingly good fun in this bitchy girls'

---

[2] And even then, some of the narrative leaps that Denver makes stretch credibility.

novel, as in some of Jackie Collins' other books. But Collins does create one memorable character, the portly, sarcastic, over-dressed, publicity maven Fanny Bernstein: 'this woman in the outrageous purple caftan with the huge earrings, orange hair and loud mouth, was hilarious' (352). A woman in her fifties who knows every celeb (and has shtupped most of them), who can work the P.R. game like a pro, who can effortlessly orchestrate gossip, Bernstein is a welcome breath of fresh air (I mean, Poison perfume).

★

GODDESS OF VENGEANCE

After the commercials, a bathroom break, and checking your phone, we're back with yet another installment in the *Lucky Santangelo* series. *Goddess of Vengeance* (2011) is More Of The Same in the *Lucky Santangelo* books (with a great title! – once again with the Sicilian revenge theme). By now, it's clear that the works in the second half of the *Lucky Santangelo* sequence are much more soap opera-ish, much more relationship stories, much more about who's dating/ doing/ divorcing who(m).

There are other plots, and villains/ rivals, however, in *Goddess of Vengeance* – step up Armand Jordan, the Prince of a small, Middle Eastern, oil-rich nation who lives in the Land of MacDonald's as a business tycoon (tho' he periodically slinks back to the strictly Islamic kingdom, to placate his pa, the King, from whom he hopes to inherit plenty of wealth some day). Of course, Jordan is a total worm to women (hiring expensive call girls and getting them to do unpleasant stuff, including to each other), and of course he has his sights set on the Keys resort in Las Vegas, Lucky Santangelo's pet project (which she ain't selling! *Bet on it*). But Jordan is obsessed with buying the Keys resort, going beyond what a sane businessman would do. So, yes folks, *Goddess of Vengeance* features yet another Lucky-and-Vegas-hotel plot (thirty years, no less, after the publication of the first *Lucky Santangelo* novel in 1981, which also included a Vegas hotel plot).

Meanwhile, Lucky Santangelo's daughter Max (*née* Maria), introduced in *Drop Dead Beautiful*, is blossoming into the familiar

Collinsian Wild Child: she's seventeen and she wants to Do It, the Big 'It', to Go All The Way, preferably with The One, that all-important major boy-babe who'll take her to Heaven and back (or maybe not back!). On the night of an out-of-control party at the Santangelos' Malibu pad (while mom and dad are away), Max gets her prize, on the sand on the beach at Malibu, with The One – in the form of superstar Billy Milena (recently split and divorcing from Madonna-ish star Venus Maria, Lucky's best friend).

As well as Max Santangelo (and her stoner, teenage chums Cookie and Harry), Billy Milena, and Venus Maria, other characters in *Goddess of Vengeance* include the newbie (introduced in *Poor Little Bitch Girl*), Denver Jones, a lawyer who's actually 'normal', or 'real' – or, anyway, not a celeb or model or groupie or hooker or gangster (Denver is the new inamorata of Bobby Santangelo, who has his own problems – they met in *Poor Little Bitch Girl*). Denver spends much of *Goddess of Vengeance* angsting about whether Bobby is The One. It's Collins' way of introducing a fairly straight soul into the wacky world of celebs, Hollywood stars and wise guys (so that Denver finds it all a little intimidating. When she meets Lennie and Lucky in Vegas, for instance, she's stunned by how amazing this famous couple is, how nice – and how in love). And there's Jorge, a new addition to Venus's stud farm.

★

In some respects, *Goddess of Vengeance* is the least compelling entry in the *Lucky Santangelo* series thus far: maybe, by this time, we sweet, tender readers have become very familiar with the ingredients (that is, if you read the *Lucky Santangelo* novels back-to-back, as I have done. However, if you read them as they came out, every few years, it wouldn't be the same). Also, Armand Jordan, the chief villain/ obstacle in *Goddess of Vengeance,* is basically a Bonnatti character in all but name (and origins): an insensitive, arrogant jerk, a drug user (coke = paranoia), an aggressive tycoon and cruel to women (there is also the hint, not taken up/ resolved really, that Jordan might be yet another of Gino Santangelo's illegitimate offspring, from a one-nighter with Jordan's mom way back in 1968. Peggy has a D.N.A. test, but decides not to pursue the issue).

Meanwhile, the new charas introduced in *Goddess of Vengeance*, such as Denver Jones (returning from *Poor Little Bitch Girl*), Bobby Santangelo's new squeeze, and Jorge, Venus Maria's new beau, aren't as appealing as some of Jackie Collins' other characters. (I missed the loud, out-of-control supermodels, for instance. Max Santangelo, tho' out-to-lunch, is way too nice! Well, she *is* Lucky's offspring, so she isn't allowed to be *too* wild).

★

As to the finale of *Goddess of Vengeance*, it comprised another crazee night in Las Vegas, as all roads lead (improbably) to the villa that Armand Jordan's staying in at the Cavendish Hotel on the Strip. Cocaine, speedballs, vodka, a suitcase full of money, Vegas lowlifes, blowjobs and naked hookers with giant tits – it's pretty much your regular evening in Jackie Collins' World of Sleaze.

It all turns out as expected – except for the bust-up and knife fight outside the villa, with Lucky in the fray, Jordan's luckless assistant Fouad, and even Lucky's daughter Max (who's been doing actor Billy Milena in the villa opposite).

The epilogue of *Goddess of Vengeance* winds up the plotlines with the customary Collinsian sense of justice/ morality/ ethics. The bad endure icky ends (Jordan's killed execution-style, for an infraction in his dodgy past), and the good get to live another day (for ex: Lucky and Lennie take the family to the South of France, where the so-in-love husband and wife re-enact a moment on vacation when they did the deed on a raft in the ocean).

★

Memorable lines in *Goddess of Vengeance*:

> Family indeed. They'd stab you in the back and bury the corpse if they thought they could get away with it. (288)

★

> Why do I feel that I'm in the middle of a Charles Dickens novel, transported back in time? Oh sure, I'm an avid reader – that's what you do when you're not allowed out of the house.
>
> Jackie Collins, *Confessions of a Wild Child* (16)

In 2013, Jackie Collins opted to go back to the origins of her signature character, Lucky Santangelo, with *Confessions of a Wild Child*. An unusual move, perhaps, tho' not unknown.[3] Unfortunately, as Collins' note at the start of *Confessions of a Wild Child* acknowledged, she had already covered Lucky's teenage years in the novel *Chances* (1981), and *Confessions of a Wild Child* ran thru the same scenarios, the same characters, and the same issues as the Lucky teen years chapters in *Chances*. Well, of course, it would be idiotic to depart radically from the story of Lucky, but *Confessions of a Wild Child* didn't seem add that much that was new, in the end (or new enough to justify even writing the book).[4] Scenes were explored in some more detail, true, and there were additional characters (more boys for Lucky to fool around with, for instance, and a girl who's drowned in the family swimming pool following a party that Lucky attends in L.A.), but too much of *Confessions of a Wild Child* was material we had already read (or knew about). *Viz.*, the life in L.A.... the boarding school in Switzerland... the nighttime escapades with Olympia Stanislopoulos... the new boarding school in Connecticut... the South of France jaunt, with Gino Santangelo and Dimitri Stanislopoulos turning up furious to collect their wayward daughters... the Las Vegas period, and the arranged marriage with the dim, boring senator's son Craven Richmond...

Lucky Santangelo's characterization wasn't altered, either, for the origins story in *Confessions of a Wild Child*: she is still super-cool, super-beautiful, a rebel, loves the Rolling Stones, enjoys dating boys (practising 'Almost' – going nearly all the way, but stopping short of coitus, which she's saving for The One), still lusts after Marco (Gino's right-hand man in Vegas, tho' he thinks she's too young), and is still full of ambition to follow her dad in the hotel business.

The choice of narrative voice in *Confessions of a Wild Child* is

---

[3] It was mirrored in many blockbuster movies, particularly the superhero movies, which went back to the origins of their lead characters in the 2000s and 2010s.

[4] Note to reader: don't read *Confessions of a Wild Child* right after *Chances*.

irritating: it's first person, present tense. The continuous present tense is a tricky viewpoint to deliver; it sort of suits Lucky's inner life, but also seems clunky and awkward:

> Oh yes, dreams do come true. Marco is at the airport, waiting to meet me. I stare at him,
> He stares right through me.
> Oh my God! He doesn't even recognize me. (37)

The timeline for *Confessions of a Wild Child* isn't stated. As with the later *Lucky Santangelo* books, Jackie Collins prefers to keep dates and years vague. But we know from *Chances* and *Lucky* that Lucky was born in 1950, and her mom was killed in 1955. So when *Confessions of a Wild Child* opens with Lucky a week before her fifteenth birthday (cited on page one), we know it's meant to be 1965. Except Collins includes ways of speaking, jargon and language that read more like the 1980s or 1990s.

Meanwhile, pop culture, such a huge part of teenagers' lives in the West in the 1960s, is barely touched on in *Confessions of a Wild Child*. There is a reference to *Cosmopolitan* magazine (which wasn't founded as we know it by Helen Gurley Brown until 1965), and Lucky wears a Rolling Stones Tee shirt, but little else (10). Even when the action moves to the South of France, and Juan les Pins and St Tropez, which we know were major hang-outs for young people and youth culture in the Sixties,[5] as well as Brigitte Bardot and the French film scene, Collins keeps references to names, places and culture vague.

Jackie Collins also coyly glosses over the details of the story of Lucky Santangelo's sexual experiences (which have been more explicit in other versions of the Santangelo legendarium). When Lucky masturbates Ursi[6] in the novel *Chances*, and he comes over her hand, she's delighted (she 'feels the power', and she wants more [507]); but in *Confessions of a Wild Child*, Collins refrains from describing such fooling around which, for a Collins novel, is curiously prudish.

Like many a romantic yarn, *Confessions of a Wild Child* builds up to a wedding. Only this is an arranged marriage, as Gino Santangelo does a deal with Peter and Betty Richmond (Washington, D.C. politicos), so that his wayward daughter Lucky will be reined in by

---

5 Andrew Loog Oldham and Donald Cammell were there, for example, and the Stones holed up near Nice at Keith Richards' place.
6 He has 'long floppy hair and kind of a bad boy look' (26).

getting hitched to their son Craven. Lucky resists, of course, but she's only sixteen and not quite the fully-fledged, 'don't fuck with me' Santangelo yet. It's either marriage or back to yet another private boarding school: that's the choice that Gino sets for her (there's no chance that the One She Wants, Marco, is going to consider her, not when she's the daughter of his boss!). Lucky opts for the Richmond marital deal,[7] because she reckons she'll be freer (and the thought of going back to school again – ugh!).

In the end, *Confessions of a Wild Child* is too lightweight, too insubstantial, to contribute much to what we've already enjoyed in the *Lucky Santangelo* series. The *Lucky Santangelo* books may be Jackie Collins's masterwork (the first half of the series is, perhaps), but *Confessions of a Wild Child* just doesn't have the heat, the juice, the fire we might hope for.

★

THE SANTANGELOS

> ...a story about the Santangelo family. And what a story it was. A murder in Chicago. An assassination in Palm Springs. A lethal car crash. Suicide bombers in Vegas.
>
> Jackie Collins, *The Santangelos* (517)

So we come to the last book that the Queen of Hollywood published in her lifetime, *The Santangelos* (2015): it's the last of the Big Collins Novels, and it's the Final Book in the *Lucky Santangelo* series, 34 years after the publication of the first *Lucky Santangelo* book, *Chances*, in 1981.

The Santangelos picks up from the end of *Goddess of Vengeance*, with the same charas in the Santangelo clan (Lucky, Lennie, Bobby, Max and Gino); their lovers/ friends/ relatives (Denver, Carolyn, M.J.); and some of the same opponents – such as King Emir, king of Akramshar. Plus the usual retinue of out-of-control supermodels (Athena), desperate-for-a-comeback actresses (Willow Price), nice screenwriters and possible lovers (Sam), movie agents (Eddie Falcon), private dicks (Chris Warwick), horny, Italian photo-

---

[7] There is blackmail behind it – Gino has piccies of Peter Richmond and Hollywood star Marabelle Blue going at it. Lucky also finds out that Gino is apparently having a fling with Richmond's wife Betty, which repulses her.

graphers (Carlo), and sleazebag journos (Jeff Williams).

So the primary plot of *The Santangelos* has King Emir planning payback for the death of his son Armand Jordan (which formed the finale of the previous *Santangelo* novel, *Goddess of Vengeance*). Also in the running as chaos-makers are Alejandro and Rafael; Alejandro performs the out-of-control bastard role - young, rich, egotistical, superficial, aggressive. The son of a drug lord (Pablo), Alejandro fancies himself as a Hollywood film producer - he's shallowly impressed by fame and celebrity. So he's gonna use dad's millions to back a movie (Rafael is the sensible one of the pair of sort of brothers, the long-suffering nanny to Alejandro).

Is Jackie Collins getting product placement money for *The Santangelos*? So many mentions of Uber taxis! And I-Phones! And, in her recent novels, American Airlines, Apple computers, Ferrari, Mercedes and B.M.W. cars, etc.

In *The Santangelos*, Lucky Santangelo is depicted as very much the Italian-American matriarch of an expanding family, the den mother to beat all den mothers ('don't fuck with a Santangelo'). Lucky is as strong as ever in *The Santangelos*, on top of everything, and nothing escapes her beady, possessive eye (*bet on it!*).

How old is Lucky Santangelo in *The Santangelos*? Hmmm - if she's born in 1950 (as previous novels have it), and *The Santangelos* is set in 2015, then she'd be 65 (but she's portrayed as sort of ageless - in her 50s at most). And Gino Santangelo seems to be in his late 90s. However, once again, Jackie Collins doesn't lock the novel into dates (tho' there are cultural references which pin it down to at least the 2000s, and possibly the 2010s).

The Santangelos takes a while to get going (longer than usual in a Jackie Collins outing): the preliminary goals and scenarios don't grip the reader like some of Collins' earlier first acts of novels (which is where the urge to turn the pages usually starts). Lucky Santangelo's plan is to build another resort in Las Vegas (*another*?!), but this time with a movie studio attached to it (Vegas is of course already a movie set (actually it's many movie sets), and employs plenty of movie and theme park technology, and a theme park approach to vacations and resorts). Husband Lennie Golden is writing and directing his independent movies (as usual). Daughter Max is starting out on her career - beginning with modelling jobs in London and Italy (and trying to edge out of the shadow of two super-successful parents (Lennie and Lucky), and an over-bearing supermodel chum and party girl, Athena). Bobby Santangelo is overseeing more openings of clubs (in Chicago), while having relationship trouble being apart from District Attorney girlfriend Denver Jones (*is she good enough for him?* she wonders; while he gripes: *how come she puts her job first every time?*). Bad girl Willow Price is planning a comeback in movies with an independent pic financed by criminal Alejandro and written by nice guy Sam. (Willow takes on the role of Venus Maria in previous *Santangelo* books, and charas such as Lina (*Dangerous Kiss*), Lola (*Hollywood Divorces*), and Claudia (*The World Is Full of Married Men*) – beautiful, ambitious and charismatic but also wayward, hedonistic, lazy and self-destructive).

The inciting incident in the plot of *The Santangelos* occurs when Gino Santangelo is gunned down in Palm Springs (this is definitely the moment when *The Santangelos* comes alive). For a while I wondered if Jackie Collins would allow Gino the Ram to die peacefully in his sleep. After all, he'd suffered plenty of grief (deaths of wives, sons, etc), but he was an Italian mobster, after all, and a peaceful death doesn't make for great drama (also, he has bumped off several victims). So, in Jackie Collins' re-run of the assassination attempt in *The Godfather*, Gino is shot by a guy while he's out jogging with his pocket-venus wife Paige (yes, Gino is jogging in his late nineties!).

So Gino the Ram is dead!

Gino? Dead?

It doesn't seem possible, kiddo! But what can I tell ya? – he's gone...

Gino. Father. Fighter. Ladies' man. Tough guy. Business titan. Man of the world. (464)

And Lucky Santangelo, for one, is furious. Discovering the word 'VENGEANCE' on a note delivered to her beloved daddy Gino Santangelo (which he placed in his safe) is hardly necessary (151): we know by now that vengeance is a major theme in Collinsworld. After all, Collins reminds us of the Santangelo family motto in her epigraph to *The Santangelos*: *never fuck with a Santangelo!*

Curiously, there isn't a heart-warming scene between father and daughter before Gino Santangelo is killed. You'd imagine that Jackie Collins would allow the two main characters in her *Lucky Santangelo* series to have one last drink on the hotel terrace in Las Vegas (to give Gino's death added emotional poignance). And it would've been entertaining to meet Gino for One Last Time. A missed opportunity, then, definitely (which a TV or film adaptation would likely feature).

But no, they don't meet in *The Santangelos* – they speak once on the phone (planning to catch up the following week (in Vegas, of course) – Lucky wants to tell papa about her scheme of building a hotel-cum-film-studio).8

When Gino Santangelo dies, the family convenes (even tho' they're all over the world). Lucky Santangelo finds herself realizing that she never liked Paige (Gino's 4th wife), and only put up with her because daddy married her. (That Paige is entertaining celebrity mourners very soon after the murder sickens Lucky. Paige also has a lover lined up – Darlene – to fill the Gino-gap).

The death of Gino Santangelo is as good a reason as any for Jackie Collins to wheel in some of the characters from her many books: so there are mentions of actor Nick Angel (from *American Star*), Al King the singer and Dallas (from way back in 1977 – *Lovers and Gamblers*), Jack Python (from *Hollywood Husbands*), and busty Gina Germaine (from *Hollywood Wives*).9 It's enjoyable when Collins activates the inter-connectedness of her fictional world (she could do this more often, as some authors do).

Meanwhile, Bobby S., Lucky's firstborn, is the target of a scam that gets him arrested for murder. It's Rafael and Alejandro, the drug lord's sons, who have the authorities closing in on them for their narcotics trafficking, so they launch a pre-emptive strike against the Santangelos (Bobby is dating Denver Jones, the D.A. who's got the drug czars in her sights). The idea was to drug Bobby and blackmail him with a rape and battery scenario, but the goon they hired goes too far, and kills the call-girl Nadia. Thus, Bobby is arrested for murder in Chicago (which provides a key subplot in *The Santangelos*).

The storylines in *The Santangelos* take familiar trails through the Collinsian Glitterverse: Lucky Santangelo, for instance, hires a private detective (Chris Warwick) to hunt down Gino's killer (she used to employ Boogie for that – Warwick is really the same character). As usual, the private detective is cool, calm, methodical and persistent, and always gets the job done (if only detectives in Collinsworld were running our governments!).

---

8 Gino Santangelo's response would probably be: *you're nuts, kiddo!* (Pause) *It's a great idea!*
9 If the timeline was set in stone, some of these characters would be 30 or 40 years older.

❤

For the finale of *The Santangelos*, Jackie Collins uses two set-pieces, which she is fond of: the social/ relationship set-piece plot (Gino the Ram's funeral and memorial celebration in Las Vegas), and the thriller plot set-piece (the murder of Gino/ the revenge plot). And for good measure, a giant auto pile-up on the desert highway to Vegas (to eliminate some characters). Collins acts as the Goddess ruling over her fictional world – with a flick of her pen across the page, people expire.

All roads lead to Las Vegas in Jackie Collins' final novel and the last *Lucky Santangelo* tale – apart from a side-strip to London and Roma (following Max's modelling career), *The Santangelos* is a Los Angeles novel and a Las Vegas novel: the Collins Heartland. I mean, if it's Gino Santangelo, it's gotta be either Gotham or Vegas; and if it's Lucky S., it's gotta be Gotham, L.A. or Vegas.

❤

The finale of *The Santangelos* plays out as expected: in the Gino Santangelo's death-revenge plot, Lucky Santangelo kills the guy who ordered her father's demise – King Emir. The incident takes place on the forty-story balcony of the Magiriano Hotel in Las Vegas: in a struggle, the King falls (thus, Jackie Collins plays it both ways – it was an accident, but it was also murder). Stupidly, the King rattles off a full confession to Lucky (they are alone) – that he killed Gino, etc, in the gloating manner of a Hollywood movie villain.[10]

We know that Lucky Santangelo is going to claim revenge for her father's murder ('never fuck with a Santangelo') – just as she did with her mother's killer, Enzio Bonnatti. (It's a little irresponsible that Lucky pushes King Emir off the building, with so many people gathered below for the funeral service, who might get hit. Jackie Collins makes something of that, too, by having the body splat right next to Craven Richmond, Lucky's hapless and useless first husband. Instantly, Craven collapses on the floor as a gibbering wreck. As he would).

This is also Jackie Collins' version of another 9/11 terrorist plot – King Emir's plan to kill Lucky at Gino Santangelo's funeral service involves suicide bombers (they will die for the cause, but be honoured, the King reassures them, as heroes).

Lucky Santangelo senses that summat's up when King Emir's entourage is discovered to be staying the Magiriano Hotel. And then

---

10 Villains never learn! Instead of talking, kill, kill, kill!

to be leaving the day of the funeral service. But with the King and his bodyguards staying behind. The clincher is Lucky discovering the note the King sent to the manager, on the same printed card she found in Gino's safe with the word 'vengeance' on it.

Meanwhile, the car crash in the desert on the way to Las Vegas clears the deck of a coupla no-goods – the drug lord's playboy son Alejandro, and another playboy, the evil Dante from the Dolcezza fashion company. The girls travelling with them survive: Willow and Max're thrown free of the car (the truck driver in the rig that smashes into them, plus the hitchhiker girl giving the guy a second blowjob, also expire, as well as a B.M.W. full of young and high teens (bar one) heading back from Vegas).

So Willow Price and Max're put into a local hospital in nearby Barstow, with the news hounds descending on Willow (again with the media and *paparazzi* issue), and Max's in a coma. Jackie Collins indulges herself with a snitch from the fairy tale *Sleeping Beauty*, and has the Prince, Billy Melina, wake Princess Max from the coma after several days.

Omitting a scene of the funeral service means that Gino Santangelo's life isn't celebrated in *The Santangelos* – instead, we have the *Lucky Santangelo* novels themselves for that. Altho' Lucky reminisces about Gino, there are fewer memorials than one might expect (altho' everybody says they'll miss him). Of course, being in his late nineties, most of his contemporaries are long dead (including Uncle Costa). There's a brief resumé of Gino's life from Costa, as Lucky recalls her uncle's stories:

> ...tales of Gino's misspent youth – racketeering, loan-sharking, owning a fancy speakeasy during prohibition, a lengthy stint in jail, countless women, then finally Vegas, where he'd turned things around and become a legitimate businessman building hotels and creating an empire. (120)

❤

The epilogue of *The Santangelos* plays out as expected, with pride of place being given to Lucky Santangelo (and Lennie Golden), as the final entry in the 2015 novel. In the brief plot summaries (a few short paras each), we discover: ★ that Willow Price's still determined to climb back to the top of the pile in Hollywood (she's still with ageing actor Ralph Maestro, from *Poor Little Bitch Girl*) ★ that Tariq and Peggy opt to stay in the U.S.A. ★ that Max and Billy Melina get together (they're engaged in Italy) ★ that Chris Warwick hooks up with a rich, older woman ★ that Denver ends up with Sam

★ that Bobby and Venus defy Lucky and continue their romance (on the down-low) ★ that Rafael ends up in Oz (but alone) ★ that Pammy (Willow's mom) marries sleazy hack Jeff Williams (they're publishing a tell-all biog of Willow called *Poor Little Bad Girl*) ★ and that Paige expires during an S/M session in Paris that goes wrong[11] (making this the last of Collins' death-at-orgasm scenes). And the last line of Collins' last novel reads: 'They [Lucky and Lennie] had each other, and that was all that really mattered' (535).

Thus, *The Santangelos* isn't quite wholly satisfying – as the final book in the *Lucky Santangelo* saga, that is (and as a revenge tale, it isn't Sophocles or Jacobean tragedy). The death of Gino Santangelo might've been milked for deeper emotions, and the resolutions of the ten-novel series are a little flimsy. There's a wan, underwhelming aspect to the finale of the series of *Lucky Santangelo* books, which could so with some red-blooded, Italian-Sicilian-American passion. It's not an all-out, operatic, spectacular finish.

---

[11] Why does Paige die? Seems a little harsh – because she stood up to Lucky over Gino's funeral? Because Lucky never really liked her? Because she squirrelled Lucky's daddy away in boring Palm Springs?

Jackie Collins

A Novel By
The Author of CHANCES

Hollywood Wives

Twelve

The Hollywood Novel Series

Los Angeles is at the end of America – the last place, the extreme. It has extreme people, extreme buildings, extreme cars.

Kit Carson (1983)

I spent two miserable years in California. But it was Barbara Stanwyck who said: 'The best place to be miserable is California.'

Andrei Konchalovsky (1986)

HOLLYWOOD WIVES

> Tits and sand – that's what we used to call sex and violence in Hollywood.
>
> Burt Lancaster (1983)

Hollywood Wives (1983) was one of Jackie Collins' biggest successes. The first entry in the *Hollywood Wives* series (which included *Hollywood Husbands, Hollywood Kids, Hollywood Divorces* and *Hollywood Wives: The New Generation*), it was soon turned into a glossy, all-star, American television mini-series (in 1985).

Hollywood Wives is another of Jackie Collins' ensemble novels, in which we follow a group of characters. Many of them are 'Hollywood Wives' or 'Hollywood Girlfriends' (with the odd 'Hollywood Maid' and 'Hollywood Mother' included). Most of the characters are in romantic relationships (that're often falling apart or starting up).

Parents and children are not a key ingredient of *Hollywood Wives*, as they are in many Jackie Collins books (but there are one or two, such as George and his daughter Karen Lancaster, who're Hollywood royalty, and the subplot of Sadie La Salle's twin sons, Deke and Buddy).

The *Hollywood* series includes:

- ▼ *Hollywood Wives* (1983)
- ▼ *Hollywood Husbands* (1986)
- ▼ *Hollywood Kids* (1994)
- ▼ *Hollywood Wives: The New Generation* (2001)
- ▼ *Hollywood Divorces* (2003)

Who are the 'Hollywood Wives'? Miz.[1] Collins explains:

> The three women were firm friends. They moved in the same circles and had the same interests – clothes, money and sex. (141)
> Pretty, and blonde. Groomed, and plasticized. The perfect Beverly Hills look. (357)

What do they do? Principally, it seems, they bitch, they live to bitch, they love to bitch:

> The lunch passed in a flurry of gossip, innuendo and general bitchery. Reputations, love affairs, talent and looks were casually pulled to pieces. (145)

---

[1] Collins has her female characters called 'Miz.' (not Miss or Ms.) when she wants to be formal.

What do they look like? Via Elaine Conti, Jackie Collins describes the Hollywood Wives this:

> The upper-echelon ladies of Beverly Hills, Bel Air and other suitably monied locations were out in full force. Saint Laurent, Dio, Blass, and de la Renta, rustled expensively on perfect bodies. And if they weren't perfect they made a damned good try. Electrolysis, body firming, cellulite control, vein removing, fat removing. All these things had taken place on one or the other of the bodies milling around. Tit renovation, teeth capping, snatch tightening, eyelid lifting, nose bobbing, ass raising. All these things and more. (235)

What are the locations of *Hollywood Wives*? The Beverly Hills Hotel. The Beverly Wilshire Hotel. Ma Maison (every other scene seems to take place in the restaurant). The Bistro. Morton's. A Century City apartment. With side-trips to Malibu, and the beach.

If Jackie Collins was getting product placement hand-outs for *Hollywood Wives*, the following would be recipients: Ma Maison, the Beverly Hills Hotel, Ferrari, Volkswagen, Armani and Gucci. We all know about product placement in movies (which can off-set costs considerably), but in novels? (In some later novels, like *The Santangelos*, certain brands (Apple, B.M.W., American Airlines, Mercedes) are referenced many times).

Karen Lancaster is a Hollywood Princess, the daughter of former studio mogul George Lancaster. She has a liaison with Ross Conti in Malibu (Conti is mesmerized by Lancaster's famous nipples, which she displays bra-less every chance she gets). Lancaster seems to be a professional Hollywood Wife – or, rather, a Hollywood Girlfriend, perpetually in relationships, tho' she doesn't have a career.

And there's dear, old Gina Germaine, with the big-boobed, airhead image, but who can be as business-like and practical when she needs to be (like blackmailing a director for a role in a movie).

> Gina Germaine. Fluffy. Blonde. Dumb. And worse. A movie star (34).
> Gina Germaine was a cliché. She was also a hot, blonde, sexy, big breasted WONDERFUL LAY. (363).

The wives/ girlfriends come out better in *Hollywood Wives* than the husbands/ boyfriends. Among the guys, the actors are the worst: Ross Conti, Buddy Hudson, etc, are depicted as selfish, narcissistic, smug, childish, etc. Sure, they might be talented, but their treatment of the women in their lives is shabby (Ross with Elaine and Karen, Buddy with Angel, etc). In Jackie Collins' fictional world, if you fall for an actor, be prepared to always be second to his profession and his ego (no matter *what* he says!).

Here are more of *Hollywood Wives*' characters: Buddy Hudson, a wannabe actor, desperate to be the new John Travolta or Al Pacino (this is the early Eighties). Unfortunately, no one else seems to think that Hudson is hot stuff – apart from his new and rather innocent, non-streetwise bride, Angel (who adores him). So Hudson does the dispiriting rounds of casting agents and auditions, like every other actor and wannabe star in Tinseltown. Buddy has a troubled past – a smothering mother (with whom he has sex, although she wasn't his real mom). A runaway at 16, he gets into the usual sleazy world of acting as an escort to women, of trashy, Hollywood parties, and drink and drugs (one of his friends, Tony, 14, is raped, killed and dumped in San Francisco, at a particularly OTT party. Another friend, Randy, ends up dead following a drug binge with on-off girlfriend Shelly, a scenario that Collins often revisits)[2].

And all the while, Buddy Hudson is lying through his teeth to his new bride Angel about getting this or that acting role (when he only has forty bucks in his pocket). But he's doing many of the right things – going to auditions, visiting agents, attending acting classes (with Joy Byron, the ageing acting coach with whom he has a fling, of course. Jackie Collins used Byron again, ten years later, in the same scenario of an eroticized tutor-pupil relationship, in *American Star*, 1993).

Angel, meanwhile, is too perfect for her own good – too pure, too naïve, too trusting. She doesn't seem bothered by Buddy Hudson's sleazy past (tho' she doesn't know everything – yet); she simply believes in him. Angel is also another wannabe actress. (A mild, suburban girl, Angel is shocked when she goes on vacation in Hawaii with her friend who makes a pass at her in bed. On the rebound from this experience, she meets Buddy).

Ross Conti is an ageing actor (of the Kirk Douglas, Tony Curtis, Paul Newman[3] type), eager to climb back to the top. He's vain, shallow, egotistical, and promiscuous (all essential attributes of Collins' take on actors). Ross's Hollywood Wife, Elaine Conti, is keen, too – for the success, for the fame, and for the money. And to be invited to the best dinner parties, and to be seen at the finest

---

2 The sleazy aspects of Buddy's life are completely glossed over in the TV mini-series.
3 The famous, crinkly blue eyes link him to Steve McQueen as well as Paul Newman.

restaurants. Elaine is the frustrated Collinsian wife, hoping against hope that her man is going to blossom into a Real Man again. (Elaine is so sexually frustrated (Ross hasn't been near her for months), that, in one of the funnier scenes in *Hollywood Wives*, she comes during her exercise class, as the women do 'the Snake' pose – crawling on the floor – and the pressure on her clitoris is too much).

Neil Gray is a hotshot, British film director, whose new project, *Street People*, is something that everyone in town wants to be a part of. Married to Montana Gray (who wrote the script), Gray has a drink problem, and is also lecherous (he has several affairs, including with actress Gina Germaine, who of course desperately wants a part in his new movie). Montana is another of Jackie Collins' many women-in-a-man's-world characters – this time, a screenwriter and would-be director (where everybody says she has two things against her: she's from Back East, and she's a woman). Montana realizes that the guys are edging her out of her own movie – one of the reasons that she opts to start directing herself.

There's a Lucky Santangelo character in each Jackie Collins book. In *Hollywood Wives*, the lucky girl is Montana Gray – so she's described as a leopard, in her late twenties, with the mandatory tiger eyes and 'wide, sensual mouth', and the unique fashion sense (silver bangles, hoop earrings, cowboy boots, loose shirts. Collins' alter-egos often use the gypsy look, including Lucky Santangelo). Plus, Gray is Collins' sort of woman: a woman on the up, a woman taking charge of her life, a woman who's trying to make it in the man's world of the film business (by writing her screenplay, and then directing). Lucky picked up that strand of Collinsian ambition in the 1990 novel *Lady Boss*, running a film studio.

Oliver Easterne is an amusing portrait of a cutthroat film producer who's obsessed with cleanliness. Every opportunity he gets he's wiping up messes, polishing forks or emptying ashtrays. Easterne is also the producer type who happily kisses ass (it's part of a producer's job, Jackie Collins notes), and is smug knowing that most of the money coming in from the movie *Street People* will go to him, rather than anyone else like the director or the actors. Which is the case in the movie business. (In the *Hollywood Wives* TV series, Rod Steiger played Easterne as a stereotypical film producer with the swagger and the cigar, with only a hint of dandyism).

Jackie Collins' depiction of the casting process of the fictional film *Street People* in *Hollywood Wives* is entertaining and a fairly good reflection of what goes on in casting. Of course it's exaggerated, but the portrayal of the power plays between film producers, film directors, agents, big stars and unknown actors is spot-on (Collins had been here many times as an actress herself in the 1950s-1960s). Collins is particularly good at how people in the film industry hide their real feelings and put on smiley masks or bullshit their way thru showbiz. (How George Lancaster bows out of the show, at the thought of a mere woman directing the film; how Ross Conti gets the gig in the end, altho' with a miserable pay-cut; how Buddy Hudson passes the screen test and gets to play Vinny; and how Gina Germaine is cast by Easterne as the female lead, no matter how inappropriate she is (with her gigantic chest). And how, after all of that work, the whole production is cancelled in the end. And how Easterne, *not* Montana Gray the writer, owns the rights to the screenplay).

★

The thriller plot in *Hollywood Wives* is provided by Deke Andrews, a psycho who chops up his family in Philly then flees to Gotham and other places. It's not Jackie Collins' most compelling criminal/ psycho plotting, and Andrews, another loner freak in the Travis Bickle/ *Taxi Driver* mode,[4] is not especially engaging, either. (Meanwhile, Detective Leon Rosemont is pursuing the murder case, having a connection to one of the victims, the hooker Joey, as does Deke. That is, Joey clings onto Rosemont, and they have a romance of sorts, with Rosemont persuading himself that it's all one way, and it's her fault).

But there's simply too much of Deke Andrews driving across the Land of the Free in *Hollywood Wives*, leaving a trail of slashed hookers and secretaries in his wake, and prattling on about being 'The Keeper Of The Order' and other Judæo-Christian garbage (which Andrews uses to justify his insanity). We get the point, but it's overdone. (The 1985 television version also included *far* too much of Andrews traversing the continent).

There're two blackmail scams in *Hollywood Wives* – Gina Germaine films her sex sessions with Neil Gray, in order to force him to put her in the movie *Street People*, and Ross Conti is photographed tupping Karen Lancaster (by a weasel with the silly name Little S. Shitz). In Collins Land, you never go to the cops in a blackmail case. (In the event, the photos of Conti enhance his

---
4 He even has his hair shaved off.

career's rebirth).

Another layer to *Hollywood Wives* is the quotation from the Rod Stewart song 'Passion':

> In the bars and the cafés – Passion,
> In the streets and the alleys – Passion
> ('lyrics used with kind permission', of course!).

★

In the middle of *Hollywood Wives*, Jackie Collins has all of the multiple plots and characters simmering along nicely in her giant witch's cauldron of a Hollywood novel. How Collins works in a book is very familiar: for example, in a romantic couple, one character will inch forward, while another slips back. Thus, Buddy Hudson is granted a screen-test for the *Street People* flick (a big deal, because he has been going after this job – and any job – for ages); but he can't share the elation with his new wife Angel, because she's so pissed at him abandoning her for days on end, she walks out on him (getting a room in a house on Fountain and a job in a hair salon on Fairfax, and later moving in with the gay couple Koko and Adrian).

Jackie Collins does this all the time in her fiction – she is a passionate devotee of irony and oppositions. Here's another example from the Buddy-Angel plot-line in *Hollywood Wives*: Buddy has been busting his gut to get a part in *Street People*, but Angel, wandering onto the beach at Malibu, is accosted by none other than Oliver Easterne, the big shot film producer who is behind *Street People*, and he wants her to appear in the movie! Using the immortal words everybody's achin' t' hear in Hollywood: *you are going to be a star!*

Thus, without trying at all – without, actually, doing anything other than being herself, Angel is picked to appear front and centre in *Street People*, while Buddy has to go thru shlepping to auditions, lying his way in to see Montana Gray (the writer and casting director).

Some of the more entertaining sections of *Hollywood Wives* are those involving the hyper-innocent Angel Hudson and the hyper-camp hairdresser Koko (who acts as a mother hen clucking around his Princess Cinders). Jackie Collins' writing comes alive when she's speaking in the voice and persona of bitchy celebrity watchers and gossip hounds (as well as make-up artists and hairdressers – she loves that relationship between the pamperer and the pampered). It's like a fairy godmother coaching Cinderella (with all the gay/ camp/

theatrical associations). So Koko is giving Angel a newbie's guide to life in Tinseltown, where cynicism and aggression is mandatory, coupled with a sense of awe and subservience in the presence of True Celebrity.

Angel Hudson is a tough study, tho' – she doesn't even know what a bar mitvah is! Or who Mario Puzo is! (Which's heresy in Collins Land!). Koko can't believe that anybody could be so naïve, but he's happy to show Angel the ropes. Poor Angel, now pregnant and separated from her new but very disappointing husband Buddy Hudson, just wants to stay out of the way and be left alone to nurse her wounds. But Koko grabs the phone off her and tells Mrs Liderman that, yes, Angel *will* go the Big Party, the centrepiece of *Hollywood Wives*.

★

So, the set-piece in *Hollywood Wives* is a Grand Hollywood Party, one of Jackie Collins' safe-and-sound stand-bys. Always works: because it has: (1) a legitimate reason to bring together all of the characters; (2) endless possibilities for misunderstandings, revelations, and full-scale bitchery (all of the stuff that Collins' fiction thrives on); (3) lengthy build-up scenes (what to wear? Who's your date? Who's doing the catering? The music? The flowers? And where to sit everyone?); (4) plus some celebrity spotting (Liza Minnelli! Hi, baby! *Oooh*, Richard Gere! Look, honey – is that Sean Connery over there?!).

In *Hollywood Wives*, it's the Contis who're honouring veteran actor George Lancaster (a sexist bore, according to Montana Gray, who doesn't really want him in her movie), and his wife, the horsey, scary (and scarily rich) Pamela London. But the real reason that Elaine Conti is stepping up to be the Hollywood Hostess of the Moment is to persuade super-agent Sadie La Salle to take on her hubby Ross, to promote his flagging acting career (unfortunately, Ross and Sadie go way back, and tho' she carries a flame for him still, after 26 years, he treated her like §&¡% back then, leaving her for another woman. La Salle seethes about this, for much of the novel).

The Big Hollywood Party gives Jackie Collins ample opportunities for comic scenes (like Oliver Easterne in the restroom cleaning himself and Pamela London thinking he's jerking off); bust-ups (Elaine throws her husband Ross Conti out of the house when she finds out about the affair[5] he's having with Karen Lancaster in her

---

[5] But Elaine is also tupping her exercise class instructor, who gives massages.

Century City apartment);[6] and misunderstandings (the estranged husband and wife Angel and Buddy finally meeting, but being with different dates).

Celebrity spotting is to the max in the Ma Maison scene in *Hollywood Wives* (one of many scenes set in the restaurant). Buddy Hudson is jazzed to see Shakira Caine (Mrs Michael Caine),[7] Stephanie Powers,[8] Robert Wagner, Roger Moore's wife Louisa, Dudley Moore, Jack Lemmon, Clint Eastwood, Tom Selleck, Sidney Poitier, etc.

Angel attends the party and is dazzled:

> She spotted James Caan, and Elliott Gould, and Liza Minnelli, and Richard Gere. RICHARD GERE!! She could die now and feel perfectly satisfied. (356)

Meanwhile, Jackie Collins lets nothing stop her from delivering a crude, *Playboy*-style comedic skit: at the moment of orgasm, Neil Gray has a heart attack and finds himself unable to pull out of Gina Germaine's 'super-cunt' (as she's known around town). No matter what the cute, Asian hooker (joining them for a threesome) tries, Gina cannot dislodge the near-dead Gray from her famous caboose (and of course she becomes hysterical). It leads to a trip to the hospital, ructions between Montana and Neil, and the delay of the principal photography of *Street People* (in the event, Montana steps into the breach and takes up the director's helm, which she's always wanted to do).

So Neil Gray receives severe punishment for adultery (you just don't fool around on a to-die-for and multi-talented woman like Montana Gray); so Montana, *very* miffed, shtupps Buddy Hudson after a night of walking on the beach at Malibu; and Gina Germaine tries to laugh off the fact that everybody in Tinseltown knows the whole, degrading story.

Yes, the fate of Neil Gray is harsh: the lesson is: don't fuck around with blonde floosies when you're married to the main author-identification figure and Lucky Santangelo stand-in – Montana Gray.

---

[6] There's a fun sequence where Ross Conti visits Karen Lancaster and her out-size nipples at Century City: it's one of those security-obsessed complexes where you need a key just to use the elevator. Jackie Collins is very good at depicting the minor irritations of modern life.

[7] Collins is fond of including Shakira and Michael Caine, the Roger Moores, the Lazars, the Poitiers, the Wilders, the Kopelsons, and the Davises in her books.

[8] Powers appeared in the TV series of *Hollywood Wives*.

Oh, and don't drink (but deny it). And when you're told, following your heart attack, *no drink, no drugs, no sex, no excessive exercise,* don't sneak off and stop at a bar for some alcohol. Thus, Gray has a heart attack in the bar's car lot.

★

At the Big Hollywood Party, cut up into the usual short sections comprising several paragraphs each, Jackie Collins offers some examples of overhead conversations:

> 'He pays me, I think it turns him on,' said the redhead in the mink-trimmed cape.
> 'I buy them dresses, take them to Acapulco – I have to give them head too?' asked an outraged stud.
> '...she's like a Barbie doll – you wind her up and she buys new clothes...'
> '...he'd fuck a bush if he thought it would invest...'
> 'The biggest prick I ever knew had the smallest!' exclaimed a soignée middle-aged woman in a chic black dress.
> 'If it cost him a nickel to shit he'd vomit,' said a fast-talking producer.
> 'Every day she comes to my office, locks the door, gets under the desk and sucks my cock,' said the head of a studio.
> 'You know what the bum says to me? He says – don't fuck on my property – you want to screw around do it on a bed someone else paid for...'

Alas, not one of those lines of bitchery were used in the television adaptation of *Hollywood Wives*.

★

Who is the character that gets the best lines in *Hollywood Wives*? The character that Jackie Collins seems to enjoy writing in-the-voice-of the most? Actually, it's Ross Conti, the ageing actor desperate for a decent role to re-launch his flagging career. Collins uses Conti as her mouthpiece for the bitchiest thoughts and the sassiest retorts in *Hollywood Wives*. For example:

He felt like a struggling starlet. Not that starlets struggled, they merely lay back, opened their legs, and welcomed America. (450)

Can't the dumb schmuck see I'm the only actor for his lousy movie? (470)

★

THE FINALE.

So, who is Deke Andrews' target in La-La Land in *Hollywood Wives*? Why is the weirdo travelling across the continent, making for Barstow, CA, and then Hollywood, CA? Jackie Collins loves to tease the reader with her thriller plots – her key technique being to conjure a massive threat and then to withhold just who the target is.

Oh, we know that Deke Andrews is going to be caught and/ or killed (when super-moralizer Jackie Collins runs the show, you can be sure of that! Bet on it, as Lucky Santangelo would say). And we also know that Collins is going to push the jeopardy several notches into the red until it's resolved (there are plenty of seemingly helpless women to use as potential victims). So Collins has Andrews chopping up victims[9] in Las Vegas and Barstow before he points his old, brown van towards Tinseltown.

In the end, the thriller plot in *Hollywood Wives* turns upon the issue of adoption: Sadie La Salle gets pregnant by the love of her life Ross Conti way back when, giving birth to twin boys: Deke Andrews and Buddy Hudson. The babies are sold for adoption. The ironies here include La Salle being the new agent for Hudson and promising to launch him as a star, not realizing he is her son (the same way she did with Conti, by plastering billboards all across the U.S. of A. saying, 'who is Buddy Hudson?'). Cleverly, in a Hitchcockian moment, Collins exploits the billboards when she has Andrews discovering one of them in La Salle's Beverly Hills home (he mistakes the photograph of Hudson for himself, precipitating a deeper dive into identity confusion).

Deke Andrews is allowed by Jackie Collins to continue his rampage of violence and madness for a long time in *Hollywood Wives* before he's caught (despite having Detective Rosemont on his tail – at the cost of his marriage: when he's on vacation with his wife Millie, he's still working on the case; she leaves). So after tying up and beating Sadie La Salle in her home, and stabbing her assistant Ferdie Cartwright[10] to death at the front door, psycho Andrews heads for Angel Hudson (whom he's convinced is an incarnation of his beloved Joey, the hooker that he seems to have forgotten that he slaughtered back in Philly!). And on the way he has a car crash with Ross Conti in his Rolls (the outcome of this incident is delayed for a long time).

Poor Angel Hudson – she's pregnant, abandoned by her husband Buddy, and then pounced upon by a fearsome psychotic murderer! The finale of *Hollywood Wives* involves Angel, naked, tied to the bed and just about to be mounted by Deke Andrews, with Sadie La

---

9 Yes, the police and security services can't capture a serial killer running amok.
10 Who preys upon underage boys. Thus, more Collinsian justice.

Salle (also bound), watching in horror, and Buddy and Leon Rosemont arriving at the last minute, for the expected rescue.

★

There are further minor knots in the plot which're undone positively in the finale of *Hollywood Wives*: like Buddy Hudson discovering that his mother had adopted him, so it wasn't incest when she climbed on top of him and did the dirty. Also, Butterball, the guy involved in the murder of his teenage friend Tony (now going under the name of Wolfie Schweicker, a Tinseltown socialite), is killed by one of his casual pick-ups in Hollywood. So justice is dealt out in the usual moral manner in Collins Land.

The rest of the *dénouement* of *Hollywood Wives* is predictable: Ross Conti is re-united with his wife Elaine (and his star rises further when the *paparazzi* photos go public); Sadie La Salle goes back to agenting; Gina Germaine is run outta town by the gossip rags (ending up with a French New Wave director in Paris); Karen Lancaster gets hitched to Brit rocker Josh Speed (the wedding provides the final scene); and Montana Gray heads for Gotham (after leaving a pile of real fæces on the office desk of cleanliness fanatic Oliver Easterne, for screwing her on her own movie).

Buddy Hudson and Angel get the last pages of *Hollywood Wives* (the top billing, so to speak), as they travel to the Lancaster-Speed nuptials, accompanied by Sadie La Salle ('Buddy wore Armani. Of course. Angel wore maternity. What else?'). On the way, the contractions start for Angel. So here's our Happy Ending to *Hollywood Wives*, with the birth of twin boys.

★

The plotting is a little uneven in *Hollywood Wives*, as the Goddess Collins orchestrates her large cast of charas and their stories. For instance, it stretches belief that Angel and Buddy keep missing each other's phone calls (or that druggie Shelly[11] answers every time that Angel calls Buddy).[12]

And Buddy Hudson is a ditz: on the important day when Angel will be moving in with him (after weeks of cajoling), he decides to travel to San Diego (arranging to have Angel picked up by a limo and taken to his new digs). Not only that, he also hopes, while in San Diego, to make the peace with his mom, *and* go to the cops

---

[11] Shelly is especially vindictive towards Angel, lying to her repeatedly, and guarding Buddy possessively.
[12] It was also unconvincing in the TV series, which milked the premise too much.

regarding his friend Tony, who was killed. All that in one day, *and* driving to and from San Diego – assuming there are no holds-up on the freeway! (As if!).

★

HOLLYWOOD HUSBANDS

INTRO: ROUND AND ROUND.
The 'Hollywood Husbands' of the title of this 1986 follow-up novel to 1983's *Hollywood Wives* are three middle-aged guys who go back a long way: Jack Python, the handsome, intelligent, cynical TV talk show host *à la* Letterman, Donahue or Leno; Howard Soloman, the cocaine-snorting, neurotic studio boss of Orpheus Studios (*à la* Don Simpson or Jeffrey Katzenberg); and Mannon Cable, the Burt Reynolds-a-like movie star. All three are getting on in years, still chasing women, still married or living with women they don't particularly like; they are conceited, self-obsessed, and ego-maniacs; very famous and powerful – Hollywood Royalty – but they're also bored and insecure.

Apart from these three guys, *Hollywood Husbands* contains the usual troupe of Jackie Collins characters, from ageing, sex-mad TV star Silver Anderson, to her unruly, punky daughter Heaven who wants to be a pop star, to Wes Money, the twentysomething bar boy (and fabulous lover) on the make, to Nora, the chain-smoking, world-weary, long-suffering publicist, to the perpetually drugged-out, aged, Hollywood wife Ida White, one of the more amusing characters in *Hollywood Husbands*.

There are plenty of Hollywood Wives and Girlfriends in the second *Hollywood* novel, including Poppy and Melanie-Shanna, Whitney, Jade, Clarissa, Beverly, etc. Really, *Hollywood Husbands* is *Hollywood Wives 2*, as it's just as much about the wives, ex-wives and girlfriends as it is about the guys. It's a sister – or brother – novel to *Hollywood Wives* (that 1983 novel inaugurated the long-running *Hollywood* series).

And there are the usual Jackie Collins settings in *Hollywood Husbands*: wild, Hollywood parties; dinner parties and restaurants; business meetings; weekends in Vegas; and Malibu (for walks on the beach), etc.

And the usual Jackie Collins activities:
- putting on make-up
- dressing for going out
- shopping on Melrose
- worrying about jobs
- watching television
- driving around the Hollywood Hills
- people haunted by the past
- a little crime and dodgy dealings
- some sex
- and some drugs.

Hollywood Husbands is another ensemble piece, with the text flitting between a large group of characters like a pilled-up hostess at one of her famous Tinseltown parties. Each segment of a chapter relates one main event before the narrative shifts swiftly to the next one. The structure cuts down on really getting into one character and their lives, into motivations and back-story, or presenting characters with complexity and depth; but the benefits are the breathless pace, the continuous sense of action, as if the novel is afraid of being boring, or getting bored with itself.

Hollywood Husbands presents a carousel of erotic relationships in the Jackie Collins manner, with the usual romances and bust-ups, and the lusts-from-afar, and the sex sessions with hookers. We've got:

- men who want to get back with their ex-wives (Mannon Cable)
- men who decide to stop fooling around when they meet the woman of their dreams (Jack Python)
- men who lust after other men's wives (Howard Soloman)
- powerful women who fall for younger men (Silver Anderson)
- and Hollywood Wives who want to please their husbands (Poppy Soloman).

Lovers are swapped, characters get together and fall apart continuously in *Hollywood Husbands*. But it's not random: Jackie Collins plans the exchanges of love and lovers so they have some irony or counter-point. For instance, studio boss Howard Soloman has lusted after Mannon Cable's ex-wife Whitney Valentine since forever, but is hesitant to make a move on her because she's his best friend's ex-wife, and Mannon dotes on Whitney. Then, when Howard is very close to making Whitney, on location in Arizona,

Mannon all of a sudden doesn't care much, because he's now seeing Clarissa Browning, who was until very recently Jack Python's lover.

And so it goes on. Very soap opera-ish, very melodramatic, very day-time TV. But it works – after all, filmmakers such as Woody Allen use this kind of erotic irony in the relationships he creates in movie after movie. It's classic stuff – the morals and lessons learned include:

(1) What you thought you really wanted, you don't, after all;

(2) The person you thought would make you happy doesn't, after all;

(3) Just when you thought it couldn't get any worse, it gets worse;

(4) Just when you thought life couldn't be any more horrible, it's suddenly, miraculously, FANTASTIC.

In Jackie Collins' fantasy world of sex-death-glitter-gore-fashion-Hollywood-romance-violence-glamour-beauty-and-lots-of-$$$$, you often get what you want, but if you do, it's rarely what you thought it was going to be (the subject of thousands of pop songs). There are Winners and Losers, yes, but the outcome is more complicated than simply dividing up characters into Winners and Losers. Occasionally, Collins will close one of her sex-and-crime-and-drugs fairy tales with an out-and-out Happy Ending (like the finale of *American Star*), but more typical is a complicated ending, with characters not having it all their own way.

As in fairy tales, patience is rewarded. And so is sheer hard work – and ambition. And humility. And truth – not being phony.

RICH AND FAMOUS PEOPLE ARE BORING.

You'll notice right away that Jackie Collins and her narrators are sceptical and critical and ironic about *all* of her characters, *including* her heroes and heroines, and the characters that the narrators seem to empathize with. Collins' narrators make bitchy remarks and put-downs of her characters that provide some of the funniest moments in her books. And you won't find J.R.R. Tolkien talking about Frodo, Gandalf and Aragorn like that, or Thomas Hardy discussing Tess Durbeyfield or Jude Fawley like that, or Jane Austen discussing *dear*, sensitive Elizabeth Bennet like that. Oh no. No, no, no.

Turns out that rich and famous and powerful people are just like everyone else. *Boring*. Wes Money, the kid from the streets of L.A., realizes that at a star-studded dinner party that forms the set-piece of *Hollywood Husbands*:

> Here he was, surrounded by the rich and famous, and once he got talking to them, he realized they were just as boring as the rest of the population. (263)

THE BIG FINISH.

1986's *Hollywood Husbands* closes with the second set-piece, the Big Finish at the climactic party on New Year's Eve on billionaire Zachary Klinger's yacht (there's a lengthy yacht sequence in *Lucky*, and again in *The Power Trip*). Many of the plot-lines are resolved here, some in action, some in dialogue – for instance:

- the will-she-won't-she romance between supermodel Jade Johnson and talk show host Jack Python (plus the re-appearance of Jade's ex, the English fop Lord Mark Rand)
- the tangled relationships between Mannon Cable, his wife Melanie-Shanna, his new lover Clarissa Brown, and his ex-wife, Whitney Valentine
- the hatred of Silver Anderson for Klinger, and Klinger trying to get Silver
- a related plot-strand – Heaven being revealed as Klinger's daughter, and Silver avoiding her, etc.

The action in *Hollywood Husbands* is literally explosive, when a load of fireworks explode and fires rage around the yacht, and everyone dives for the lifeboats. It's *Titanic* time. Yet it occurs off-screen. Why? Because it's the *relationships* that count, not the action, and the relationships have already been dealt with in the party scenes.

And *Hollywood Husbands* pays off the mystery identity of the character in the flashbacks: sometimes Jackie Collins withholds the identity of the short flashbacks. *Hollywood Husbands* is unusual in only having flashbacks about one character. And she is only called 'the girl' in those italicized paragraphs.

Turns out it was Clarissa Brown Wot Done It – the Serious Actress who insists on shtupping her co-stars because it's good for the performance (!). So it was Clarissa who was 'the girl' in the flashbacks set 'somewhere in the Seventies', and 'somewhere in the Mid-West'. Her life was miserable and violent – repeatedly raped and abused. So she torches the house where the goons live and kills them. And she does it a number of times. Ms Collins ends each flashback like this:

> *Quietly, methodically, she shook the gasoline around the house. Lighting the first match was easy...* (233)

And Clarissa B. gets her own back on the glitterati in Hollywood by setting fire to the yacht and lighting the fireworks. As the narrator of *Hollywood Husbands* puts it, the people on that yacht form the cream of Hollywood – 'This was the most headline-making drama possible, with the most expensive cast ever assembled' (493). Yes, it's even better than a movie: 'No movie could beat *this* story' (493).

The coda of *Hollywood Husbands*, set a few weeks later, in February, 1986 (and also 9 months later), ties up some of the loose ends, the silliest being Jade's wedding to Lord Rand: in the middle of it, just as Jade's about to say 'I do', Jack Python appears with a helicopter and whisks Jade away (oh, you had to be there, darling!).

But Jackie Collins knows that if you've stayed with the 1986 book this far, you'll go along with some over-the-top action and humour. It's the same with a movie: in the last couple of reels in a big movie (certainly the ones made in recent times), the action gets loud, chaotic and wild. And the audience goes along for the ride (if you're still resisting the movie after one hour and twenty minutes, you've been wasting your time!).

★

Some memorable lines in *Hollywood Wives*:

> *I wouldn't even fuck her if she crawled to my trailer on her hands and knees and begged for it. Well... maybe if she begged.*

> There was nothing like success for putting the hard-on back in a man's life. (9)

★

HOLLYWOOD KIDS

Hollywood Kids (1994) was another business-as-usual novel for Jacqueline Jill Collins. Priced $28.00 (£17.99) in hardback, it was a 600-page book (but in 12-point type, with far fewer words per page than the average novel). Another in Collins' *Hollywood* series, *Hollywood Kids* was sort of about the children of big, Hollywood stars, film producers and the like, but as some of the main characters were in their thirties (like actor Bobby Rush), they weren't really 'kids' (Rush and his dad, Jerry Rush, were clearly modelled on father-and-son actors such as Kirk and Michael Douglas, while Jordanna Levitt's pa was a Clint Eastwood-a-like guy).

For the central five kids of the title, the theme was: how bad was it having a famous ma or pa? With all the privilege and wealth and fast cars came the œdipal conflicts, the high expectations (and disappointments), the lack of praise and respect, and so on. (J.J. Collins has mined this seam in many books).

Hollywood Kids was another novel with a thriller plot driving some of the narrative – in this case, an out-of-control movie actor turned psycho who kills his co-star in front of six witnesses while working on a movie. Once out of prison, Zane Ricca begins eliminating the people who put him away (they all happen to be women), one by one (so it's another twist on *The Count of Monte Cristo*, which Collins has employed several times).

Along the way in *Hollywood Kids* there are the usual old relationships falling apart and new ones being formed; the usual sleazy stuff (Cheryl and her friend Grant take over a call-girl business); gangsters (New York mob boss Luca Carlotti and his lackeys); journalists and TV news presenters (Kennedy and Rosa); and a Los Angeles setting (I guess it has to be L.A. if the book's called *Hollywood Kids*. It couldn't really be Wisconsin, could it?).

Not classic Jackie Collins by any means, *Hollywood Kids* was still enjoyable, with enough action and bitchiness and witty dialogue to keep it afloat for the duration. Afterwards, *Hollywood Kids* wasn't particularly memorable – none of the characters, except perhaps Jordanna and Kennedy (the two charas that Collins' narrator seems to identify with most), stay with you. And the climactic stuff with the kidnapping of the two women, being held hostage in a basement somewhere up in those sleazy Hollywood Hills, was routine TV cop show or police thriller stuff.

Déjà vu.
Again.

So I started in on *Hollywood Wives: The New Generation* (2001) right after reading 2008's *Married Lovers*, with *déjà vu* kicking in rapidly (by page 25). In *Married Lovers*, Lucy Lyons in an actress married to a powerful writer-director husband trying to get her own script off the ground but her husband won't help; so she secretly goes to a scuzzy apartment in Venice (Venice in Cali, not Italy), to use a young screenwriter (name of Marlon),[13] who has a taut body.

Now get this: in *Hollywood Wives: The New Generation*, Taylor Singer is an actress married to an Oscar-winning writer-producer-director who secretly goes to a shabby, Venice beachfront place to work on her project with a young, hunky scriptwriter. The scenarios are identical in many other respects (about the only difference is that in *Married Lovers,* Lyons holds back from getting it on with Marlon; instead, the heroine, Cameron Paradise does, and there's no talk between the lovers in either novel, it's just sex; but in*Hollywood Wives: The New Generation,* Singer takes her writer).

What else have we got in this sequel to Jackie Collins' most successful novel, *Hollywood Wives*? A mega-star Lissa Roman, in music and movies (think Whitney Huston, Beyoncé, Madonna) ★ her bride-to-be daughter Nicci who's having doubts (about marriage – what else?) ★ Nicci's fiancé film director Evan Richter who's uptight, a momma's boy and cheating on her ★ Brian Richter, the bad boy brother (and film director) that Nicci secretly fancies ★ Taylor Singer, an actress trying get her own project off the ground ★ her husband, successful but conservative film director Larry Singer ★ rugged, ex-cop private detective Michael Scorsinni ★ his loving but rather plain girlfriend ★ Michael's detective buddy and his wife Amber ★ and assorted boyfriends, girlfriends, wives and husbands.

The on-running thriller plot in *Hollywood Wives: The New Generation* is a kidnapping story (Jackie Collins has used kidnapping b4, in *Hollywood Kids* and several times in the *Lucky Santangelo* series, and all the way back to 1977's *Lovers and Gamblers*), but it doesn't offer much of interest. Ex-con and hate-all-humans Eric

---

13 It's amazing that Collins can have a character called Marlon, who was probably named after Marlon Brando (in real life as in a novel), and the author, Collins, had an affair with Brando! Again and again, we would love to read Collins' autobiography!

Vernon organizes the job with a bunch of misfits from a topless bar (!). And of course because the target is Nicci, the second author-identification figure (after Lissa Roman), he hasn't a chance.

The epilogue to *Hollywood Wives: The New Generation* rounds everything off exactly as you would expect, and exactly as a reader would want. The bad guys get punished, the good guys win out, the romances that're longed-for happen (chiefly, Lissa 'n' Michael, 'n' Nicci 'n' Brian), and the ones that don't, don't. And even if a romance doesn't fly, it doesn't always matter. For instance, Saffron gets another boyfriend (they littter the boulevards in L.A.), and also a star part in a TV series. The narrator cracks wise:

The stud didn't last.
The TV series did. (487)

And in Hollywood, a successful TV series can be far more satisfying than twenty studs in a row (as any actor'll tell you).

There's not a lot to say about *Hollywood Wives: The New Generation*, apart from the fact that it breezes by adequately. Vintage it ain't, memorable it ain't, but it did give rise to the most satisfying adaptation of Jackie Collins' work on screen, the 2003 TV mini-series. For that reason alone, *The New Generation* of *Hollywood Wives* is significant.

★

HOLLYWOOD DIVORCES

2003's *Hollywood Divorces* was another addition to the series of *Hollywood* novels by Jackie Collins about the City of Dreams begun with *Hollywood Wives* in 1983 (but really extending back to early works like *Sinners* in 1972). Despite the title, and the emphasis on couples breaking up, *Hollywood Divorces* contained the usual romantic musical chairs and erotic encounters of Collinsiana (like *The World Is Full of Divorced Women*) – and just as many new romances as relationships falling apart (in the world of the merry-go-round of relationships, of Love and Strife, there have to be as many couples ending as beginning).

Hollywood Divorces was diverting, but it wasn't pristine Jackie

Collins. Too much of it was by-the-numbers – but that may be because this was about the seventh Collins book in a row I'd read. Hell, *any* author gets repetitive after a while. Yes, even the holiest, sacredest and bestest of them all, like William Shakespeare or Homer, repeat themselves. (Read *As You Like It* then *Twelfth Night* then *A Midsummer Night's Dream* then *Love's Labour's Lost* then *Much Ado About Nothing* then *The Comedy of Errors*, one after another. Works of genius, for sure, but they repeat. A lot).

All of the characters presented in *Hollywood Divorces* were the familiar Jackie Collins types: there's the young, Latino super-babe Lola Sanchez (think J. Lo). The thirtysomething, English actress Shelby Cheney (think Kate Winslet or Natasha Richardson). The ageing action star who's hitting the skids with drink and drugs, Shelby's husband Linc Blackwood (think Bruce Willis or Steven Seagal). Bad boy actor Nick (think Billy Bob Thornton or Sean Penn – again). 19 year-old film director Cat Harrison. Cat's soon-to-be-ex-husband Jump Jagger, a rock 'n' roller (of course! With a name like that!). Super-agent Merrill, old but powerful. His young assistant Jonas. Long-suffering publicist Faye. Pete the tall, quiet stunt guy. Nasty Hispanic stud and film director Tony Sanchez.[14] Dull-as-dishwater ex-tennis player Matt Seel. And so on.

Easily the most interesting character in *Hollywood Divorces* is Cat Harrison: she's fun, smart, witty, brittle, and is following her dream. Very young for a film director (and a female film director at that), and probably inspired by Allison Anders and maybe Sofia Coppola (Anders, for instance, drew on her own life for her movies, such as *Gas, Food, Lodging* and *Mi Vida Loca,* as Cat does in her first film, *Wild Child*, a favourite Collins title, which she used for one of her last novels).

While Lola Sanchez is a hopelessly neurotic and OTT diva (but with the body of a Goddess, naturally), and Shelby Cheney is just too damn nice and idealistic for her own good in *Hollywood Divorces*, Cat Harrison knows what she wants, and goes for it. It's refreshing, for instance, when Cat surprises her husband rocker Jump on tour in Australia only to find out that he's been fooling around (on a rock tour? surely not?!), that she dumps him immediately and for good. And she doesn't soften, as so many lit'ry and romance heroines do. It really is curtains for her and Jump. Cat's decisiveness

---

[14] I wonder if Collins picked the name Tony Sanchez because he was part of the Rolling Stones' coterie in the late 1960s, associated in particular with Anita Pallenberg and Keef Richards. There's also Jump Jagger here, too.

– or, rather, her will-power in sticking to her decisions – is appealing (attributes she shares with Lucky Santangelo, of course).

By comparison, poor Shelby Cheney indulges her self-destructive and jealous husband Linc Blackwood's every whim, and Lola simply can't resist Mr Stud, Tony.

We know that Lola and Tony will come to a bad end, that Linc Blackwood will self-destruct in alcohol and pills, and that Cat Harrison will end up with either Nick or Jonas (or maybe neither).

The theme is *Hollywood Divorces* is once again about improving your life, via man-woman relationships: exchanging the men in your life for better ones. Better men, better relationships. Trading *up*, honey. After all, the men that the three main female characters are dating (or stuck with) aren't what they want. Lola Sanchez has a particularly dull husband: Matt Seel does little more than watch sport on TV. And dabbles in writing a script. And hopes to take acting classes and become an actor. But he doesn't do any of that, doesn't get off his heiny on the couch (sound familiar?). And when Lola is shooting a movie, Matt is scarily pathetic, whining at Lola like a kid, asking what he's supposed to do while she works.

Matt Seel is a caricature, sure, as the Dull Husband From Hell; he is described hilariously: 'he stood around like a dressed extra at a funeral and had absolutely nothing to say' (418).

So when Matt Seel wakes up from his comatose lifestyle in *Hollywood Divorces* and dresses up all in black like a ninja assassin and heads off to kill Lola's bad boy lover Tony Sanchez, it's utterly unconvincing. Because Matt is so *not* capable of doing anything like that. Not even thinking of it, let alone carrying it out. (It's one of those cases when an author searches around their cast of characters, wondering how to stoke up the dramatic heat in their story as it chugs towards the end, and choosing the wrong character, or using a character in the wrong way).

That particular narrative nugget comes in quite late in *Hollywood Divorces,* as if our Mistress of Fantasy, Jackie Collins, is coming around to the climax of the book: we know that Tony Sanchez has to die, because not only is he Bad News, he has a boxer killed simply because the guy danced too close to Lola at a nightclub (jealousy that becomes just a tad extreme). But having Matt Seel provide the impetus for the climax stretches belief.

As to locations, *Hollywood Divorces* – what a surprise! – takes place in Los Angeles and New York, with side trips to London and

Las Vegas (and, briefly, Australia. However, the book opened with an extended sojourn in South France, at the Cannes Film Festival). By now it's absolutely the done thing in a Jackie Collins book to jump in a Ferrari and drive to Las Vegas for the weekend (right after fucking on the beach in the dark off the Pacific Coast Highway). We've all done it (but not all of us wrote and published a book about it).

Adaptations of Jackie Collins' novels
(this page and over).

The Stud (1978).

The Bitch (1979).

Yesterday's Hero (1979).

The World Is Full of Married Men (1979).

Thirteen

Jackie Collins At the Movies (and On TV Too)

No movie could beat *this* story.

Jackie Collins, *Hollywood Husbands*

TV AND FILM ADAPTATIONS OF JACKIE COLLINS

The fiction of Jackie Collins has been served fairly poorly by television and film producers and directors and writers (and all the rest of the hundreds of people involved in film and TV production). Of the ten or so adaptations of Collins' books, none of been anywhere near classic or compelling, and most are regarded now as terrible. Some have been absolutely abysmal – *The Bitch* and *The Stud*; some have been mediocre – *Paris Connections* and *Lucky Chances*; some have been successful and much-watched (but still disappointing), like *Hollywood Wives;* and only one has got anywhere near nailing the flavour, the wit, the glamour and the *high velocity* of Collins' prose: *Hollywood Wives: The New Generation.*

Speed – yes, this is what the novels of Jackie Collins demand, and what they don't get. Or have I been watching too much Japanese animation, which can deliver entire movies in 22 minutes?! Or Hong Kong action movies, which *really* zing along, as fast as a sword thrown by a *kung fu* star thru a monster's neck. By comparison, North American television and movies appear *so slow*. Even TV shows and movies that're celebrated for being 'flashy' or 'trendy' are *so slow* in terms of *storytelling*. I don't mean the *editing*, I mean the *pace* and the *storytelling*. Self-conscious, tricksy and often rapid editing simply disguises the fact that there's not much going on – you just get four short shots of the same boring thing from different angles: a shot of a guy from a regular angle; a shot of said guy from under his nose; a third shot from through window blinds; and a fourth shot from the ceiling, the mandatory, look-at-me overhead shot of idiot film students (which wastes half-an-hour to set up). OK, I get it! – Dave the Slob is drinking a glass of beer! Big fucking deal!

By contrast, Japanese *animé* speeds along at a rapid pace, yet there is also time for interludes, for plot points, characterization and conversations. By the time a North American TV show has got past the exposition and is building (slowly) to the first dramatic or action highpoint, a Japanese animated show has *already* introduced all the major charas, plus their relationships, plus their goals and motives, plus some flashbacks, and staged an outstanding action sequence, *and* they've killed off the monster, raided the fridge, and slaughtered twenty ninja, with the heroes at the end drenched in the light of a molten, golden sunset like an atomic bomb over Tokyo...

The fiction of Jackie Collins – can't anybody in TV or movies *see* this? – aches for a zippy, zingy, spicy sort of filmmaking. It needs a film editor who can keep up with a manic film director like Tsui Hark, the dragon master of Chinese cinema, who can *cut cut cut* those scenes down to their most exciting moments. (Leave out that dead air! No need for pauses – we've got planes bound for Vegas to catch here!).

I'm not talking about *rushing* thru a Jackie Collins novel, or missing out anything that's crucial to the plot, or not having time for interludes and quietness. I'm talking about capturing how Collins' characters interact, how they talk, how they move. Lucky Santangelo does not sit behind a desk issuing orders – she is a dynamic, glamorous woman who can handle a gun and rarely lets anybody get in her way!

Oh, and while we're at it, can't anybody deliver the *dialogue* in a Jackie Collins novel? We are talking about a *fast,* uptempo delivery here, boys! We are talking about characters who spice their lines up with jokes and bitchiness all the time, kiddo.

Usually, critics (and audiences) over-emphasize dialogue (they *listen* to TV, not watch it), while many important filmmakers and scriptwriters regard dialogue as only a small ingredient in a movie. For instance, screenwriters talk much more about characters, and structure, and scenes, than about dialogue, and filmmakers like Akira Kurosawa say if they wanted to simply get a 'message' across, they would put it on a placard. And a movie or a TV show is images, music, sounds, movement, colour and a thousand other things, as well as dialogue.

But in a Jackie Collins book, dialogue is where much of the story takes place, and where much of the fun is. So you have to nail the dialogue. If Jackie Collins were Samuel Beckett, she might've sat on the set while her books were being filmed in 1979/ 1985/ 1990/ 2010/ etc, and offered some advice. Beckett was famously obsessive about the *exact* wording of his plays, about pauses and beats (Woody Allen is rumoured to be similar).[1] No way would Beckett allow actors to perform his texts that veered away far at all from the written word.

Ah, but Jackie Collins I guess was just too nice, and certainly she wasn't a bit of a tyrant like Samuel Beckett (or Woody Allen or

---

[1] Some actors have recalled that Woody Allen can be pedantic when it comes to delivering lines: 'there's a reason for the comma in that speech', he has been known to remark.

Andrei Tarkovsky) could be. Lucky Santangelo says to a film producer (Eddie Kane) in the book *Lady Boss*: 'you're fired!' But Collins wouldn't do that to the production companies adapting her work. And yet, have you seen *The Bitch* or *The Stud*?! *Someone* should've been fired! (Or killed, as in *Bullets Over Broadway,* 1994).

Also, Jackie Collins likes to swear. Or rather, her *characters* like to swear. A lot.

She's a female equivalent of Henry Miller or Norman Mailer, where swearing comes naturally. In which case, capturing the true flavour of a Collins novel automatically means broadcasting after the watershed, or an 'R' rating (forget about 'NC-17', no major studio bothers with 'NC-17' at all).[2] But television broadcasters reserve 'bad language' for their prestige shows, and the odd niche drama (and even prestige TV doesn't allow as much 'bad language' as Collins puts in her works). Theatrical releases are sometimes seen as more 'explicit' in terms of language, and issues such as nudity, sexuality, violence, etc. But here, too, the adaptations of Collins' work have pulled back from reproducing her dialogue.

'No movie could beat *this* story', remarks the narrator of *Hollywood Husbands* – and it's partly why the movies and TV shows of Jackie Collins' novels don't work: because the books are so much better!

Luckily, we have Jackie Collins novels. The TV shows and the movies adapted from her work have been *very* disappointing. But the novels are so much like movies or TV shows anyway, it doesn't matter.

★

Jackie Collins has worked as a screenwriter and a producer: Collins' has screenplay credits on the two *Lucky Santangelo* TV series: *Lady Boss* and *Lucky Chances*, and on two early movies: *The Stud* (co-writers were David Humphries and Christopher Stagg), and *Yesterday's Hero*. And Collins has producer credits on *Lucky Chances, Jackie Collins Presents, Hollywood Wives: The New Generation* and *Paris Connections*.

---

2 For some critics, the 'NC-17' rating was effectively a form of censorship. It was a form of economic censorship, because an 'NC-17' rating meant death at the box office, and a studio wouldn't promote an 'NC-17' rated film the same way they would an 'R' rated film (the studios, anyway, demand 'R' rated films the contract). Indeed, between 1990 and 2002, the major Hollywood distributors had only released two North American films with an 'NC-17' rating: *Henry and June* and *Showgirls* (foreign films were occasionally distributed under 'NC-17').

However, it has to be acknowledged, great screenwriters such as Robert Towne, Ingmar Bergman and William Goldman have nothing to worry about: Jackie Collins' work as a scriptwriter is rather timid and plain. Unadventurous – Collins is not going to drastically modify her own work as Hayao Miyazaki does, or treat the original material (the novel) as simply one element in a creative collaboration, as Orson Welles does. Instead, Collins' work as a screenwriter sticks to the formulaic structures of North American television (which's partly why both *Lucky Chances* and *Lady Boss*, two crucial works in the adaptations of Collins' fiction, are underwhelming. And these were productions in which Collins has writer and producer credit).

★

HOW TO MAKE A JACKIE COLLINS MOVIE

In movies, equivalents for Jackie Collins' novels include backstage dramas, and satires about Hollywood and show business such as *42nd Street* (1933),[3] *Boogie Nights* (1997) and *Showgirls* (1995) (other movies of this type would include *The Bad and the Beautiful, The Barefoot Contessa, Chicago, Sunset Boulevard, L.A. Confidential, Singin' In the Rain, A Star Is Born, 54,*[4] *The Player, Contempt,*[5] *Ed*

---

[3] The 1933 backstage musical *42nd Street* (directed by Lloyd Bacon) is an absolute delight, and a total classic. If you haven't seen it: you must. One aspect that's really enjoyable about *42nd Street*, like other comedies of the period (screwball or otherwise), is the *speed* of the movie, the rapidfire exchanges of dialogue. Man, so many movies today are s-o s-l-o-w, but the best 1930s comedies (the Marx Brothers' movies, for instance, or *The Thin Man* movies, or *Bringing Up Baby*), are joyously swift.

[4] Steve Rubell, of Studio 54 (the subject of the 1998 movie *54*), would select the beautiful, fashionable people for the entry into the famous nightclub (certainly an inspiration for Collins). If you were famous, you were still not guaranteed entry, tho' celebs who partied there included Mick Jagger, Michael Jackson, Diana Vreeland (editor of *Vogue*), Andy Warhol, Liz Taylor, Liza Minnelli, Truman Capote, Jack Nicholson, Ryan O'Neal, Elliott Gould and Jerry Hall.

[5] *Le Mépris* (a.k.a. *Contempt*, a.k.a., *A Ghost At Noon,* 1963) was another of Jean-Luc Godard's films about films, in particular the contemporary Hollywood film industry. Witty, sexy, cynical, philosophical, *Contempt* has it all – including Brigitte Bardot.

Wood,[6] Bugsy,[7] Chaplin, and The Last Tycoon[8]).

Few would count Jackie Collins' books among the great satires or send-ups of Hollywood – either of the film and media industry in Hollywood/ L.A. (like *The Day of the Locust* by Nathanael West or *The Last Tycoon* by F, Scott Fitzgerald), or of the role of Hollywood in contemporary, North American culture and global culture. But Collins does capture some of the Los Angeles lifestyle, the lives of the rich and famous, and some aspects of Tinseltown and its movie industry. (To be fair, these are *novels*, and if you want in-depth accounts of how film studios do business, read the standard film history books,[9] or look at the trades like *Variety* and *Hollywood Reporter*. The readers of Collins' books probably don't want to get into the crazy accounting systems of Hollywood, for instance, or have lengthy breakdowns of budgets, casting, contracts and deals).

American Grafitti, Grease, Happy Days, The Last Picture Show – those are movies and TV shows looking back at the 1950s from the 1970s. More fitting for Collins Land perhaps are movies of the 1990s looking back at the 1970s, which chime with Jackie Collins' 1990s books like *Thrill!* and *American Star*. *Boogie Nights* is one, and another one which really captures the atmosphere of suburban North America in the Seventies, with kids hanging out, and high school, and drugs, and, above all, music, is *Dazed and Confused* (1993), an indie favourite. Indeed, why not have a Hollywood musical based on a Collins novel? Preferably directed by John Waters, or Bob Fosse.

Among more recent movies, *Showgirls* (Paul Verhoeven, 1995) is more like a Jackie Collins novel than Collins' own books. I *love*

---

6 *Ed Wood* (1994) starred Johnny Depp (delivering an outstanding performance) as film director Ed Wood, maker of cult classics such as *Glen or Glenda* and *Plan 9 From Outer Space*, an eternal optimist who believed in himself, made films on minuscule budgets in a few days, raising finance from any source and however he could. *Ed Wood* evoked Hollywood settings of the 1950s which were right out of Collins' *Santangelo* novels.

7 A movie starring Warren Beatty about the movie-an'-gangster foundation of Las Vegas – this is pure Jackie Collins!

8 *The Last Tycoon* (1976) was a disappointing F. Scott Fitzgerald adaptation starring Robert de Niro.

9 For a study of cinema, there is one book that towers above *every other book* on film (even tho' the competition is fierce!): David A. Cook's *A History of Narrative Film*. David Bordwell and Kristin Thompson have written many great books on cinema: *Film Art: An Introduction, Narration In the Fiction Film, Film History: An Introduction, The Classical Hollywood Cinema: Film Style and Mode of Production to 1960* and *Storytelling In the New Hollywood* I would also recommend Bruce Kawin's *How Movies Work*, Gerald Mast's *Film Theory and Criticism: Introductory Readings*, and Mast & Kawin's *A Short History of the Movies*.

Showgirls! But it is routinely regarded as a flop (economically), a kitschy, silly movie. Of course it is! That's why it's wonderful! But as a depiction of a young woman on the make - Nomi Malone (Elizabeth Berkley)[10] - it is pure Collins - Nomi hitches a ride from the suburbs of N. America to the Bright Lights of Las Vegas, climbing the ladder from lap dancer and pole dancer to showgirl in the chorus then finally to being the star of the show. It's all there - the ambition, the greed, the rivalries, the bitching, the gossip, the dancing, the nudity, the sex, the casinos. Wonderful, truly wonderful.

And the energy and verve of *Showgirls* is hypnotizing. *Showgirls* also captures a side of contemporary, North American life which Jackie Collins has attempted in her books: the gritty, dangerous streets, the sense of being driven by ambition to lift oneself out of mediocrity and boredom into something glittering and famous. Of course, Las Vegas embodies all of that, and also the hollowness of it all.

Joe Eszterhas, at least in the late 1980s and early 1990s, was the screenwriter for Jackie Collins: he wrote *Basic Instinct* and *Showgirls*. And Eszterhas is also a Collinsian character in himself - earning mega buck$ for his flashy, trashy, sensational script work (much to the irritation of fellow writers and journos)![11]

Boogie Nights (Paul Thomas Anderson, 1997) is an incredibly impressive comedy about the 1970s porn industry which has many affinities with Jackie Collins' world. But, as with *Showgirls*, *Boogie Nights* is way more entertaining and funny and wild than Collins' adaptations. And believable - even though *Boogie Nights* is an OTT comedy. *Boogie Nights* has many Collinsian elements, including the L.A setting, a seemingly endless round of sex, drugs, violence, drugs, and more drugs, sleazy nightclubs, betrayals, vengeance, crime, and Seventies disco music (the soundtrack for *Boogie Nights* is just sublime - the best thing about the movies based on Collins' books in the 1970s are the soundtracks).

Some of the more sensational movies of Oliver Stone correspond with the world of Jackie Collins - I'm thinking of the

---

10 As the driven, one-time innocent but now super-cynical Nomi, I think Elizabeth Berkley is brilliant (though critics lampooned Berkley as well as the movie). Most of all, Berkley has the fierce energy of one of Jackie Collins' wild women who will stop at nothing to get what they want.

11 According to David Thomson (in *A Biographical Dictionary of Film*), Joe Eszterhas was 'large, hirsute, florid, reflective, anecdotal, self-deprecating (he admitted he had done script doctoring for as little as $600,000 a week), and someone to make the Korda family young again' (227).

world of 'greed is good' big business in *Wall Street* (both Charlie Sheen and Michael Douglas are Collins-style actors), or the cynical schlock of *U-Turn*, where everyone's corrupt, and of course the rock star biopic *The Doors*, which has many Collinsian scenes – including the totally dumb scene of getting head in an elevator!

The movies of Woody Allen contain many Collinsian scenes and characters, and a line in bitchy, witty dialogue which's in the tradition of sophisticated, uptown New York humour. Allen's movies and Collins' books share numerous elements: ensemble structures of many characters; intertwining stories; the erotic dalliance of swapping partners; thriller, gangster and shlocky ingredients; a passionate love of Hollywood cinema (including its long history); exaggerated romanticism; a passion for music; hotels, restaurants and apartments (there are a huge no. of restaurant scenes in both Allen[12] and Collins); and contemporary urban settings (New York of course for Allen, but also L.A., London and Paris – both Collins and Allen are devotees of living in great cities).

Woody Allen's movies are like Jackie Collins' novels with intellectual humour and Grand Themes attached; Collins' books're like Allen's films with more sex, more gossip, more lowbrow pop culture, and better clothes.[13] Allen has directed films about the perfect murder, too, a very Collinsian theme. (Lennie and Lucky go see a Woody Allen movie in *Lady Boss*).

The gangster flicks directed by Martin Scorsese (and his imitators, such as Quentin Tarantino and Abel Ferrara), would seem to be covering similar territory to Jackie Collins' books: *GoodFellas* and *Casino* in particular (and *Pulp Fiction*; meanwhile, *Taxi Driver* is an early version of the Collinsian psycho, who had already appeared in books like *Sinners*). However, Scorsese's films are much more reticent in depicting sexuality on screen than Collins in her books, though not violence of course: Scorsese's movies, like so many contemporary Hollywood pictures, revel in portraying graphic violence on screen. (And female charas are poorly portrayed).

And then there's *The Godfather* (Francis Coppola, 1972) – in this case, contrary to the usual thinking, the movie is far superior to the book. Mario Puzo acknowledged that the novel wasn't the best he could do, and if he'd known so many people were going to read it,

---

12 Allen is well-known for frequently eating out.
13 The costumes in many Allen films are somewhat frumpy, tweedy, preppy, and old-fashioned.

he would have done a better job.[14] But *The Godfather* movie is far superior on numerous levels to Jackie Collins' books - and most bestselling novels. But Collins' work doesn't present itself so solemnly and seriously, either.

The Godfather is one of Jackie Collins' favourite books, and she says she re-reads it regularly (that's typical of Collins to admit that – while other writers talk about re-reading the classics, like *Great Expectations* or *Wuthering Heights* – Mel Brooks says he reads *War and Peace* regularly – for Collins, it's *The Godfather!*). It's easy to see the influence of both *The Godfather* the book and the movie on Collins' work - and not only in her depiction of the world of gangsters in the *Lucky Santangelo* series.

If you enjoy movies about wise guys, macho posturing, men with guns, homoerotic brotherhoods, murderous psychopaths, Sicilian revenge, Las Vegas, and the films of Francis Coppola, Martin Scorsese, Abel Ferrara, Brian de Palma, Jonathan Demme, John Woo and Ringo Lam, you will enjoy *Jane Austen's Mafia!*[15] (1998). It's very funny; the humour is in the *Airplane!* and *Naked Gun* vein - director Jim Abrahams is the 'A' in the Zucker-Abrahams-Zucker team.

In *The Godfather*, Don Corleone famously drew the line at narcotics: thieving, racketeering, extortion and other crimes were OK for da Corleone family bizniz, but not drugs. The way that distinction was made in *The Godfather* seemed so serious, coming from Marlon Brando (despite the hypocrisy of it). In *Jane Austen's Mafia!,* the Don laments the old days: 'we steal things, we kill and dismember people. Now it's all drugs. Where's the honour?'

The hugely successful *Emmanuelle* movies of the 1970s have the jet-setting, exotic locales for softcore porn which chimes with Jackie Collins' fictional world (though not the pretentious, French philosophizing about sex in the *Emmanuelle* books and films – Collins never does that; thankfully. Who needs sermonizing lectures and Existential philosophy in the midst of a good fuck? Only French intellectuals!).

---

14 Mario Puzo said later that he liked the book, but he 'wished like hell I'd written it better'. He reckoned he had written 'below my gifts in that book' (1972, 41). Puzo had sold the book rights to Paramount for $12,500 – a very small figure in view of how much $$$$ the movie eventually made. But Puzo needed that money. His agency William Morris had told him to hold off for a better offer. But this was before the paperback rights for *The Godfather* had been sold for $410,000.

15 *Jane Austen's Mafia!* (a.k.a. *Mafia!*, 1998) was wr. by Greg Norberg, Michael McManus and Jim Abrahams, prod. by Bob Levy and Peter Abrams, and dir. by Jim Abrahams.

Classic Brit flick *Performance* (1970, directed by Donald Cammell & Nic Roeg), is another pic with close affinities with Jackie Collins' Glamland - particularly the depiction of a rock star's decadent, reclusive and sexy lifestyle. And it's Mick Jagger in the lead role - never better, in a piece of perfect casting (Jagger is definitely the model for some of Collins' characters. However, in *Performance*, old Rubber Lips is definitely *not* playing himself. Jagger is nothing like the character of rock star Turner, as anybody who knows anything about Jagger can see!).[16]

And the utterly wonderful Anita Pallenberg in *Performance* is a Jackie Collins character if ever there was one. Pallenberg plays the bad girl (Pherber) who leads wise guy James Fox (Chas) astray with teasing, mercurial brilliance. Pallenberg is an extraordinary woman by any standards - powerful, erotic, beautiful, quirky, eccentric, very smart and very confident (she was also a key influence in the Rolling Stones' circle, and had relationships with Keef Richards and Brian Jones). Pallenberg is Lucky Santangelo more than Lucky herself - Pallenberg was an original 'wild child': a fashion model, expelled from school, hanging out in New York with Andy Warhol and Jasper Johns, and the *dolce vita* set in Roma, a seductive, dangerous force of nature, and more (see Appendix).

And London's gangland has never been portrayed more impressively than in *Performance.* Now if just one Jackie Collins film adaptation were anywhere near the level of quality of *Performance*, that *really* would be something! (Director Donald Cammell was another Brit who ended up in the Hollywood Hills. A little like a Collins character himself, Cammell's lover was China Kong, the daughter of Marlon Brando's other half).

There's a group of movies which have clear links to Jackie Collins' books, in terms of casting, style and content, and that's the 'erotic thrillers' (a.k.a. neo-noirs)[17] - particularly the ones of the 1990s: *The Last Seduction, Kill Me Again, Body of Evidence, Disclosure, Wild Things, Red Rock West,* and the one that made them really big - *Basic Instinct* (if Sharon Stone's character Catherine Trammel isn't a classic Jackie Collins character, I don't know who is. In Collins' *Lovers & Players*, the two Russian hooker characters 'had

---

16 Elements of Keef Richards and Brian Jones, according to Marianne Faithfull and Anita Pallenberg, were influences on the way that Jagger played Turner. Actually, it's Donald Cammell's interpretation of what it would be like being Jagger.
17 Prior to that 1990s group, there were 1980s movies like *Body Heat, The Postman Always Rings Twice,* and *Fatal Attraction.*

seen *Basic Instinct* several times. Both women fancied themselves in the Sharon Stone role. Tough, fearless, sexy, predatory...' [315]).

Basic Instinct (Paul Verhoeven, 1992) contains pretty much every Jackie Collins cliché: a powerful woman, ambiguous and deadly, the pussy flash, bisexuality and rough sex, an ageing, Hollywood star (Michael Douglas), who's part of Hollywood royalty (son of Kirk), classy city setting (Frisco),[18] chases, a murder mystery, cops, pop psychology, etc. Only the ending wasn't *à la* Collins: *she* wouldn't let Trammell get away with it. In Collins' moral universe, Trammell would have to be punished – by death. (But not by the electric chair after the usual course of justice – someone she'd wronged in the past would seek revenge).

Billionaire producer Hamilton Heckerling urges fading star Lucy Lyons to 'do a Sharon – flash your snatch' to kick-start her career (in *Married Lovers*, 219). Lyons is pissed that the only movie anybody remembers her making was *Blue Sapphire*, where she went nude. By the end of *Married Lovers*, Lyons has caved in to sequelitis, just as Stone did with *Basic Instinct 2,* and makes *Blue Sapphire 2.*

Other Collinsian movies would include *The Bodyguard* (1992), *Dreamgirls* (2006), *The Player* (1992),[19] *Short Cuts* (1993), and *Celebrity* (1998).[20]

There are other movies which capture the look and feel, the sleaze and glamour, of a Jackie Collins novel: Hong Kong action movies. The contemporary thrillers of Chinese action cinema present a world of gamblers, crooks, hookers, intense fire-fights, operatically, hysterically emotional confrontations, and super-cool gangsters diving in slow motion while blasting away with two guns. For trashy, sexy, fun movies, with super-fast cutting, insane camerawork, black humour, ultra-violence, and OTT outbursts of emotion, few cinemas can beat Hong Kong cinema. The *Naked Killer* movies, *Heroic Trio, My Father Is a Hero,* and the incendiary thrillers

---

18 Tho' Collins has very seldom used San Francisco.
19 *The Player* (1992) was a slick satire on contemporary Hollywood, written and produced by Michael Tolkin. *The Player* was a film about film people made by film people and full of film references. One of the selling points of the piece in its marketing was the number of Hollywood stars that appeared in cameos and walk-on parts; spot the celeb was advertized as part of the pleasure of *The Player:* in the background (and foreground) one saw Angelica Huston, Malcolm McDowell, Max von Sydow, Bruce Willis, Susan Sarandon, Burt Reynolds, Martin Scorsese and Nick Nolte, among many others.
20 1998's *Celebrity* (released through Miramax), was Woody Allen's version of a Jackie Collins novel. Well, not exactly! – it was another of Allen's ensemble pieces about the love lives of contemporary New Yorkers. Collins has often cited Allen's movies in her works.

of Tsui Hark, Tony Ching Siu-tung, Ringo Lam, Jackie Chan and John Woo.

Naked Killer (1992) is a Hong Kong knock-off of *Basic Instinct*. It's classy trash; it's paper-thin, has no more meaning than a plastic cup, and is gloriously, gleefully violent. *Naked Killer* is perfect midnite movie fare, guaranteed to play like gangbusters in movie houses of the sleazier cities of this little, green planet. Star Chingmy Yau as *femme fatale* Kitty is sensational in thigh-high, black boots and a fitted, red mini-dress. Shoulder-length dark hair, a pouty, lipsticked mouth, Yau's Kitty is a female revenge fantasy in hooker clothing.

Yet another form of cinema that would suit Jackie Collins' fiction is the Bollywood musical, the *masala* (spice) film – the best Bollywood musical movies have the glam, the clothes, the comedy, the speed, the pace and the energy to match the novels. But of course, the most obvious equivalents with Jackie Collins' fictional world is a TV series or mini-series, those glossy, slick, dumb H.B.O. series.

★

What a movie adaptation of a Jackie Collins book really needs is *fantastic editing*. Assuming that -->

(1) the script was pretty good (easily the most difficult task)
(2) and assuming that a decent cast could be obtained
(3) and assuming that there was a killer soundtrack
(4) and assuming the production values, the look, the costumes, the make-up, the hair, the locations, the cars and all the rest were in place

<-- then editing and pacing would be among the most important ingredients.

Why? Because Jackie Collins' novels have a very rapid pace. What lets down the adaptations of Collins' work in TV and film is the s-l-o-w pacing (among other elements). A Collins novel needs to be uptempo – both *within* scenes and, most vital of all, how scenes *connect together*. A variety of editing devices, which in other contexts can be flashy and gimmicky and redundant, would be essential. Flash cuts, jump cuts, shock cuts, dissolves, slo-mo, superimpositions, step-motion and whatever else a team of veteran editors could come up with – *anything* necessary to get across the sensationalized, sexy and sleazy world of a Collins story. (Maybe Sam Peckinpah and his team should edit it (if only!), but Tsui Hark, Wong Jing or Paul Verhoeven should direct it).

In short, a Jackie Collins movie or TV adaptation should capture the way that Collins writes: fast, fast fast. The way she writes dialogue. Rapid-fire. The way she jumps from scene to scene.

But there's no need to adapt a Jackie Collins novel for film or TV, because the books are already so movie-ish, so TV-like, and so vivid. 'All of my books have the potential to become movies, it's just a question of finding a studio who wants to get behind me and put up the money to make the movie', Jackie Collins noted.

Yes – this is the crux of it: adaptations of Jackie Collins' work perhaps fall short because the books are *already* as filmic as you can get with the written word.

★

Censorship and ratings is an issue – because Jackie Collins' books are not only 'R' rated, they are, if you *really* filmed them as they were written, 'NC-17' rated. No TV network is going to make (let alone broadcast) an 'NC-17' version of a Jackie Collins novel! And even the 'R' rated elements are mild on TV, compared to the books. Forget about the portrayals of sex and drugs and violence, which're all far tamer in the TV shows and movies than in the novels, the biggest casualty that I miss is Collins' dialogue. Television will allow some swearing, but not reams of it. What a pity, because Collins' barbed, bitchy dialogue is one of the key strengths of her fiction.

★

Despite being an awful movie, the success of *The Stud* led to a cycle of Jackie Collins adaptations in the late 1970s: the sequel, *The Bitch*, *The World Is Full of Married Men* and *Yesterday's Hero*. Unfortunately, two of these movies – *The World Is Full of Married Men* and *Yesterday's Hero* – are not available widely, so I have focussed on *The Stud* and *The Bitch*.

The Collins films of this period were based at Pinewood Studios. They featured mainly British casts, and soundtracks of mainly pop songs (with disco prominent).

★

THE BITCH: THE BOOK AND THE MOVIE

The film adaptation of Jackie Collins' 1979 book, *The Bitch* (1979), is a piece of shit. That's Hollywood jargon for one of the most dreadful movies you could ever hope to avoid. I saw it in 1980 at a cinema in Hereford, England. God knows why I paid money to see this heap of dreck.[21] (Collins acknowledged how bad the movie was in her note on the 2012 reprint of *The Bitch*: '*The Bitch* is a fun book – a lot better than the movie!').

How did this movie ever make money in Great Britain? Or anywhere? Apparently it did well at the box office (but distributors and P.R. people and film studios *always* say that). I guess it was so cheap to make, so the negative cost-to-profit ratio was potentially good, as with movies like *American Graffiti* or *Breathless* (but oh no, *The Bitch* is not in that class!).

The movie of *The Bitch* is bad, bad, bad. BAD. On *every* level.

Where to begin? Shall we even bother? No point.

The book was clearly hurled from the window (or written after the fact), and the filmmakers decided to take just a few elements from it and do their own thing.

Which's great! Fantastic! Fucking wonderful!

If the movie was good, that is.

But it's not.

You can forgive a lot in an adaptation from a novel to the screen *if the final movie is fab*. Orson Welles and his team chucked away most of *Badge of Courage* by Whit Masterson when they made *Touch of Evil* in 1957 for Universal, and re-wrote it, but it didn't matter, because the movie was a *tour-de-force* of cinema. Same with *The Lady From Shanghai* (based on *If I Die Before I Wake* by Sherwood King), another classic Orson Welles movie.[22] In fact, there are many great movies that've been produced from terrible books.

Of course, *The Bitch* as a *book* isn't exactly *War and Peace* or *Catcher In the Rye*. It's meant to be an entertaining yarn set in the world of the rich and famous in New York, Las Vegas and London.

---

[21] Yes I do, it was a date with Alison.
[22] Rita Hayworth was a classic Jackie Collins personality: the screen goddess of *Gilda* (her biggest hit), Hayworth was one of the top stars of the time, and a pin-up icon for the US forces during WW2. Orson Welles, separated from Hayworth at the time of making *The Lady From Shanghai*, had Hayworth cut her hair short, dyed white blonde, and look older than she had done in previous films (much to the horror and fury of Columbia boss Harry Cohn, one of the inspirations for the movie mogul in *The Godfather*). The smiling, voluptuous screen idol of *Gilda* was replaced by an icy blonde *femme fatale*.

But the *movie* of *The Bitch* stinks in every way.

The star, Joan Collins is... Joan Collins, as ever. She's always Joan Collins, and she plays Joan Collins as well as anybody (she was 46 when she made this flick).

But there's no acting going on here. No directing. No scriptwriting. No editing. No sound mixing.

Little surprise that director Gerry O'Hara had written (and directed) episodes of TV series *The Professionals* and *The Avengers* (but had worked mostly as an assistant director). *The Bitch* resembles a bad TV episode of a bad TV series but with more nudity than the TV broadcasters allow. It is so shoddy it beggars belief.

As for the credits, Gerry O'Hara has the script credit on *The Bitch*. It was produced by Ronald Kass, Oscar Lerman (Jackie Collins' husband), Edward Simons, and John Quested. Appearing alongside Jackie's sister (the only name in the film)[23] were Ian Hendry, Kenneth Haigh, Antonio Catafora, Pamela Salem, Sue Lloyd, and John Ratzenerger. Released Sept 19, 1979. 94 mins.

What *should* the film of *The Bitch* be like? It should be *Boogie Nights* or *Saturday Night Fever* or *Showgirls*.

The Bitch is a truly terrible movie but not one of those films that're 'so bad they're good'. This is plain garbage.

Let's not bother anymore with this movie, but I can draw attention to one or two of the 100s of flaws. First off, Las Vegas in the book is left out entirely, so there's no sense of a threat to would-be tycoon Nico Constantine. Instead, he explains about the ring at the airport – but there's not even a shot of the friggin' ring! Let's *see* the sodding MacGuffin, at least![24]

So the threat in The *Bitch* is transferred to some London gangsters, and we all know that British gangsters in movies are sooooooo dull, apart from two pictures: *Brighton Rock* (1947) and *Performance* (1970), the only two British gangster flicks worth anything (yet they persist in being produced).

But the London mob are introduced way too late in *The Bitch*, which scuppers the thriller plot. Doesn't help either that the actor playing Nico (Antonio Cantafora) has about as much charisma as a used teabag. The film really could've done with spending a little

---

[23] Trivia: two bit parts are played by Mick Jagger's brother Chris and a young Bill Nighy, an actor who's now in every other film coming out of Hollywood or Britain.

[24] See the *Lord of the Rings* movies for a textbook example of how to make a tiny ring look Big and Important!

more money above the line, on the talent appearing in front of the camera, and obtaining a more suitable and more well-known actor for Nico. (For instance, Omar Shariff - oh, obvious casting, I know, but Shariff is great, and so right for the role - he could play the businessman with shady dealings, and also the playboy aspect, and the lover).

Meanwhile, Fontaine Khaled is supposed to be the Super Bitch. But not in this film, and not as played by Jackie Collins' elder sister, Joan. Anything that was good in the novel (yes, I am *defending* Jackie Collins' novel!), is thrown away by the filmmakers. The whole thing. Instead, Fontaine in this 1979 adaptation comes across a rather nice woman who has occasional moments of irritation.

The Bitch's budget's low,[25] but that's no excuse for a bad movie (I won't bother to list the magnificent movies made on a tenth of *The Bitch*'s budget. *Rashomon* (1950 - $40,000) and *The Seventh Seal* (1957 - $150,000) will do for now).

Some beautiful people would be nice, to alleviate the horrors elsewhere in this 1979 flick - the people in *The Bitch* are supposed to be the rich and the famous, the jet-setters, the in-crowd. But they're so dowdy and dreary. *The Bitch* portrays Britain's upper-classes and the international jet-set as a bunch of ugly losers. The film adds a sort of orgy at the country house in the book - nude people fooling about in the swimming pool, but it doesn't work (the orgy scene has the look of a re-shoot, one of those scenes added by the film producers when they viewed the movie and realized it stank, and desperately tried to spice it up).[26]

And the disco and the dancing! Oh man, this is so <u>*not*</u> *Saturday Night Fever*! If only! Execrable dancing and choreography. *The Bitch* of course cashes in on the disco movement of the late 1970s (but because movies take a while to make, it was released after the main action had passed). In fact, all four of the Collins adaptations of the late 1970s feature plenty of disco music.

So there *is* a stack of music in *The Bitch*, which's the best thing about it[27] (though not the theme song, which includes lyrics by Don

---

[25] $600,000, according to *People* magazine.
[26] As happened with the films of Walerian Borowczyk, and another 1979 flick, *Caligula*.
[27] I have an old audio cassette of *The Bitch* soundtrack (Warwick Records, 1979), which features: Gloria Gaynor ('I Will Survive'), Herbie Hancock, the Real Thing, Linda Lewis, the Dooleys, the Hunters, Gonzales, the Stylistics, Quantum Jump, Inner Circle, the Drifters, Deborah Washington, Gibson Brothers, George Chandler, Len Boone, Players Association, Leo Sayer, Olympic Runners, and the Three Degrees ('Giving Up, Giving In').

Black): the Stylistics, Blondie, the Drifters, Herbie Hancock, the Three Degrees, Deborah Washington and Gloria Gaynor ('I Will Survive', *of course*). Dick Rowe was music supervisor (with original music by Biddu).

And the sex in the movie – as flaccid and limp and dry and cold as death itself.

★

THE STUD

What about *The Stud* (Quentin Masters, 1978)? *The Stud* (produced by Ronald Kass, Oscar Lerman, Edward Simons, and George Walker) is important for a number of reasons in the world of Jackie Collins – it was the first film adaptation of one of her books, and it has a screenplay credit for Collins (along with two other writers – David Humphries and Christopher Stagg).

Unfortunately, *The Stud* is a piece of cack, a truly God-awful movie. It is badly conceived, badly scripted,[28] badly cast, badly performed, badly directed, badly edited, badly dubbed, badly scored and badly presented. It is an all-round, 100% DUD.

I can point out a few things amiss with the 1978 film of the 1969 novel *The Stud*:

The SCRIPT and the STORY.

There isn't a story. None at all.

Tony Blake runs a nightclub for his boss Fontaine Khaled, with whom he's having an affair. That's it.

Oh, there is a tiny bit more: Tony has a fling with the daughter of some aristocratic folks. And plans to set up another nightclub, so he'll be his own boss.

OK, it doesn't matter if there isn't a story worth speaking of in *The Stud*. Plenty of wonderful movies satisfy if there are other things going for them.

Like CHARACTERS.

A good bunch of characters can be fascinating and entertaining.

The characters in *The Stud* movie are *so* dull, you can't believe it. They are supposed to be, one guesses (one hopes), the wealthy,

---

[28] But *three* writers are credited for this car wreck. Didn't they read each other's drafts? Didn't someone among them think, actually, this is awful?

switched-on, jet-setting Beautiful People of London in the 1970s. But they are so boring, so unutterably vapid.

CASTING. What a truly *dreadful* cast in The Stud! Yes, Oliver Tobias looks nice, and Joan Collins is as glam as ever. But with these woefully *under*-written parts to play, there's not a lot going on anywhere.

And the actors assembled around them in The Stud are just terrible. At least give the audience some eye-candy! Let's have some tall, handsome hunks, at least! And some luscious women! Oh no, no, no, The Stud does *not* provide that.

You simply do not care in the slightest about these vacuous, middle-class twits and upper-class jerks. Let them all die in a train pile-up in the first minute of the film! Who gives a *fuck*?

TECHNICAL ELEMENTS. The look, the sets, the costumes, the lighting, the sound – all the production value elements of The Stud are appallingly, embarrassingly bad. No, you can't blame the low budget. That's no excuse here. You're shooting in London for Christ's sake! One of the most exciting cities on Earth! You've got a trip to Paris!

What? You can't make London look like a million dollars! It IS a million dollars! It's a BILLION dollars! It's fucking London! (And this is using the supposedly amazing film technicians in Britain who contribuited to the *James Bond* and *Star Wars* movies in this era).

The dancing. As with The Bitch, the dancing and disco scenes, which are filler for this movie, are horrible[29]

SEX. Oh hell, do you really want to know? The sex scenes in The Stud are as limp and feeble as the rest of the movie.

THEMES. There aren't any.

IDEAS. There aren't any.

DIALOGUE. Why oh why can't filmmakers capture Jackie Collins' spicy, witty and *rapid-fire* dialogue on screen? Shjt, if the actors can't deliver it, at least have the editors (led by David Campling) cut the film a little *faster*, for Chrissake!

F-A-S-T-E-R!!!

MUSIC. As with The Bitch, the soundtrack is easily the best part of The Stud. No, not the incidental music by Biddhu, who did both Stud 'n' Bitch movies (the soundtrack becomes truly weird in the drug-addled, swimming pool romp). But the soundtrack, which includes Odyssey, Hot Chocolate, 10CC ('I'm Not In Love',

---

[29] Flick Colby was choreographer.

inevitably[30]), Rod Stewart, KC and the Sunshine Band, Rose Royce, David Soul, Leo Sayer ('You Make Me Feel Like Dancing'), Tina Charles, Heatwave, and Manfred Mann. (Martin Machat and Biddu were music co-ordinators).

There's a cameo from Jackie Collins in the movie of *The Stud* – in the montage of photos and letters from Tony Blake's conquests, Collins is in there, with a signed photo ('Tony, nobody does it better!' – a reference to the *James Bond* movie of a year earlier, 1977, *The Spy Who Loved Me*, and it's fab theme song by Carly Simon. Oh, if *only* a Jackie Collins movie had the laughs, the humour, the style, the silliness, the stunts, the glamour, the women, and the OTT-ness of a *James Bond* movie!!).

THE WORLD IS FULL OF MARRIED MEN.

The World Is Full of Married Men was produced by New Realm/ Married Men, produced by Malcolm Fancey, Adrienne Scott and Oscar Lerman, written by Jackie Collins and Terry Howard, DP: Ray Parslow, edited by David Campling, art dir. by Tony Curtis, with music by Frank Musker and Dominic Bugatti. In the cast were Anthony Franciosa, Carroll Baker, Sherrie Cronn, Paul Nicholas, Gareth Hunt, Georgina Hale, Anthony Steel, John Nolan and Jean Gilpin. Bonnie Tyler and the dance troupe Hot Gossip also appeared. Released June 3, 1979. 107 mins.

The soundtrack for *The World Is Full of Married Men* included: Tavares, Bill Withers, Edwin Starr, Hot Gossip, Gladys Knight, Shalamar, Heatwave, the Emotions, Taste of Honey, Nora Hendricks, the Three Degrees, Billy Ocean, etc, plus Bonne Tyler's title song. Many are disco songs of the era, along with Paul Nicholas, Sarah Brightman, and Barry Manilow. (Ronco released a double vinyl album for the film with 28 tracks).

YESTERDAY'S HERO.

Yesterday's Hero was produced by Packer Organisation/ Cinema Seven Productions/ Elliott Kastner Production, Collins scripted the film, Elliott Kastner, Oscar Lerman and Ken Regna produced, and Neil Leifer directed. DP: Brian West, music by Stanley Myers,[31]

---

30 And used in *The Streetwalker* (*La Marge*, Walerian Borowczyk, 1976).
31 Myers was best-known for *The Deer Hunter, Insignificance, My Beautiful Laundrette, Dreamchild, Castaway, Track 29, The Witches,* and *Heart of Darkness*.

casting by Allan Foenander, editing by Tony Gibbs,[32] and prod. design by Keith Wilson. In the cast were Suzanne Somers, Ian McShane, Adam Faith, Paul Nicholas, Sam Kydd, Trevor Thomas, Glynis Barber, Sandy Ratcliff and Alan Lake.

Yesterday's Hero was set in the world of British sport, featuring characters who drew on soccer stars such as George Best (like the lead role, Rod Turner, played by Ian McShane). *Yesterday's Hero* depicts bad boy and drinker Turner hoping to have another shot at success (the plot is similar to *Rocky*).

Like other Jackie Collins adaptations of the period, *Yesterday's Hero* featured a soundtrack of contemporary pop songs, including 'Razzle Dazzle' by Heatwave, 'You Bet Your Love' by Herbie Hancock, 'Ring My Bell' by Anita Ward (a disco classic), 'Wanted' by the Dooleys, 'Duke of Earl' by Darts, 'Get Off' by Foxy, 'Hold the Line' by Toto, and the title song by Paul Nicholas. Other acts included: Bill Withers, Peter Brown, Suzanne Sommers, Phoebe Snow and Bobby Caldwell. Released Nov 22, 1979. 95 mins.

Reviews were mixed to poor: 'irresistibly bad' (*Time Out*) and 'totally uninteresting' (*Halliwell*).

---

[32] He cut *A Bridge Too Far, Fiddler On the Roof, Dune, Ronin, Agnes of God, Dogs of War, Rollerball, Tom Jones, Petulia, Juggernaut, The Knack, Jesus Christ Superstar, Walkabout* and *Performance*.

Hollywood Wives (1985),
this page and over.

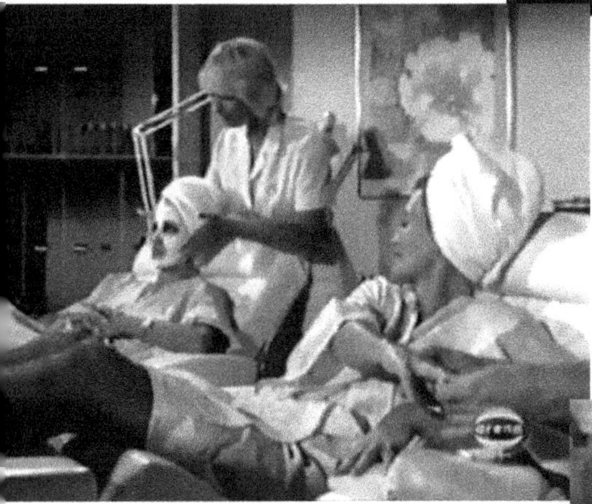

Lucky Chances (1990).

Lady Boss (1992).

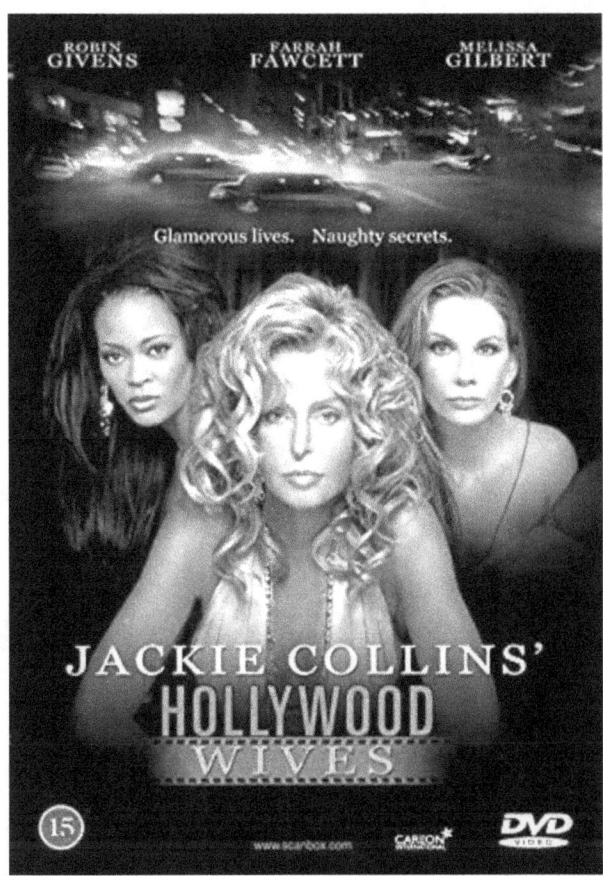

Hollywood Wives: The New Generation (2003).

Paris Connections (2010).

LUCKY CHANCES AND *LADY BOSS*

LUCKY CHANCES

The TV series *Lucky Chances* (1990) was Jackie Collins' version of one of her favourite books and movies, *The Godfather*. Produced by Susan Baerwald, William Peters and Collins for N.B.C. (she also wrote the screenplay), dir. by Buzz Kulik, music by Billy Goldenberg, DP: Gayne Rescher, casting by Meryl O'Loughlin, prod. des. by Jan Scott, and costumes by Buffy Snyder. *Lucky Chances* combined the first two *Lucky Santangelo* books, *Chances* (1981) and *Lucky* (1985).

Remember that phrase Jackie Collins uses when lovers are passionate about each other? - *heat*. Well, *Lucky Chances* ain't got *heat*, it's as cold as concrete. *Nobody does anything*: like previous adaptations of Jackie Collins' work, *Lucky Chances* mainly consisted of really dull, wealthy people in yet another restaurant scene, yet another hotel suite, yet another ritzy party, and yet another poolside chat.

And who would you cast as Lucky Santangelo - in 1990, or now? Very difficult. Because Lucky is one helluva human being:

> Lucky Santangelo.
> Dangerous.
> Stubborn.
> Strong.
> Crazy.
> Sensual.
> Everything. (*Lucky*, 637)

She's gotta look like a million dollars, move like a panther, be a leader, a career woman, a daughter, a schoolgirl, and an assassin. To put it in Jackie Collins' lingo: every woman'd wanna*be* her, and every guy'd wanna *fuck* her.

Well, actress Nichollette Sheridan is no Lucky Santangelo - not mine, not yours, and probably not for thousands of viewers. Where is the gutsy Lucky? The sexy, slinky Lucky? The super-confident Lucky? The lonely, troubled Lucky? Not here, folks. (Go thru the list of actresses of this period, however, and you'll soon discover that this was a very tough role to cast. Start with the obvious ones: Michelle Pfeiffer, Kim Basinger, Bridget Fonda, Madonna, Mia Farrow, Dianne Wiest, Julia Roberts, Meg Ryan, Sharon Stone, etc. None fit.

Maybe Linda Fiorentino[1]).

Lucky Chances was never more than routine television. It might've explored similar territory to Mario Puzo's 1969 novel, but of course it was a million miles away from the 1972 Paramount movie *The Godfather*, which still tops many people's lists of their favourite movies, and has been more influential on the portrayal of gangsters and the mafia in popular culture than any other movie (or book). *The Godfather* is a majestic piece of cinema (and all the more amazing because of its very troubled production history).

It's unfair to place the *Lucky Chances* TV movie alongside *The Godfather*, but this is clearly what Jackie Collins was aiming for, in both the *Lucky Santangelo* novels, and in this TV version of the first two books, which Collins scripted (incidentally, *Lucky Chances* was broadcast the same year as *The Godfather 3* was released, 1990. Same year as *GoodFellas*. And a year later *Bugsy* came out, which included the founding of Las Vegas, and starred Warren Beatty, one of the key Collinsian stars, as Bugsy Siegel).

Lucky Chances was a glossy, slick TV production, but never rose above being anything more than mildly entertaining and diverting. The direction (by Buzz Kulik)[2] was indifferent, the performances were uninspired (Vincent Irizarry's Gino was by far the most engaging, switched-on performance),[3] and the production design, costume design, camerawork, make-up, hair,[4] editing, and other technical elements[5] were pleasing but lacked imagination, texture, depth, and detail. This's nothing to do with the budget, but partly down to the pressures of TV production, the schedule, the resources, and of course the talents of the filmmakers.

You have to admit too that that the quality of the screenplay by Jackie Collins was adequate but nothing more. *Lucky Chances* turned out to be a rather superficial and unengaging production. Every twist or turn of the plot was wholly predictable (but not

---

[1] Fantastic in *The Last Seduction*.
[2] Kulik's a veteran of numerous TV shows, but this was clearly just another job for him.
[3] You probably won't recognize many of the actors in *Lucky Chances*. The more well-known ones included Sandra Bullock, Stephanie Beacham, and David McCallum.
[4] The hair (by Carolyn Elias and Barbara Lampson) seemed shoddy to me – late 1980s Big Hair (of course – what Jackie Collins TV show hasn't got Big Hair?), but the men's hair, particularly the ageing-up, was crudely done.
[5] The heads of some of the key departments included Jan Scott, Jack Taylor, Meryl O'Loughlin, Buffy Snyder, David Beatty, Gayne Resher, Carolyn Elias, Alan Fama, and Billy Goldenberg.

satisfyingly predictable), and the characters were in the main stereotypes which were under-written and not fleshed out by the actors. Also, the tone of the piece was too much the same, with little variation between scenes, so that the show comprised a series of the same sort of scenes, running on and on (very common in TV).

Television production is a giant machine, as we know, that has to feed the perpetually hungry maw of TV. And *Lucky Chances* really did look like something manufactured on an assembly line: get onto the set, rehearse the lines quickly, light the set, shoot a master shot (3 takes), a two-shot (2 takes), three close-ups (5 takes), then move on – strike the set, it's lunch already. You could see from even one or two minutes that there was no inspiration or imagination going on here, that this was a by-the-numbers television production.

Which would be OK, but you always hope for summat more, don't you? (well, I do!). *Lucky Chances* would pass for average television, but it would be another 13 years b4 Jackie Collins finally had a TV production that got close to embodying her fiction: *Hollywood Wives: The New Generation*.

Another drawback with *Lucky Chances* was the lack of a strong dramatic storyline. The first part of *Lucky Chances* was all about Gino Santangelo, the second was about his wayward daughter Lucky. But structurally, it was weak: the TV mini-series flashed up with dates '1947', '1952', etc, but a simple chronology doesn't count as a dramatic structure.

And there were no threats to the stability: Enzio Bonnatti (Michael Nader) and his cronies, the arch rivals of the Santangelos, would show up (always uninvited), and scowl and mouth off, but nothing happened. It was just talk, endless talk. Everything in *Lucky Chances* felt like a set-up for something that would happen later. Well, you can take 20 or 30 minutes of slow setting up (but even in a 90 minute movie that's too much), but not two hours. And *Lucky Chances* also felt like a show with every other scene missing; I didn't see it when it aired on N.B.C. in 1990: maybe it made more sense being interrupted with commercial breaks for General Motors or vacations in Atlantic City.

Remember Sonny in *The Godfather* promoting the family getting into narcotics, and old man Vito Corleone nixing the notion? There was an olde worlde self-righteousness about that decision, wasn't there? As if it was OK to be a mafia family that kills its rivals, that runs rackets in money, gambling, drink, and protection, etc, but will draw the line at drugs. *Lucky Chances* had the same holier-than-thou ethics, so that Gino Santangelo won't get into drugs or prostitution.[6]

★

LADY BOSS

Lucky Chances was followed up by *Lady Boss* (1992), produced by Steven R. McGlothen, Robert M. Sertner, Randy Sutter, and Frank von Zerneck, directed by Charles Jarrott, and scripted by Jackie Collins from her 1990 novel. Music[7] was by Dana Kaproff, Chuck Arnold was DP, Christopher Cooke edited, casting by Susan Glicksman and Fern Orenstein, Leonard Bram was first A.D., sets by K.C. Fox, Clancy T. Troutman was supervising sound editor, costumes by L. Paul Dafelmair and Jane Janiger, make-up by Richard Arias, and hair by Nina Paskowitz (yes, you have to credit the people who did the hair, make-up and costumes on a Jackie Collins picture!).

Kim Delaney was Lucky Santangelo; also appearing in the huge cast were Yvette Mimieux, Jack Scalla, Alan Rachins, Phil Morris, Joseph Cortese, Joan Rivers and Donald Trump.[8] In the cast of *Lady Boss* there are no serious names, like Angie Dickinson or Anthony Hopkins in the 1985 *Hollywood Wives* adaptation (Rivers was in a minor role).

Lady Boss is intended as a sequel to *Lucky Chances*: there are summaries of what happened in *Lucky Chances*, for instance, to keep the audience up-to-date.

But listen, kiddo, there's a glaring omission (a biggie among many): where the XXXX is Gino Santangelo? Big Daddy storms into the *Lady Boss* novel on the sixth page, but in the TV adaptation, minute after minute goes by... *and no Gino!* An hour goes by – *still no Gino!* (Yes, he is briefly mentioned in dialogue at the top of the

---

[6] Tho', actually, he does deliver some drugs in the novel of *Chances* (but only once).
[7] The music in *Lady Boss* (by Dana Kaproff), with its slinky saxophones, sounds like the score of a 1970s porno flick (which might be appropriate for a Jackie Collins yarn, but not for a TV series of the early 1990s).
[8] Yes, a cameo from the future President of the U.S.A.!

show, but is that enough? No!).[9]

Among the other elements dropped from *Lady Boss* are: actresses Leslie Kane and Abe's girlfriend Inga, actor Billy Milena, exec Ben Harrison, the brothel subplot, Venus Maria's back-story, Deena Swanson's troubled youth, Lennie Golden retreating to Gotham then the French Riviera, Emilio's actress girlfriend Rita, Franklin with star Johnny Romano, Venus marrying Cooper Turner – and Gino Santangelo, age 79, is at the party in the finale, with Paige (and Gino marries Paige).

Unfortunately, as with other Jackie Collins adaptations for the small screen, *Lady Boss* is spoilt by indifferent and uninspired staging and direction, bland music (where are the pop songs of the 1980s?), a too-similar tone (with few variations), and some stale performances. Instead of the zing of Collins' prose, we get boringly blocked scenes.[10]

Take a crucial scene in *Lady Boss*, where the story really starts (some 25 minutes into the show): Lucky Santangelo and her lawyer (Morton Sharkey)[11] visit the ageing patriarch and studio mogul Abe Panther. This is the scene where the quest of the main character is laid out (like Albus Dumbledore outlining Harry Potter's task in *Harry Potter*, or the chief in a cop show telling his team what they've got to do): to get her eager, Italian-American mitts on Panther Studios, Lucky's got to go under-cover and dish the dirt on its dodgy dealings.

But how *dull* is the filming of this scene! Lucky and Sharkey walk in, and sit at a big desk, with old Panther on the other side of it. They talk. The former mogul stands up, goes over to a cupboard to fetch a cigar (every mogul should have a cigar!), and Lucky follows him (while prating about the sorry state his studio's in). Then they sit down again. And talk some more.[12] Dynamic, this ain't.

Much of *Lady Boss* is this mechanical. True, some scenes are filmed in master shots and sequence shots, giving the actors room to explore the drama. But then the filmmaking reverts to singles and over-the-shoulder shots. Boring!

---

9 Lucky announces that Gino's coming to Cali in the last minutes, but by then it's far too late!
10 I missed the Gotham settings of the *Lady Boss* novel: now the TV series begins with Lucky and co. already settled into a swanky Malibu manse. *Lady Boss* does go to New York, but only for brief scenes).
11 Yes, Collins has a lawyer called Sharkey!
12 In the novel, Lucky quotes Panther's two qualities needed for a movie star: 'likability' and fuckability' (28). Well, that doesn't appear in the scene!

Oh yes, *Lady Boss* is a television production, I know that – and it's definitely limited by a TV schedule, and is filming scenes against the clock. But why does everything have to boil down to: master shot; two-shot; close-up; close-up; close-up; over-the-shoulder; close-up? And why does the action and movement within shots, and the staging, have to be so static? Collins' prose has a verve, a dynamism, about it, which nobody seems able to translate into something that works on screen.

Alas, *Lady Boss* contains nothing like the scene at Abigaile Stolli's Hollywood party – when a well-known feminist, Mona Sykes, gets into a heated argument with a black politician, Andrew J. Burnley:

> 'CUNT!'
> The forbidden word, said loudly and with great venom, shocked the entire table into silence.
> 'What did you call me, you black prick?' screamed the feminist, clearly in a fury.
> 'I called you a cunt, and that's what you are,' the black politician yelled back. (157)

And of course soon after stunning everybody they're making out in the car.

Readers will have their own view of what Lucky Santangelo looks, talks, dresses and acts like, and some viewers will no doubt have been disappointed with the *Lucky Santangelo* television adaptations. Certainly, Kim Delaney has the long, gypsy curls of Lucky, something of the Italian-American look, and she looks great in swimwear. But the panther/ tiger qualities of Lucky? No. The wild child, dangerous aspects of Lucky? No. The intense erotic heat of Lucky? No. The aggressive business sense of Lucky? No.

Kim Delaney, bless her, doesn't look like she could take up a gun and defend her family from nasty gangsters, or be a powerful businesswoman in man's world, or – you have to admit – that she could be Gino Santangelo's daughter.

Also, Lucky S. is re-conceived from the novel in other ways in the 1992 *Lady Boss*. Lucky, born in 1950, is 35 years-old during 1985 (when the action of the 1990 novel is set). That is, she is Lucky at the height of her powers. The TV series plays Lucky more like late twenties, and this Lucky doesn't come across as a cunning wheeler-dealer who has already been running the Santangelo operations in Las Vegas. (Meanwhile, Jack Scalla, as Lennie Golden, seems to be doing a combination of Mickey Rourke and Robert de Niro; but isn't

Golden meant to be a comedian in the style of Chevy Chase, Robin Williams and Eddie Murphy? Not a Method actor like de Niro or Rourke?).

The TV adaptation of *Lady Boss* makes numerous mistakes, including: not providing a decent introduction to characters; not explaining who they are, and their relationships to the other characters; not showing us who Lucky Santangelo is - a high-power business woman (we have little idea that she runs operations in Vegas, New York, L.A., etc); not dramatizing the key conflicts in a compelling manner; and not giving us much of an idea of what a Hollywood studio is and does (we see scenes of Lennie Golden filming a rubbish movie, but little else).

But this is a Hollywood film studio, which we know is full of egos, bitchery, weirdos and ultra-camp divas. For ex, Venus Maris is a Madonna-style superstar: but she's introduced initially as just another pretty female character: how about showing us what Venus does for a living? How about a big concert at the L.A. Forum? Or, if the budget won't stretch to that, how about depicting Venus filming a steamy video with dancers?

And it's the same with all of the characters: for instance: Martin Swanson is meant to be a business tycoon of the order of Donald Trump or Ted Turner: we see nothing of this - he's just another (slightly creepy) guy living in posh digs with a bored, jealous wife. And Santino Bonnatti is a seriously wacko psycho - but there's no evidence of that; instead, he looks like a guy who runs a truck hire company.

So *Lady Boss* is the cut-price, *Baywatch*, T. & A. version of a Jackie Collins novel - nameless, shapely women dressed in bikinis drift around the edges of the action (but not Lucky Santangelo - she sports a more demure, one-piece swimsuit - in black, of course). There are some (mild) sex scenes in *Lady Boss* (tho' in some versions they are censored out).

Another problem with *Lady Boss* is that issues are not satisfyingly dramatized. For ex, Santino Bonnatti in the *Lucky Santangelo* novels is a *really* revolting gangster, but we don't *see* that in the TV *Lady Boss*: instead, we see Bonnatti being released from the penitentiary, climbing into a limo and vowing to kill Lucky Santangelo. Fine, but very low-key - but that's all Bonnatti is allowed to do for every scene he appears in subsequently. When he threatens Eddie Kane at Panther Studios and demands his money (for the porn that Panther has been sneaking into their overseas video exports), all he does is leave a message on Kane's answering machine! And Kane quails in the background. It's *so* limp! Come on, if you're delivering a *gangster* subplot, at least do it justice! (Throw someone through a glass window! A gun in the mouth! A motorcycle chase and explosions! Anything!).

The action in the finale of *Lady Boss* is so inept your kids could do better (mine already have): there are two assassins and two targets: business tyro Martin Swanson and our heroine, Lucky Santangelo. Lucky returns to her beachside home in Malibu after the Venus Maria party at her movie studio, where she finds the skinny agent sent by Santino Bonnatti to kill her.[13] The producers/ filmmakers have no idea whatsoever on how to deliver this crucial sequence.[14] Did no one think to hire a stunt co-ordinator? Hasn't anyone realized that this is a Big Scene, and has to pay off two or more hours of television? Where's the excitement? The threat? Or, as Jackie Collins would say, the heat?

Nothing. *Rien.* Zilch.. *Nada.*

And the Swanson adultery/ betrayal sequence is no better. Ditto with the Bonnatti execution.

If it was you or me, we would go for it a little, right? These scenes require much more than half a night shoot and a budget of twenty bucks.

As if that isn't disappointing enough, the romantic reunion scene between Lucky and Lennie, which oughta be highly emotional/ sensual/ magical, is so nothingy I can't even be bothered to write, to wr — ... ... oh, *whatever*...[15]

★

It's easy to complain, so I'll offer a few suggestions of things I would do: ask for a longer lead-in time, to find exactly the right actress for Lucky; scrap the script and start over; cast more known faces (and invite real-life cameos); develop characterization much further; include some vivid flashbacks (which further enhance the characters); add some action set-pieces, fully staged (these could be from other *Lucky Santangelo* books, or Collins' other novels); feature snippets from the movies that Panther Studios produces; portray a movie studio operating at its height; and beg the

---

13 In the book, it's an inept hit-man called Link.
14 What's with the feeble drowning attempt? (In the book, it's the Pacific Ocean).
15 Insipid shit would be polite.

broadcasting nannies to allow sex scenes and 'bad language'.

★

HOLLYWOOD WIVES

Hollywood Wives (1985) was by far the biggest television/ film production of a Jackie Collins novel. *Hollywood Wives* has sold over 15 million copies, so it was a good bet for a TV series, and it is probably Collins' most well-known book (as well as one of her finest books).

The team behind *Hollywood Wives* included some high power collaborators, such as executive producers Aaron Spelling and Douglas Cramer, and producers Howard Koch, Steven Milkis, E. Duke Vincent, Robert McCullogh and J. David Williams. (Spelling, for example, is one of the most successful producers in North American television; Spelling's vast number of shows include *Charlie's Angels, Hart To Hart, Beverly Hills, 90210, Charmed* and *Dynasty*).

Robert McCullogh wrote the script; Robert Day directed; William Spencer was DP; editing by Fred Chulack and Ray Daniels (supervising editor: John Woodcock); casting by Lynn Stalmaster; art dir. by John Chilberg; costumes by Nolan Miller; hair by Hazel Catmull *et al*; make-up by Stephen Abrums *et al*; the composer was Lalo Schiffrin (b. 1932, he has an amazing run of credits, including *Enter the Dragon, Dirty Harry, Mission: Impossible* and *Bullitt*).[16] Rocky Moriana was music supervisor.

The cast of *Hollywood Wives* was the best to appear in a Jackie Collins adaptation, including Anthony Hopkins, Joanna Cassidy, Stephanie Powers, Candice Bergen,[17] Angie Dickinson,[18] Robert Stack, Mary Crosby, Roddy McDowall, Suzanne Somers, Rod Steiger, Andrew Stevens, Catherine Mary Stewart, Frances Bergen, and Steve Forrest.

Hollywood Wives is a starry, glossy, and in places very camp and

---

16 But the Rod Stewart song 'Passion' in the novel wasn't used. Too pricey for the rights maybe?
17 The novel refers to Bergen twice. And Bergen, being married to director Louis Malle, is certainly a Collinsian figure.
18 Dickinson is mentioned in the book – chatting with Johnny Carson (and also in *Hollywood Husbands*, as one of Wes Money's objects of lust).

plastic[19] adaptation of a Jackie Collins novel. *Hollywood Wives* receives the North American television approach, with recognizable actors, on-the-nose dialogue, easy-to-identify characters, and a soap opera dramatic structure.

Yet that doesn't quite capture the witty, bitchy, slick style of a Jackie Collins novel.

Style-wise, *Hollywood Wives* exhibits the familiar approach of U.S. television drama of the period: sets that're too big, un-lived-in, and fake, 1980s Big Hair, indifferent music, acting-by-numbers, and unimaginative, straightforward plotting[20]

The acting style in *Hollywood Wives* ranges from barely passable to downright dreadful. Steve Forrest, playing Ross Conti, is hilarious to watch in his reaction shots as he plays the Hollywood has-been as a 'little boy lost'.

Hollywood Wives was conceived and presented in the so-familiar format of glossy, North American television. Every scene is over-lit (altho' *Hollywood Wives* was filmed on celluloid not video), with light blasting into every part of the settings (William Spencer was DP), every scene is staged in medium close-ups or medium long shots (just like a TV soap opera, down to the cretinously dull establishing shots outside each location), the staging is flabby and utterly uninspired (actors stand about spouting dialogue), the dialogue is hopelessly obvious and on the nail (yet there's very little 'bad language' – the meat and veg of Collins' prose style), and of course North American TV cuts back on the sex and violence and drug use and all of the elements which can appear in 'R' rated movies but not on TV (where movies are often censored/ edited, even when they're rated 'G' or 'PG').

Every scene in *Hollywood Wives* looks like every other scene – *Hollywood Wives* is alarmingly flat, dramatically. There *is* no drama – and even the rising stings of music running up to a commercial break by Lalo Schifrin and co. offer no suspense. It's blanded-out, an airbrushed, censored version of a Jackie Collins novel. So much of it is so nothingy you can't believe it.

The dialogue in a Jackie Collins adaptation should be zappy and zingy, it should be delivered fast and brashly, but in *Hollywood Wives*, ah, no, not again with the standard delivery of lines! Can't

---

19 Plastic and camp in the Andy Warhol, Pop Art manner.
20 The storytelling doesn't possess an ounce of passion or insight, and the characters come across as paper-thin. Scenes are filmed in the most boring manner.

anybody reproduce the way that Collins writes dialogue? It's one of the chief pleasures of a Collins novel!

It's true that *Hollywood Wives* is a 'PG' rated, TV version of a distinctly 'R' rated novel – but it's not the censoring of sex, drugs, language, etc, which scuppers the tube's adaptation of the novel: it's that it's a poor piece of television full stop.

For camp value, for trashy value, *Hollywood Wives* was potentially a good runner – but, once again, it was the wrong kind of camp! I mean, it was *boring* camp, instead of being glitzy, sensational, sexy camp. Sadly, this was *not The Rocky Horror Picture Show* or *Grease* or a John Waters movie (if only! Indeed, why didn't someone hire Waters or Andy Warhol or even, God forbid, Russ Meyer, to direct a Collins movie?!).

Yes, even with talents like Howard Koch, Aaron Spelling and Douglas Cramer contributing to *Hollywood Wives*, it still didn't translate the heat and bitchiness of a Jackie Collins novel, or of this particular novel.

★

Altho' *Hollywood Wives* was three long TV movies in all, it still dropped many elements from the *Hollywood Wives* novel of 1983. Gone were the back-stories of charas such as Ross Conti, Montana Gray, Sadie La Salle, Angel Hudson, etc (a pity, because of some the back-stories go back to Hollywood in the 1950s, which would be fun to see recreated). Some of the back-stories, however, were put into present-tense scenes – Angel is menaced at a supermarket, for example, which sort of correlates with her experiences in the past.

The violence was heavily toned down in the TV version of *Hollywood Wives*: Deke Andrews chops up his family with a machete in the book. The crime scene's so gruesome it sickens the detective assigned to investigate the multiple murder. The story of Detective Rosemont pursuing the case was also left out (instead, there are short, boring and repetitive scenes of Andrews crossing the continent and acting nasty). And also the young hooker Joey, that Andrews befriends, and who the detective is linked to, is excised.

Hollywood Wives cuts back on the camp elements of the 1983 novel (while adding its own camp value, of course). In the book, there are some very camp gay characters, including trannies (and dressed in some outrageous costumes!). In the TV series, most of that is ditched: instead, it relies on the performance of the ever-wonderful Roddy McDowall to deliver the homosexual undercurrents, as Jason Swandle (which McDowall does with restraint). James 'Gypsy' Haake plays the hairdresser Koko in a very over-the-top manner, a caricature of a cliché of a stereotype of a camp hair stylist (we don't see Koko's partner, Adrian, or Angel staying with them).

The Big Set-piece in *Hollywood Wives*, the party held at the Contis' home, lost the opportunity to include some real stars in cameos (they are mentioned in the novel).

Elaine's life in the TV version of *Hollywood Wives* includes the shoplifting subplot, but not her flings with her exercise instructor and others. Neil Gray has a heart attack, but of course the television adaptation missed out the bit where Gray's weiner is trapped inside Gina's 'super-cunt'. Montana spends the night with Buddy after the party, but they don't make love, as they do in the novel. Meanwhile, the important beat in the novel of Montana taking over the directing reins of her script, is left out.

The most successful plot-line in *Hollywood Wives* is the one with Anthony Hopkins as the film director Neil Gray and Suzanne Somers (she appeared in *Yesterday's Hero*) as the actress Gina Germaine who's desperate for a role in Hopkins' film *Final Reunion*[21] (along with Andrew Stevens' Buddy Hudson). Gina shtupps Gray, begging him to cast her in *Final Reunion* (eventually resorting to blackmail – video-taping their sex sessions. There's a *lot* of blackmail in Jackie Collins' fiction!). Hopkins invests the role of the Brit film director with just enough energy to make it vaguely convincing,[22] while Somers is great as the sex kitten actress Gina on the make.

Hollywood Wives doesn't encourage the audience to care a jot about any of the charas or their storylines. While some of the roles are nicely cast – Catherine Mary Stewart is a convincing innocent in the big city, Rod Steiger[23] is a striking movie mogul, for example (plus Hopkins and Somers) – these parts are easily within the range of the performers, who have all been better elsewhere (and nobody is encouraged to do more than the bare minimum). Well, yes this *is* North American television, a factory for manufacturing programming that can hold viewers in between the all-important commercial breaks (television runs on advertizing). But you always hope for

---

21 It's *Street People* in the novel.
22 In the novel, Gray is likened to Richard Burton, and Hopkins, who has also been compared to Burton, uses a bit of a Burtonesque voice.
23 Alas, the more extreme aspects of Oliver Easterne's personality, like his obsessive cleanliness, didn't make it into the TV version.

Something More, particularly with a drama mini-series, with a starry cast, where more money (presum-ably) has been spent (at least to assemble that cast).

The least successful section of *Hollywood Wives* has Andrew Stevens as Deke Andrews (with an awful, stuck-on beard),[24] as the mandatory psycho in a Jackie Collins adaptation (he's a-killin' an' a-maimin' his way across the United States of North America, every part of which looks suspiciously like it was filmed just outside Los Angeles).

Altho' she's winningly played by one of Hollywood's queens of the screen – Angie Dickinson – Sadie La Salle's plan of launching Buddy Hudson as a sex symbol to enact revenge on Ross Conti (who left her), seems very childish (and also – how could anybody dump a superstar like Angie Dickinson?! And even a young Dickinson, *circa* 1958?!). In a novel, we read and interpret characters and scenes in our own way, often skimming over flaws in the narrative or the prose; in a movie or TV show, those flubs and misconceived plots are sometimes cruelly exposed. And parts of the novel of *Hollywood Wives* just don't work on screen: the Sadie-Ross plot, the Angel-Buddy break-up plot, the Deke Andrews-mother revenge plot, etc. It's not that *Hollywood Wives* is 'unrealistic', because the *Hollywood Wives* novel is decidedly fantastical, it just doesn't convince. Worse, it's not much fun, either.

In *Hollywood Wives,* almost every character (apart from Angel Hudson) is cynical and selfish, doing nothing for no one. They are all concerned with their careers (turning to blackmail), or simple, instant gratifications (empty sex and drink[25] – the TV series draws back from depicting drug use, which has usually freaked out the U.S. TV networks, altho' it's a staple of Jackie Collins' fiction).

★

Hollywood Wives does capture the disconnection, the alienation, and the bland interactions of 1980s Los Angeles, even more so perhaps than Jackie Collins' novel. The superficial, narcissistic, selfish, empty culture (described in Jean Baudrillard's *America,* 1988). *Hollywood Wives* is a TV series of shots of people driving in cars or having boring conversations on telephones in over-lit and over-decorated rooms. It certainly delivers the car culture of L.A. – Ross Conti pulls up on Rodeo Drive and puts a quarter in a parking

---
24 Actor Andrew Stevens gets to play both Buddy Hudson and Deke Andrews – hence the joke beard and make-up.
25 Neil Gray is a boozer (as was Anthony Hopkins who played him).

meter... Elaine nervously drives around in her convertible... Buddy jams his saloon into the sidewalk, jumping out to hurry after a girl that looks like Angel... and Deke Andrews hitches rides or buys numerous vehicles as he crosses the loveless wastes of North America in search of Collinsian revenge. Meanwhile, in the age before cel phones, the internet, pagers and the like, the signature sound of *Hollywood Wives* is the ringing of a telephone.

Joanna Cassidy, as Marilee Gray, voices an important theme that is seldom discussed in Jackie Collins' fiction, but lies underneath every story: loneliness (the issue of being alone is raised in the scene where Elaine Conti is disconsolate after Ross walks out).

★

So the climax finally arrives in the TV version of *Hollywood Wives*, after four hours of indifferent/ dreadful television. The Big Scene, in the house and on the lawn at Sadie La Salle's Hollywood home, looks like it was directed by a bunch of inept, first-year drama students from U.C.L.A. It is shockingly bad – and this is a network television drama! With an all-star cast! With a budget of more than 50 cents! (The finale's staged in full daylight in a garden,[26] with zero atmosphere/ texture – come on, guys – at least film it at night in a thunderstorm! This is, after all, paying off the sleazy side of the Hollywood Dream).

So Deke Andrews turns out to be Buddy Hudson's twin brother, and both're sons of Sadie and Ross Conti. (The TV version misses out the car crash with Ross Conti, Detective Rosemont, and Andrews heading for Angel's place, where he ties her to the bed naked, and is about to rape her, etc).

The *dénouement* scenes of *Hollywood Wives* are dismal let-downs – the storylines are resolved in such a brief, can't-be-bothered fashion: Elaine Conti walks out on Ross (after putting him into a limo); Sadie La Salle says she has lots of talking to do with Buddy about his career and parentage; Easterne discusses his new movie with the press; and Buddy and Angel make up with one, chaste kiss.[27] (Only Oliver Easterne gets a big send-off – a crane shot up and away from the foyer of the hospital, which segues into a long shot of – what else? – the Hollywoodland Sign up in the Hollywood

---

26 The music in the climax is running continually, as it is throughout much of *Hollywood Wives* – and it just swamps the drama. It's another case of TV/ film producers being terrified of allowing more'n ten seconds to go by in silence or near-silence. So poor Lalo Schifrin and company have to supply minute after minute of scoring.

27 The plots're wrapped up differently in the book.

Hills). Yes – no matter how bad the 1985 TV mini-series is of Jackie Collins' 1983 novel, we always have the book!

★

HOLLYWOOD WIVES: THE NEW GENERATION

So how about *Hollywood Wives: The New Generation* (2003)? Produced by Jackie Collins, Wendy Hill-Tout, Tom Patricia, Randi Richmond, Renée Valente, Michelle Wong and Michael Jaffe for C.B.S., it was based on the 2001 book of the same name. Joyce Chopra directed and Nicole Avril wrote the screenplay (thus it's already unusual, with many women in key creative positions. A *female* director! That is so Jackie Collins!).

Farrah Fawcett headed up the cast (in one of her last roles), which also included Melissa Gilbert, Robin Givens, Dorian Harewood, Jeff Kaake, Robert Moloney, Jack Scalla, Stewart Bick and Pascale Hutton. *Hollywood Wives: The New Generation* was a follow-up to the 1983 novel, Collins' biggest hit, and the 1985 TV series.

The most significant aspect of *Hollywood Wives: The New Generation* for me was that it was the first television or movie adaptation of a Jackie Collins work which captured the breakneck pace of her fiction – in particular the continuous switching from one character and story and situation to another. It's all about the *editing*, the tempo, the rhythm, and previous adaptations of Collins' work had just been *too slow*.

No, it wasn't because the original *Hollywood Wives* was made in 1985, or *The Stud* and *The Bitch* in the late 1970s, and *Hollywood Wives: The New Generation* was much more recent (2003). (However, in some TV dramas there has been a trend for more rapid editing.) It's because Collins *never* dwells for too long on any single character or story. Her books *always* leap from one place to another. And rapidly, too.

So *Hollywood Wives: The New Generation* captured that. However, the downside was that exposition and setting up characters and situations was a little lacking. If you knew Jackie Collins' glamorous world and Hollywood itself, that was fine. If you didn't, it might have been more difficult to keep up.

That's a minor quibble, however. More problematic was the last third of *Hollywood Wives: The New Generation*, when the thriller plot – where Lissa Roman's daughter Nicci (Pascale Hutton) is kidnapped – kicked in. Oh dear, this was so run-of-the-mill, TV drama stuff, which we've seen 100s of times before. What a pity that *Hollywood Wives: The New Generation* degenerated into mechanical cop show antics.

At that point, with the storylines coalescing into the single plot of the kidnapping, the pacing and editing of *Hollywood Wives: The New Generation* became routine and predictable.

But this also illuminates how Jackie Collins' novels work in the first place: Collins uses a thriller or murder mystery ingredient to spice up her narratives, and to provide a narrative engine to drive some of the stories (and to add suspense and jeopardy). She typically introduces the thriller plot very early on (sometimes in the first chapter, as in *Hollywood Kids* and *Married Lovers*). So the reader (or viewer) knows that something is going to happen, that some character wants vengeance or to do summat nasty.

The thriller plot works in Jackie Collins' novels, I think, because it doesn't over-balance the mix. The reader can take it or leave it – it's only one ingredient among many in a Jackie Collins book.

In the 2003 C.B.S. adaptation of *Hollywood Wives: The New Generation*, however, the kidnapping plotline consumed too much screen time. It also tried to create emotional climaxes which rang false (such as the reconciliation between Lissa Roman and her daughter Nicci).

As to being a good interpretation of the 2001 novel, *Hollywood Wives: The New Generation* was OK-ish. Certainly it retained most of the key narrative elements; but then, the 2001 novel wasn't great, so novel-to-movie comparisons don't matter too much.

★

PARIS CONNECTIONS

Paris Connections (2010) was produced by Amber Entertainment and Alienor Productions to be sold thru the British supermarket Tesco (i.e., it was a direct-to-video/ direct-to-DVD movie). It was produced by Simon Bosanquet (and six other producers),[28] written by Michael Tupy, and directed by Harley Cokeliss (b. 1945).[29] It's a Madison Castelli/ *L.A. Connections* story. (Some aspects of *Paris Connections* cropped up in *The Power Trip*, a novel of 2012).

The *milieu* of *Paris Connections* was high fashion – the world of fashion shows and fashion models (the thriller plot has beautiful models being nobbled by an unseen killer. The moral? Don't step into the garden for a cigarette! Because there's a psycho lurking in the bushes! And don't walk alone at night down dark alleys! Jeez, I thought everybody knew that!).

Anthony Delon (son of Alain Delon) was Jake Sica, Trudie Styler was Olivia Kulikova, Hudson Leick was Coco De Ville, Caroline Chikezie was Nathalie de Barge, Fabien De Chalvron was Sergei Borinski, and Charles Dance was Aleksandr Borinski. Screen legend Anouk Aimée had a brief cameo as a fashion designer.

Nicole Steinwedell appeared as Madison Castelli, Jackie Collins' journo character, a good, ol' American lass who lives in Gotham and is sent to Paris for a story by her editor. (Steinwedell has some of the sass and spirit of a Jackie Collins character, and she looks the part, but she never quite connected with the material, or wasn't allowed to let rip). Other characters come from the *Madison Castelli* novels, such as Jake Sica.

But the biggest star in *Paris Connections* was undoubtedly Paris itself. What a city! With acting perfunctory, direction indifferent, staging bland, music even blander, at least Paris was up to the mark in *Paris Connections*. True, you can point a camera anywhere in Gay Paree and you get yourself a pretty image. Paris certainly never disappoints as a city of cinema – and we never get tired of seeing it!

Indeed, *Paris Connections* featured way too many second unit images of the famous sights (as padding), so at times it was more like a Jackie Collins travelogue than a dramatic movie.

Hmmm... I'd much rather see Jackie Collins herself walking

---
28 Jackie Collins, Lawrence Elman, Ileen Maisel, Shezi Nackvi, Mark Ordesky and Marie-Laure Reyre.
29 Many in the crew were French – a sort of French-American approach to Collins.

around the streets of Paris with the script of *Paris Connections* in her hand, telling us where each scene would be filmed. (Yes, I'm afraid that *Paris Connections* is the sorta movie where the production meetings, or the location scouting trips and or even (heaven forfend!), the casting sessions would be more entertaining than the movie itself).

Because, story-wise and drama-wise, *Paris Connections* was, how to put it politely, not the most compelling thriller you've seen. The charas were humdrum and stereotypical, the acting was samey, the tone was one-note (like the music), and the situations were as familiar and as unengaging as a trip to Bank of America on a rainy Wednesday morning to withdraw twenty bucks for a coffee, and about as 'much fun as a box of tampons' (a quip from the novel *The Power Trip* [249]).

Paris Connections was in short a TV movie-style thriller that're ten a penny on television channels all over the world.

But this is *Jackie Collins!* This is the *Queen of Hollywood!*

Well, maybe. But not in *this* movie.

You are waiting for something to happen, or something to engage you... But it doesn't arrive in *Paris Connections.* Unless you count the second unit imagery of Paris. In which case, book your plane ticket now!

Well, to be fair, there *is* some sorta romantic chemistry between Madison Castelli and her old boyfriend Jake Sica, including the obligatory sex scene, but not much with the other couple, Russian tycoon Alexsandr (Charles Dance) and his fashion designer *belle,* Coco De Ville (Hudson Leick).

But the script of *Paris Connections* (by Michael Tupy) is so lame, it doesn't inspire anybody to do much of anything in this direct-to-DVD movie. No one's enchanted here, because we've all seen this story, this thriller format, this murder mystery story a zillion times (even if we are in the City of Light).

Or, put it like this, if *Paris Connections* was being produced by Panther Studios under the beady eye of Lucky Santangelo, in the *Lucky Santangelo* series, she would decide (after viewing the rushes) to halt production, bring the crew back from Paris (too expensive!), order a page one rewrite, and re-cast the movie. (And shoot in Vancouver).

Who's the murderer? Do you really care? Was it the antsy, adopted son, Sergei? Was it a rival fashion designer? Nope, it was

Olivia, Aleksandr's assistant (who's the real mother of Sergei).

Clichés as ancient as this thriller plot in *Paris Connections* demand something extra, some energy, some new twist… Otherwise, why bother? Is it another case of producers and filmmakers misjudging the audience of a Jackie Collins story? Do they think readers of Collins are satisfied with low quality products? (With these feeble attempts at suspense and mystery, this nothing-in-particular script, and this indifferent kind of filmmaking?)[30]

---

[30] If you bought this movie in a supermarket (and no doubt some Collins fans did), you'd ask for your money back.

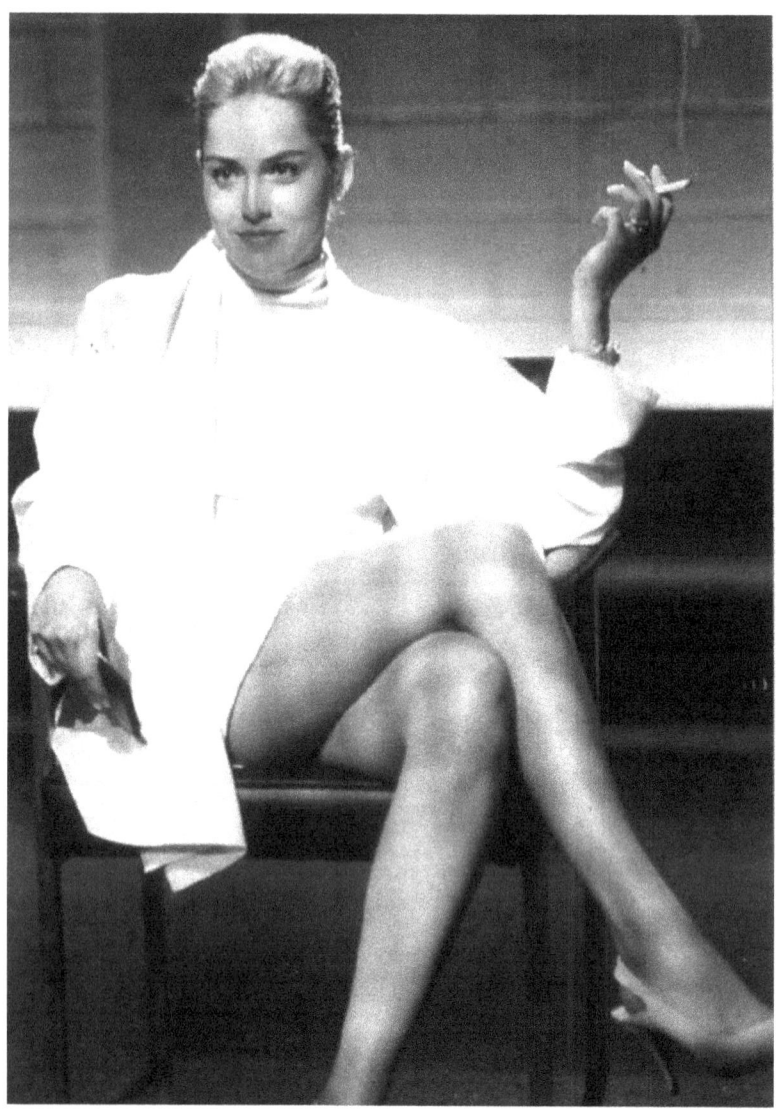

Movies that explore the same world as Jackie Collins' books (this page and over).

Basic Instinct (1992).

The Godfather (1972).

James Bond movies of the 1960s

Emmanuelle (1974)

Showgirls (1995) explores prime Jackie Collins territory:
young women in Las Vegas desperate to make it.
Sleaze, crime, murder, sex, music and glitz.
Look at the club above, there's even a panther!

You are a whore.

Boogie Nights (1998)

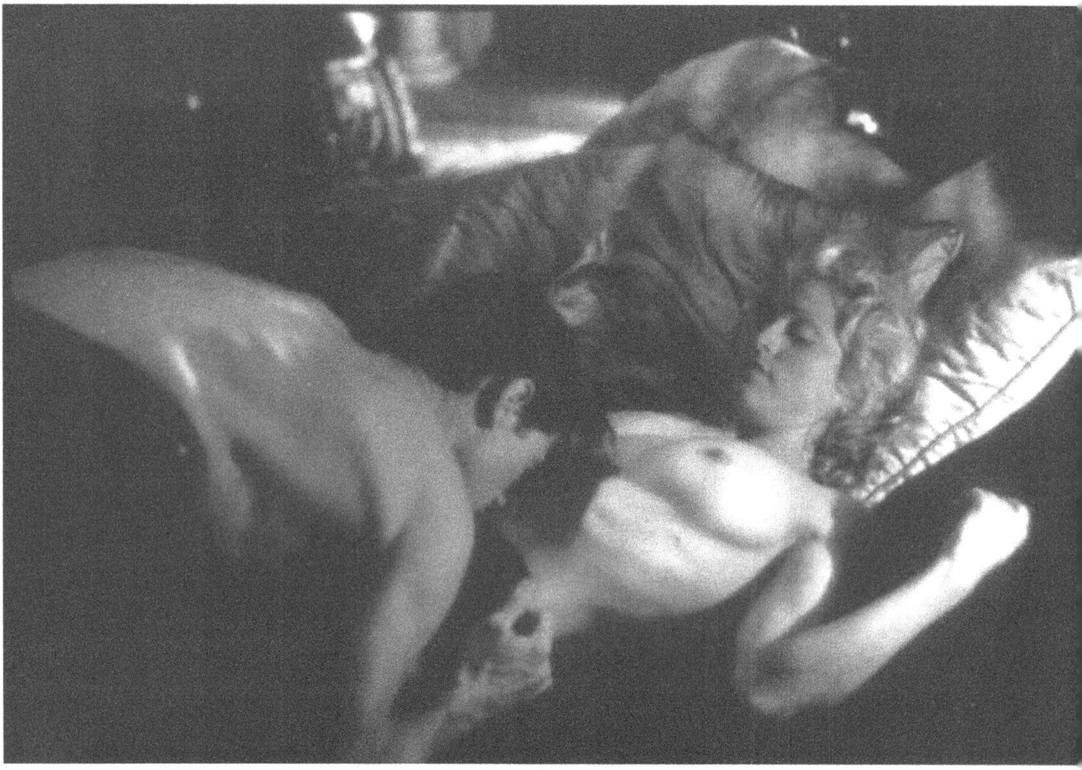

The cycle of erotic thrillers (a.k.a. neo-noir films) of the late 1980s/ early 1990s have affinities with Collins' fiction, such as Body of Evidence (1993). And the gangster flicks of Martin Scorsese explore a similar sort of criminal underworld (such as GoodFellas, 1990).

♥

The last word in this book should come from Jackie Collins (from *Hollywood Wives,* of course) – wherever you are, Jackie, have a good one!

> Goodbye California… She would miss it in her own way. The ocean and the beach. The mountains and the parks. The very seduction of living in the sun. And of course, the view from the top of their hill. That very special spread of lights laid out like fairytale land.
> Yes. She knew she would miss L.A., but as Neil would say… 'Never look back…' (594)

♥ ♥ ♥ ♥ ♥

Epilogue

Los Angeles. Present day.

He'd made it.
Big time.
Two mega-hit movies, as writer and director (with the new flick Jackie Collins, Queen of Hollywood *rolling out at Christmas).*[1]
Houses in Malibu and Maui; offices in Hollywood, Central Park West and on the Warners lot.
Voluptua, a really wild supermodel, was giving him great head in his luxurious suite in the Beverly Hills Hotel. He squirmed to feel those famous, million-dollar, Italian lips (blue lipstick, of course) wrapped around his cock.
*When the door burst open and Vincent Gianetti and two wise guys from Vegas walked in, he wasn't surprised. The presence of his ex-wife, super-bitch Frigida, flanked by five lawyers, was less welcome (*he *was paying for those sharks!).*
He reached for his gun.
Too late.
A heartbeat away from nirvana – a gunshot – a scream – then the earthquake hit, the building collapsing around them.
What the hell, he thought, it'll make a wonderful movie.

---

[1] An action thriller and racy biopic starring Scarlett Johansson (as J.C.) and Johnny Depp, the preview at Cannes had been nuts. There's also a wild fantasy sequence where Johansson dreams she's a panther hunting and fucking in the jungle.

Appendices

Quotes By Jackie Collins

I am still shocking people today, and I don't know why. Is it because I'm a woman talking about sex and men? One magazine said that no one writes sex in the back of a Bentley better than Jackie Collins.

People are intrigued by fame, power and wealth and I think Hollywood is the only place where you get all three together.

Do not copy my style! The first rule of writing is write about what you know, not what you think you know. So, think about what you've done in your life and write about that.

I don't believe in writing anything that I don't know about or haven't researched about personally. I like to transport the reader to places, and in order to do that I have to do the research.

I have this theory that people in Hollywood don't read. They read *Vanity Fair* and then consider themselves terribly well read. I think I can basically write about anybody without getting caught.

I write about real people in disguise. If anything, my characters are toned down - the truth is much more bizarre.

I have written 20 books, and each one is like having a baby. Writing is not easy; some people want to write books but just can't put a story together. I can put together a story that interests both me and my readers.

I really fall in love with my characters, even the bad ones. I love getting together with them. They tell me what to do; they take me on a wild and wonderful trip.

I think I'm a born storyteller. Inspiration is all around me. I can read a newspaper article and come up with an idea for a book.

❤

Ideas are all around me. If I wasn't interested in them myself, I don't think anyone else would be either.

❤

I write synopses after the book is completed. I can't write it beforehand, because I don't know what the book's about. I invent something for my publisher because he asks for one, but the final book ends up very differently.

❤

If you want to achieve your dreams, you must follow them, and the best way to follow them is not to think about wanting to be very rich, but to think about doing something that you really want to do.

❤

Whatever you have a passion for, then you must do. If you want to write, write about something you know about.

❤

I write about the American dream: if you set your mind to do something, you can do it.

Quotes From Jackie Collins' Books

Never fuck with a Santangelo.

He *knew* there was a better life out there somewhere. And he *knew* the only way to get it was with money.

Bingo! Everyone was for sale. All you had to do was establish a price.

You've always gotta have a plan, an' you always gotta stick to it.

She looked down at him like a mother who'd just caught her son jacking off over a naked picture of HItler.

Men. They were either gay, into kinky sex, cheating on their wives, momma's boys, jerks, drug users, cheats, pimps, or actors - the worst kind.

'Paying for pussy? In *this* town!' he'd exclaimed. 'LA is a free pussy heaven!'

Fucking was his favourite pastime, second only to making money.

Falling in love is like getting hit by a large truck and yet not being mortally wounded. Just sick to your stomach, high one minute, low the next. Starving hungry but unable to eat. Hot, cold, forever horny, full of hope and enthusiasm, with momentary depressions that wipe you out.

'…he'd fuck a bush if he thought it would invest…'

Getting old was a bitch, but it was better than the alternative.

Real-Life Jackie Collins Characters

ANITA PALLENBERG.

Anita Pallenberg had relationships with the Italian photographer/painter Mario Schifano,[2] Brian Jones, and later Keith Richards (from 1967 to 1979). A former fashion model, Pallenberg had been an assistant to Jasper Johns in New York City, and hung out with Andy Warhol and Larry Rivers. Pallenberg was a scenester, a woman on the scene, at parties, hanging out with artists and celebrities (before she met the Stones, Pallenberg was already a veteran of the *dolce vita* scene in Rome and the Factory scene in Gotham).

Anita Pallenberg was already a worldy-wise woman by the time of appearing in *Performance* (more than most in the cast, including Mick Jagger and James Fox); she spoke five languages,[3] and was of German, Swiss and Italian descent[4] (and came from a wealthy family: her mother Paula Wiederhold was German, her father Arnaldo Pallenberg was an Italian travel agent and artist.[5] She was born in Roma). Her childhood was spent in France, Germany and Spain; she hitchhiked around Europe; she studied[6] in New York and Rome (she went by boat to Gotham from Rome in 1963);[7] and she settled in London.

> Anita in those days was absolutely electrifying. Whenever she came into a room, every head would turn to look at her. There was something kittenish about her, a sense of mischief - of naughtiness. (Christopher

---

[2] Mario Schifano later had an affair with Marianne Faithfull, adding further layers to what Philip Norman dubbed 'the 'Mick-Keith sexual labyrinth' (1984, 373). Pallenberg stood in for models for Schifano when they were indisposed or late.
[3] Her father sent her to a German school (partly to learn German), which she resented. But later she appreciated being able to speak five languages.
[4] Her ancestors included the Symbolist artist Arnold Böcklin - her great-great-grandfather. Anita Pallenberg's father and grandfather were also painters (based in Rome).
[5] Aristocratic, but not rich.
[6] Anita Pallenberg was expelled from school at 16. She studied medicine, graphic design and picture restoration as a teenager.
[7] Anita Pallenberg has recounted that she hung out with some of the *dolce vita* set - Federico Fellini, Pier Paolo Pasolini, Luchino Visconti, Alberto Moravia *et al.*

Gibbs)[8]

For photographer Gered Mankowitz, Anita Pallenberg was 'the epitome of the incredibly beautiful, incredibly stylish Sixties woman,' but he also regarded her as 'evil and manipulative and wicked' (ib., 91). Linda Keith (Keith Richard's girlfriend) admired Pallenberg: 'she was the most wonderful and powerful person. I have huge respect and admiration and love for her' (ib., 91).

Philip Norman described Anita Pallenberg in his superb biography of Mick Jagger thus:

> Anita was stunningly beautiful in the crop-haired, snub-nosed, long-legged way that perfectly suited sixties fashion, but with an extra, almost feral quality, 'like a cheetah', John Dunbar recalls. She was formidably intelligent, fluent in four languages, and knowledgable about art and the obscurer ways of German and European literature. She also had a recklessness and appetite for devilment that would cause more than one of her new rock 'n' roll friends to suspect her of being a witch. (193-4)

MICK JAGGER.

Mick Jagger is a Jackie Collins character *par excellence.* If you made up a person like Jagger, a nice, middle class kid from Dartford in Kent, England who became a pop superstar, nobody would believe you. If you added the wild history of the Rolling Stones to the personality of ol' Rubber Lips, readers would laugh it off as pure lies.

Mick Jagger is a rock 'n' roll icon, caricatured in the press for his odd looks (huge lips) and Mockney, mid-Atlantic drawl. He's known on first-name terms, as 'Mick', like Eric (Clapton), David (Bowie), Marc (Bolan), Jimi (Hendrix), and Bob (Dylan). While Keef Richards and Ron Wood were the party animals in the Stones, hanging out all night after the gig, taking drugs, Jagger looked after himself. A keep-fit fanatic, Jagger was still strutting around the stage in his 60s. In 1993, Jagger had 7 children with 3 mothers, homes in New York, Texas, Mustique and the Loire, and was worth over $75 million.

Check out one area of the life of Mick Jagger: his love life – the subject of tabloid gossip for half a century. As with Warren Beatty and Charlie Sheen, the number of women that Jagger is reckoned to have dated is legendary, and includes model Chrissie Shrimpton (sister of Jean); Marianne Faithfull;[9] Bianca Pérez-Mora Macias [10] (they married in 1971 and separated in 1977; they have one child, Jade Sheena Jezebel); model Apollonia von Ravenstein; 18 year-old starlet Mia Farrow; Patti Boyd (who also dated George Harrison, Eric Clapton and Ron Wood); Mackenzie Phillips; model Jerry Hall (they dated in 1977; married in 1990; the marriage was annulled in 1999; they have four children);[11] singer Linda Ronstadt; Luciana Gimenez, a 29 year-old thong model from Rio (they have one child, Lucas Maurice Morad); Carinthia West (a 25 year-old model and photographer); Valerie Perrine, a Texan actress;

---
8 In P. Norman, 1984, 165.
9 Mick Jagger apparently had a threesome with Marianne Faithfull and one of the local women in a Tangiers brothel.
10 She had been engaged to Michael Caine.
11 Jagger wooed Jerry Hall away from singer Bryan Ferry.

Victoria Vicuna, a Venezuelan model (both in the early 1980s); Bebe Buell (mother of actress Liv Tyler); actress Angelina Jolie; heiress Sabrina Guinness; Dana Gillespie; L'Wren Scott, a 34 year-old American stylist (1967-2014); 19 year-old model Sophie Dahl (grand-daughter of Roald Dahl); TV star Amanda de Cadenet; Irish singer Andrea Corr, 22; Carla Bruni (at the time Eric Clapton's squeeze); actress Marsha Hunt (they had one child, Karis); 'the Pisces Apple lady' (Chris O'Dell), who had liaisons with George Harrison and Ringo Starr as well as Jagger; Pat Andrews and Suki Potier (Brian Jones's girlfriends); Tina Turner (backstage at a 1960s gig in Bristol's Colston Hall, apparently); one of the Ikettes, Pat Arnold; another Ikette, Clauda Linnear; Uschi Obermaier (Keith Richards' girlfriend); Linda McCartney (according to Bill Wyman), before she met Paul; Cecilia Nixon; plus a host of groupies (often these were young American (Californian) women who were happy to spend a night (or just a few hours) at Cheyne Walk or a Parisian hotel; they had names like Susie Suck, Miss Mercy, Suzie Creamcheese, Kathy Kleevage, and of course the Plaster Casters).

Indeed, it might be easier to say who in the Western world *hasn't* tupped Mick Jagger! ('In the oversexed world of rock, in the whole annals of show business, Jagger's reputation as a modern Casanova is unequalled,' noted Philip Norman [7]).

DAVID BOWIE.

Los Angeles seems to be the perfect city for David Bowie – a modern city, an entertainment capital, with a focus on Hollywood and music. And, as many pop acts from Britain found from the 1960s onwards, L.A. is a terrific Party Town (many of the famous escapades in pop and rock legend have occurred in L.A.).[12]

Hollywood was a mythical place to David Bowie long before he visited Amerika, as it has been for millions of people from Europe. Hollywood, tho', and Los Angeles, became loathed as well as loved, and after living there in the mid-1970s, Bowie was put off the place for life. But Bowie certainly caught the sleaze and glitter of the streets of West Hollywood in songs such as 'Cracked Actor' (and, if you wander around Sunset and Vine,[13] they're still very much like that). Indeed, like much of the output of the Doors or 'California Love' by Tupac Shakur, 'Cracked Actor', 'Drive-In Saturday' and other Bowie songs about La-La Land have become classic L.A. tracks, like musical equivalents of Kenneth Anger's much-thumbed *Hollywood Babylon* book.

'Cracked Actor' receives an outstanding performance in the *Ziggy Stardust* movie of 1973. It was composed in the Beverly Hills Hotel (of course! – where all of Jackie Collins' characters stay – and where else is David Bowie going to hole up in Los Angeles? The only other alternative is the Chateau Marmont[14] (the Continental Hyatt 'Riot' Hotel being just too rowdy).)

---

12 Many Brit acts ended up in L.A., such as Fleetwood Mac, John Lydon, Billy Idol and even Steven Morrissey (even tho' Mozzer has fulminated many times about the superficiality and stupidity of the U.S.A. in his songs and interviews!).
13 'You caught yourself a trick down on Sunset and Vine, | But since he pinned you baby, you're a porcupine', Bowie sings in 'Cracked Actor'.
14 But, being on Sunset Boulevard, that's just too close to the scary, sleazy streets for our Bromley lad.

Paranoia, drugs (cocaine), alienation, depression, nefarious incidents, and dabblings in occultism – the L.A. years of David Bowie seem to have been filled with many ingredients one would expect in a clichéd account of a 1970s rock star living in the U.S.A. or on tour. But Bowie's experience in La-La Land seems to have been much bleaker and more depressing than, say, Led Zeppelin and the Who (those 1970s supergroups whose laddish pranks and jolly japes have become legendary).

DINO DE LAURENTIIS.

Dino de Laurentiis (1918-2010) was probably the most well-known Italian producer of recent times, a formidable mogul who moved from Italian movies (*Il Bandito, Bitter Rice, Anna, Europa '51, La Lupa, La Strada*), to North American co-productions (*War and Peace, Ulysses*), to international movies (*Barabbas, Bandits In Rome, Serpico, Barbarella, Three Days of the Condor* and *The Valachi Papers*), and epics (*The Bible, Waterloo, The Bounty* and *Dune*). De Laurentiis has produced all-out commercial ventures (such as *King Kong, Death Wish, Hurricane, Orca the Killer Whale, Flash Gordon, Conan the Barbarian, Year of the Dragon, Body of Evidence, Desperate Hours* and *Hannibal*), but also movies by art maestros like Ingmar Bergman, Federico Fellini, Luchino Visconti, Michael Cimino, Pier Paolo Pasolini, Milos Forman, David Lynch, Vittorio de Sica and Robert Altman (such as *Buffalo Bill, Face To Face, Lo Straniero,* and *Blue Velvet*). In North America in the 1980s de Laurentiis founded D.E.G. (De Laurentiis Entertainment Group) in North Carolina, which flourished until it ended in 1988 (with, some said, debts of $200 million).

Dino de Laurentiis' career is truly remarkable – and long-running (he began producing during the German Occupation of Italy). He formed Real Cine in 1941 (when he was 23), produced *Il Bandito* (Alberto Lattuada, 1946), when he was 28, and married actress Silvana Mangano, one of the Queens of Italian cinema. With Carlo Ponti, de Laurentiis formed Ponti-De Laurentiis in 1950 (they own the Farnesina Studios in Rome). De Laurentiis created Dinocittà outside Rome, where *The Bible, The Great War* and *Barabbas* were based.

JOE LEVINE.

Joe Levine (1905-1987) was the kind of film producer that Jean-Luc Godard satirized in his movies (such as *Contempt,* which Levine produced). Bostonian Levine was famous for his straight-talkin' attitude towards filmmaking, which included plenty of swearing ('sometimes, I guess, I even scare people because I use four-letter words… That's the way I've always lived my life', Levine confessed in the book published to accompany *A Bridge Too Far*). Skilful marketing campaigns were one of Levine's strong points; he worked thru his Embassy Pictures company (Levine had begun in movie distribution, in New England; he launched Embassy in the late 1940s; Embassy was sold to Avco in the late 1960s for a huge profit, where it became Avco-Embassy).

OTHERS.

Prince (1958-2016) is another classic Jackie Collins persona – a super-funky pop star who's so phenomenally talented he makes everybody else look like losers (and he put on the finest show you'll see! I saw Prince at the L.A. Forum in 2011 – probably the best concert ever).

'Swifty' Lazar, the famous agent, may be another inspiration – small, bald with thick glasses, he was famous for his Oscar parties, had clients like Madonna, Lauren Bacall, Cole Porter and Ernest Hemingway, and called people 'kiddo' (like Gino Santangelo).

Porn star Traci Lords (b. 1968) is a perfect Jackie Collins character – with a life story so amazing it wouldn't be believed in a Collins book: the small-town girl from Ohio who ran away to Tinseltown to appear in 80 or so porn films between 1985 and 1986 (plus numerous photo shoots), Lords was at the centre of a controversy which exploded over being a minor. The shake-up and climate of paranoia threatened the adult movie industry to its core. And yet Lords went on to appear in mainstream movies and television.

Fans On Jackie Collins

READERS' REVIEWS ON THE AMAZON WEBSITE

LOVERS & PLAYERS

I love it! There is the usual assortment of Sex, Drugs, Money, Crime, Blackmail... This novel about sex, family and relationships is her best ever.
❤

Secrets, lies, murder, betrayal and sex make up exciting ingredients for *Lovers & Players*. This book kept my attention from the first page to the last. Jackie Collins is now one of my favorite authors!!!

There wasn't a boring moment in this book! Jackie sure does know how to tell a story.
❤

I was concerned that I had 'out-grown' Jackie Collins, or lost my interest when her new book came out. BUT - WOW - she got me again! FABULOUS - FANTASTIC - I did not see any of it coming! Bravo! I fell in love all over again. Thanks for another great book!
❤

I like how the book isn't just about sex. It's a cheerful story that DOES have sex and bad habits in it, but it's got some things to remember: Surviving a tough childhood IS possible, and leaning on someone/ asking for help is OK; pursuing dreams is a good thing; why some people turn out the way they do and why superficial sex and bad habits ultimately don't satisfy.
❤

The kind of book you buy in an airport and read once. Though I was genuinely surprised at the end, this book was just too repetitive to enjoy. Seeing the same phrases and descriptions over and over again made this book just bearable. If you don't mind redundance then this might be just the book for you

AMERICAN STAR

This is one of my favorite books of all time. I'm not a huge Jackie Collins fan, I've read some of her stuff and most of it just isn't my cup of tea. This one though! WOW! It's such a great story, peppered with flashbacks and different points-of-view. You just WANT Nick and Lauren to get together and just when you think they might, some tragedy yet again looms, ripping them apart. It's a smooth read, and hard to put down, so make sure you have lots of time on your hands because you won't want to stop reading.
❤

This is a great book. I really enjoyed it. After I started to read it I realized that I had read it before and I enjoyed it just as much as the first time. This is one of my favorite Jackie Collins books. Really great characters!!! You can't go wrong with this book!!

❤
I loved this book. I could not put it down and since the first time I read it, I have read it twice more. There are some great plotlines in this book that keep you on your toes.

❤
American Star is simply fantastic. There are no other words for it. It has everything a reader could possibly want from a good read. It's not typical Collins. *AmericanStar* tells a love story which I found completely unforgettable. It's truly stunning.

❤
I absolutely love Jackie Collins, but I think that this book fell short at the ending.

I didn't like how Lauren eluded Nick for the entire book, even up to the last few pages. She seemed a bit too pretentious and untouchable. I thought she loved him?

Otherwise, I loved Nick and empathized with his pain. I had hoped Lauren would have been more of a likeable character.

THRILL!

For the past 2 years, I have read nothing BUT Jackie Collins, not in any particular order. This is my absolute favorite of the non-Santangelo novels! The characters, good or bad, are very interesting, the events are paced very well. Nothing is EVER boring here. Lara and Joey are lovable characters, the book twists and turns and is hard to predict. Wait until you see what the bad guys/ girls get! Close to the end, you cannot put it down, the suspense will drive you nuts! Excellent read, if you haven't read Jackie Collins, DO IT! You will always get a THRILL!

❤
I'm really hooked on Jackie Collins! I really love the Santangelo series, but THRILL I just loved. It was along the same lines, a major page-turner. I had it read in 2 days! I was up all night reading.

❤
The most spellbinding novel since *Chances*. I just couldn't put it down. The charachters of Lara and Joey were breathtakingly portrayed in this superb novel. Way to go Jackie.

❤
I like Jackie's novels for the pure entertainment. This one just doesn't live up to her other books. Our heroine Lara was just not that interesting and I didn't really feel good about Joey either. It is okay, but her other books are so much better that I would not bother with this one.

❤
This book isn't as good as Jackie's other books. It uses her same storylines over and over. By the way, does it seem like she has about 15 different plots that she uses over and over in her books?

HOLLYWOOD WIVES: THE NEW GENERATION

Granted, Jackie Collins is not the best writer in the world, and she doesn't pretend to be. Her characters are clichéd and their dialogue is at times painful to read. What she does write here, however, is a juicy page-turner, a delicious guilty pleasure. I couldn't wait to see what was going to happen next, and when I got to the end I was satisfied, yet sad that the adventure was over. This is definitely one of Collins' best novels in a long time. Still, nothing has been able to top the original *Hollywood Wives* for interesting characters, shocking surprises and jaw-dropping twists and turns.

❤
If you enjoy reading about sex, cheating spouses, drug abusers, a cast of characters with no depth and a plot that just doesn't add up, then this is the novel for you. If you're like me, you will not enjoy this novel as much as the first *Hollywood Wives,* there is not much of anything here to enjoy. I just couldn't get a feel for any of the characters. It's amazing how Ms. Collins ties up the story in a neat little package when in fact the story just doesn't make any sense. I've been reading Ms. Collins' work for a long time and this has been the most lacking one to date – but decide for yourselves!!!

❤
This book is very much like her other 30 or so books, movie stars, affairs, kidnappings, and a deranged person. I was very disappointed because I thought she could have come up with some newer ideas. Do not get me wrong it is fun to read but JACKIE please find some newer things to write about or at least reveal who these people are in real life, maybe then we can appreciate it more.

❤
It may have been trashy, brainless, tawdry melodrama but I loved this book! Jackie

takes all the stereotypes of Hollywood celebrities and throws them together into a glamor-packed soup of gossip and subplots! Like a 500-page tabloid! The characters are all true-to-form spoiled, self-obsessed divas. The goings-on are appropriately scandalous. The many talents and many husbands, the wild rich kids, the gay followers, it's all here!

Bibliography

JACKIE COLLINS

The World Is Full Of Married Men (1968), Pan Books, 2010
The Stud (1969), Pan Books, 1984
Sinners (1971), Pan Books, London, 1984
The Love Killers (a.k.a. *Lovehead*) (1974), Simon & Schuster, London, 2012
The World Is Full Of Divorced Women (1975), Simon & Schuster, London, 2012
Lovers & Gamblers (1977), Pan, London, 2009
The Bitch (1979), Pan Books, London, 1984
Chances (1981), Simon & Schuster, London, 2012
Hollywood Wives (1983), Simon & Schuster, London, 2012
Lucky (1985), Pan Books, London, 1986
Hollywood Husbands (1986), Pan Books, London, 1987
Rock Star (1988), Pan Books, 1989
"A Special Interview With Jackie Collins", in *Rock Star*
Lady Boss (1990), Pan Books, London, 1991
American Star (1993), Book Club Associates, London, 1993
Hollywood Kids (1994), Macmillan, London, 1994
Vendetta: Lucky's Revenge (1996), Pan Books, London, 2007
L.A. Connections (1998), Pan Books, London, 1999
Thrill! (1998), Macmillan, London, 1998
Dangerous Kiss (1999), Macmillan, 1999
Lethal Seduction (2000), Simon & Schuster, London, 2000
Hollywood Wives: The New Generation (2001), Pocket Books, London, 2002
Deadly Embrace (2002), Pocket Books, London, 2003
Hollywood Divorces (2003), Simon & Schuster, London, 2014
Lovers & Players (2005), Simon & Schuster, London, 2005
Drop Dead Beautiful (2007), Simon & Schuster, London, 2007
Married Lovers (2008), Pocket Books, London, 2009
Poor Little Bitch Girl (2009), Simon & Schuster, London, 2009
Goddess of Vengeance (2011), Simon & Schuster, London, 2011
The Power Trip (2012), Simon & Schuster, London, 2012
Confessions of a Wild Child (2014), St Martin's Press, 2014
The Lucky Santangelo Cookbook (2014), Simon & Schuster, London, 2014

The Santangelos (2015), Simon & Schuster, London, 2015

Website: jackiecollins.com

OTHERS

Connie Alderson: *Magazines Teenagers Read*, Pergmanon, 1986
Alison Assiter & Avedon Carol, eds. *Bad Girls and Dirty Pictures: The Challenge to Reclaim Feminism*, Pluto Press, 1993
L. Barbach, ed. *Erotic Interludes*, Futura, 1988
Frances Bonner *et al*, eds. *Imagining Women Cultural Representations and Gender*, Polity Press, Cambridge, 1992
P. Booth. *Big Apple*, Futura, 1984
Brian Braithwaite & Joan Barrell: *The Business of Women's Magazines*, Kogan Page, 1988
S. Bright, ed. *Totally Herotica*, Quality Paperback Book Club, New York, 1995
Judith Butler: *Gender Trouble: Feminism and the Subversion of Identity*, Routledge, 1990
—. & J.W. Scott, eds. *Feminists Theorise the Political*, Routledge, 1992
Hélène Cixous: *A Hélène Cixous Reader*, ed. Susan Sellers, Routledge, 1994
Eric Clark: *The Want Makers*, Hodder & Stoughton, 1988
Alice Courtney & Thomas Whipple: *Sex Stereotyping in Advertising*, Lexington Books, Lexington, 1983
Mary Daly: *Pure Lust: Elemental Feminist Philosophy*, Women's Press, 1984
G. Day & C. Bloch, eds. *Perspectives on Pornography: Sexuality in Film and Literature*, Macmillan, 1988
Andrea Dworkin. *Our Blood: Prophecies and Discourses On Sexual Politics*, Women's Press, 1982
—. *Pornography: Men Possessing Women*, Women's Press 1984
—. *Intercourse*, Arrow 1988
—. & Catherine MacKinnon: *Pornography and Civil Rights: A New Day for Women's Equality*, Organizing Against Pornography, Minneapolis 1988
Richard Dyer: *Stars*, British Film Institute, 1979
—*Only Entertainment*, Routledge, 1992
B. Fowler. *The Alienated Reader: Women and Popular Romantic Literature In the 20th Century*, Harvester Wheatsheaf, 1991
Nancy Friday: *Forbidden Flowers: More Women's Sexual Fantasies*, Arrow, 1993
Jane Gallop: *Thinking Through the Body*, Columbia University Press, New York, 1988
Lorraine Gamman & Margaret Marshment, eds. *The Female Gaze: Women as Viewers of Popular Culture*, Women's Press, 1988
Pamela Church Gibson & Roma Gibson, ed. *Dirty Looks: Women, Pornography, Power*, British Film Institute, 1993
C. Gledhill, ed. *Stardom: Industry of Desire*, Routledge, 1991
Robert Goldman: *Reading Ads Socially*, Routledge, 1992
R.S. Green. "Born Lucky", *The Guardian*, Feb 23, 2016
Gabriele Griffin *et al*, eds. *Stirring It: Challenges For Feminism*, Taylor &

Francis, 1994

Elizabeth Grosz: *Sexual Subversions*, Allen & Unwin, 1989

—. "Fetishization", in E. Wright, 1992

—. *Volatile Bodies,* Indiana University Press, Bloomington, IN, 1994

—. *Space, Time and Perversion,* Routledge, London, 1995

R. Harris. *The Rich and the Beautiful,* Magnum, 1979

L. Hart. *Fatal Women: Lesbian Sexuality and the Mark of Aggression,* Princeton University Press, Princeton, NJ, 1994

—. *Between the Body and the Flesh: Performing Sadomasochism,* Columbia University Press, New York, NY, 1998

Anne Hollander: *Seeing Through Clothes,* Viking Press, New York, 1980

S. Howard, *Kiss of the Falcon,* Mills & Boon, 1990

Maggie Humm: *Feminisms: A Reader,* Harvester Wheatsheaf, 1992

—. *Feminist Criticism: Women as Contemporary Critics,* Harvester, 1986

Luce Irigaray: *The Irigaray Reader,* ed. Margaret Whitford, Blackwell, Oxford, 1991

—. *Je, tu, nous: Toward a Culture of Difference,* tr. Alison Martin, Routledge, 1993

—. *Thinking the Difference: For a Peaceful Revolution,* Athlone Press, 1994

Mary Jacobus, ed. *Women Writing and Writing About Women,* Croom Helm, 1979

Sut Jhally: *The Codes of Advertising: Fetishism and the Political Economy of Meaning in the Consumer Society,* Routledge, New York, 1990

E. Jong, *Fear of Flying,* Granada, 1974

J. Krantz. *Mistral's Daughter,* Corgi, London, 1984

Julia Kristeva: *About Chinese Women,* tr. A. Barrows, Boyars, 1977

—. *Desire in Language: A Semiotic Approach to Literature and Art,* ed. Leon Roudiez, tr. Thomas Gora, Alice Jardine & Leon Roudiez, Blackwell, 1982

—. *The Kristeva Reader,* ed. Toril Moi, Blackwell, 1986

Annette Kuhn: *The Power of the Image: Essays on Representation and Sexuality,* Routledge, 1985

Jacques Lacan and the *Ecole Freudienne: Feminine Sexuality,* ed. Juliet Mitchell and Jacqueline Rose, Macmillan, 1982

Robin Lakoff & Raquel Scherr: *Face Value: The Politics of Beauty,* Routledge, Boston, 1984

D.H. Lawrence. *A Selection From Phoenix,* Penguin, 1971

L. Leigh. *Greed,* Bantam Books, 1992

J. Lydon. *Rotten: No Irish, No Blacks, No Dogs: The Authorized Autobiography of Johnny Rotten of the Sex Pistols,* Hodder & Stoughton, London, 1993

Elaine Marks & Isabelle de Courtivron, eds. *New French Feminisms: an Anthology,* Harvester Wheatsheaf, 1981

Kate Millet: *Sexual Politics,* Doubleday, New York, 1970

Trevor Millum: *Images of Woman: Advertising in Women's Magazines,* Chatto, 1975

Toril Moi: *Sexual/ Textual Politics: Feminist Literary Theory,* Methuen, 1985

R. Murray. *Images In the Dark: An Encyclopedia of Gay and Lesbian Film and Video,* Titan Books, London, 1998

Kathy Myers: *Understains: The Sense and Seduction of Advertising,* Comedia, 1986

Lynda Nead: *Female Nude: Art, Obscenity and Sexuality,* Routledge, 1992

P. Norman. *The Stones,* Elm Tree, 1972

—. *Sympathy For the Devil: The Rolling Stones Story*, Linden Press, New York, NY, 1984

—. *Mick Jagger,* HarperCollins, 2012

M. Puzo. *The Godfather,* Putnam's Sons, New York, NY, 1969

—. *The Godfather Papers and Other Confessions*, Putnam's Sons, New York, NY, 1972

Janice Radway: *Reading the Romance: Feminism and the Representation of Women in Popular Culture*, University of North Carolina Press, Chapel Hill, 1984

Adrienne Rich: *Blood, Bread and Poetry,* Virago, 1980

Elaine Showalter, ed. *The New Feminist Criticism,* Virago, 1986

T. Southern & M. Hoffenberg, *Candy,* Putnam's Sons, New York, NY, 1964

Dale Spender: *The Writing or the Sex? why you don't have to read women's writing to know it's no good,* Pergamon Press, New York, 1989

Susan Rubin Suleiman, ed. *The Female Body in Western Culture: Contemporary Perspectives*, Harvard University Press, Cambridge, Mass., 1986

K. Thompson. *Storytelling In the New Hollywood,* Harvard University Press, Cambridge, MA, 1999

D. Thomson. *A Biographical Dictionary of Film,* Deutsch, London, 1995

—. *The Big Screen,* Allen Lane, 2012

G. Tremlett. *Rock Gold: The Music Millionaires,* Unwin Hyman, London, 1990

Cynthia White: *Women's Magazines 1693-1968*, Michael Joseph, 1970

Judith Williamson. *Decoding Advertisements*, Marion Boyars, 1978

—. *Consuming Passion: The Dynamics of Popular Culture*, Marion Boyars, 1986

Janice Winship: *Inside Women's Magazines*, Pandora, 1987

Elizabeth Wright, ed. *Feminism and Psychoanalysis: A Critical Dictionary*, Blackwell, Oxford, 1992

T. Zanetta & H. Edwards. *Stardust: The Life and Times of David Bowie*, Michael Joseph, London, 1986

Jack Zipes: *Don't Bet on the Prince: Contemporary Feminist Fairy Tales in North American and England*, Gower 1986

—. *The Brothers Grimm*, Routledge, 1989

CRESCENT MOON PUBLISHING

web: www.crmoon.com e-mail: cresmopub@yahoo.co.uk

ARTS, PAINTING, SCULPTURE

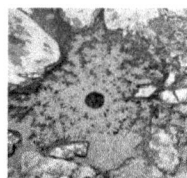

The Art of Andy Goldsworthy
Andy Goldsworthy: Touching Nature
Andy Goldsworthy in Close-Up
Andy Goldsworthy: Pocket Guide
Andy Goldsworthy In America
Land Art: A Complete Guide
The Art of Richard Long
Richard Long: Pocket Guide
Land Art In the UK
Land Art in Close-Up
Land Art In the U.S.A.
Land Art: Pocket Guide
Installation Art in Close-Up
Minimal Art and Artists In the 1960s and After
Colourfield Painting
Land Art DVD, TV documentary
Andy Goldsworthy DVD, TV documentary

The Erotic Object: Sexuality in Sculpture From Prehistory to the Present Day
Sex in Art: Pornography and Pleasure in Painting and Sculpture
Postwar Art
Sacred Gardens: The Garden in Myth, Religion and Art
Glorification: Religious Abstraction in Renaissance and 20th Century Art
Early Netherlandish Painting
Leonardo da Vinci
Piero della Francesca
Giovanni Bellini
Fra Angelico: Art and Religion in the Renaissance
Mark Rothko: The Art of Transcendence
Frank Stella: American Abstract Artist
Jasper Johns
Brice Marden

Alison Wilding: The Embrace of Sculpture
Vincent van Gogh: Visionary Landscapes
Eric Gill: Nuptials of God
Constantin Brancusi: Sculpting the Essence of Things

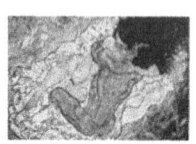

Max Beckmann
Caravaggio
Gustave Moreau
Egon Schiele: Sex and Death In Purple Stockings
Delizioso Fotografico Fervore: Works In Process 1
Sacro Cuore: Works In Process 2
The Light Eternal: J.M.W. Turner
The Madonna Glorified: Karen Arthurs

LITERATURE

J.R.R. Tolkien: The Books, The Films, The Whole Cultural Phenomenon
J.R.R. Tolkien: Pocket Guide
Tolkien's Heroic Quest
The *Earthsea* Books of Ursula Le Guin
Beauties, Beasts and Enchantment: Classic French Fairy Tales
German Popular Stories by the Brothers Grimm
Philip Pullman and *His Dark Materials*
Sexing Hardy: Thomas Hardy and Feminism
Thomas Hardy's *Tess of the d'Urbervilles*
Thomas Hardy's *Jude the Obscure*
Thomas Hardy: The Tragic Novels
Love and Tragedy: Thomas Hardy
The Poetry of Landscape in Hardy
Wessex Revisited: Thomas Hardy and John Cowper Powys
Wolfgang Iser: Essays and Interviews
Petrarch, Dante and the Troubadours
Maurice Sendak and the Art of Children's Book Illustration
Andrea Dworkin
Cixous, Irigaray, Kristeva: The *Jouissance* of French Feminism
Julia Kristeva: Art, Love, Melancholy, Philosophy, Semiotics and Psychoanalysis
Hélene Cixous I Love You: The *Jouissance* of Writing
Luce Irigaray: Lips, Kissing, and the Politics of Sexual Difference
Peter Redgrove: Here Comes the Flood
Peter Redgrove: Sex-Magic-Poetry-Cornwall
Lawrence Durrell: Between Love and Death, East and West
Love, Culture & Poetry: Lawrence Durrell
Cavafy: Anatomy of a Soul
German Romantic Poetry: Goethe, Novalis, Heine, Hölderlin
Feminism and Shakespeare
Shakespeare: Love, Poetry & Magic
The Passion of D.H. Lawrence
D.H. Lawrence: Symbolic Landscapes
D.H. Lawrence: Infinite Sensual Violence
Rimbaud: Arthur Rimbaud and the Magic of Poetry
The Ecstasies of John Cowper Powys
Sensualism and Mythology: The Wessex Novels of John Cowper Powys
Amorous Life: John Cowper Powys and the Manifestation of Affectivity (H.W. Fawkner)
Postmodern Powys: New Essays on John Cowper Powys (Joe Boulter)
Rethinking Powys: Critical Essays on John Cowper Powys
Paul Bowles & Bernardo Bertolucci
Rainer Maria Rilke
Joseph Conrad: *Heart of Darkness*
In the Dim Void: Samuel Beckett
Samuel Beckett Goes into the Silence
André Gide: Fiction and Fervour
Jackie Collins and the Blockbuster Novel
Blinded By Her Light: The Love-Poetry of Robert Graves
The Passion of Colours: Travels In Mediterranean Lands
Poetic Forms

MEDIA, CINEMA, FEMINISM and CULTURAL STUDIES

J.R.R. Tolkien: The Books, The Films, The Whole Cultural Phenomenon
J.R.R. Tolkien: Pocket Guide
The *Lord of the Rings* Movies: Pocket Guide
The Cinema of Hayao Miyazaki
Hayao Miyazaki: *Princess Mononoke*: Pocket Movie Guide
Hayao Miyazaki: *Spirited Away*: Pocket Movie Guide
Tim Burton : Hallowe'en For Hollywood
Ken Russell
Ken Russell: *Tommy*: Pocket Movie Guide
The Ghost Dance: The Origins of Religion
The Peyote Cult

Cixous, Irigaray, Kristeva: The *Jouissance* of French Feminism
Julia Kristeva: Art, Love, Melancholy, Philosophy, Semiotics and Psychoanalysis
Luce Irigaray: Lips, Kissing, and the Politics of Sexual Difference
Hélene Cixous I Love You: The *Jouissance* of Writing
Andrea Dworkin
'Cosmo Woman': The World of Women's Magazines
Women in Pop Music
HomeGround: The Kate Bush Anthology
Discovering the Goddess (Geoffrey Ashe)
The Poetry of Cinema
The Sacred Cinema of Andrei Tarkovsky
Andrei Tarkovsky: Pocket Guide
Andrei Tarkovsky: *Mirror*: Pocket Movie Guide
Andrei Tarkovsky: *The Sacrifice*: Pocket Movie Guide
Walerian Borowczyk: Cinema of Erotic Dreams
Jean-Luc Godard: The Passion of Cinema
Jean-Luc Godard: *Hail Mary*: Pocket Movie Guide
Jean-Luc Godard: *Contempt*: Pocket Movie Guide
Jean-Luc Godard: *Pierrot le Fou*: Pocket Movie Guide
John Hughes and Eighties Cinema
Ferris Bueller's Day Off: Pocket Movie Guide
Jean-Luc Godard: Pocket Guide
The Cinema of Richard Linklater
Liv Tyler: Star In Ascendance
Blade Runner and the Films of Philip K. Dick
Paul Bowles and Bernardo Bertolucci
Media Hell: Radio, TV and the Press
An Open Letter to the BBC
Detonation Britain: Nuclear War in the UK
Feminism and Shakespeare
Wild Zones: Pornography, Art and Feminism
Sex in Art: Pornography and Pleasure in Painting and Sculpture
Sexing Hardy: Thomas Hardy and Feminism

The Light Eternal is a model monograph, an exemplary job. The subject matter of the book is beautifully organised and dead on beam. (Lawrence Durrell)
It is amazing for me to see my work treated with such passion and respect. (Andrea Dworkin)

CRESCENT MOON PUBLISHING
P.O. Box 1312, Maidstone, Kent, ME14 5XU, Great Britain. www.crmoon.com

cresmopub@yahoo.co.uk   www.crescentmoon.org.uk

www.ingramcontent.com/pod-product-compliance
Lightning Source LLC
Chambersburg PA
CBHW050119170426
43197CB00011B/1641